WITHDRAWN

POETRY THEMES

POETRY THEMES

*A bibliographical index to subject anthologies
and related criticism in the English language,
1875-1975*

compiled by

PETER MARCAN
BA ALA

CLIVE BINGLEY LINNET BOOKS
LONDON   HAMDEN · CONN

FIRST PUBLISHED 1977 BY CLIVE BINGLEY LTD
16 PEMBRIDGE ROAD LONDON W11 UK
SIMULTANEOUSLY PUBLISHED IN THE USA BY
LINNET BOOKS AN IMPRINT OF THE SHOE STRING PRESS INC
995 SHERMAN AVENUE HAMDEN CONNECTICUT 06514
SET IN 9 ON 10 POINT PRESS ROMAN BY ALLSET
AND PRINTED AND BOUND IN THE UK BY
REDWOOD BURN LTD OF TROWBRIDGE AND ESHER
COPYRIGHT © PETER MARCAN 1977
ALL RIGHTS RESERVED
BINGLEY ISBN: 0 85157 232 4
LINNET ISBN: 0 208 01545 0

Library of Congress Cataloging in Publication Data

Marcan, Peter.
    Poetry themes.

    1. Poetry—Indexes.   2. Poetry—Themes, motives—
Indexes.   I. Title.
PN1022.M3   016.821008   77-22483
ISBN 0-208-01545-0

CONTENTS

ACKNOWLEDGEMENTS

Many librarians and publishers have helped indirectly with the compilation of this work. I am grateful to the staff of the British Museum Library where the majority of the items annotated were seen. I am grateful to the staff of Westminster Public Libraries, the London Library and the library of the University of London, Senate House who checked their catalogues for me on a number of occasions.

I must thank the following librarians who provided me with information in writing: Margaret Deas of the National Library of Scotland, P Henchy of the National Library of Ireland, Gareth O Watts of the National Library of Wales, William Hodges of the Bodleian, Muriel Austen of the Poetry Society, Michael FitzGerald of the Royal Aeronautical Society, Catherine Pickett of the India Office Library, Pamela Gilbert of the entomological library at the Natural History Museum, Valerie A Ross of Barnet Public Libraries, S K Barker of Camden Public Libraries, J P Wells, of Oxford City Library, Anthony Shearman of Edinburgh Public Library, and P N Allen of Birmingham Reference Library.

The following publishers kindly provided me with information on their books: Aims for Freedom and Enterprise, Batsford, Blackie, Exley Publications, Hodder and Stoughton, Macmillan, Frederick Muller, Latimer, Oxford University Press, Secker and Warburg, A Wheaton, Wolfe, and Yoseloff.

I am grateful to Bill Hannah for his assistance with the compilation of the author/compiler index.

P M

INTRODUCTION

The primary aim of this bibliography is to provide a subject approach to poetry on a scale which has not been previously attempted. Existing poetry indexes are virtually all of American origin (see Appendix), and cover as a rule only the general anthology. The search through many volumes for an elusive item can be time-consuming and much valuable material available only in the subject or thematised collection is lost. I have attempted to index in this work such subject anthologies which bring together poetry on one subject or a group of related subjects.

I have excluded subject-based collections by individual poets—this is a vast and as yet unexplored field. I have also excluded anthologies consisting entirely of prose or drama extracts. Inevitably many anthologies contain both poetry and prose. Such collections are not always easy to trace. The prose is often wide ranging, consisting of extracts from novels, plays, histories, philosophical works, biographies, letters and diaries with a sprinkling of short quotations, maxims and proverbs. Subsequently these collections will often be classified under the subject. Nevertheless I have included as many such anthologies as I have been able to discover over a research period of two years.

It is my hope that this bibliography will be of use to librarians in their efforts to trace and locate poetry and literary items, to recitalists, broadcasters and anthologisers looking for off-beat material, to authors and speech-makers looking for ideas, and to teachers and students concerned with the thematic approach.

Some anthologies are profusely illustrated and are intended as gift books; others appear in limited editions and have a particular bibliographic interest for the dealer and collector. Other anthologies are intended for children or for school use. Indeed the range of presentation is wide. The range of subjects covered is correspondingly wide, as shown by the classification scheme used in this book, although there is naturally a predilection for certain 'poetic' subjects—love, for example, or religion, war, nature and the sea. Chronologically many anthologies will range from the sixteenth to the twentieth century. Many, however, will include some extracts from medieval literature and from the Bible. While the vast proportion of material in each anthology is taken from literature in the English language, some items might come from foreign literatures, and a few of the anthologies indexed are in fact of a completely international nature. In addition to poetry and prose of known authorship, some anthologies contain anonymous ballad and folksong material, and a number of items listed here are devoted entirely to this type of material.

Critical literature in the form of books, articles and theses has also been included. Much obscure material can often be traced in this secondary literature. Theses, being the outcome of scholarly research at a high level, are inevitably equipped with references and bibliographies. The critical literature cited will be of interest to the student of poetry, providing sources for thematic and comparative studies, and indicating possible fields for further research. It should be pointed out that some anthologies themselves have long scholarly introductions together with notes and glossaries.

Most of the items indexed fall within the time-scale 1875-1975, though some material published during 1976 which came to my notice during the course of compilation has been included. Some pre-1875 material, going back in a few cases to about 1850, has been included, when of particular interest.

The sources for this bibliography have been extensive and range from the standard bibliographic indexes, which provided the backbone of the entries, to more specialised catalogues, special collections, and subject bibliographies. The published library catalogues of Harvard University Library, The London Library, Glasgow and Pittsburgh Public Libraries were found useful, the latter two particularly so for nineteenth century material. Three special collections, for which there do not exist published catalogues, were consulted. These are the library of the Poetry Society, the special collection of poetry books in Victoria branch library, Westminster, and the special collection of books on literature in general at Poplar branch library, Tower Hamlets, London. Two particularly useful sources for ballad and folksong material were: *The Vaughan Williams library catalogue of the English Folk Dance and Song Society* (Mansell, 1973); and *A bibliography of North American folklore and folksong*, by Charles Haywood (New York, Greenberg, 1951).

Special subject bibliographies yielded some items not traced elsewhere. Critical literature was traced through the *Cambridge bibliography of English literature* and the *Annual bibliography of English language and literature* (1920-   ) and various specialised retrospective bibliographies. Theses were traced through *Dissertations in English and American literatures: theses accepted by American, British and German universities, 1865-1964* (Bowker, 1968), compiled by Lawrence F MacNamee; the Aslib *Index of theses accepted for higher degrees in the universities of Great Britain and Ireland (1953-   )*; the *Retrospective index to theses of Great Britain and Ireland, 1716-1950*, Vol I (European Bibliographical Center/The Clio Press, 1975); and the American *Comprehensive dissertation index, 1861-1972* (Xerox University Microfilms, 1973).

Commonwealth thesis material was traced through *Critical writings on Commonwealth literatures: a selective bibliography to 1970 with lists of theses and dissertations*, compiled by William H New (University of Pennsylvania Press, 1975).

None of this thesis material has been examined.

The classification scheme adopted for the arrangement of items is my own, but is based on fairly conventional classification notions. There are

viii

three main sections: the life of man, covering the world of religion, emotional life, social life and organisation, and the world of the arts; history and general geographical description; and the world of science and natural history.

Entries provide full bibliographical details, with notes on different editions and re-issues. Heading of chapters or sections are given in full. Annotations cover the type and range of material included. It is to be regretted that space did not permit a detailed listing of unusual items of particular interest. Some anthologies consist almost entirely of items by famous, or unknown and obscure writers. In such cases this information will be given in the annotation. Otherwise it may be assumed that the anthologies contain a mixture of items by both known and unknown writers. As all my inspection of books was carried out in English libraries, it is inevitable that more annotations will exist for books published in the United Kingdom than in America.

CLASSIFICATION SCHEME

THE WORLD OF KNOWLEDGE

BOOKS AND LIBRARIES

1 IRELAND, Alexander
The book-lover's enchiridion: thoughts on the solace and companionship
of books, selected and chronologically arranged by Philobiblos. London,
Simpkin & Marshall, 1883. ix, 237pp.
The book-lover's enchiridion. American edition, revised and enlarged.
Philadelphia, J B Lippincott, 1883. 312pp.
The book-lover's enchiridion: thoughts on the solace and companionship
of books and topics incidental thereto, garned from writers of every age for
the help and betterment of all readers by Alexander Ireland. 3rd ed. London,
Simpkin & Marshall, 1883. xv, 478pp.
The book-lover's enchiridion: thoughts on the solace and companionship
of books and topics incidental thereto, gathered from the best writers of
every age and arranged in chronological order, by Alexander Ireland. 4th ed.
London, Simpkin & Marshall, 1884. xvi, 492pp.
The book-lover's enchiridion: thoughts on the solace and companionship
of books and topics indidental thereto, gathered from the writings of the
greatest thinkers from Cicero, Petrarch and Montaigne to Carlyle, Emerson
and Ruskin by Alexander Ireland. 5th ed. London, Simpkin & Marshall,
1888. xviii, 511pp.

2 LANG, Andrew
Ballads of books, edited by Andrew Lang. London, Longmans, 1888.
157pp.
A recast, with a few omissions, of the volume with the same title edited by
Brander Matthews.

3 LANGFORD, John Alfred
The praise of books as said and sung by English authors, selected with a
preliminary essay on books by John Alfred Langford. London, Cassell,
Petter & Galpin, 1880. 165pp.
Prose extracts and poetry on books, literature, knowledge, from the six-
teenth to nineteenth century.

4 LEONARD, R M
The book lover's anthology, edited by R M Leonard. London, Oxford
University Press, 1911. 408pp. Notes (pp 369-399).

Poetry and prose from the sixteenth to the nineteenth century covering a
wide range of subjects: books, libraries, the Bible, book collecting, learning,
knowledge, etc. The compiler acknowledges some debt to the collections of
Ireland, Matthews and Roberts.

5 MADDOCK, L W
   Silent friendships: an anthology in praise of books, compiled by L W
Maddock. Hadlow (Kent), Tudor Publishing Company, 1931. 29pp.
Mostly prose extracts.

6 MATTHEWS, Brander
   Ballads of books, chosen by Brander Matthews. New York, George J
Coombes, 1887. 174pp, front. (Books for the Bibliophile Series).
Frontispiece engraving: 'The bibliophile' by Van S Finxt.

7 ROBERTS, William
   Book verse: an anthology of poems of books and bookmen from the
earliest times to recent years, edited by W Roberts. London, Elliot Stock,
1896. 213pp.

8 RUDDY, Howard S
   Book-lover's verse: being songs of books and bookmen, compiled from
English and American authors by Howard S Ruddy. Indianapolis, Bowen-
Merrill, 1899. xvii, 223pp.

9 SANFORD, A P, and SCHAUFFLER, Robert Haven
   The magic of books, compiled and edited by A P Sanford and Robert
Haven Schauffler. New York, Dodd & Mead, 1929. xvii, 424pp. (Our
American Holidays Series).

10 STEVENS, Norman D
   Library humour: a bibliothecal miscellany to 1970, edited and indexed
by Norman D Stevens. Metuchen, Scarecrow Press, 1971. 427pp.
Prose and poetry pieces taken mostly from American and English librarianship journals.

11 STONE, Edward L
   Book-lover's bouquet, gathered by Edward L Stone. New York, W E
Rudge, 1931. 35pp.
Limited edition: 500 copies on Hand and Arrows paper, in Centaur type.

12 SWAN, H
   In praise of books: an encheiridion for the booklover, compiled by
H Swan. London, George Routledge; New York, E P Dutton, [1905].
118pp. (Routledges Miniature Reference Library).
Poetry and prose extracts from the sixteenth to twentieth century. Alpha-
betical arrangement by author's name. A miniature book.

13 THOMPSON, James
   Books: an anthology, compiled by James Thompson. London, Anne
Bingley, 1968. 47pp.

Headings: Books are for ever; Books are all very well; Books are good for you; Books are a comfort; Away with books; Old books, new books; All sorts of books; Book-lovers; Libraries and librarians.
Prose and poetry extracts and pieces from the sixteenth to twentieth century. List of sources: pp 39-45.
Anne Bingley is a registered imprint of Clive Bingley Ltd.

14 [TIMPERLEY, C H]
Songs of the press and other poems relative to the art of printers and printing; also of authors, books, booksellers, bookbinders, editors, critics, newspapers, etc, original and selected with notes, biographical and literary. London, Fisher, 1845. 208pp.
Glossary of technical terms.

15 TREWIN, J C
In praise of books: an anthology of pleasure, compiled by J C Trewin. London, Frederick Muller, 1958. 48pp, illus.
Prose and poetry extracts from the seventeenth to twentieth century.

16 WHITE, Gleeson
Book song: an anthology of poems of books and bookmen from modern authors, edited by Gleeson White. London, Elliot Stock, 1893. xviii, 185pp. (The Booklovers Library).

See also: 289

RELIGION

RELIGION IN GENERAL

17 ADAMS, H G
A cyclopaedia of sacred poetical quotations, consisting of choice passages from the sacred poetry of all ages and countries, classified and arranged for facility of reference under subject headings illustrated by striking passages from scripture, edited by H G Adams. London, Groombridge, 1854. 735pp. Emphasis on the seventeenth and nineteenth centuries. Originally issued in eleven parts.

18 BASSET, Elizabeth
Love is my meaning: an anthology of assurance, collected by Elizabeth Basset, foreword by the Queen Mother. London, Darton, Longman & Todd, 1975. 272pp.
Poetry and prose on religious themes from the Bible to the twentieth century, with an emphasis on the twentieth century.

19 BEAUMONT, Timothy
Modern religious verse, selected by Timothy Beaumont. London, Studio Vista, 1966. 48pp. (The Pocket Poets).
Familiar and unfamiliar poets.

20 BEECHING, H C
Lyra sacra: a book of religious verse, selected and arranged by H C Beeching. London, Methuen, 1895. xx, 364pp. Notes (pp 337-356). Mostly familiar poets of the sixteenth, seventeenth and nineteenth centuries.
Second edition: 1903. xxii, 381pp.

21 BIRNIE, Ian H, and ELLIOTT, John
Confrontation [compiled by] Ian H Birnie and John Elliott. London, New York, McGraw Hill, 1975. xii, 187pp, illus.
A compilation of twentieth century texts and photographs for use by sixth form and college students in discussion of religious belief and behaviour.

22 BROWN, Carleton
Religious lyrics of the fifteenth century, edited by Carleton Brown. Oxford, Clarendon Press, 1939. xxxi, 394pp.
Notes (pp 293-351). Glossary (pp 352-394).
Headings: Dialogues between the blessed Virgin and child; Marian laments; Songs and prayers to the blessed Virgin; Hymns to the Trinity; Hymns to

4

God the father, creator; Hymns and prayers to Christ; Songs of the annunciation; Songs of the nativity; Songs for epiphany; Hymns and songs of the
passion; Appeals to man from the cross; Complaints of Christ; Easter songs;
Songs of the Eucharist; The mysteries of the faith; Occasional prayers and
songs; Prayers to the guardian angel; Two prayers by Lydgate against the
pestilence; Songs of penitence; Songs of old age; Songs of mortality; Songs
against fortune; Songs of the decadence of virtue; Songs against vice; Proverbs and moral sentences.

23 BROWN, Carleton
Religious lyrics of the fourteenth century, edited by Carleton Brown.
Oxford, Clarendon Press, 1924. xxii, 358pp.
Notes (pp 241-288). Glossary (pp 289-358).
Headings: Lyrics of the beginning of the century; Lyrics from MS Harley
2253; Hymns by Friar William Herebert from Phillipps MS 8336; Miscel-
laneous lyrics before 1350; A group of lyrics collected by Bishop Sheppey
in Merton College, Oxford—MS 248; Miscellaneous lyrics of the mid-
century; Lyrics from the commonplace book of John Grimestone; Lyrics
of the school of Richard Rolle, from Cambridge University—Dd 564;
Miscellaneous lyrics from about 1375; The 'Vernon' series of refrain poets;
Miscellaneous lyrics of the end of the century.
Second edition: 1952, xxii, 365pp.
Contains no new collected material but the glossary has been extensively
revised.

24 BULLETT, Gerald
The pattern of courtesy: an anthology continuing the Testament of
Light, made and edited by Gerald Bullett. London, Dent, 1943. [135]pp.
Notes.
Prose extracts and poetry from all periods. Writings on the religious and
philosophical approach to life.
Reissued with the title 'The testament of light', 1938. Contains
different preliminary matter.

25 BULLETT, Gerald
The testament of light: an anthology, made and edited by Gerald Bullett.
London, Dent, 1932. [172]pp. Notes.
Prose extracts and poetry of all periods.
Second edition: 1933. Four items displaced by new material.
Third edition: 1938. One further displacement and correction of mis-
takes in text and notes.

26 CAMPLING, Christopher, and DAVIS, Michael
Words for worship, compiled by Christopher Campling and Michael
Davis. London, Edward Arnold, 1969. xvi, [373]pp. Music.
Contents and headings: Bible readings (items 1-106)—references to biblical
passages for the year; Prayers (items 107-604); Readings (items 605-825)—
The life, death and ressurection of Jesus Christ; The Christian Church and
Christian activity and worship; God and nature; God and mankind; Attitudes

to God, to life and to ourselves; The body; Challenge and action; Freedom and love; Attitudes to other people; Helping other people; Disciples, saints and crusaders; People and society; Wealth; Suffering; Death and eternity; Fables and legends; Short readings (quotations).
Readings consist of poetry and prose extracts, all of the twentieth century; includes some modern hymns with music.

27 CECIL, David
   The Oxford book of Christian verse, chosen and edited by Lord David Cecil. Oxford, Clarendon Press, 1940. xxvii, 560pp.
Covers poetry from the Middle Ages to the nineteenth century, with an emphasis on the seventeenth century.

28 CLARK, Thomas Curtis
   The golden book of religious verse: the golden book of faith, compiled by Thomas Curtis Clark. Carden City, New York, Garden City Publishing Company, 1937. 273pp.

29 COLQUHOUN, F Mary
   Songs of Christian warfare, arranged by F Mary Colquhoun. Edinburgh, Andrew Elliot, [1887]. 158pp.
Minor nineteenth century verse.

30 COMPER, Frances M M
   Spiritual songs from English manuscripts of the fourteenth to sixteenth centuries, edited by Frances M M Comper; with a preface by Herbert J C Grierson. London, Society for Promoting Christian Knowledge, [1936]. xxiii, 293pp. Glossary.
Headings: The incarnation; The nativity; Theme of the passion; Orisons to the Holy Trinity and to our Lady and Saint John; Eucharist and Mass. pp 255-282: notes on religious poetry manuscript collections in major British libraries and in private ownership.

31 COOKE, George Willis
   The poets of transcendentalism: an anthology edited by George Willis Cooke, with an introductory essay and biographical notes. Boston, New York, Houghton Mifflin, 1903. 341pp.
American nineteenth century poetry.

32 CROSSE, Gordon
   Everyman's book of sacred verse, edited with notes by Gordon Crosse. London, A R Mowbray, 1923. ix, 265pp. Notes (pp 214-253).
Compiler acknowledges debt to the anthologies of Quiller-Couch, Palgrave, Dean Beeching and to Trench's 'Household book of English poetry'.

33 DE-LA-NOY, Michael
   The fields of praise: an anthology of religious poetry, compiled by Michael-de-la-Noy. Oxford, Religious Education Press, 1968. xi, 82pp.
Mostly twentieth century English poetry on religious and philosophical subjects (love, death, joy and sadness, etc).

34 DRIVER, Tom F, and PACK, Robert
    Poems of doubt and belief: an anthology of modern religious poetry,
edited by Tom F Driver and Robert Pack. New York, Macmillan, 1964.
xxi, 258pp.
American and English poetry.

35 ESCOTT, Harry
    Minstrels of Christ: contemporary Christian verse, compiled by Harry
Escott. London, Epworth Press, 1941. 76pp. (Wayside Books no 7).
Headings: The mystery of faith; The historical revelation; The Christian
life; Through nature to God.
Unfamiliar poets.

36 FULLER, Alfred J
    Golden thoughts from the great writers: a volume of selected devotional
poetry and extracts, arranged by Alfred J Fuller. London, E Nister; New
York, Dutton, [1898]. 192pp, illus (some col). Biographical notes.
Well known poets from the seventeenth to nineteenth century.

37 GARNETT, Emmeline
    The wheel: an anthology of religious verse, compiled by Emmeline
Garnett. London, Burns & Oates, Macmillan, 1965. xix, 235pp.
Headings: One O one was God alone; Lonesome valley; Four thousand
winters; Comfort ye my people; Christmas Eve and twelve of the clock;
And let the new year in; Seek him in the kingdom of anxiety; Are there
anybody here like Mary-a-weeping?; Nineteen hundred and fourty nails;
Death and darkness, get you packing; The spirit is running, the darkness
is ending; And the city was pure gold.
Poetry of the Middle Ages to the twentieth century. Includes some psalms
and some extracts from medieval mystery plays (the Chester, Wakefield
and York cycles).

38 GELL, E M
    The blessed company: daily links for members of the church, compiled
by the Hon Mrs Gell. London, A R Mowbray; Milwaukee, The Young
Churchman Company, 1916. viii, 119pp.
Headings: Advent and Christmastide: the church's mission; New year and
season of the epiphany: God's dues; The season of Lent: conditions of
membership; Easter, Ascension, Whitsuntide: the life of Christ; The season
of Trinity: the spiritual structure; The church's ideals.
Extracts from the Bible and from mostly nineteenth century poetry for
each day of the week, throughout the year.

39 GELL, E M
    The cloud of witness: a daily sequence of great thoughts from many
minds following the Christian season, compiled by Mrs Lyttelton Gell.
London, Henry Frowde, 1891. xv, 552pp.
Poetry and prose extracts of all periods, with an emphasis on the nineteenth century, covering a wide range of philosophical themes.

40 GLEANINGS FROM THE SACRED POETS,
with biographical notices of the authors. Edinburgh, London, Gall &
Inglis, [1875]. xvi, 400pp, illus.
Covers poetry from the Middle Ages to the nineteenth century.
   Reissued: 1881. This issue has a red embossed cover and coloured
decorative borders.

41 GOUDGE, Elizabeth
   A book of faith, compiled by Elizabeth Goudge. London, Hodder &
Stoughton, 1976. 352pp.
Headings: Faith in God the creator; All created things speak to us, with
their many voices, of the word of God who created them; The loving and
beloved creatures who share our hope; Faith in God the redeemer; Not
only the saints and heroes, but the men and women who day by day illu-
mine life for the rest of us . . . ; The children and the lovers keep faith
alive in us; Faith, hope and charity; Men and women of faith speak to us
of other gifts of the spirit, given to our giving; Faith maintained in darkness and tribulation; Faith maintained as old age carries us forward through
death to resurrection and to hopes of heaven.
Wide ranging anthology covering all periods, but with an emphasis on the
twentieth century. Includes some classical and foreign items in translation. Poetry and some prose.

42 HAZO, Samuel John
   A selection of contemporary religious poetry, compiled by Samuel John
Hazo. Glen Rock, (New Jersey), Paulist Press, 1963. 128pp. (Deus Books).

43 HILL, Caroline Miles
   The world's great religious poetry, edited by Caroline Miles Hill. New
York, Macmillan, 1923. xxxix, 836pp.

44 HILTON, Donald H
   Words to share: an anthology of poetry and prose for use in Christian
education and worship, compiled by Donald H Hilton. Nutfield (Surrey),
Denholm House Press, 1974. 191pp.
Headings: This is my life; Family and friends; Town and around; All the
year round; The created universe; The world is a circle.
Provides references to thematically related passages in the Bible.

45 HORDER, W Garrett
   The treasury of American sacred song with notes explanatory and bio-
graphical, selected and edited by W Garrett Horder. London, New York,
Henry Frowde, 1896. x, 387pp.
Nineteenth century American poetry.
   Revised and enlarged edition: 1900. x, 401pp.

46 HUELIN, Gordon
   All in good faith: an anthology in words and pictures of Western
Christianity, edited by Gordon Huelin. London, Leslie Frewin, 1966.
280pp, illus.

Poetry and prose; mainly prose with an emphasis on the history of the church, with extracts from twentieth century historical works.

47 KAUFFMAN, Donald T
   The treasury of religious verse [compiled by] Donald T Kauffman. Westwood, (New Jersey), Revell, 1962. 371pp.

48 KENNEDY, Charles W
   Early English Christian poetry, translated into alliterative verse by Charles W Kennedy with critical commentary. London, Hollis & Carter, 1952. xi, 292pp.
   Contains: Genesis (extracts); Christ and Satan (extracts); Dream of the Rood (entire); Andreas (entire); Elene (entire); Physiologus (extracts); Phoenix (entire); Be domes daege (entire).

49 L, H L
   Lyra christiana: a treasury of sacred poetry, edited by H L L. London, Nelson, 1888. 562pp.
   Nineteenth century poetry; each poem prefaced with a short quotation from the Bible.

50 LAUDAMUS TE:
   a cycle of poems to the praise and glory of God, composed in His honour (in the English language) by the poets of six continents and humbly presented in the book form by Manifold. London, Manifold, 1967. xii, 135pp.

51 LAWSON, James Gilchrist
   Best loved religious poems, gleaned from many sources by James Gilchrist Lawson. New York, Revell, 1933. 256pp.

52 LAWSON, James Gilchrist
   The world's best religious quotations, compiled by James Gilchrist Lawson. London, Kingsgate Press, 1932. 192pp.
   Stanzas of poetry and short prose quotes from all periods, covering a wide range of subjects.

53 LEIGHTON, Richard
   The early English carols, edited by Richard Leighton. Oxford, Clarendon Press, 1935. cxlv, 461pp. Bibliography of original sources. Notes (pp 351-454).
   Headings: Introduction: the carol as a genre; The carol as dance-song; The Latin background of the carol; The carol as popular song; The carol and popular religion. Carols: of advent, of the nativity, of St Stephen, of St John the Evangelist, of the Innocents, of St Thomas of Canterbury, of the New Year, of the Epiphany, of the board's head, of holly and ivy, lullaby carols, of the passion, to the virgin, of the annunciation, of Christ's pleading, of Christ's love, to Christ, of purgatory, of saints, of the mass, of religious counsel, of moral consent, of doomsday, of mortality, satirical carols, carols of women, of marriage, of childhood, picaresque carols, convivial

carols, carols of ale and hunting, political carols, amorous carols, humourous carols.

54 LEONARD, Henry C
Sacred songs of the world, translated from one hundred and twenty languages, edited by Henry C Leonard. London, Elliot Stock, 1889. 223pp.
Much of the material is medieval and earlier.

55 LEONARD, R M
Religious poems, selected by R M Leonard. London, Oxford University Press, 1914. 128pp. Notes. (Oxford Garlands).
Poetry by well-known poets from the sixteenth to the nineteenth century.

56 MacILWAINE, W
Lyra hibernica sacra: an anthology of religious verse written by Irishmen, compiled by W MacIlwaine. Belfast, M'caw, Stevenson & Orr; Dublin, Hodges, Foster & Figgis; London, Bell, 1878. ix, 366pp.
Mostly nineteenth century poetry.
Second edition: 1879. 398pp. Contains a few additions.

57 MARCHANT, James
Anthology of God, chosen by Sir James Marchant; with an introduction by the late Lord Long of Lambeth. London, Cassell, 1946. 156pp.
Headings: The being of God; God in nature; The soul's search for God; The presence of God; God and man; The love of God; Home to God.
Poetry of the seventeenth and nineteenth centuries, mainly the nineteenth, by familiar and unfamiliar poets.

58 MAY, G Lacey
English religious verse: an anthology, compiled with an introduction by G Lacey May. London, Dent, 1937. xix, 299pp. (Everyman's Library no 937).
Poetry from the middle ages to the twentieth century 'by which Englishmen have expressed their hungering for God'. Well-known poets.

59 MAY, G Lacey
A little book of religious verse, compiled by the Rev G Lacey May.
London, Society for Promoting Christian Knowledge, 1935. 95pp.
Headings: Part I: God; Our Lord Jesus Christ; The holy spirit; The holy catholic church; Part II: The holy eucharist; The saints; The blessed Virgin Mary; Man's source and destiny; Death; The intermediate state; Heaven and hell; The curse of sin; Repentance and forgiveness of sin; The daily life and work; Prayer; Intercession; Suffering; Children; Angels; The Christian chacacter.
Seventeenth and nineteenth century poetry by well-known poets.

60 MEAD, Frank S
Encyclopedia of religious quotations, edited and compiled by Frank S Mead. London, Peter Davies, 1965. 534pp.
Prose and poetry extracts and quotes of all periods covering a wide range of subjects. Includes extracts from the Bible.

61 MORRISON, James Dalton
   Masterpieces of religious verse, edited by James Dalton Morrison. New
York, London, Harper, 1948. 701pp.
Headings: God; Jesus; Man; The Christian life; The kingdom of God; The
nation and the nations; Death and immortality.
English and American poetry of the seventeenth and nineteenth centuries,
with an emphasis on the nineteenth. Double columns; 2006 numbered
items.

62 O'BRIEN, Irene
   Poems of worship, chosen by Irene O'Brien. Oxford, Blackwell, 1969.
xiii, 82pp.
Headings: Sun, moon and stars; Day and night; Rain; God's wonderful
night; Music and song; Birds and beasts; Trees and flowers; Spring, summer,
autumn, winter; Easter, harvest, Christmas; The Lord Jesus; School; Home;
People who work for us; I am wonderfully made; Playtime.
Mostly extracts of twentieth century verse which the compiler had found
suitable to read to infants and lower juniors in the act of worship.

63 O'CONNELL, John R
   Lyra martyrum: the poetry of the English martyrs 1503-1681: an
anthology, gathered together by Sir John R O'Connell; with a foreword by
Cardinal Bourne. London, Burns, Oates & Washbourne, 1934. 123pp.
Biographical notes.
Poems by Sir Thomas More, Philip Howard, Earl of Arundel, Henry Walpole,
Robert Southwell (twenty-six poems), John Thulis and Nicholas Postgate.

64 PALGRAVE, Francis T
   A treasury of sacred song, selected from the English lyrical poetry of
four centuries, with notes explanatory and biographical by Francis T
Palgrave. Oxford, Clarendon Press, 1889. ix, 374pp. Notes (pp 329-361).
Nineteenth century poetry: pp 194-325.

65 PARKER, T H, and TESKEY, F J
   Let there be God: an anthology of modern religious poetry, compiled
by T H Parker and F J Teskey. Oxford, Religious Education Press, 1968.
157pp, col plates. Biographical notes.
Headings: What shall it profit a man . . .?; In the beginning; Of man's first
disobedience; And the waters covered the face of the earth; Out of Egypt;
I bring you good tidings of great joy; He was a man; Oh death, where is
thy sting?; Seek and ye shall find.
'Implicit in every poem is the realization that man needs God as much as
God needs man.' Plates are reproductions of twentieth century religious
paintings.

66 PLOTZ, Helen
   The earth is the Lord's: poems of the spirit, compiled by Helen Plotz;
illustrated with wood engravings by Clare Deighton. New York, Crowell,
[1965]. xiv, 223pp, illus.

67 THE POETRY OF THE SABBATH:
   Being a collection of all the best poems on the Sabbath and its sanctities.
London, Houlston & Wright, 1865. 200pp.
Poetry from the seventeenth to nineteenth century.

68 SAMPSON, Ashley
   The Englishman's religion: an anthology, edited with an introduction
by Ashley Sampson. London, Allen and Unwin, 1948. 122pp.
Prose and poetry from the sixteenth to nineteenth century; mostly prose.

69 SCHAFF, Philip, and GILMAN, Arthur
   A library of religious poetry: a collection of the best poems of all ages
and tongues, with biographical and literary notes, edited by Philip Shaff
and Arthur Gilman. London, Sampson Low, Marston, Searle & Rivington,
1881. 1004pp.
Headings: The poet; The poet and nature; The poet as narrator; The poet
sings of country; Scriptural places, scenes and characters; The poet contemplates life and experience; The dramatist's view of life and duty; The poet
contemplates the family life; The Christian epic; The poet with God
(pp 465-591); The poet contemplates the saviour (pp 597-791); The poet
contemplates the holy spirit; The poet in the face of trial and sorrow; The
poet in view of death and the judgement; The poet's vision of hell, purgatory
and paradise; The poet in view of heaven.

70 SHEED, F J
   Poetry and life: an anthology of English Catholic poetry, compiled by
F J Sheed. London, Sheed and Ward, 1943. xvii, 187pp. Biographical notes.
Headings: Part I: The context of human life: God, and the creation and the
fall of man, The incarnation; Passion and redemption; The last judgement.
Part II. The life of man: The kind of being man is; The kind of thing life is;
Love, marriage and virginity; The beauty of the world; The pain of the
world; Religion: the soul and God, the soul and Christ, the blessed Virgin,
the church, the Reformation; Death; After death.
Covers the work of twenty-six poets, mainly of the sixteenth, seventeenth
and nineteenth centuries.

71 SHIPLEY, Orby
   Lyra eucharistica: hymns and verses on the holy communion, ancient
and modern with other poems, edited by the Rev Orby Shipley. London,
Longman, Green, Longman, Roberts & Green, 1863. xxviii, 271pp.
Headings: The preparation; Oblation; The consecration; The communion;
The thanksgiving.
Nineteenth century poetry and old hymns, mostly translated from Latin
and German.

72 SOMERVELL, R U
   Thank God: an anthology of praise, compiled by R U Somervell.
London, James Clarke, [1964], 63pp.
Headings: Daily praises for a month (pp 7-41); Praises for special occa-
sions: Morning; Evening; Sunday; Communion; Christmas; New Year; Good

Friday; Easter Day; Whitsunday; In illness; In sorrow; In loneliness; In old age.
Poetry and prose extracts from the Bible and the saints.

73 SOUTHGATE, Henry
   Suggestive thoughts on religious subjects: a dictionary of quotations and selected passages from the best writers, ancient and modern for the use of the clergy and others, compiled and analytically arranged by Henry Southgate. 2nd ed. London, Charles Griffin, 1881. xix, 447pp.
Contains a considerable number of extracts from the writings of nineteenth century clergymen.

74 STEWART, George
   Dedication: an anthology of the will of God, collected by George Stewart. New York, Association Press, 1931. xxxvi, 142pp.

75 STREAMER, Volney
   Voices of doubt and trust, selected by Volney Streamer. New York, Brentanos, 1897. xxi, 215pp.

76 THOMAS, Ronald Stuart
   The Penguin book of religious verse, introduced and edited by R S Thomas. Harmondsworth, (Middx), Penguin, 1963. 191pp.
Headings: God; Self; Nothing; It; All.
American and English poetry from the sixteenth to twentieth century, by well-known poets.

77 TRAPP, Jacob
   Modern religious poems: a contemporary anthology, edited by Jacob Trapp. New York, Harper & Row, 1964. 304pp.

78 VINCENT, Louis
   The little brown company: an anthology of Franciscan poetry and prose, gathered by Louis Vincent. London, Martin Hopkinson, 1925. xii, 136pp.
Limited edition: 500 copies. Mostly nineteenth and early twentieth century poetry connected with St Francis.

79 WALLIS, C L
   Treasury of poems for worship and devotion, edited by C L Wallis. New York, Harper, 1959. 378pp.
Headings: Poet's petition; To God, the father; Thou crystal Christ; The varied ministries of nature; By day and night; The home circle; God's far-ranging kingdom; Disciplines of the spiritual life; Petitions of doubt and protest; Through deep waters; Towards the larger life; With thankful hearts.
Poetry from the seventeenth to twentieth century.

80 WATTS, Neville
   Love songs of Sion: a selection of devotional verse from Old English sources, adapted by Neville Watts. London, Burns, Oates & Washbourne, 1924. xxiii, 167pp.
Headings: Of holy mass and communion; Of our blessed Lord's love; Of

14

our blessed Lord's passion; Of our Lady; Of the four last things.
Verse taken mainly from fifteenth century manuscripts and rewritten in a
twentieth century style.

81 WILLMOTT, Robert Aris
    Sacred poetry, selected and edited by Robert Aris Willmott; with
seventy-nine illustrations by Holman Hunt, J D Watson, Sir John Gilbert,
J Wolf and other artists. London, Routledge, 1893. 440pp, illus.
Mostly nineteenth and seventeenth century poetry by well-known poets.

82 WINTLE, W James
    Pilgrim songs on the king's highway, selected by W James Wintle.
London, John Ouseley, [1911], 286pp, plates.
Poetry of the seventeenth and nineteenth centuries.

83 WOOD, Phyllis Taunton
    The heavenly vision: an anthology, compiled by Phillis Taunton Wood.
London, Student Christian Movement Press, 1935. 158pp.
Headings: Vision and aspiration (the growth from childhood to a con-
scious faith); Vision and adoration (the experience of those whose vision
has become clear enough for them to enjoy and adore God); Vision and
action (the activity which is the result of vision).
Poetry and prose extracts of all periods, with an emphasis on the seventeenth and nineteenth centuries. Prose includes extracts from philosophers,
saints and mystics.

84 WOODS, Ralph Louis
    The world treasury of religious quotation: diverse beliefs, conviction,
comments, dissents and opinions from ancient and modern sources, compiled and edited by Ralph Louis Woods. New York, Hawthorne Books,
[1965]. xv, 1106pp.

85 WRIGHT, Kate A
    Sacred poems of the nineteenth century, edited by Kate A Wright.
Birmingham, C Combridge; London, Simpkin, Marshall, Hamilton & Kent,
[1898]. 280pp.
Mostly unfamiliar poetry.

See also: 1398, 1433, 1454

Studies and criticism

86 ABBEY, C J
    Religious thought in Old English verse, by Rev C J Abbey. London,
Sampson Low, 1892. 456pp.
A descriptive study with many complete examples, ranging from Caedmon
to the eighteenth century.

87 APPLETON, Sarah S
    Theology and poetry in the Middle English lyric. PhD thesis, Ohio
State University, 1961.

88 BENZIGER, J
Images of eternity: studies in the poetry of religious vision from Wordsworth to T S Eliot, by J Benziger. Carbondale, Southern Illinois University Press, 1962. 324pp. Bibliography. Notes.
Chapters: The transcendentalizing experiences; Wordsworth, Shelley; Keats; Tennyson; Browning; Arnold; Modern instances: Yates, Stevens, Eliot; The ennobling interchange.

89 BROWN, Dorothy I
Religion in the non-dramatic poetry of the reign of Queen Elizabeth I, with the exception of the works of Spenser. PhD thesis, Colorado University, 1950.

90 BUSAILAH, Reja E
Christian themes in the formulaic tradition of Old English poetry. PhD thesis, New York University, 1972.

91 CARPENTER, W Boyd
The religious spirit in the poets, by the Rev W Boyd Carpenter. London, Isbister, 1900. 247pp.
Chapters: Kinship between religion and poetry; Religion and literary inspiration; The genuine and superficial religious element; Edmund Spenser; Marlowe's 'Faustus'; Shakespeare's 'Tempest'; Milton's 'Comus'; 'The Ancient Mariner'; Tennyson; Tennyson's 'In Memoriam'; Browning.

92 CHRISTIAN THEMES IN CONTEMPORARY POETS:
a study of English poetry of the twentieth century. London, S C M Press, 1965. 208pp. Bibliography (mainly primary works).
Chapters: Introduction—some aspects of the twentieth century background of belief; The search for a pattern—poetry of Edwin Muir; The mystery of suffering—poetry of David Gascoyne; The affirmative way—poetry of Charles Williams; The analysis of guilt—poetry of W H Auden; The world in creation—poetry of Norman Nicholson; The holiness of the heart's affections—poetry of Anne Riddler; Image and form; Event and image.

93 COX, Ernest H
Certain Middle English poetic survivals in the religious and semi-religious poetry of the sixteenth century. PhD thesis, University of N Carolina, 1936.

94 DOUGHTY, W L
Studies in the religious poetry of the seventeenth century, by W L Doughty. London, Epworth Press, 1946. 200pp. Notes. References.
Covers the poetry of Henry Vaughan, Francis Quarles, Richard Crashaw, Sir John Davies, Henry More, Thomas Traherne.

95 FAIRCHILD, Hoxie Neal
Religious trends in English poetry, by Hoxie Neal Fairchild. New York, Columbia University Press. 6 vols. Bibliographies. References in footnotes. Indices of subjects.

Vol I–1700-1740: Protestantism and the cult of sentiment. 1939. 592pp.
Vol II–1740-1780: Religious sentimentalism in the age of Johnson. 1942.
406pp. Vol III–1780-1830: Romantic faith. 1949. 549pp. Vol IV–1830-
1880: Christianity and romanticism in the Victorian era. 1957. 592pp.
Vol V–1880-1920: Gods in a changing poetry. 1962. 663pp. Vol VI–
1920-1965: Valley of dry bones. 1968. 525pp.

96 GAFFNEY, S J C
Theology in English poetry. PhD thesis. National University of Ireland,
1941.

97 GRANT, J P G
Poetry and theology: Christian and Platonist attitudes to the fall of
man in seventeenth century devotional poets. DPhil, University of
Sussex, 1966.

98 GRAY, Douglas
Themes and images in the medieval English religious lyric, by Douglas
Gray. London, Routledge & Kegan Paul, 1972. x, 300pp, plates. Notes
and references (pp 227-294).
Chapters: Part I–The background; The inherited tradition; Medieval
devotion; The English lyrics. Part II–The scheme of redemption; Christ
and the Virgin Mary; Annunciation and nativity; The passion; Resurrection
and assumption. Part III–The life of this world; The Christian life; Death
and the last things.
A lucid account of the subject with many examples. Plates are reproductions of medieval manuscripts.

99 HARRIS, Patricia H
The anonymous English religious lyric: a handbook. PhD thesis,
University of Missouri, 1969.

100 HORNING, Sister Mary Eulogia
Evidences of romantic treatment of religious elements in late eighteenth
century minor poetry 1771-1800. PhD thesis, Catholic University of America,
Washington, 1933. 103pp.

101 LEACH, Elsie
Commercial imagery in early seventeenth century English religious
poetry. PhD thesis, University of California, Los Angeles, 1951.

102 MacAULIFFE, M M
The poetry of the Catholic revival. MA thesis, National University of
Ireland, 1938.

103 MARTZ, Louis L
The poetry of meditation: a study in English religious literature of
the seventeenth century, by Louis L Martz. New Haven, Yale University
Press, 1954. xiv, 375pp. Bibliography. (Yale Studies in English, Vol 125).
Chapters: Part I–The art of meditation; The method of meditation;
Meditation on the life of Christ; Self knowledge–the spiritual combat;
Problems in puritan meditation: Richard Baxter. Part II–Robert Southwell

and the seventeenth century; John Donne in meditation: the 'anniversaries'; George Herbert: in the presence of a friend; George Herbert: the unity of the temple. Conclusion—'Unity of being' and the meditative style.

104 McKEOUGH, Mary N
Religious lyric verse in fifteenth century England. PhD Thesis, National University of Ireland, 1941.

105 MILLER, Joseph Hillis
The disappearance of God: five nineteenth century writers, by Joseph Hollis Miller. Cambridge (Mass.), Belknap Press of Harvard University Press, 1963. ix, 367pp. References in footnotes.
Covers: De Quincey, Emily Brontë, Gerald Manley Hopkins, Robert Browning and Mathew Arnold.

106 MORGAN, K E
Christian themes in English poetry of the twentieth century. PhD thesis, University of Liverpool, 1963.

107 NORBERT, Mother Mary
The reflection of religion in English medieval verse romances. PhD thesis, Bryn Mawr University, 1940.

108 PATTERSON, F A
The Middle English penitential lyric: a study and collection of early religious verse. New York, Columbia University Press, 1911. ix, 203pp.

109 PEAKE, L S
Theology in the English poets of the Victorian era. BLitt thesis, Oxford University, 1926.

110 SAMPSON, Herbert C
The Anglican tradition in eighteenth century verse. PhD thesis, Michigan State University, 1965.

111 SCHOLES, Kenneth A
The Elizabethan devotional lyric. PhD thesis, University of California, Berkeley, 1956.

112 SELZ, William A
Conventional imagery in religious verse of the English Renaissance. PhD thesis, Harvard University, 1944.

113 STUART, Charles Macaulay
Vision of Christ in the poets: selected studies of the Christian faith as interpreted by Milton, Wordsworth, the Brownings, Tennyson, Whittier, Longfellow, Lowell, edited by Charles Macaulay Stuart; with an introduction by Professor C W Pearson. Cincinnati, Curts & Jennings; New York, Eaton & Mains, 1896. 304pp, front, port.

114 THORNBURG, Robert B
A survey of sixteenth century English religious verse. PhD thesis, Pennsylvania University, 1956.

115

116 UNDERWOOD, J J
   The English religious lyric in the Middle Ages. MA thesis, National
University of Ireland, 1937.

117 WEBER, Sarah Appleton
   Theology and poetry in the Middle English lyric: a study of sacred
history and aesthetic form. Columbus, Ohio State University Press,
1969. 292pp.

118 WHITE, Natalie E
   The English liturgical refrain lyric before 1450 with special reference
to the fourteenth century. PhD thesis, Stanford University, 1945.

119 WILDER, Amos N
   Modern poetry and the Christian tradition: a study in the relation
of Christianity to culture. New York, Scribner, 1952. 287pp.

120 WILDER, Amos N
   The spiritual aspects of the new poetry, by Amos N Wilder. New York,
London, Harper, 1940. xix, 262pp. Bibliography.
Part I—Modernist and traditionalist. Part II—Factors making for negation.
Part III—Alternative faiths: the cult of the irrational with a note on Hart
Crane; The new pantheism; The nihilism of Mr Robinson Jeffers; The
primitivism of D H Lawrence; Ethical motives; Revolutionary and prole-
tarian poetry: Kenneth Patchen; W B Yeats and the Christian option;
Mr T S Eliot and the anglo-catholic option; The pit from which we are
dragged.

121 WILSON, J H
   Christian theology in Old English poetry. PhD thesis, Tulane University,
1965.

122 WOOLF, Rosemary
   The English religious lyric in the Middle Ages, by Rosemary Woolf.
Oxford, Clarendon Press, 1968. xi, 426pp, plates, illus. References in
footnotes.

THE SCRIPTURES

The Bible in general

123 HORDER, W Garrett
   The poets' Bible, selected and edited by W Garrett Horder. New Testa-
ment section. London, Isbister, 1881, 489pp.
Poetry of the seventeenth and nineteenth centuries, covering all episodes
in the gospels.
   Second edition: 1883. xxx, 504pp.
   Third edition: London, Ward, Lock & Bowden, 1895. xviii, 504pp.

124 HORDER, W Garrett
The poets' Bible, selected and edited by W Garrett Horder. Old Testament section. London, Isbister, 1889. 608pp.
Poetry mainly of the seventeenth and nineteenth centuries covering many episodes in the Old Testament.

Studies and criticism

125 ALLEN, M J
The book of Job in Middle English literature, 1100-1500. PhD thesis, London University, 1970.

126 HEBAISHA, H A K
Biblical poems from 1538-1638, with special reference to poems on David and on Job. PhD thesis, University of London, 1966.

127 JONES, P R
The treatment of Old Testament characters and incidents in Old and Middle English poetry and drama. MA thesis, University of Wales, 1958.

128 RIGGIO, Milla B
Genesis and Exodus: structure and narrative style in medieval Latin and Old English biblical poetry. PhD thesis, Harvard University, 1972.

129 ROSTON, Murray
Prophet and poet: the Bible and the growth of romanticism, by Murray Roston. London, Faber, 1965. 204pp. Bibliography. References in footnotes.
Chapters: Hebraism and classicism; The laminated bible; Nature refined; Patriarchal nobility; Enthusiastic devotions; The boundless universe; The bible poeticized; The trumpet of a prophecy.

130 SHROEDER, Peter R
The narrative style in Old English biblical poetry. PhD thesis, Harvard University, 1967.

131 SIEGEL, Ben
Elements of the Old Testament in early seventeenth century English poetry. PhD thesis, University of Southern California, 1957.

132 SIGER, Leonard
The image of Job in the Renaissance. PhD thesis, Johns Hopkins University, 1960.

133 SIMMONS, B
Some aspects of the treatment of the psalms and of the song of Solomon in English eighteenth century literature. MA thesis, University of London, 1937.

134 STEVENSON, J C
The influence of the Bible on English literature of the seventeenth century. MA thesis, University of Birmingham, 1914.

Jesus Christ

135 ASTLE, Cedric
    The Gospel in English literature: a classical anthology of prose and
poetry on the life of Christ, compiled by Cedric Astle. London, Skeffing-
ton, 1950. 236pp.
Headings: The father; The son; The master; The servant; The saviour; The
king.
Poetry and prose from the sixteenth to the nineteenth century.

136 AULT, Norman
    The poet's life of Christ, compiled, arranged and decorated by Norman
Ault. London, Oxford University Press, 1922. xxviii, 272pp, illus.
Poetry from the Middle Ages to the twentieth century, covering all aspects
of Christ's life.

137 COLVILE, Kenneth N
    A little book of the passion: an anthology of prose and verse chosen by
Kenneth N Colvile. London, Philip Allan, 1928. xii, 164pp.
Headings: The preparation; The garden; Halls of judgment; Golgotha; The
sepulchre; The divine love.
Poetry from the seventeenth to nineteenth century.

138 CLARK, Thomas Curtis, and CLARK, Hazel Davis
    Christ in poetry, compiled and edited by Thomas Curtis Clark and Hazel
Davis Clark. New York, Association Press, [1952]. 412pp.

139 CLARK, Thomas Curtis
    The Master of men: quotable poems about Jesus, compiled by Thomas
Curtis Clarke. New York, R R Smith, 1930, 243pp.

140 CROW, Martha Foote
    Christ in the poetry of today: an anthology from American poets, com-
piled by Martha Foote Crow. New York, Womans Press, 1917. 207pp.
    Second, revised edition: 1918. 227pp.
    Third, revised edition: 1923. 314pp.
    Fourth, revised edition: compiled and reassembled by Elvira Slack . . .
1928. 287pp.

141 ELLIOTT, H B
    The life and the way: the story of Christ, compiled from the poets
by H B Elliott; with an introduction by John Oxenham. London, Jarrolds,
1923. xv, 148pp, plates.
Headings: The story of the nativity; The childhood of Jesus; The ministry;
Holy week; Christ victorious.
Covers the work of thirty-three poets, mostly unfamiliar, of the late nineteenth and early twentieth centuries.

142 MARCHANT, James
    Anthology of Jesus, arranged and edited by Sir James Marchant.
London, Cassell, 1926. xi, 393pp.

Covers all aspects of the life of Christ. Poetry and prose of all periods, but with an emphasis on the nineteenth century.

143 MARY IMMACULATA, Sister
The tree and the master: an anthology of literature on the cross of Christ, edited by Sister Mary Immaculata; with a preface by W H Auden. New York, Random House, 1965. xxviii, 254pp.

144 MILLER, Basil
Beautiful poems on Jesus, compiled by Basil Miller. Kansas City, Beacon Hill Press, 1948. 342pp.
Reprinted: New York, Books for Libraries Press, 1968. (Granger Index Reprint Series).

145 SHIPLEY, Orby
Lyra messianica: hymns and verses on the life of Christ, ancient and modern with other poems, edited by The Rev Orby Shipley. London, Longman, Green. Longman, Roberts & Green, 1864. lii, 414pp.
Poetry covering all periods; half from the Middle Ages and earlier.

146 SOUTHGATE, Henry
Christus redemptor: being the life, character, and teachings of Our Blessed Lord and Saviour Jesus Christ, illustrated in many passages from the writings of ancient and modern authors, selected and analytically arranged by Henry Southgate. London, Cassell, Petter & Galpin, [1875]. xvi, 312pp.
Prose and poetry from the seventeenth to nineteenth century. Contains much material taken from the writings of nineteenth century clergymen.

See also: 123, 173

Studies and criticism

147 BATHO, E C
The life of Christ in the ballads. (in Essays and Studies, Vol 9, 1923, pp 70-97). References in footnotes.

148 BROWN, Harry M
The Christ image: concepts of Christ in contemporary American poetry. PhD thesis, Western Reserve University, 1955.

149 KELLY, Thomas Daniel
Medieval poems on the cross and crucifixion. PhD thesis, Princeton University, 1967.

150 LEMAY, Sister Marie de Lourdes
The allegory of the Christ-Knight in English literature, by Sister Marie de Lourdes Lemay. Washington, The Catholic University of America, 1932. xii, 89pp. Bibliography.

151 STUBBS, Charles William
   The Christ of English poetry: being the Hubean lectures delivered before
the University of Cambridge, 1904-5, by Charles William Stubbs. London,
Dent; New York, Dutton, 1906.
Four lectures covering: Cynewulf, William Langland, Shakespeare, and
Robert Browning.

The Virgin Mary

152 FLOOD, J M
   Ave Maria: a selection of verse and prose written in praise of the mother
of God [compiled by] J M Flood. Dublin, The Catholic Truth Society of
Ireland, 1951. 86pp.
Prose and poetry of all periods, including extracts from the Saints, histories
and the Bible.

153 MARCHANT, James
   The Madonna: an anthology, selected and edited by Sir James Marchant;
with an introduction on the Madonna in art by Sir Charles Holmes, with
numerous illustrations. London, Longmans & Green, 1928. xxxix, 206pp,
illus.
Headings: Invocation; The annunciation; The nativity; Madonna's lullaby;
The child Jesus; Joseph and Mary; Hail, full of grace; At the cross; The
second eve; The assumption and coronation; Ora Pro Nobis; The witness of
the ages.
Poetry and prose of all periods; mostly poetry. Emphasis on the writings
of the Saints, the Middle Ages, and the seventeenth and nineteenth centuries.

154 SHEED, F J
   The Mary book, assembled by F J Sheed. London, New York, Sheed &
Ward, 1950. ix, 309pp, plates (some col).
Headings: Anticipation; From the annunciation to the assumption; All
generations call her blessed.
Poetry and prose of all periods; more prose than poetry.

155 SHIPLEY, Orby
   Carmina mariana: an English anthology in verse in honour or in
relation to the blessed Virgin Mary, collected and arranged by Orby Shipley.
London, printed for the editor by Spottiswoode & Co, 1893. xxi, 439pp.
Ranges from Chaucer to Tennyson and includes some foreign material in
translation. Some items are taken from periodical literature. Includes
sixteen poems on old master paintings featuring the Madonna.
   Second series: Privately printed for the editor by John Griffin, 1902.
liv, 528pp.

156 THERESE, Sister M
   I sing of a Maiden: the Mary book of verse, edited by Sister M Therese.
New York, Macmillan, 1947. xivii, 459pp. Notes.

Studies and criticism

157 McDERMOTT, John J
Mary Magdalene in English literature from 1500 to 1650. PhD thesis, University of California, Los Angeles, 1964.

DOGMA

The fall of man   *Studies and criticism*

158 SMITH, Eric
Some versions of the fall: the myth of the fall of man in English literature, by Eric Smith; with a foreword by J I M Stewart. London, Croom Helm, 1973. xiv, 228pp, plates.

Repentance   *Studies and criticism*

159 CANFIELD, Virginia G
From Parnassus' Mount to Sion's Hill: repentance and conversion in English non-dramatic poetry of the first half of the seventeenth century. PhD thesis, Ohio State University, 1949.

160 SHAKESHAFT, M M
The treatment of the theme of repentance in religious verse, 1595-1610. MA thesis, University of London, 1961.

The devil   *Studies and criticism*

161 MOUNTFORD, W M
The devil in English literature from the Middle Ages to 1700. PhD, University of London, 1931.

162 WOOLF, R E
The devil in Old English poetry. (in Review of English Studies, Vol 4, 1953, pp 1-12).
References in footnotes. Only a few actual examples.

Day of judgement   *Studies and criticism*

163 STURM, Norbert Aloysius
Judgement day in eighteenth century poetry. PhD thesis, Case Western Reserve University, 1961.

164 MILLER, Arthur
The last man: a study of the eschatological theme in English poetry and fiction from 1806 through 1839. PhD thesis, Duke University, 1966.

165 WHITBREAD, L
The doomsday theme in Old English poetry. (in Beiträge zur Geschichte der deutschen Sprache und Literatur, (Halle), 89, 1967, pp 452-481).
References in footnotes.

166 WORKMAN, Rhea Thomas
The concept of hell in Anglo-Saxon poetry before AD 850. PhD thesis,
University of South Carolina, 1958.

Immortality

167 ADAMS, Richard W
The Middle English body and soul poems: an edition. PhD thesis,
Harvard University, 1971.

168 THE CELESTIAL COUNTRY:
Hymns and poems on the joys and glories of paradise; with illustrations
after Fra Angelico, Ghirlandajo, Botticelli, Lippi, Bernardino Luini, Benozzo
Gozzoli, and Carpaccio. London, Seeley, 1900. vii, 96pp, plates.
Pieces by the saints and seventeenth century poets.

169 COBLENTZ, Stanton A
Unseen wings: the living poetry of man's immortality, compiled by
Stanton A Coblentz. New York, The Beechhurst Press, 1949. 282pp.

170 G, N
The testament of immortality: an anthology selected and arranged by
N G; with a preface by T S Eliot. London, Faber, 1940. 280pp.
Prose and poetry of all periods, including extracts from the Bible, the saints
and philosophers.

171 HAZARD, Marshall Curtiss
The immortal hope: the witness of the great poets of all ages to the life
beyond, compiled by M C Hazard; with an introduction by Newell Dwight
Hillis and with sixteen full page half-tone illustrations from the original
paintings by celebrated artists. New York, A L Burt, [1906]. xxviii, 303pp,
plates.

172 HAZARD, Marshall Curtiss
The tearless land: a collection of poems on heaven, compiled by Marshall
Curtiss Hazard. Boston, Chicago, Congregational Sunday-School and
Publishing Society, [1896]. 303pp.

173 HERNAMAN, Claudia Frances
Lyra consolationis from the poets of the seventeenth, eighteenth and
nineteenth centuries, selected and arranged by Claudia Frances Hernaman.
London, Longmans, 1890. 228pp.
Headings: Death and burial; Communion of saints; Near the end of life's
journey; Children; Words of cheer; Resurrection; Ascension; Second coming.
Poetry based on Christ's crucifixion, death, burial and ascension.

174 ROSS, Peter V
If a man dies, shall he live again?—the poets' answer, edited by Peter V
Ross. San Francisco, W J Marnell, 1931. 165pp.

175 SITWELL, Constance
   Seek paradise [compiled by] Constance Sitwell. London, Cape, 1948.
174pp.
Prose and poetry extracts of all periods on heaven and immortality; mostly prose.

See also: Death 375-385

Studies and criticism

176 OSMOND, R E
   The relationship between body and soul in seventeenth century non-dramatic literature. PhD thesis, Cambridge University, 1968.

177 WARR, Nancy Nairn
   The body-soul debate in seventeenth century poetry. PhD thesis, The University of New Mexico, 1969.

178 WEATHERHEAD, M A
   The contribution of Victorian poets to the development of the idea of immortality. MA thesis, University of Manchester, 1926.

THE RELIGIOUS LIFE

Prayers and graces

179 ARMSTRONG, O V and ARMSTRONG, Helen
   Prayer poems, compiled by O V Armstrong and Helen Armstrong. New York, Nashville, Abingdon-Cokesbury Press, [1942]. 256pp.

180 DIXON, Henry Lancelot
   Saying grace, historically considered and numerous forms of grace taken from ancient and modern sources with appendices, by Henry Lancelot Dixon. Oxford, London, James Parker, 1903. xvi, 263pp.
Headings: Part I—Introduction on saying grace; Part II—Ancient forms of grace; Part III—Oxford and Cambridge (Latin graces used by the different colleges); Part IV—Modern graces.

181 HARGER, M
   Prayers from the poets, compiled by M Harger. New York, Chicago, Fleming H Revell, [1891]. 199pp.

182 HEADLAM, Cecil and MAGNUS, Laurie
   Prayers from the poets, edited by Cecil Headlam and Laurie Magnus. London, Routledge; New York, E P Dutton, 1906. xii, 371pp. (Wayfaring Books.)
Headings: Veni, creator; Pater noster; De profundis; The conduct of life; The work of our hands; The pilgrim's progress; Love and death; Earth and heaven; Thanksgiving.
An enlarged edition of item 186.

183 HYATT, Alfred H
   A little book of graces [compiled by] Alfred Hyatt. London, Philip
Welbey, 1906. 65pp. (The Aldwych Series, No 6.)
Includes twenty-four items by John and Charles Wesley, and 'On saying
grace before meat' by Charles Lamb.

184 LAING, Allan M
   More prayers and graces: a second book of unusual piety, collected by
Allan M Laing; with illustrations by Mervyn Peake. London, Gollancz,
1957. 64pp, illus.
Short poetical stanzas and prose anecdotes, mostly humorous, by mostly
twentieth century writers.

185 LAING, Allan M
   Prayers and graces: a little book of extraordinary piety, collected by
Allan M Laing; with illustrations by Mervyn Peake. London, Gollancz,
1944. 64pp, illus.
Material similar to that in the above.

186 MAGNUS, Laurie and HEADLAM, Cecil
   Prayers from the poets: a calendar of devotion, compiled and edited by
Laurie Magnus and Cecil Headlam. Edinburgh, London, Blackwood, 1899.
369pp.
Poetry mostly of the sixteenth, seventeenth and nineteenth centuries.
Includes some classical and foreign writers in translation.

187 TRENCH, John
   The Harp book of graces: prayers at the table from the eighth century
to the present day, edited by John Trench. London, Harp Lager, 1963.
37pp.
Headings: The age of faith; Graces at Oxbridge colleges and schools; The
age of piety; The age of self-consciousness.

188 WOODS, Ralph Louis
   Poems of prayer, edited by Ralph Louis Woods. New York, Hawthorn,
1962. 287pp.
Primarily a collection of Catholic prayer poems, written by Catholics.

Studies and criticism

189 ROBBINS, Rossell Hope
   Popular prayers in Middle English verse (in Modern Philology, Vol 36,
May 1939, pp 337-50).
References in footnotes. Numerous examples.

190 ROBBINS, Rossell Hope
   Private prayers in Middle English verse. (Studies in Philology, Vol 36,
July 1939, pp 466-75.)
References in footnotes.

Mysticism

191 ALBERTSON, Charles Carroll
  Lyra mystica: an anthology of mystical verse, edited by Charles Carroll Albertson; introduced by William Ralph Inge. London, Macmillan, 1932. lvi, 496pp.
All periods, but predominantly nineteenth century American and English poetry. Compiler acknowledges debt to a large number of other special and general anthologies.

192 CASHMORE, Adeline
  The mount of vision: a book of English mystical verse, selected and arranged by Adeline Cashmore; with an introduction by Alice Meynell. London, Chapman & Hall, 1910. 160pp.
Headings: The traveller; The way; Friends of the way; The open vision. Familiar poets of the seventeenth and nineteenth centuries.

193 HUNTER, Irene
  American mystical verse: an anthology, selected by Irene Hunter; preface by Zona Gale. New York, Appleton, 1925. xxiii, 308pp.
  Reprinted: New York, Books for Libraries, 1970. (Granger Index Reprint Series.)

194 NICHOLSON, D H S and LEE, A H E
  The Oxford book of English mystical verse, chosen by D H S Nicholson and A H E Lee. Oxford, Clarendon Press, 1916. 644pp.
Poetry from the sixteenth to twentieth century; the larger part is of the nineteenth century.

195 SHIPLEY, Orby
  Lyra mystica: hymns and verses on sacred subjects, ancient and modern, edited by The Rev Orby Shipley. London, Longman, Green, Longman, Roberts and Green, 1865. xiv, 434pp

Studies and criticism

196 FILES, Harold G
  Some aspects of eighteenth century mysticism in England. PhD thesis, Harvard University, 1923.

197 NEENAN, Mary P
  Some evidences of mysticism in English poetry of the nineteenth century. PhD thesis, Catholic University, 1916.

Churches, parsons, and pilgrims

198 BETJEMAN, John
  Altar and pew: Church of England verses, edited by John Betjeman. London, Edward Hulton, 1959. 47pp. (The Pocket Poets.)
Poetry from the seventeenth to twentieth century, describing churches, their priests and people.

199 CHRISTMAS, F E
　The parson in English literature: a galaxy of clerical figures, gathered from the writers of six centuries by F E Christmas. London, Hodder and Stoughton, 1950. 342pp.
Includes a significant number of poems.

See also: 418, 421, 1044, 1392

Studies and criticism

200 DITCHFIELD, P H
　The parson in literature (in Essays by Divers Hands: Transactions of the Royal Society of Literature, new series, Vol l, 1921, pp 25-60).
Covers prose and poetry from Chaucer to the nineteenth century.

201 HOLLOWAY, Julia Bolton
　The figure of the pilgrim in medieval poetry. PhD thesis, University of California, Berkeley, 1974.

RELIGIOUS FESTIVALS

Christmas

202 ANDREWS, William
　A wreath of Christmas carols and poems, chosen and edited by Williams Andrews. Hull, J R Tutin, 1906. 64pp.

203 BEECHING, H C
　A book of Christmas verse, selected by H C Beeching; with ten designs by Walter Crane. London, Methuen, 1895. xvi, 174pp, illus. Notes.
Headings: Latin hymns and early carols; Later poems and carols; Christmas merrymaking (pp 139-169).
Poetry from the seventeenth to nineteenth century.

204 BRAYBROOKE, Neville
　A partridge in a pear tree: a celebration for Christmas, arranged by Neville Braybrooke; with decorations by Barbara Jones and Henry Fawcett School. London, Darton, Longman & Todd, 1960. 196pp, plates, illus.
Poetry and prose covering a wide range of subject matter ranging from the Middle Ages to the twentieth century.

205 BREWTON, Sara W and BREWTON, John E
　Christmas bells are ringing, selected by Sara and John Brewton; illustrated by Decie Mervin. New York, Macmillan, 1951. 114pp, illus.

206 BULLEN, A H
　A Christmas garland: carols and poetry from the fifteenth century to the present time, edited by A H Bullen; with seven illustrations newly designed by Henry G Wells. London, John C Nimmo, 1885. xxxii, 278pp, illus. Notes.

Headings: Part I—Christmas chants and carols; Part II—Carmina sacra; Part III—Christmas customs and Christmas cheer; Farewell to Christmas.
Limited edition: 150 copies.

207 CARNEGIE LIBRARY SCHOOL ASSOCIATION

Christmas in poetry: carols and poems chosen by a committee of the Carnegie Library School Association. First series. New York, H W Wilson, 1922. 48pp (printed on one side of page only).
Second series: New York, H W Wilson, 1923. 42pp.

208 A CHRISTMAS ANTHOLOGY:

carols and poems, old and new. London, George Harrap, 1906. 119pp, illus.
Headings: Christmas holy; Christmas merry.
Poetry from the seventeenth to nineteenth century. Compiler acknowledges debt to 210 and 219.

209 CHRISTMAS IN ART AND SONG:

a collection of songs, carols and descriptive poems, relating to the festival of Christmas; illustrated from drawings by distinguished artists. New York, Arundel, 1880. 128pp, illus.

210 CHRISTMAS WITH THE POETS:

a collection of songs and descriptive verse relating to the festival of Christmas from the Anglo-Norman period to the present time; embellished with fifty tinted illustrations by Birket Foster and with initial letters and other ornaments. London, David Bogue, 1851. x, 189pp, illus.
Introduction is signed: H V.
Further editions: 1852, 1855, 1862.

211 CHRISTMAS, F E

A Christmas anthology, compiled by F E Christmas. London, St Hugh's Press, [1944]. 52pp, illus.
Headings: The Christmas season; Christmas Eve; Christmas Day; The First Christmas.
Twenty-two pieces of prose and poetry of the seventeenth, nineteenth and twentieth centuries.

212 COLLINS, Philip

English Christmas: an anthology, edited with an introduction by Philip Collins. London, Gordon Fraser, 1956. 96pp, illus.
Headings: The story and its meaning; Objections and reservations; Preparing for Christmas; Festivities of Christmas; Dickens and Christmas; Less Happy Christmasses; The aftermath.
Poetry and prose from the seventeenth to twentieth century.

213 THE CRADLE OF THE KING:

a Christmas anthology, by Richard Crashaw, John Bannister Tabb, Robert Stephen Hawker, Coventry Patmore, Alice Meynell, Kartharine Tynan and Francis Thompson. London, Burns & Oates, 1911. 24pp, illus.

214 DAVIS, David
A single star: an anthology of Christmas poetry, compiled and arranged by David Davis; illustrated by Margery Gill. London, The Bodley Head, 1973. 94pp, illus.
Headings: 'Christmas almost come'; Christmas Eve; Bethlehem; Christmas morning; 'Make we merry'; Christmas night; Epiphany and after; Epilogue.
Poetry from the sixteenth to twentieth century, mostly of the nineteenth and twentieth.

215 FOLEY, Daniel J
Christmas in the good old days: a Victorian album of stories, poems and pictures by the personalities who rediscovered Christmas, edited by Daniel J Foley; illustrated with sketches by Charlotte Edmands Bowden, photos by Paul E Genereux, and a portfolio of Christmas decorations drawn by Lucy Ellen Merrill in the nineteenth century. Philadelphia, Chilton, 1961. 224pp, illus. Bibliography.

216 GRIBBLE, Leonard R
A Christmas treasury in prose and verse selected and edited by Leonard R Gribble. London, Society for Promoting Christian Knowledge, 1929. 231pp.
Headings: The nativity; The season; Festivities, feasts and friends; Tales and legends; Old gleanings.
Poetry and prose from the seventeenth to the twentieth century.

217 GRIGSON, Geoffrey
The three kings: a Christmas book of carols, poems and pieces, chosen with an account of the legend by Geoffrey Grigson. London, Gordon Fraser, 1958. 77pp, illus.
Poetry and prose from the Middle Ages to the twentieth century. Illustrations are reproductions of paintings and sculpture.

218 HYETT, Florence B
Fifty Christmas poems for children, selected by Florence B Hyett. New York, Appleton; Oxford, Blackwell, 1923. 68pp.

219 JEWITT, W Henry
The nativity in art and song: its varied treatment with pen and pencil, ancient and modern, with illustrative notes, historical and legendary by W Henry Jewitt. London. Elliot Stock, 1898. xiv, 198pp, illus.
Headings: The story of the nativity; Treatment of the story in verse; The angel hosts and their worship; The wise men from the East; The presentation in the temple; Cradle songs; The joyousness with which the festival of the Lord's nativity has been associated; Legends in connection with Christmastide and the child Christ.
Covers all periods from the middle ages to the nineteenth century. Illustrations are the compiler's own sketches of religious masterpieces.

220 KELLEHER, D L
   An anthology of Christmas prose and verse, collected by D L Kelleher, with new stories and poems by Humbert Wolfe, Martin Armstrong, T F Powys, Helen Beauclerk, etc. London, Cresset Press, 1928. vii, 231pp. Prose includes: Christmas letters (pp 15-25). Poems and ballads: pp 99-159; Carols (with music): pp 169-198.

221 KNIGHT, William
   The poets on Christmas, selected and edited by William Knight. London, Christian Knowledge Society, 1907. 192pp.

222 McNAUGHT, Rosamund Livingstone
   Christmas selections for readings and recitations, compiled by Rosamund Livingstone McNaught. Philadelphia, Penn Publishing, 1906. 202pp.

223 REEVES, James
   The Christmas book, chosen and compiled by James Reeves; illustrated by Raymond Briggs. London, Heinemann; New York, Dutton, 1968. 191pp, illus.
Prose and poetry on all aspects of Christmas from the seventeenth to the twentieth century.

224 ROHDE, Eleanour Sinclair
   Christmas, compiled by Eleanour Sinclair Rohde. London, The Medici Society, 1930. 61pp, plates.
Consists of twenty-five religious poems, mainly of the sixteenth and seventeenth centuries. Plates are reproductions of Renaissance paintings.

225 ROLLINS, Charlemae Hill
   Christmas gif': an anthology of Christmas poems, songs and stories written by and about Negroes, edited by Charlemae Hill Rollins; line drawings by Tom O'Sullivan. Chicago, Follet, [1963]. 119pp, illus.

226 SCHAUFFLER, Robert Haven
   Christmas: its origin, celebration and significance as related in prose and poetry, edited by Robert Haven Schauffler. New York, Moffat & Yard, 1907. xiii, 325pp. (Our American Holidays Series.)

227 SHIPMAN, Dorothy Middlebrook
   Stardust and holly: poems and songs of Christmas, selected by Dorothy Middlebrook Shipman. New York, Macmillan, 1932. xxiv, 235pp.

228 SNELL, Ada Laura Fonda
   The first Noel: animal songs of the Nativity, compiled by Ada Laura Fonda Snell; illustrated by Sybil Clark Fonda. New York, Bookman Associates, [1956]. 43pp, illus.

See also: 53, 1714

32

The Christmas carol   Studies and criticism

229 BRICE, Douglas
   The folk carol of England, by Douglas Brice. London, Herbert Jenkins,
1967. xviii, 174pp. Music. Bibliography.
Chapters: The English carol; The ballad; Folk poetry; 'Adeste fideles';
Medieval poetry, its return and vindication; The folk carol today.

230 NETTEL, Reginald
   Christmas and its carols, by Reginald Nettel. London, Faith Press,
1960. 144pp. Music.
Chapters: Found behind a bookcase; Possible theory of origins; The mould-
ing of purpose; The polyphonic carols; Wassail; In time of change; The new
Christmas; In the age of Dickens; Carols in America; The carol revival.

231 PHILLIPS, William J
   Carols: their origin, music and connection with mystery plays, by
William J Phillips; with a foreword by Sir Frederick Bridge. London, Rout-
ledge; New York, Dutton, 1921. xv, 134pp. Music.
Chapters: Origins of carols and mystery plays; Carols and dancing; Mystery
plays; Connection of carols with mystery plays; Carols of the Virgin Mary;
The narrative or story-telling carols; Carols of nature; Trees; Spring carols;
Lullabies and cradle-songs; The childhood of Christ; Numeral carols; The
wassails; Angels and shepherds; Epiphany; Welcome to Christmas; Farewell
to Christmas; The music of the carols.

232 ROUTLEY, Erik
   The English carol, by Erik Routley. London, Herbert Jenkins, 1958.
272pp. Music. Bibliography.
Chapters: Part I—the singing ages: The medieval manuscript carols; The
ballad carol; The music of the ballad carols; Part 2—the great controversy:
medieval genius for play; The wrath of the puritans; Christmas hymns.
Part 3—the return of the carol: The nineteenth century; Carols from other
countries; Carols today.

Easter

233 CARNEGIE LIBRARY SCHOOL ASSOCIATION
   Easter in poetry: poems chosen by a committee of the Carnegie Library
School Association. New York, H W Wilson, 1926. 54pp. Printed on one
side of the page only.

234 CHRISTMAS, F E
   An Easter anthology, compiled by F E Christmas. London, St Hughs
Press, 1946. 52pp, illus.
Headings: Easter in nature (ten items); Easter in the soul (thirteen items).
Poetry and prose, mostly of the nineteenth century.

235 EASTER POEMS:
   a religious anthology by George Herbert, Richard Crashaw, Henry
Vaughan, John Bannister Tabb, Edward Caswall, Alfred Noyes, Frederick

William Faber, Katharine Tynan, and Francis Thompson. London, Burns & Oates. [1914]. 24pp, illus.

236 KNIGHT, William
    An Easter anthology, collected, arranged and edited by William Knight. London, Sidgwick and Jackson, 1912. 219pp.
Religious verse; includes poetry on the events which preceded the crucifixion and which came after the Resurrection.

237 RICE, Susan Tracy
    Easter: its history, celebration, spirit and significance as related in prose and verse, compiled by Susan Tracy Rice; edited by Robert Haven Schauffler. New York, Moffat & Yard, 1916. xxvi, 261pp. (Our American Holidays Series.)

NON-CONFORMISTS

Quakers

238 JENKINS, Charles Francis
    Quaker poems: a collection of verse relating to the Society of Friends, compiled by Charles Francis Jenkins. Philadelphia, John C Winston, 1893. 258pp, illus, ports.
Headings: The friends; Personal poems; New England; At meeting; Death; Quaker schools.
English and American poetry of the nineteenth century.

Studies and criticism

239 KEITH, Philip M
    The idea of quakerism in American literature. PhD thesis, Pennsylvania University, 1971.

MYTHS AND LEGENDS

CLASSICAL

General

240 BULFINCH, Thomas
   Poetry of the age of fable, collected by Thomas Bulfinch. Boston,
J E Tilton, 1863. ix, 250pp, illus.
Poetry from the seventeenth to nineteenth century, by mostly well-known
poets. Collection is based on the poetical quotations in the compiler's
'The age of fable'.

Studies and criticism

241 (BIBLIOGRAPHY) BROWN, Huntington
   The classical tradition in English literature: a bibliography (in Harvard
Studies and Notes in Philology and Literature, xviii, 1953, pp 7-46).

242 BUSH, Douglas
   Mythology and the Renaissance tradition in English poetry, by Douglas
Bush. Minnesota, University of Minnesota Press; London, Oxford Univer-
sity Press, 1932. vii, 360pp.
Bibliography (pp 325-344): chronological checklist of mythology poems
up to 1680.

243 BUSH, Douglas
   Mythology and the romantic tradition in English poetry, by Douglas
Bush. Cambridge (Mass), Harvard University Press, 1937. xvi, 647pp.
Bibliography (pp 595-627): chronological checklist of mythology poems
1681-1935.

244 BUSH, Douglas
   Pagan myth and the Christian tradition in English poetry, by Douglas
Bush. Philadelphia, American Philosophical Society, 1968. 112pp. Bibliography. References in footnotes. (Memoirs of the American Philosophical Society, Vol 72.)

245 CLARKE, Helen Archibald
   Ancient myths and modern poets, by Helen Archibald Clarke. New
York, Baker & Taylor, 1910. 360pp, plates.

246 COLLINS, John Churton
Greek influence on English poetry, by the late John Churton Collins; edited with preface by Michael Macmillan. London, Pitman, 1910. vii, 127pp.

247 (BIBLIOGRAPHY) GUILD, E C A
A list of poems illustrating Greek mythology in the English poetry of the nineteenth century, by E C A Guild. Brunswick, 1891. (Bowdoin College Library Bibliographical Contributions, No 1, 1891.)

248 (BIBLIOGRAPHY) LAW, Helen Hull
Bibliography of Greek myth in English poetry, by Helen Hull Law. New York, The Service Bureau for Classical Teachers, 1932. 36pp. (Bulletin XXVII.)
Supplement: 1941. 19pp.
Revised edition: 1955. 39pp;

249 LEA, E M
Classical mythology and classical subjects in the work of some of the nineteenth century poets. MA thesis, Birmingham University, 1921.

250 NORTON, Dan S and RUSHTON, Peters
Classical myths in English literature, by Dan S Norton and Peters Rushton; with an introduction by Charles Grosvenor Osgood. New York, Rinehart, 1952. 444pp, illus.

251 O'ROURKE, E
The use of mythological subjects in modern poetry, by E O'Rourke. London, University of London Press, 1912. 62pp.

252 WILLIAMS, E A
The classical element in English poetry of the nineteenth century. MA thesis, University of Wales, 1908.

Special themes   Studies and criticism

253 LE COMTE, Edward Semple
Endymion in England: the literary history of a Greek myth, by Edward Semple Le Comte. New York, Kings Crown Press, 1944. xxi, 180pp. References in footnotes.

254 OSENBURG, Frederic C
The ideas of the golden age and the decay of the world in the English Renaissance. PhD thesis, Illinois University, 1939.

255 ST CLAIR, Foster York
The myth of the golden age from Spenser to Milton. PhD thesis, Harvard University, 1931.

See also: 273-276

256 REES, Compton
The Hercules myth in Renaissance poetry and prose. PhD thesis, Rice University, 1962.

257 MERIVALE, Patricia
Pan, the goat-god: his myth in modern times, by Patricia Merivale. Cambridge (Mass), Harvard University Press, 1969. xv, 286pp, plates, illus.

258 KAPLAN, Marion
The phoenix in Elizabethan poetry. PhD thesis, Los Angeles, University of California, 1964.

259 AWAD, Lewis
The theme of Prometheus in English and French literature. PhD thesis, Princeton University, 1953.

260 RAIZIS, Marios Byron
The Prometheus theme in British and American poetry. PhD thesis, New York University, 1966.

261 ATWOOD, Elmer Bagby
English versions of the Historia Trojana. PhD thesis, University of Virginia, 1932.

262 HINTON, Norman Dexter
A study of medieval English poems relating to the destruction of Troy. PhD thesis, University of Wisconsin, 1957.

POST-CLASSICAL

General *Studies and criticism*

263 GUERBER, H A
Myths and legends of the Middle Ages: their origin and influence on literature and art, by H A Guerber. London, Harrap, 1909. xv, 404pp.

Special themes *Studies and criticism: Don Juan*

264 NOZICK, M
The Don Juan theme in the twentieth century. PhD thesis, Columbia University, 1953.

265 WORTHINGTON, Mabel P
Don Juan: theme and development in the nineteenth century. PhD thesis, Columbia University, 1953.

Studies and criticism: King Arthur

266 BRINKLEY, Roberta Florence
Arthurian legend in the seventeenth century, by Roberta Florence Brinkley. Baltimore, John Hopkins Press; London, Oxford University

Press, 1934. xi, 228pp. Bibliography (pp 197-224). (John Hopkins Monographs in Literary History series Vol 3.)

267 (BIBLIOGRAPHY) CLWYD LIBRARY SERVICE
Catalogue of the collection of Arthurian literature. 1974. 142pp.

268 (BIBLIOGRAPHY) FLINTSHIRE COUNTY LIBRARY
The legend of King Arthur: a list of books in the Flintshire County Library, compiled by E R Harries. 1963. (182)pp.

269 (BIBLIOGRAPHY) INTERNATIONAL ARTHURIAN SOCIETY
Bibliographical bulletin of the International Arthurian Society. Vol 1, 1949—
Abstracts of articles and books.

270 MERRIMAN, James D
The flower of kings: a study of the Arthurian legend in England between 1485 and 1835. PhD thesis, Columbia University, 1962.

271 (BIBLIOGRAPHY) NEWBERRY LIBRARY, CHICAGO
The Arthurian legend: a check list of books, compiled by J D Harding. 1933. 120pp.
Supplement: 1938. iv, 90pp.

272 REID, Margaret Jane Cornfute
The Arthurian legend: comparison of treatment in modern and medieval literature, by Margaret Jane Cornfute Reid. London, Oliver and Boyd, 1960. ciii, 277pp. Bibliography.

Studies and criticism: Paradise

273 ANDERSON, Heather J
The medieval terrestial paradise. PhD thesis, Buffalo University, 1973.

274 ARMSTRONG, John
The paradise myth, by John Armstrong. London, Oxford University Press, 1969. xii, 153pp, plates. References in footnotes.

275 COTTON, Nancy
Paradise: the failure of an ideal. PhD thesis, New Mexico University, 1971.

276 GIAMATTI, Angelo B
The earthly paradise in the Renaissance epic. PhD thesis, Yale University, 1964.

Robin Hood

277 DOBSON, Barrie and TAYLOR, John
Rhymes of Robyn Hood: an introduction to the English outlaw, by Barrie Dobson and John Taylor. London, Heinemann, 1976. 336pp. Bibliography.

A selection of texts with short introductions and a long general introduction. Appendices: titles and first lines of Robin Hood ballads; The Sloane manuscript life of Robin Hood; A selection of proverbs of Robin Hood; A select list of Robin Hood place-names.

278 GUTCH, John Mathew
    A lytell geste of Robin Hode with other ancient and modern ballads and songs relating to this celebrated yeoman to which is prefixed his history and character, grounded upon other documents than those made use of by his former biographer 'Mister Ritson', edited by John Mathew Gutch; and adorned with cuts by F W Fairholt. London, Longman, Brown, Green & Longman, 1847. 2 vols, illus.

279 GUTCH, John Mathew
    Robin Hood: a collection of poems, songs and ballads illustrated with notes by John Mathew Gutch and life by John Hicklin. London, William Tegg, 1867. xxvii, 367pp.

280 RITSON, Joseph
    Robin Hood: a collection of all the ancient poems, songs and ballads, edited by J Ritson. 1823 edition reprinted with a new introduction by Jim Lees. Wakefield (Yorkshire), EP Publishing, 1972. vii, iii-x, lxxiv, 240pp.
    Originally published: 1795. 2 vols with wood engravings by Thomas Bewick.

Studies and criticism

281 CLAWSON, William Hall
    The gest of Robin Hood, by William Hall Clawson. Toronto, University of Toronto Library, 1909. 129pp. (University of Toronto Studies. Philological Series.)
Part of a PhD thesis, Harvard University, 1907 on the Robin Hood ballads.

282 (BIBLIOGRAPHY) GABLE, J Harris
    Bibliography of Robin Hood, compiled by J Harris Gable. Lincoln (Nebr), 1939. 163pp, illus (facsims). (University of Nebraska Studies in Language, Literature and Criticism, No 17.)

283 NELSON, Malcom A
    The Robin Hood tradition in English literature in the sixteenth and seventeenth century. PhD thesis, North Western University, 1961.

Studies and criticism: Tristram

284 MALONE, Mary Elizabeth
    Treatments of the Tristram legend in Victorian poetry. PhD thesis, East Texas State University, 1970.

Studies and criticism: The Wandering Jew

285 FULMER, Oliver Bryan
  The wandering Jew in English romantic poetry. PhD thesis, Tulane University, 1965.

THE ETHICAL WORLD

CHASTITY

286 BRUSER, Fredelle
Concept of chastity in literature, chiefly non-dramatic of the English renaissance. PhD thesis, Radcliffe University, 1948.

287 LANHAM, Margaret
Chastity: a study of sexual morality in the English medieval romances. PhD thesis, Vanderbilt University, 1947.

CONSCIENCE

288 FIELD, C
The dweller in the innermost: an anthology of conscience, compiled by C Field; with an introduction by Gilbert Thomas. London, Headley Bros, 1917. 128pp, illus.
Poetry and prose extracts from the sixteenth to twentieth century. Includes some classical and foreign writers in translation. Arranged alphabetically by author's name.

LIFE IN GENERAL

GENERAL

289 ARMSTRONG, Martin
The major pleasures of life, selected and arranged by Martin Armstrong. London, Victor Gollancz, 1934. 672pp.
Headings: The pleasures; Books and writers; Art and artists; Love; Music and musicians; Architecture; Contemplation; Food; Drink; Nature and the simple life.
Poetry and prose of all periods; includes some extracts from the Bible.

290 BRIDGES, Robert Seymour
The spirit of man: an anthology in English and French from the philosophers and poets, made by the poet laureate in 1915 and dedicated by gracious permission to His Majesty the King. London, Longmans, 1916. [196]pp.
Headings: Book I—Dissatisfaction; Retirement; Spiritual desire; Idea of God; Spiritual love and praise. Book II—The muses; Beauty is truth; Fairyland; Romance; Childhood; Ideal love; Nature; Spring and lovers; Youth and age. Book III—Mortality; Melancholy; Sorrow; Sin; Ethics and conduct; Philosophies and humanities. Book IV—Loving kindness; Sympathies; Christian charity; Myths; Christian virtue; Vocation and active virtue; Social virtue and freedom; Heroism; The happy warrior; Life in death; The heavenly kingdom. Covers prose and poetry of all periods; mostly well-known poets.
Reprinted 1973, with an introduction by W H Auden. [247]pp.

291 GOLLANCZ, Victor
From darkness to light: a confession of faith in the form of an anthology, compiled by Victor Gollancz. London, Victor Gollancz, 1956, 668pp.
Headings: 1—From darkness to light; Hope and trust; Serenity; Joy and praise. 2—The unity of goodness in things evil; Divine and human; Divine benevolence and compassion; So panteth my soul after thee O God; The glories of the children of God. 3—The trust, reason and beyond reason; The soul's memory; Vision and sacrament; Time and eternity. 4—Religion and religion; Crime and punishment; War and peace. 5—The just life for man; The The one thing needful; The just thing needful; Desirable things.
A wide ranging anthology covering all periods with an emphasis on Classical writers, the Bible and the philosophers.

41

292 GOLLANCZ, Victor
   The new year of grace: an anthology for youth and age, compiled and
edited by Victor Gollancz. London, Victor Gollancz, 1961. 510pp.
Based on 'The year of grace'; same headings but with running commentary.
Some items have been omitted, others shortened or lengthened; new
material amounts to about one quarter of the whole.

293 GOLLANCZ, Victor
   The year of grace: passages chosen and arranged to express a mood
about God and man, by Victor Gollancz. London, Victor Gollancz, 1950.
576pp. Music.
Headings: First part— God's mercy and love; A reading of Christ; Joy and
praise. Second part—Good and evil; Sin and repentance; Man, fellow-
worker with God. Third part—The relation of man to man. Fourth part—
Acceptance; Man's dignity and responsibility; Activity; Integrity; Humility;
Freedom. Fifth part—The self; Intimations; The many and the one.
A wide ranging anthology covering all periods, including classical writers
and the Bible, philosophers and poets.

294 GOUDGE, Elizabeth
   A book of comfort, an anthology, [compiled] by Elizabeth Goudge.
London, Michael Joseph, 1964. 334pp.
Headings: Part I—We are comforted when we consider the glory and wis-
dom of creation, and both by the sight and the remembrance of all crea-
tures of the earth. Part II—The comfort we have in delighting in each
other; Children; Lovers; Saints and heroes; Ordinary folk. Part III—The
comfort of faith. Part IV—Comfort in tribulation; In illness; In old age;
When facing bereavement and death; In darkness and aridity; The comfort
of repentance and forgiveness; The comfort of the world of prayers.
Part V—The comfort we have in living in the world of the imagination;
Heaven; Angels; The world of the poet; The world of ships and the sea;
The fairy world; The world of home; To end with, a few comic verses.
Poetry and prose, with an emphasis on the nineteenth and twentieth
centuries.

295 GREEN, A Romney
   A craftsman's anthology, [compiled] by A Romney Green; edited and
abridged by Joan Yeo. London, Allen and Unwin, 1948. 294pp.
Headings: Life, by land and sea; Portraits and pictures; Nature; Man and
woman; Oneself and others; Consciousness of mortality; Consciousness of
immortality; Great men; Inter pares; De ise Ipso; Poetry and religion; Art
and science; Education; Sub-history; Social disease; England; The future.
Poetry and prose of all periods, with an emphasis on philosophers.

296 HADFIELD, John
   A book of beauty: an anthology of words and pictures, compiled by
John Hadfield. London, Hulton Press, 1952. 255pp, illus (some col).
Music.

Part I: The invisible sun ('illustrates the course of human life from birth to death'). Part II: Look at the stars ('Some indications of the beauty which can be found outside ourselves—in the sights, sounds and sense of things devised by nature and art').

Poetry and prose from the sixteenth to twentieth century; mostly familiar writers. pp 243-253: notes on the illustrations (paintings and sculpture).

Reprinted: London, Harrap, 1976.

For an account of the creation and success of this anthology see: The case-history of a quiet bestseller, by John Hadfield (in The Bookseller, August 14th, 1976, pp 1295-1299).

297 HADFIELD, John

A book of delights: an anthology of words and pictures, compiled by John Hadfield. London, Hulton Press, 1954. 256pp, illus (mostly col). Music.

Headings: Awakening; Delights of the senses; Being and doing; Loving (pp 128-183); Dreaming (pp 184-199); Making; Understanding; Falling asleep (pp 228-243).

Prose and poetry from the sixteenth to twentieth century. Compiler has attempted to . . 'illustrate in the context of common experiences the ever-presence of delight, the immanence of happiness'. pp 245-253: notes on the illustrations.

298 HADFIELD, John

A book of joy: an anthology of words and pictures, compiled by John Hadfield. London, Vista Books, 1962. 256pp, illus (mostly col).

Poetry and prose from the sixteenth to twentieth century. . . . . 'Joy is a transcendent emotion: it is something which goes beyond pleasure, even beyond delight'. pp 242-250: notes on the illustrations.

299 HADFIELD, John

A book of pleasures: an anthology of words and pictures, compiled by John Hadfield. London, Vista Books, 1960. 256pp, illus (mostly col).

Headings: Daybreak; Creature comforts (food and drink) (pp 16-41); Notes and voices (music and birdsong) (pp 42-50); Green thoughts; Beasts, birds and fishes; The weather; Home and away (places); Occasions; Affairs of the heart (pp 133-166); Vanities; Actions (sports) (pp 177-215); Reactions; Nightfall.

Prose and poetry from the seventeenth to twentieth century. pp 241-250: notes on the illustrations.

300 HADFIELD, John

Love for life: an anthology of words and pictures, compiled by John Hadfield for members of the Book Society. London, The Book Society, 1961. 207pp, illus (mostly col).

Book is a 'distillation' of the previous anthologies. pp 197-204: notes on the illustrations.

301 MACAULAY, Rose
The minor pleasures of life, selected and arranged by Rose Macaulay.
London, Victor Gollancz, 1934. 75lpp.
A 'bedside' anthology of prose and poetry on many subjects. 104 subject
headings (eg bells, conversation, dancing, eccentricity, gossip, hot baths,
old age, reading, smoking, street music, taverns, etc). Emphasis on the
seventeenth and eighteenth centuries.

302 OSGOOD, Margaret Cushing
The city without walls: an anthology setting forth the drama of life,
arranged by Margaret Cushing Osgood. London, Jonathan Cape. 1932.
764pp.
Headings: I know that I am; The creation; Hymns of praise; Jesus Christ;
Satan and hell; Divine love and compassion; Buddha; The saints (pp 194-
238); Spiritual teachers (pp 243-306); Earth; Water; Fire; Heavenly bodies;
Sleep; Music and dance; Eternity and time; Human love; Questionings and
doubts; Calamity and despair; Old age; Death; Lamentation; Wisdom;
Silence and meditation; Vision; Runes and charms; Prayers.
Poetry and prose of all periods; includes some foreign material in trans-
lation.

303 QUILLER-COUCH, A T
The pilgrim's way: a little scrip of good counsel for travellers, chosen
by A T Quiller-Couch. London, Seeley, 1906. viii, 330pp.
Headings: Childhood; Youth; The fore-runners; Divine love; Human love;
Marriage and children; House and garden; Work and the daily round;
Divinity in man; Nature; The stars; The strength of manhood; The grace of
manhood; The freeman; The citizen; Content; Wisdom; Prayer and praise;
Charity; Some exemplars; Bereavement and consolation; Age; Death.
Poetry and prose of all periods, including some foreign writers in trans-
lation.

304 STANLEY, Arthur
The testament of man: an anthology of the spirit, by Arthur Stanley.
London, Victor Gollancz, 1936. ix, 662pp.
Prose and poetry of all periods, from records of ancient people to the
twentieth century. The collection represents: 'man's interpretation of the
world according to his higher nature . . . the divinity of man sometimes
breaks out in unexpected places, and the gifts of fellowship, chivalry and
self-sacrifice are not confined to any time or any class.'

305 WOODS, Ralph Louis
A treasury of contentment: inspirational selections in which man af-
firms life's worth and celebrates its rewards, compiled and edited by Ralph
Louis Woods. New York, Trident, 1969. 381pp.

See also: Religion, especially 24, 25, 33, 41, 62; Consolation 655-659;
Peace 660-666; 705

CONFLICT

306 HACKER, Geoffrey and others
Conflict 1, [compiled] by Geoffrey Hacker, James Learmonth, and
Rony Robinson. Sunbury-on-Thames (Middx), Nelson, 1969. 162pp,
illus. Bibliographies (further reading). Filmographies.
Headings: Section 1 The home—Earliest years; Childhood; Adolescence;
Leaving home. Section 2 School—Going to school; Boys and girls; Teachers
and pupils; After school.
Twentieth century poetry and prose; more prose than poetry; intended for
school use.

307 HACKER, Geoffrey and others
Conflict 2, [compiled] by Geoffrey Hacker, James Learmonth and
Rony Robinson. Sunbury-on-Thames (Middx), Nelson, 1969. 166pp,
illus. Bibliographies (further reading). Filmographies.
Headings: Self . . ; . . . Versus . . ; . . . Society . . ; . . . and the system.
Twentieth century poetry and prose; more prose than poetry; intended for
school use.

308 LEARMONTH, James and ROBINSON, Rony
Conflict 3, [compiled] by James Learmonth and Rony Robinson. Sun-
bury-on-Thames (Middx), Nelson, 1976. 157pp.
Headings: Marriage—Who will it be?; Shall we call the whole thing off?;
Children: Do we need children?; Do children need us?
Twentieth century poetry and prose, including extracts from newspapers.
Intended for schools.

309 SKULL, John
Conflict and compassion: a selection of poems, edited by John Skull.
London, Hutchinson Educational, 1969. 122pp.
Headings: Some of our human problems; The bomb; War; Innocent victims
of war; The influence of environment; Social misfits; Mental sickness;
Colour discrimination; Road accidents; Graver casualties; Old age; Materi-
alism; Town planning; Humanity.
Twentieth century poetry, mostly by well-known poets.

DISCRIMINATION

310 FOSTER, John L
Black and white: an anthology, compiled by John L Foster. Exeter,
A Wheaton, 1976. 83pp. (Dimensions series.)
Headings: Childhood and adolescence; Strange lands, new cultures; Living
together; Side by side.
Twentieth century prose, poetry and drama by black writers.

311 PARKER, T H and TESKEY, F J
Discrimination, compiled by T H Parker and F J Teskey. Glasgow, Blackie, 1970. 58pp. (Themes to Explore series.)
Headings: Opinions, reasoned and uninformed; The individual discriminates; Society discriminates; Does God discriminate?
Twentieth century poetry. Intended for schools.

PEOPLE (FICTIONAL AND HISTORICAL)

312 C, C and G, D
A national gallery: being a collection of English characters, compiled by C C and D G. London, Martin Secker, 1933. vii, 536pp.
Poetry and prose extracts from the sixteenth century to the twentieth. Interprets character 'in a wide sense to include couples and families as well as individuals, and dogs and wet days, as well as worthy, wicked or ideal men and women.'

313 PARKER, Elinor
One hundred poems about people, selected by Elinor Parker; illustrated by Ismar David. New York, Crowell, 1955. 234pp, illus.
Headings: Under twenty; My fair lady; Lives in sunshine; From the hills, from the roads, from the sea; 'All that's past'; People from history; From story book and legend; Some strange characters; The poet himself.
Nineteenth and twentieth century poetry. Intended for children.

314 STANLEY, Arthur
Good company, selected by Arthur Stanley. London, Victor Gollancz, 1941. 288pp.
Headings: A blush of boys; A bevy of ladies; A muster of peacocks; A school of clerks; An unkindness of ravens; A gaggle of geese.
Prose and poetry from the sixteenth to twentieth century. Includes some classical and medieval writers. Known and unknown authors; mostly prose.

315 WALE, William
What great men have said about great men: a dictionary of quotations, [compiled] by William Wale. London, Swan Sonnenschein, 1902. 482pp.
Good coverage of statesmen and writers and poets. Substantial extracts of prose and poetry, including complete sonnets.
Reprinted: Detroit, Gale Research, 1968.

See also: Epitaphs 398-422

Studies and criticism

316 HOPKINS, Kenneth
Portraits in satire, by Kenneth Hopkins. London, Barrie Books, 1958. 290pp, plates (ports). Bibliography (primary sources and biographical works).

Chapters cover the work of eighteenth century verse satirists: Charles
Churchill, Christopher Anstey, William Mason and others; The 'Rolliard'
and the poetry of the Anti-Jacobin; Peter Pindar.

Heroes and 'tough' characters

317 BALDWIN, Michael
Billy the kid: an anthology of tough verse, edited by Michael Baldwin.
London, Hutchinson Educational. 1963. 176pp, illus.

318 COLE, William
Rough men, tough men: poems of action and adventure, [compiled] by
William Cole; illustrated by Enrico Arno. New York, Viking, 1969. 255pp,
illus.
Intended for children.

319 COLLINS, Vere Henry
Poems of action, selected by V H Collins. Oxford, Clarendon Press,
1918. 160pp.

INVECTIVE

320 GRIGSON, Geoffrey
Unrespectable verse, edited by Geoffrey Grigson. London, Allen Lane,
1971. xxv, 335pp.
Contains outrages, lampoons, insults and vitriolic pieces from the Middle
Ages to the nineteenth century.

321 KINGSMILL, Hugh
An anthology of invective and abuse, compiled and edited with critical
and historical comments by Hugh Kingsmill. London, Eyre & Spottiswoode,
1929. 221pp.
Prose and verse from the sixteenth to the twentieth century.

322 KINGSMILL, Hugh
More invective, edited with critical and historical comments by Hugh
Kingsmill. London, Eyre & Spottiswoode, 1930. xi, 205pp.

323 MUIR, Frank
The Frank Muir book: an irreverent companion to social history. London,
Heinemann, 1976. 327pp.
Headings: Music; Education; Literature; Theatre; Art; Food and drink.
Short prose and poetry extracts from all periods with a running commen-
tary.

324 SCOTT, Francis Reginald
The blasted pine: an anthology of satire, invective and disrespectful
verse, chiefly by Canadian writers, edited by Francis Reginald Scott.
Toronto, Macmillan, 1957. xxix, 138pp, illus.

THE HUMAN LIFE CYCLE

BABIES

325 BAIRD, Jane
This starry stranger: an anthology of babyhood, [compiled] by Jane Baird; with a foreword by Compton Mackenzie, and decorations by A H Watson. London, Frederick Muller, 1951. 176pp, illus.
Headings: Before the beginning; New born; The Christmas baby; Babyhood; Cradle songs; The nursery; Fathers and mothers.
Poetry and some prose from the Middle Ages to the twentieth century.

326 DIMSDALE, C D
Babies: a miscellany of the literature on infancy, [edited] by C D Dimsdale. London, Golden Galley Press, 1948. 56pp, plates. (Clipper Books Series, No 1.)
Headings: News for parents; Cherubs; Babyhood; From fiction; Lullaby; Grievous loss; Folklore; Just nonsense.
Prose and poetry, mostly of the nineteenth and twentieth centuries. Plates are photographs of babies.

327 FORD, Robert
Ballads of babyland—English and American, selected and edited with notes by Robert Ford. Paisley, Alexander Gardner, 1905. xx, 348pp.
Biographical notes: pp 323-340.
Nineteenth century verse.

328 FORD, Robert
Ballads of bairnhood, selected and edited with notes by Robert Ford. Paisley, London, Alexander Gardner. 1894. xix, 348pp. Biographical notes: pp 319-348.
All nineteenth century Scottish verse.
   Reprinted: 1913.

329 HOVDE, Louise
The cradle book of verse: an anthology of baby poetry, chosen by Louise Hovde. New York, G H Doran, 1927. xvi, 301pp, col front.
   Reprinted: New York, Books for Libraries Press, 1972. (Granger Index reprint series.)

330 PENDERED, Mary
My baby: a little record for mothers, compiled by Mary Pendered. London, Sisley, [1908]. 126pp.
Short extracts of nineteenth and twentieth century poetry. Blank pages opposite each page of text.

331 REYHER, Becky
Babies keep coming: an anthology, edited by Becky Reyher. New York, London, McGraw-Hill, 1947. xx, 538pp, illus.
Headings: Life everlasting; The spring and the summer; Announcement; Birth; Another baby; Their sex and name and number; Babies are wonderful, but . . . ; Sh-sh, the psychologists might hear you; Their ways—and ours; Father has a baby too; Motherhood; Expert advice; So you think it is hard on you; The nurse; Not bread alone; The Christ Child; Good night.
English and American prose and verse, mostly of the twentieth century; more prose than verse.

332 WINN, Marie
The baby reader: 56 selections from world literature about babies, and their mothers, admirers and adversaries, compiled by Marie Winn. New York, Simon & Schuster, 1973. 352pp, illus.

333 WARING, Lady Clementine
Mother and babe: an anthology for mothers, compiled by Lady Clementine Waring. London, Putnam, 1933. 288pp.
Headings: Waiting; The new marvel; The new beauty; The new ecstasy; The new mystery; The new responsibilities; The new homage; The new sorrows; The new prayers; Carols and songs; The christening; Scolding songs; Bedtime; Lullabies; Fairies and folklore.
Mostly nineteenth and twentieth century poetry; some prose.

Lullabies

334 BUDD, F E
A book of lullabies, 1300-1900, chosen and edited by F E Budd. London, Scholartis Press, 1930. 128pp. Introduction: pp 1-25.
Sixty-three pieces, mostly by well-known poets.

335 COMMINS, D B
Lullabies of the world, compiled by D B Commins. New York, Random House, 1967. 267pp. Music.
Lullabies are given in their original languages and in English translation.

336 GOSSET, Adelaide L J
Lullabies of the four nations: a coronal of song with renderings from the Welsh and Gaelic, arranged by Adelaide L J Gosset. London, Alexander Moring, 1915. xix, 278pp, plates. Notes and sources: pp 247-271.

Headings: Of hope and joyousness; Of pensiveness and ruth; Of the sun, moon and stars; Of the winds and the sea; Of birds; Of bogies; Lullabies addressed to the infant Christ; Echoes of the Christ child.
Covers original and traditional poetry from the fifteenth to twentieth century from England, Wales, Scotland and Ireland.

337 REED, Gwendolyn E
Songs the sandman sings, compiled by Gwendolyn E Reed; drawings by Peggy Owens Skillen. New York, Atheneum, 1969. 42pp, illus.
A collection of lullabies and other poems for the child who is reluctant to go to bed.

338 SMITH, Elva S
A book of lullabies, compiled by Elva S Smith; with illustrations from famous paintings. Boston, Lothrop, Lee and Shepard, 1925. xxii, 563pp, front, plates.

339 STRETTEL, Alma
Lullabies of many lands, collected and rendered into English by Alma Strettel; with seventy-five illustrations by Emily J Harding. London, George Allen, 1894. 127pp, illus.
Several items each from European countries and Russia. Compiler acknowledges debt to the researches of friends in the foreign countries.

See also: 452

Studies and criticism

340 DAIKEN, Leslie
The lullaby book, by Leslie Daiken; musical research by Mary Hills and Sebastian Brown. London, Edmund Ward, 1959. 64pp, illus. Music.
Chapters: The essence of lullaby; The child-muse and the muse-child; Ways and means of singing baby to sleep; Sleep personified; The folk-lore of the cradle; The origin of lulling; Lullabies from many lands; Lullaby for a doll; Lullabies for the infant Jesus.
A short study of the traditional folk lullaby. Includes many examples with music.

CHILDREN

341 BAKER, George Cornelius
When men were boys: a collection of poetry about boys written by noted poets, edited by George Cornelius Baker. New York, Association Press, 1926. xviii, 211pp, front., plates.

342 BARNETT, P A
The children's way: a book of verses about children, selected and arranged by Mrs P A Barnett. London, Jarrold, [1910]. 222pp.

Mostly nineteenth century poetry dealing with children, the relationship
of parents to children and of grown-up persons to their parents. Chronological arrangement.

343 BURKE, Thomas
   Children in verse: 50 songs of playful childhood, collected and edited by
Thomas Burke; with illustrations in colour and black and white by Honor
C Appleton. London, Duckworth, 1913. 135pp, illus.
Nineteenth century verse.

344 BURKE, Thomas
   The small people: a little book of verse about children for their elders,
chosen, edited and arranged by Thomas Burke. London, Chapman & Hall,
1910. 220pp.
Headings: Prefatory; The spirit of childhood; Small people in the nursery;
Small people here and there; Grown tired of play.
Mostly nineteenth century poetry.

345 COLE, William
   Beastly boys and ghastly girls: poems collected by William Cole; draw-
ings by Tomi Ungerer. London, Methuen; Cleveland, World Publishing
Company, 1964. 125pp, illus.
Twentieth century American and English verse about rebellious, naughty
and unconventional children.

346 ELWES, Hervey
   The modern child, compiled by Hervey Elwes; with a foreword by L
Allen Harker. London, T N Foulis, 1908. xxv, 246pp.
Headings: Childhood; Frightening things; Little girls; Boys; Grown-ups;
Lessons; Out of doors; Sea-side children; Child-friends; Religion; Entertain-
ments; London; Children's books; Christmas; 'Lost awhile'.
Poetry and prose of the nineteenth century by mostly unknown writers.

347 HILDITCH, Gwen
   In praise of children: an anthology for friends, compiled by Gwen Hil-
ditch. London, Frederick Muller, 1950. 63pp, illus.
Prose and poetry extracts, mostly of the nineteenth and twentieth centurie

348 HOPKINS, Lee Bennett
   Girls can too!: a book of poems, compiled by Lee Bennett Hopkins;
illustrated by Emily McCully. New York, F Watts, 1972. 43pp, illus.
Poems intended for children, all testifying to the fact that girls do things
as well as boys, if not better.

349 IVOR-PARRY, Edith
   In the garden of childhood: an anthology of prose and verse for all
childlovers, together with a tabulated journal for the insertion of various
events in a child's life, spaces for photographs, blank pages for notes and
other records, [compiled] by Edith Ivor-Parry; with a foreword by

Katharine Tynan. London, Routledge; New York, E P Dutton, 1913.
183pp; 64pp.
Mostly nineteenth century poetry.

350 LEONARD, R M
Poems on children, selected by R M Leonard. London, Oxford University Press, 1914. 128pp. (Oxford Garlands.)
Headings: The beginning of life; Poems addressed to individual children;
Elegies and epitaphs; Distress suffered by bereaved parents; Parental responsibility; Cradle songs; Tributes of poets of a certain age to youthful
and ripening charms.
Poetry from the sixteenth to the twentieth century mostly by well-known
poets.

351 MEYNELL, Wilfrid
The child set in the midst by modern poets, edited by Wilfrid Meynell,
with a facsimile of the MS of 'The toys' by Coventry Patmore. London,
Leadenhall Press; New York, Scribner, 1892. xxiii, 195pp.
Nineteenth century poetry, all concerned with the worship of the child.
Mostly familiar poets. Preface consists of an essay on the child in English
poetry.

352 MILES, Susan
Childhood in verse and prose: an anthology chosen by Susan Miles.
London, Oxford University Press, 1923. 408pp.
Headings: This tender age; The Christ-child; Babes and sucklings; 'O yonge
freshe' folkes, he and she; 'The joyes and griefes of parents'; 'Pleased with
a rattle, tickled with a straw.; Meat and drink; 'Beasts and all cattle, worms
and feathered fowls'; 'The earth is full of thy riches'; 'New wax is best for
printyng'; 'Precept upon precept'; 'The cockpit of learning'; 'Young toilers';
'Early sorrows'; 'Fear knows him well'; 'Fancies from afar'; 'Theologia
Innocentium'; 'Remembered innocence'; 'Immortal children'.
Poetry and prose from the fourteenth to the twentieth century.

353 ROBERTSON, Eric S
The children of the poets: an anthology from English and American
writers of three centuries, edited with an introduction by Eric S Robertson.
New York, London, White & Allen, [1891]. xxxv, 460pp.

354 (BIBLIOGRAPHY) SHAW, John Mackay
Childhood in poetry: a catalogue of the books of English and American
poets in the library of the Florida State University, with lists of poems that
relate to childhood and notes by John Mackay Shaw. Tallahassee, Robert
M Strozier Library, Florida State University, 1962. 8 vols.
Based on the compiler's own collection, which attempts 'to bring together
the books in which first appeared those poems that relate to childhood, or
which have been read to or by children from the earliest days of our language
to the present.' Extensive contents listings are given. Includes a key-word
title index.

355 WITHERS, Percy
   The garland of childhood: a little book for all lovers of children, com-
piled by Percy Withers. London, Grant Richards, 1910. 338pp.
Headings: Out of the deep; The child in the cradle; The new possession;
The salt of the earth; The unborn years; Childhood; Young barbarians and
others; Non anglicised angels; All in a garden fair; Joy and wonder and
dreams; And pain; In retrospect.
Mostly nineteenth and early twentieth century poetry; some prose extracts.

356 WOOD, L S
   A book of English verse on infancy and childhood, chosen by L S Wood.
London, Macmillan, 1921. xvii, 365pp. Notes (pp 331-353). Introduction:
pp ix-xvii.
Poetry from the seventeenth to twentieth century.

See also: 308, 376, 418, 420, 657, 663, 707, 809

Studies and criticism

357 BABENROTH, A Charles
   Wordsworth's treatment of childhood in the light of English poetry from
Prior to Crabbe, by A Charles Babenroth. New York, Columbia University
Press, 1922. vii, 401pp.

358 COVENEY, Peter
   The image of childhood: the individual and society: a study of the theme
in English literature, by Peter Coveney; revised edition with an introduction
by F R Lewis. Harmondsworth (Middx), Penguin, 1967. 361pp. (Peregrine
Books.)
Chapter 2—Blake's Innocence and Experience; Chapter 3—Wordsworth
and Coleridge.
   Poor monkey, London, Rockliff, 1957. Title of first edition of this
book.

359 GRAEFFE, Lotte Burchardt
   The child in medieval English literature from 1200 to 1400. PhD thesis,
University of Florida, 1965.

360 HALL, E M
   Childhood in English poetry. MA thesis, University of Wales, 1921.

361 HOWARD, John Douglas
   The child hero in the poetry of Blake, Shelley, Byron, Coleridge and
Wordsworth. PhD thesis, University of Maryland, 1967.

362 JANNEY, F Lamar
   Childhood in English non-dramatic literature from 1557 to 1798, by
F Lamar Janney. Greifswald, Abel, 1925. 136pp. Originally presented as
a thesis at Johns Hopkins University, 1924.

363 ROLLER, Bert
Children in American poetry, 1610-1900. PhD thesis, Peabody University, 1930.

364 SCOTT, A
Childhood in English poetry. MA thesis, University of Belfast, 1935.

365 SINANOGLOU, Leah P
For such is the kingdom of heaven: childhood in seventeenth century English literature. PhD thesis, Columbia University, 1971.

366 WHITING, W A
Studies in the treatment of the child in English literature. MA thesis, London University, 1921.

367 WHITTAKER, P H
On child life in medieval English literature. MA thesis, Liverpool University, 1932.

YOUTH AND ADOLESCENCE

368 MILES, Susan
An anthology of youth in verse and prose, chosen by Susan Miles. London, John Lane The Bodley Head, 1925. xxxvii, 386pp. Sources and notes: pp 333-376.
Headings: The spring time of life; Young men and maidens; Realms of gold; Freakish youth; Among all lovely things; Jest and youthful jollity; The blood-warme aye; The aims and ends of burning youth; Young love.
Mostly little known verse from the sixteenth to the eighteenth century.

369 PARKER, T H and TESKEY, F J
The adolescent, compiled by T H Parker and F J Teskey. London, Blackie. 1970. 58pp, illus. (Themes to Explore Series.)
Headings: Becoming aware; And the family; After school—work; After school—leisure.
Twentieth century poetry, intended for school use.

370 SAMUDA, Mike
Adolescence: an anthology, compiled by Mike Samuda. Exeter, A Wheaton, 1976. 80pp, illus. (Dimensions series.)
Headings: The agony; Discovery; Parents and conflict; Escape; The meaning of it all; Grown up?
Mostly twentieth century prose and drama.

371 WOOD, L S
Youth and maidenhood: a book of English verse, chosen by L S Wood. London, Dent, 1925. xxxi, 320pp.
Poetry from the sixteenth to twentieth century.

OLD AGE

372 MAXWELL, Marjorie Eleanor
  The blessings of old age: an anthology gathered and arranged by Marjorie Eleanor Maxwell. London, Faber, 1954. 224pp.
Headings: Youth and age; Portraits; Memories; Harvest home; Tares among
the wheat; Farewell; The ever-burning torch.
Poetry and prose from the Bible (26 items) and from the sixteenth century
to twentieth century. Some Greek pieces in translation. The compiler
acknowledges debt to other anthologies, like the 'Golden treasury', the
Oxford anthologies, and 'Come hither'.

373 SEARLE, Chris
  Elders: a collection of poems by elder citizens, compiled by Chris
Searle; photographs by Ron McCormick. London, Reality Press, c/o
Centerprise, 1973. 40pp, illus.
24 poems about old age, pensions, retirement, death and the past.

374 SENIOR CITIZENS POETRY:
  an anthology. (Chichester), Janay, 1972. 157pp.
Poetry by old people, mostly reflecting on old age, the past and the future.

See also: 309, 629

DEATH

375 CURTISS, Mina
  Olive, cypress and palm: an anthology of love and death, compiled by
Mina Curtiss. New York, Harcourt & Brace, 1930. xvii, 296pp.
Headings: Oh, doe not die; Fare thee well, great heart; I weep for Adonis—
he is dead; Underneath this stone doth lye as much beautie as could dye;
Oh, he is gone and I am here; But you return no more; Thou wast all that
to me, love; Alter? when the hills do; All the flowers of the spring; Your
monument shall be my gentle verse.
Poetry from the sixteenth to nineteenth century.

376 DENT, M V
  Innocence and death, [compiled] by M V Dent. London, Methuen,
1911. xiii, 183pp.
Mostly nineteenth century poetry and prose extracts on the death of young
children. Includes some epitaphs.

377 THE DUAL LAND:
  being a collection of verses from many sources for the great family of
those who have been, who are, or who may be bereaved. London, Elliot
Stock, 1900. 459pp.
Part I: Death and separation; Part II: Paradise—the intermediate state;
Part III: Resurrection—reunion; Part IV: Eternity—god all in all.
Mostly nineteenth century poetry and verse. Double columns.

378 LAMONT, Corliss
Man answers death: an anthology of poetry, edited by Corliss Lamont.
New York, Putnam, 1936. xvii. 283pp.
Second and enlarged edition: with an introduction by Louis Unter-
meyer. New York, Philosophical Library; London, Watts, 1952. xvi,
330pp.
Headings: If a man dies, shall he live again?; When death is, we are not;
All men are mortal; We who are about to die; Fare thee well, great heart;
Here lies a most beautiful lady; Nothing can touch him further; Death,
thou shalt die!; I stand alone and think; Natural immortalities; The sting of
transiency; Let us live then and be glad.
Covers poetry of all periods, from the Bible and classics to the twentieth
century.

379 MAGNUS, Laurie and HEADLAM, Cecil
Flowers of the cave, compiled and edited by Laurie Magnus and Cecil
Headlam. Edinburgh, London, William Blackwood, 1900. xvii, 309pp.
Consists of 125 numbered items of all periods, from the Bible and classics
to the nineteenth century. Includes some French poems in the original.

380 POOL, Phoebe
Poems of death: verses, chosen by Phoebe Pool; with original lithographs
by Michael Ayrton. London, Frederick Muller, 1945. 112pp, illus. (New
Excursions into English Poetry.)
Poetry of the sixteenth to twentieth century, with an emphasis on the six-
teenth and seventeenth.

See also: Immortality 167-178; 350; Consolation 655-659; 636

Studies and criticism

381a BOURGEOIS, V E
Laments for the dead in medieval narrative poetry. BLitt thesis, University of Oxford, 1957.

381b COLLMER, Robert George
The concept of death in the poetry of Donne, Herbert, Crashaw and
Vaughan. PhD thesis, University of Pennsylvania, 1953.

382 FACKLER, Miriam Ernestine
Death: idea and image in some later Victorian lyrists. PhD thesis, University of Colorado, 1955.

383 FELDERMAN, Edric D
Dread, transfiguration and stammering: speculative essays on the death
fear in literature. PhD thesis, Buffalo University, 1969.

384 PECHEUX, M Christopher
Aspects of the treatment of death in Middle English poetry. PhD thesis,
Catholic University of America, 1952.

385 WIMBERLEY, Lowry Charles
Death and burial lore in the English and Scottish ballads, by Lowry
Charles Wimberley. University of Nebraska, 1927. 138pp. (University of
Nebraska Studies in Languages, Literature and Criticism, No 8.)

Elegies

386 BAILEY, John Cann
English elegies, edited by J C Bailey. London, John Lane, The Bodley
Head, 1900. xliv, 236pp. (The Bodley Head Anthologies.)
Elegies from the sixteenth to nineteenth century; all are addressed to dead
friends, lovers, children, etc.

387 BALDWIN, James
The book of elegies, edited with notes by James Baldwin. Boston, Silver
& Burdett, 1893. 304pp. (Select English Classics, Volume 3.)

388 DRAPER, John W
A century of broadside elegies: being ninety English and ten Scotch
broadsides illustrating the biography and manners of the seventeenth century photographically reproduced, and edited with an introduction and
notes by John W Draper. London, Ingpen & Grant, 1928. xviii, 218pp,
plates.
Limited edition: 275 copies for sale. Each piece accompanied with notes
and a glossary.

389 HARRISON, Thomas Perrin
The pastoral elegy: an anthology, edited with introduction, commentary
and notes by Thomas Perrin Harrison; English translations by Harry Joshua
Leon. New York, Octagon Books, 1968. 311pp. Notes.
pp 25-157: foreign writers, Ronsard, Petrarch, Boccacio, etc. pp 174-250:
poets from the sixteenth to nineteenth century: Spenser, Drummond,
Milton, Pope, Philips, Gay, Shelley, Arnold.

390 LEONARD, R M
Elegies and epitaphs, selected by R M Leonard. London, Oxford University Press, 1915. 128pp. Notes. (Oxford Garlands.)
Poetry from the seventeenth to the twentieth century by mostly well-known
poets. Covers: pieces on literary figures, on personal friends of the poets;
pieces inspired by battle and women, dirges, poems on children and autobiographical items.

See also: 350, 635, 997

Studies and criticism

391 BENNETT, Alvin L
The Renaissance personal elegy and the rhetorical tradition. PhD thesis,
Texas University, 1952.

392 BRIGHT, Michael H
The nineteenth century English pastoral elegy. PhD thesis, Tulane University, 1969.

393 DRAPER, John W
The funeral elegy and the rise of English Romanticism, by John W Draper. New York, New York University Press, 1929. xv, 358pp, plates. References in footnotes.
Chapters: The problem; The funeral elegy and the Cavaliers; —and the puritans; —in liturgic use; —in the reign of Charles II; —in the American colonies; —and the Neo-Classical compromise; —in Scotland; —in the reign of Queen Anne; —in the reign of George I; —in the reign of George II; —and the use of English romanticism.

394 FISHER, J
The elegy in the eighteenth century. BLitt thesis, Oxford University, 1929.

395 HENSON, Robert E
Sorry after a godly manner: a study of the puritan funeral elegy in New England 1625-1722. PhD thesis, University of California, Los Angeles, 1957.

396 LEBANS, W M
The English funeral elegy and its classical predecessors. PhD thesis, University of London, 1972.

397 TROMLY, Frederic B
The English funeral elegy from 1307-1614. PhD thesis, Chicago University, 1970.

Epitaphs

398 ANDREWS, William
Curious epitaphs collected from the graveyards of Great Britain and Ireland, with biographical, genealogical and historical notes, by William Andrews. London, Hamilton Adams, 1883. 182pp. Bibliography.
Headings: Epitaphs on parish clerks and sextons; Typographical epitaphs; Epitaphs on sportsmen; Epitaphs on tradesmen; Bacchanalian epitaphs; Punning epitaphs; Epitaphs on musicians and actors; Epitaphs on notable persons; Miscellaneous epitaphs.
Bibliography (pp 157-172) covers mostly nineteenth century collections, both general and regional.
Second edition: London, William Andrews, 1899. 241pp. This edition has no bibliography.

399 BEABLE, W H
Epitaphs: graveyard humour and eulogy, compiled by W H Beable; London, Simpkin, Marshall, Hamilton & Kent, 1925. 246pp.

Headings: About epitaphs; Ancient epitaphs; Curious epitaphs; Miscellaneous epitaphs.
Reprinted: Detroit, Singing Tree Press, 1971.

400 BOX, Charles
Elegies and epitaphs: a comprehensive review of the origin, design and character of monumental inscriptions and other necrological literature, whether in the form of elegiac verse or less ambitious prose, to which are appended fully three hundred epitaphs or mottoes classified to suit the exigencies of different times of life; also dissertations upon ancient and modern cemeteries and disused burial-grounds, etc, elegies and epitaphs on celebrated persons, Latin and musical epitaphs, by Charles Box. Gloucester, H Osborne, 1892. x, 299pp.
Chapter and section headings: The elegy; The epitaph; Elegies and epitaphs on celebrated persons; Mortuary monuments and inscriptions; Past condition of metropiltan places of sepulture; The cemetery; Scriptural texts and mottoes; Quaint relics and cuiosities; Professional epitaphs; Latin and musical inscriptions (with musical notation); Miscellaneous epitaphs,with thoughts on death, resurrection, etc; Concluding section contains poems of a philosophical nature on life and death.
A general miscellany of information, poetry and epitaphs.

401 BRISCOE, John Potter
Gleanings from God's acre: being a collection of epitaphs, [compiled] by John Potter Briscoe; with an essay on epitaphs by Dr Samuel Johnson. Edinburgh, Oliphant, Anderson & Ferrier, 1883. 160pp.

402 BROWN, Raymond Lamont
A book of epitaphs by Raymond Lamont Brown. Newton Abbott (Devon), David and Charles, 1967. 126pp.
Headings: Churchyard humour; Just for the famous; The epitaphs of Robert Burns; The epitaphs of slaves, and birds and animals; From distant lands; From tinker and tailor to soldier and sailor; Pluto's favourite miscellany.

403 DIPROSE, John
Diprose's book of epitaphs: humourous, eccentric, ancient and remarkable. London, Diprose & Bateman, [1879]. 80pp.

404 EATON, Arthur Wentworth
Funny epitaphs, collected by Arthur Wentworth Eaton. Boston, The Mutual Book Company, 1900. 96pp.

405 GOLDSMID, Edmund Marsden
A collection of epitaphs and inscriptions, interesting either from historical associations, or quaintness of wording, edited by E M Goldsmid. Edinburgh, privately printed for the author, 1885. (Collection Adamantaea Vol 12.) Limited edition: 350 copies. 2 vols.

406 HOWE, W H
   Everybody's book of epitaphs: being for the most part what the living think of the dead, compiled by W H Howe. London, Saxon, [1895]. 192pp. (Everybody's Book Series, Vol 17.)
   Headings: Brief epitaphs; Epitaphs of celebrated persons; Curious epitaphs.

407 HUNT, Cecil
   Here I lie, [compiled] by Cecil Hunt; with illustrations in imaginative mood by Maurice Arthur. London, Cape, 1932. 111pp, illus.
   A miscellaneous collection consisting of items which the compiler had noted down at random over the years.

408 HUNT, Cecil
   Last words: a collection of singular, authentic words, [compiled] by Cecil Hunt. London, Methuen, 1944. 88pp

409 KIPPAX, John R
   Graveyard literature; a choice collection of American epitaphs, with remarks on monumental inscriptions and the obsequies of various nations, by John R Kippax. Chicago, S C Griggs, 1877. 213pp.
   Headings: Epitaphs on eminent personages; Admonitory epitaphs; Devotional epitaphs; Adulatory, laudatory and bombastic epitaphs; Professional epitaphs; Ludicrous, eccentric and ridiculous epitaphs; Punning and satirical epitaphs; Miscellaneous epitaphs.
   Reprinted: Detroit, Singing Tree Press, 1969.

410 LINDLEY, Joyce and LINDLEY, Kenneth
   Urns and angels: an anthology of epitaphs and engravings, compiled from material collected by J and K Lindley. Wiltshire, Pointing Finger Press, 1964. 17pp, illus.
   Brief, one stanza long epitaphs. Limited edition: twenty-two numbered copies. Printed in Modern No 20 and Grotesque No 18 on Basingwerk Parchment.

411 LOARING, Henry James
   Epitaphs: quaint, curious and elegant, with remarks on the obsequies of various nations, compiled and collected by Henry James Loaring. London, William Tegg, [1876]. 262pp.
   Headings: Elegant epitaphs; Professional epitaphs; Witty and grotesque; Miscellaneous epitaphs.

412 PETERSON, Gail
   The last laugh: a completely new collection of funny, old epitaphs, disinterred by Gail Peterson; revitalized with likeness by John Trotta.
   Kansas City, Hallmark Editions, [1968]. 62pp, col illus.

413 PETTIGREW, Thomas Joseph
   Chronicles of the tombs: a collection of epitaphs preceded by an essay on epitaphs and other monumental inscriptions, with incidental observations on sepulchral antiquities, by Thomas Joseph Pettigrew. London, Bell, 1888. 529pp.

pp 1-272: The essay (containing many examples). Headings (of the collec-
tion): Royal epitaphs; Epitaphs on nobility, warriors and statesmen;
Epitaphs of Ecclesiasticus; Epitaphs on poets; Miscellaneous epitaphs;
Ludicrous and eccentric epitaphs.

414 PIKE, Robert E
  Granite laughter and marble tears: epitaphs of old New England, [com-
piled] by Robert E Pike. Brattleboro (Vt), Stephen Bye Press, 1938. 80pp,
illus.

415 REDER, Philip
  Epitaphs, [compiled] by Philip Reder; illustrations by Andrew Dodds.
London, Michael Joseph, 1969. 124pp, illus.
Headings: Curious, odd and grotesque; Trades, pastimes and occupations;
Long lives and many children; Beautiful, plaintive and pathetic; Deaths
most violent and peculiar.

416 SPIEGL, Fritz
  A small book of grave humour: comic and curious memorial inscriptions,
collected by Fritz Spiegl and recreated by Jane Knights. London, Pan
Books, by arrangement with Scouse Press, 1971. 188pp.
Only a few of the epitaphs are rhyming. The pages are shaped as tomb-
stones and recreate the original inscription styles.

417 STEWART, Aubrey
  English epigrams and epitaphs, selected by Aubrey Stewart, with illustrations and notes. London, Chapman & Hall, 1897. 282pp, illus. Notes
(pp 243-268).
Epitaphs: pp 145-240.

418 SUFFLING, Ernest R
  Epitaphia: being a collection of 1300 British epitaphs, grave and gay,
historical and curious, annotated with biographical notes, anecdotes, etc,
with an introduction upon modes of burial and a general survey of interments in the British Isles from medieval times, together with an account of
peculiar interments, church folk-lore, and a short chapter on American
epitaphs, by Ernest R Suffling. London, L Upcott Gill, 1909. 496pp.
Headings: Burial customs; Some strange burials; Ancient burials; Epitaphs
of Saxon times; Miscellaneous epitaphs; Laudatory; Bombastic; Admonitory or contemplative; Denunciation or invective; Epigrammatic; Punning
epitaphs; Brevity; Witty epitaphs; Profane epitaphs; Anagrams, chrono-
grams, puzzles; Mistakes; Wives, husbands; Large families; Epitaphs on
children; Longevity; Eating; Drinking; Epitaphs on animals; Clergy; Sailors;
Soldiers; Blind or afflicted; Heart and skull burial; Parish clerks; Illiterate
epitaphs; Beautiful epitaphs; Absurd epitaphs; Sportsmen; Various modes
of death; Death by drowning; Death by lightning; Death by murder;
Deaths by accident; Hanging; Scriptural; Lovers; Epitaphs on the poor;
Quaint epitaphs; Professional men; Various trades and callings; Anglers;
Metaphor; Irish epitaphs; Scottish epitaphs; Scottish covenanters;

Continental; Remarkable persons and events; Eccentric epitaphs; American epitaphs.
A wide ranging collection of considerable importance. Running commentary.

419 TEGG, William
Epitaphs, witty, grotesque, elegant, etc. together with a selection of epigrams, compiled and edited by William Tegg. London, William Tegg, 1875. 112pp.

420 UNGER, Frederic W
Epitaphs: a unique collection of post-mortem comment, obituary wit and quaint and gruesome fancy, [compiled] by Frederic W Unger. London, Gay and Bird; Philadelphia, Penn Publishing Company, 1906. 169pp.
Headings: Unconscious humour; Deliberate humour; Conjugal epitaphs; Derogatory; Epitaphs on occupations; Conversational epitaphs; Punning epitaphs; Bacchanalian epitaphs; Epitaphs on infants and children; Brief epitaphs; Pathetic epitaphs; Epitaphs on celebrated persons; Miscellaneous epitaphs; Epitaphs by Max Adeter.

421 WALLIS, Charles L
Stories on stone: a book of American epitaphs, [compiled] by Charles L Wallis. New York, Oxford University Press, 1954. xv, 272pp, illus. Bibliography.
Headings: American stone shadows; Farewell to arms; Home is the sailor; O pioneers! Lo, the poor Indian! Out where the West begins; Freed from bondage; Heaven's my destination; Sermons in stone; Ministers; The God haters; Doctors and patients; Victims of chance and circumstance; Crime and punishment; Each by his own trade; The course of true love; A word or two for mother; Brief candles; Fraternal god; Written with an iron pen; The unlettered muse; Grave figures; The philosopher's stone; Momento mori; Requiescat in pace; Here lies; Man's best friend.
Collection designed to represent each decade in American history and all parts of the country.

Studies and criticism

422 MOORE, Earl A
The epitaph as a literary form in England and America. PhD thesis, Indiana University, 1931.

THE FAMILY AND HOME

GENERAL

423 ADAMS, Anthony and JONES, Esmor
Just outside, [compiled] by Anthony Adams and Esmor Jones. London,
Nelson, 1973. 63pp, illus. (Nelson's Humanities Scheme, Phase One.)
Headings: The street; Inside the house; The family; Friends; Occasions.
Twentieth century prose and poetry. Intended for schools.

424 JOHNSTONE, Johanna and KARMILLER, Murray
Family tree: an anthology of the world's most distinguished fiction and
non-fiction about family relationships with sources ranging from the Bible
to the 'New Yorker', compiled and edited by Johanna Johnston and Murray
Karmiller. Cleveland, New York, The World Publishing Company, [1967].
522pp.
Headings: Husbands and wives; Fathers and sons; Fathers and daughters;
Mothers and sons; Mothers and daughters; Brothers and sisters; Aunts,
uncles, nieces, nephews and cousins; Grandmothers and grandfathers;
Parents and children; Family gatherings.
Mostly prose; some poetry.

425 JONES, Rhodri
Families, edited by Rhodri Jones; photographs by John Krish. London,
Heinemann Educational, 1971. 56pp. (Preludes Series—for younger readers.)
Twentieth century poetry and verse.

426 JONES, Rhodri
Generations, edited by Rhodri Jones. London, Heinemann Educational,
1969. 72pp.
Headings: Growing up; Love and marriage; The family circle; Growing old.
Twentieth century poetry.

427 RANDOLF, Anson Davies Fitz
Home life in song with the poets of today, [compiled by A D F Randolf].
New York, the compiler, [1879]. 271pp.
Headings: Babyhood; Childhood and youth; Home life in the country;
Home life in the town; Grandfather and grandmother; Looking backward.
English and American nineteenth century poetry.
   Second edition (?): [1886]. 312pp, illus, plates.

See also: 418, 1587

Studies and criticism

428 BRIDGES, William E
The family circle in American verse: the use and fall of an image. PhD thesis, Brown University, 1963.

MOTHERS

429 AYER, Mary Allette
Our mothers, compiled by Mary Allette Ayer. Boston, Lothrop, Lee & Shepard, [1916]. xv, 222p

430 BISHOP, Bette
The beauty of motherhood: selected writing about the joys of being a mother, compiled by Bette Bishop; coloured illustrations by Frieda D Senn. Kansas City, Hallmark Editions, [1967]. 62pp, col illus.

431 CARNEGIE LIBRARY SCHOOL ASSOCIATION
Mother's day in poetry: poems chosen by a committee of the Carnegie Library School Association. New York, Wilson, 1926. 49pp.
Poems printed on one side of the pages only.

432 EXLEY, Richard, and EXLEY, Helen
To Mum: a gift book written by children for mothers everywhere, edited by Richard and Helen Exley. Watford (Herts), Exley Publications, 1976. 64pp, illus (some col).
Entries based on contributions from children all over the world. Mostly short prose extracts, but includes some verse.

433 GILL, Katie May
Poems for mother, edited by Katie May Gill. New York, H Harrison, 1940. 386pp.

434 HUCKEL, Elizabeth Johnson
Songs of motherhood, selected by Elizabeth Johnson Huckel. New York, Macmillan, 1904. 111pp.

435 McCRACKEN, E
To mother: an anthology of mother verse, [compiled] by E McCracken; with an introduction by Kate Douglas Wiggin. Boston, Houghton, 1917. 195pp, illus.

436 MINER, Caroline Eyring
There's always mother, compiled by Caroline Miner. Salt Lake City, Deseret Book Company, 1968. x, 135pp.

437 RICE, Susan Tracy
Mother's day: its history, origin, celebration, spirit and significance as related in prose and verse, compiled by Susan Tracy Rice; edited by R H

Schauffler. New York, Moffat & Yard, 1915. x, 363pp. (Our American Holidays Series.)

438 RICE, Susan Tracy
Mothers in verse and prose: a book of remembrance, compiled by Susan Tracy Rice; edited by Robert Haven Schauffler. New York, Moffat & Yard, 1916. 357pp, plates, ports.

439 WAGNER, Ruth H
Garlands for mother, compiled by Ruth H Wagner; designed and illustrated by Byron Barton. Norwalk (Conn), C R Gibson, 1968. 89pp, illus.

FATHERS

440 DICKSON, Margarette Ball and others
Book of father verse, edited by Margarette Ball Dickson . . . Katie M Gill and Alpheus Butler . . . Minneapolis, Argus, 1942. 358pp.
American poetry of the twentieth century.

441 DOUD, Margaret and PARSLEY, Cleo M
Father: an anthology of verse, collected and arranged by Margaret Doud and Cleo M Parsley. New York, Dutton, [1931]. xx, 209pp.

442 EXLEY, Richard and EXLEY, Helen
To Dad: a gift book written by children for fathers, edited by Richard and Helen Exley. Watford (Herts), Exley Publications, 1976. 63pp, illus (some col).
Entries based on contributions from children all over the world. Mostly short prose extracts.

443 RICE, Wallace and RICE, Frances
To my Dad, compiled by Wallace and Frances Rice; decorations by Elizabeth Ivins Jones. New York, Barse and Hopkins [1956]. 94pp, illus.
Prose and poetry extracts from Shakespeare to the twentieth century; includes a number of twentieth century American poems.

444 SCHWARTZ, Alvin
To be a father: stories, letters, essays, poems and proverbs on the delights and despairs of fatherhood, compiled by Alvin Schwartz. New York, Crown, 1967. xix, 249pp.

445 SEYMOUR, Peter S
A father's love: tributes, priase and wisdom about dads and their offspring, selected by Peter S Seymour; illustrated by Carl Cassler. Kansas City, Hallmark Editions [1972]. [unpaged].

446 WOODS, Ralph Lewis
Laurels for father: great tributes in prose and poetry, edited by Ralph Lewis Woods. [Norwalk, Conn.], C R Gibson, 1968. 83pp.

GRANDPARENTS

447 EXLEY, Richard and EXLEY, Helen
   Grandmas and Grandpas: a gift book written by grandchildren for their
grandparents, edited by Richard and Helen Exley. Watford (Herts), Exley
Publications, 1976. 64pp, illus, (some col).
Entries based on contributions from children all over the world. Mostly
short prose extracts.

BEDROOMS AND BEDS

448 COLE, Hubert
   The bedside book of bedrooms, edited by Hubert Cole. London, Heinemann, 1962. 386pp.
Headings: Nursery days; Single beds and bachelor quarters; Getting out,
getting in, getting off; Double beds and married bliss; Things that go bomp
in the night; Scratch singles and mixed doubles; Send for the doctor.
Wide ranging in subject matter, covering everything that has happened in
bedrooms. Mostly prose.

449 GRAY, Cecil and GRAY, Margery
   The bed, or the cleriophiles Vade Mecum, [compiled] by Cecil and
Margery Gray; decorated by Michael Ayrton. London, Nicholson &
Watson, 1946. 280pp, illus.
Headings: Beds of antiquity; Medieval beds; Renaissance, baroque and
rococo beds; Romantic and modern beds.
Prose and poetry extracts; poetry mostly of an erotic nature. Chronologi-
cally wider ranging than 448.

SLEEP AND DREAMS

450 DE LA MARE, Walter
   Behold, this dreamer: of reverie, night, sleep, dream, love-dreams,
nightmare, death, the unconscious, the imagination, divination, the artist
and kindred subjects, [compiled] by Walter De la Mare. London, Faber,
1939. 702pp.
Headings: Day-dreaming; Evening and night; Waking and watching; Bed;
On sleep; The drowsy approaches; Childhood and sleep; Sleeping; Lullaby
my liking, my dear; That not impossible She; Dreams dreamed; Dreams
feigned; How and why; The stuff of dreams; Apparition, hallucination,
chance?; This bourne . . . ; That glassy interval; The turning of the tide;
The Phoenix; The life of things; The silent pool; Reason and imagination;
The artist; Animus and Anima; Conclusion.
A wide ranging anthology covering poetry and prose of all periods.

451 HILL, Brian
   Such stuff as dreams, compiled by Brian Hill; with a foreword by Calvin
S Hall. London, Hart Davis, 1967. 214pp.
Headings: The curtain grows thin; Pleasant dreams; Bloody deeds; Night-
mares and unpleasant dreams; A miscellany; Dreams in legend and fiction.
Mostly prose extracts.

452 LAING, Allan M
   The sleep book: an anthology for the pillow, collected by Allan M Laing.
London, Frederick Muller, 1948. 150pp.
Headings: Sleep; Wooing sleep; Lie-a beds; Whom she avoids; Invocations;
Lullabies; The stuff of dreams; Sleepy philosophy.
Poetry and some prose passages; a number of twentieth century pieces.

453 PHILLIPS, Catherine Alison
   An anthology of sleep, compiled by Catherine Alison Phillips. London,
Guy Chapman, 1924. 217pp.
Headings: Falling asleep; Sleep's power and attributes; Sleep in tragedy;
The figure and abode of sleep; Sleep in death; Dreams; Vida es sueno; Sleep
and nature; Sleeping children; The sleeping mistress; The sleep of love; The
sleepy lover; Sleeplessness; Sleepless grief; Sleepless love; The sleep of sin
and spiritual danger; Trances, spells and charms; Nightmares; Awakening.
Introduction (pp 9-14).
A wide ranging anthology from classical authors to the twentieth century.

454 ST JOHN, John and ST JOHN, Diana
   The small hours; an entertainment for the sleepless, compiled by John
and Diana St John. London, Heinemann, 1957. 262pp.
Headings: Part One—The courtship of sleep; Physic, potions and possets;
Counting sheep; The promotion of yawns; Sleeping under difficulties.
Part Two—Sleep from the bookshelf: some restful diversions for the wake-
ful (pp 129-253).
Part One consists mostly of prose passages; part two mostly of poetry on
sleep, night, etc, ranging from the Bible to the twentieth century.

455 STEWART, Carol
   Poems of sleep and dream, chosen by Carol Stewart; with original litho-
graphs by Robert Colquhoun, London, Frederick Muller, 1947. 127pp.
Poetry ranging from the Bible to the twentieth century.

See also: 297; Lullabies 334-340; 661; 1593

Studies and criticism

456 BLEETH, Kenneth A
   Narrator and landscape in the medieval dream vision. PhD thesis, Harvard University, 1970.

457 EHRENSPERGER, Edward C
Dreams in Middle English literature. PhD thesis, Harvard University, 1921.

458 HIEATT, Constance Bodkin
Realism of dream visions: the poetic exploitation of the dream experience in Chaucer and his contemporaries, by Constance Bodkin Hieatt. The Hague, Paris, Mouton, 1967. 120pp. Bibliography. (De Propietatibus Litterarum, Series Practica, 2.)

459 REEVE, Richard H
Dreams in the critical theory and poetic practice of certain early nineteenth century writers. PhD thesis, University of California, Berkeley, 1932.

460 SPEARING, A C
Medieval dream poetry, by A C Spearing. London, Cambridge Universith Press, 1976. 236pp. Bibliography.
Chapters: Dreams and visions (Latin writers like Boethius and Alanus and French courtly poetry of the thirteenth and fourteenth centuries); Chaucer; The alliterative tradition ('Pearl' and 'Piers Plowman'); The Chaucerian tradition (poems by Lydgate, Clanvowe, King James I, Henryson, Dunbar, Douglas and Skelton).

461 WEIDHORN, Manfred
Dreams in seventeenth century English literature, by Manfred Weidhorn. The Hague, Paris, Mouton, 1970. 167pp. Bibliography (pp 160-165). Chapters: Major theories of the dream from Homer to Hobbes; Typical uses of the dream in Western literature; Dream visions in seventeenth century English literature—psychological, autobiographical, philosophical,—political, polemical, satirical,—moral and religious; Dream in seventeenth century English lyric poetry: neoplatonic and stoic,—complimentary and genteel,—ratiocinative and satiric,—voluptuous; Dreams in seventeenth century English dramatic and narrative works, (Shakespeare pp 107-117); Milton.

THE EMOTIONAL WORLD

LOVE AND COURTSHIP

462 ADAMS, William Davenport
Lyrics of love from Shakespeare to Tennyson, selected and arranged with notes by W D Adams. London, H S King, 1874. xx, 252pp.
Second edition: London, Kegan Paul, 1878. xx, 252pp.

463 ADLARD, John
The fruit of that forbidden tree: Restoration poems, songs and jests on the subject of sensual love, edited by John Adlard. Cheadle (Cheshire), Carcaret Press, 1975. 135pp. (Fyfield Books series.).

464 BELL, G K A
Poems of love, edited by G K A Bell. London, Routledge; New York, Dutton, 1906. 207pp. (Golden Anthologies Series.)
Light lyrics.

465 BETJEMAN, John, and TAYLOR, Geoffrey
English love poems, chosen by John Betjeman and Geoffrey Taylor. London, Faber, 1962. 220pp.
Poetry from the sixteenth to the twentieth century.

466 THE BEST LOVE POEMS:
a collection of dramatic, humorous, pathetic, sentimental and passionate poems. London, W Foulsham, [1925], 93pp.
Poetry of the sixteenth, seventeenth, and nineteenth centuries by familiar poets.

467 BLISS, Frank E
In praise of Bishop Valentine, [compiled by Frank E Bliss]. London, printed for private circulation, 1893. xiii, 158pp.
Love lyrics from the sixteenth to nineteenth century celebrating St Valentine's day. Limited edition: 125 copies printed on hand made paper and 25 copies on Japanese vellum.

468 BOLT, Sydney
Twentieth century love poetry, edited with an introduction by Sydney Bolt. London, Hutchinson Educational, 1969. 126pp. Bibliography (primary sources only).

Introduction: pp 9-31. Poetry by T S Eliot (10 poems), D H Lawrence (19 poems), Robert Graves (26 poems), and poets since 1945.

469 THE BOOK OF THE KISS
London, A L Humphreys. 1914. 16pp.
Short prose extracts and quotations. Blue borders and capital letters. Decorated paper cover.

470 BRISCOE, J Potter
Tudor and Stuart love songs, selected and edited by J Potter Briscoe.
London, Gay and Bird, 1902. xv, 142pp.

471 BRUNDAGE, Frances
Wedding bells, [compiled] by Frances Brundage. London, Raphael Tuck, [1898]. [31]pp, illus (some col).
Twenty-six short poetry extracts, mostly of the nineteenth century. Embossed, silver cover.

472 BULLEN, A H
Musa proterva: love poems of the Restoration, edited by A H Bullen.
London, privately printed, 1889. xxiii, 128pp. Limited edition of 780 copies.
Reprinted: New York, AMS Press, 1971.

473 BULLEN, A H
Speculum amantis: love poems from rare song-books and miscellanies of the seventeenth century, edited by A H Bullen. London, privately printed, 1889. xvii, 129pp. Limited edition of 500 copies.
Reprinted: New York, AMS Press, 1971.

474 BYRON, May
The garden of love: flowers gathered from the poets, by May Byron.
London, Hodder and Stoughton, [1911]. 360 pp, illus.
Headings: Spring, summer, autumn, winter.
Mostly familiar poets of the seventeenth and nineteenth centuries.

475 C, C and G, D
The English in love: a museum of illustrative verse and prose from the fourteenth to the twentieth century, assembled by C C and D G. London, Martin Secker, 1934. xi, 559pp, illus.
Headings: And this is love; To make much of time; First love; Love at first sight; Love lies dreaming; The he and she: The he; The he and the she: The she; Counsels and perfections: counsels; Counsels and perfections: perfections; Scenes and suits; Laughing love; Philanderer; The secret plague.

476 CAINE, Ralph H
Love songs of the English poets, 1300-1800, with notes by Ralph H Caine. London, Heinemann, 1892. xxv, 278pp. Biographical notes.

477 CAVALIER LYRICS
and other seventeenth century love poems. London, Chatto and Windus,
1941. 45pp. (Zodiac Books.)

478 CHANDLER, Horace Parker
The lover's year-book of poetry: a collection of love poems for every day
in the year, [compiled] by Horace Parker Chandler. Boston, Roberts, 1893.
2 vols.
Nineteenth century American and English poetry.

479 CLASSEN, Ernest and Hilditch, Neville
In praise of love: a romantic anthology, edited by Ernest Classen and
Neville Hilditch. London, Frederick Muller, 1951. 62pp, illus.
Poetry extracts and prose quotations and maxims of all periods.

480 COLE, William
Erotic poetry: the lyrics, ballads, idylls and epics of love, classical to con-
temporary, edited by William Cole; foreword by Stephen Spender. London,
Weidenfeld and Nicolson, 1964. liv, 50lpp.
Headings: Of women; Incitement and desire; Importunities and advice;
Celebrations and delights; Womanizers and seducers; The world and the
flesh; By-paths and oddities.
English and American poetry covering a wide range of subject matter. Em-
phasis on the seventeenth and twentieth centuries.

481 CONNELL, Catharine
Love poems old and new, selected by Catharine Connell. New York,
Random House, 1943. xviii, 205pp.

482 DE LA MARE, Walter
Love, [compiled] by Walter De la Mare. London, Faber, 1943. cxliv,
592pp, illus.
Headings: In the springtime; Things great and small; Children and friends;
The cause and measure; Love scrutinized; Love and poetry; First love;
She shall be called woman; Grace and beauty; Eros; The fever and the fret;
Love thwarted and unrequited; Love betrayed; Love lamented; Love and
happiness; Wild-flowers; Farewell; In absence; Constancy; Love in grief;
Love after death; Divine love.
Poetry and prose of all periods.

483 DOUGLAS, Robert W
Love songs of Scotland: jewels of the tender passion selected from the
writings of Burns, Tannahill, Scott, Ramsay, Lady Nairne, MacNeill, Jamie-
son, Hogg, Douglas Allan and others with a glossary, selected and edited
by Robert W Douglas. New York, New Amsterdam Book Company, 1901.
xv, 214pp.

484 D'OYLEY, Elizabeth
He and she: an anthology of love poems, [compiled] by Elizabeth
D'Oyley. London, Collins, 1928. 224pp.

Headings: Young love; The devout lover; The constant lover; The light
lover; The disconsolate lover; The lover maketh a portrait of his love;
The love of a man for a maid; And of a maid for a man; Love's confession;
Love's parting.
Poetry of the sixteenth, seventeenth and nineteenth centuries; mostly
familiar poets. Twenty-six anon items (songs and ballads).

485 DUPONT, Paul
Across a crowded room: an anthology of romance, edited by Paul
Dupont. London, Leslie Frewin, 1965. viii, 242pp, plates (mostly ports).
Mostly prose passages—extracts from biography, histories, letters, etc.

486 DUGDALE, Marie
A lovers manual: a small anthology of love, [compiled] by Marie Dug-
dale. Canterbury, J A Jennings, 1949. 24pp.
Anthology designed to 'hold up a standard for those who desire to love
truly'. Extracts from the Bible, Shakespeare, Wordsworth, C Rossetti and
others.

487 ELLIS, Havelock
The lovers' calendar, compiled and edited by Havelock Ellis. London,
Kegan Paul, Trench & Trübner, 1917. 423pp.
Demonstrates the course of love with nineteenth century verse by known
and unknown poets.

488 ELLWANGER, George H
Love's demesne: a garland of contemporary love-poems, gathered from
many sources by George H Ellwanger. New York, Dodd-Mead, 1896. 2
vols, xxiv, 234pp; 286pp.
American and British poetry of the nineteenth century. The compiler
aimed at including the less familiar.

489 FISK, Earl E
Lovely laughter: an anthology of seventeenth century love lyrics, edited
by Earl E Fisk; and decorated by Vera Willoughby. London, Cassell; New
York, Knopf, 1932. xvi, 137pp, col plates.
Headings: Lovely laughter; Happy, happy country swains; Gather ye rose-
buds while ye may; Beauty clear and fair; Love me less or love me more;
Battlefields of night; Witchcrafts; Love's delight; The contented lover.
Mostly familiar poets; compiler acknowledges debt to Norman Ault's 'Seven-
teenth century lyrics'. Limited edition: 999 copies issued for sale. Hand
set in Rudolph Koch's kursiv type and printed on Pannekoek paper at the
Curwen Press.

490 FRASER, Antonia
Scottish love poems: a personal anthology, [compiled by] Antonia
Fraser. Edinburgh, Canongate, 1975. 253pp.
Headings: Celebrations of love; Wooings; First love; Longing and waiting;
Encounters; Romantics; Unromantics; Marriages; The nature of love;

Obsessions; Warnings; Laments; Unrequited love; Faint hearts; Doomed love;
Farewells; Love lost; Love in abeyance; Change and paradox; Old loves;
Enduring love.
Covers all periods.
Paperback edition: Harmondsworth (Middx), Penguin, 1976.

491 GARRET, Edmund H
  Elizabethan love songs in honour of love and beautie, collected and illus-
trated by Edmund H Garret; with an introduction by Andrew Lang. London,
James R Osgood, 1893. xxxi, 178pp.

492 GELL, E M
  The more excellent way: words of the wise on the life of love: a sequence
of meditations compiled by the Hon Mrs Lyttelton Gell. London, Henry
Frowde, 1898. xiv, 319pp.
Headings: Of love's nature; Of love's essentials; Of love's graces; Of love's
capacities; Of love's dues; Of love's paradoxes; The perfect union.
Short extracts of poetry and prose. Green borders and decorative vignettes.

493 GEOFFREY, William
  The complete lover, edited and compiled by William Geoffrey. New
York, Harrison-Hilton, 1939. 291pp.
Headings: Notions of love; La Donna mobile; Advice; Love at first sight;
Noli me tangere; The kiss; Praise; Recipes; Desire; Idyll; Absence; Love
letters; Jealousy; In dispraise; Reconciliation; Declarations; Deadlock; De-
spair; Farewell; Epilogue.
Wide ranging anthology of prose extracts and poetry from many countries.
Prose consists of extracts from philosophers, letters, plays and some epi-
grams. Poetry is mainly of the seventeenth and nineteenth centuries.

494 GRIGSON, Geoffrey
  The Faber book of love poems, edited with an introduction by Geoffrey
Grigson. London, Faber, 1973. 407pp. Notes and references.
Headings: Love expected; Love begun; The plagues of loving; Love con-
tinued; Absences, doubts, division; Love renounced and love in death.
Poetry of all periods; includes some French poetry in the original.

495 HARTSHORNE, Grace
  For thee alone: poems of love, selected by Grace Hartshorne. Boston,
D Estes, [1899]. xxxvi, 294pp, plates.
Reprinted: New York, Books for libraries, 1969.

496 HADFIELD, John
  A book of love: an anthology of words and pictures, compiled by John
Hadfield. London, Edward Hulton, 1958. 256pp, illus.
  Compiler's aim was to 'illustrate the need for love, the search for love
and some of the forms of love through a free association of pictures, poems
and passages of prose'. Pieces from the seventeenth to twentieth century.
pp 243-253: notes on the illus (paintings and sculpture).

497 HADFIELD, John
  Elizabethan love songs, edited by John Hadfield; with lithographs by
John Piper. Barham Manor (Suffolk), Cupid Press, 1955. ix, 134pp, col
plates. pp 119-132: Notes on sources.
Limited edition: 660 copies.

498 HADFIELD, John
  Georgian love songs, edited by John Hadfield; with decorations by Rex
Whistler. Preston (Herts), Cupid Press, 1949. xix, 147pp, plates. pp 113-
142: notes on sources.
Limited edition: 660 copies.

499 HADFIELD, John
  Restoration love songs, edited by John Hadfield; with decorations by
Rex Whistler. Preston (Herts), Cupid Press, 1950. xx, 153pp, plates.
pp 129-147: notes on sources.
Limited edition: 660 copies.

500 HARRAP, George G
  Love lyrics from five centuries, selected by George G Harrap; with an
introduction by John Drinkwater and pictures by Baron Arild Rosenkrantz.
London, Harrap, 1932. 198pp, col plates.
Designed to 'illustrate every phase of the tender passion . . . and every kind
of lover'. Mostly familiar poets; emphasis on the nineteenth century.
Limited edition: 125 copies.

501 HARTOG, W G
  The kiss in English poetry, selected by W G Hartog; with a foreword by
Henry Simpson. London, A M Philpot, 1923. xiii, 82pp.
Light verse from the sixteenth to twentieth century. Purple boards with
velvet spine. Limited edition: 500 copies on hand-made paper.

502 HAYWARD, John
  Love's helicon: or the progress of love described in English verse, ar-
ranged and edited by John Hayward. London, Duckworth, 1940. 255pp.
Poetry of the sixteenth, seventeenth and nineteenth centuries.

503 HOWELL, Anthony
  Erotic lyrics, selected by Anthony Howell. London, Studio Vista,
1970. 64pp. (The Pocket Poets Series.)
Short poems from the seventeenth to twentieth century.

504 HULBURD, Percy
  English love lyrics, 1500-1800, selected and edited with an introduction
by Percy Hulburd. London, Walter Scott, [1891]. xxx, 221pp. (The
Canterbury Poets Series.)

505 HUMPHREYS, Arthur Lee
  A garland of love: a collection of posy-ring mottoes, [compiled by
Arthur Lee Humphreys]. London, the compiler, 1902. 74pp.
Rhyming couplets on love from the sixteenth to eighteenth century.

506 HUSTED, Helen
  Love poems of six centuries, edited by Helen Husted; introduction by
William Rose Benet. New York, Coward-McCann, 1950. 287pp.
Headings: Innocence; Desire; Fulfillment; Pain and parting; Maturity;
Love's immortality.

507 HUTTON, Edward
  A book of English love poems, chosen out of poets from Wyatt to
Arnold, by Edward Hutton. London, Methuen, 1905. xxxv, 230pp.

508 KINGSMILL, Hugh
  The worst of love: an anthology, edited with comments and an introduction by Hugh Kingsmill; illustrations in black and white by Nicolas
Bentley. London, Eyre and Spottiswoode, 1931. xxi, 242pp, illus. Biographical notes.
An anthology of bad prose and poetry connected with love from the sixteenth to twentieth century. Emphasis on the nineteenth century.

509 KISSES
  Being fragments and poetical pieces on the kiss. Edinburgh, Aungervyle
Society, 1884. (Aungervyle Society Reprints, Nos XXVIII-XXIX; nos 16
and 17 of the second series.)

510 KRANS, Horatio Sheafe
  English love poems, old and new, edited by Horatio Sheafe Krans. New
York, London, Putnam, 1909. xx, 208pp.

511 LAMPSON, Godfrey Locker
  A soldier's book of love poems, arranged by Godfrey Locker Lampson.
London, Arthur L Humphreys, 1917. xi, 188pp.
Poetry from the fifteenth to nineteenth century; familiar poets.

512 LANGBRIDGE, Frederick
  Love knots and bridal-bands: poems of wooing and wedding and valen-
tine verses, selected and arranged by Frederick Langbridge; with sixteen
coloured illustrations by G E Leslie, W F Yeames, Marcus Stone, Alice
Harvers, Harriett M Bennett, Mary S Story, John Scott, G F Wetherbee.
London, Raphael Tuck, 1883. 148pp, col plates.
Headings: Love and courtship—Love and lovers; Pro amore: In amorem;
First love; Love-making simplified; Love loyal; Amantium irae; 'No, thank
you, John'; Wooed and won; Marriage—All ye that intend; Thoughts,
fancies and homilies; Some wedding pictures; The happy pair; After years
of life together.
Nearly all nineteenth century verse. Double columned page.

513 LANGTON, Stephen
  For her namesake: an anthology of poetical addresses from devout lovers
to gentle maidens, edited by Stephen Langton. London, Herbert and Daniel,
1911. 346pp.

Poetry and verse of the sixteenth, seventeenth and nineteenth centuries arranged alphabetically by the name of the girl concerned.
New enlarged edition: 'By what sweet name?' London, Faber and Gwyer, 1925. 280pp.

514 LAYTON, Irving
Love where the nights are long: Canadian love poems, edited by Irving Layton; drawings by Harold Town. Toronto, McClelland and Stewart, 1962. 78pp, illus.

515 LEONARD, R M
Love poems, selected by R M Leonard. London, Oxford University Press, 1914. 128pp. Notes. (Oxford Garlands.)

516 LIBERTINE LYRICS
by various authors mostly of the seventeenth and eighteenth centuries; with illustrations by Erwin Schachner. New York, Peter Pauper Press. [1967]. 62pp, col illus.
'Seventeenth and eighteenth century poems which sing of the beauty of carefree (but not necessarily licentious) love. The spirit is gay and humorous' . . .

517 LOVE POEMS
by famous authors. London, Siegle and Hill, [1911]. 119pp. (Langham Booklet Series.)
Mostly nineteenth century poems. A miniature book.

518 THE LOVERS DICTIONARY:
a poetical treasury of lovers thoughts, fancies, addresses and dilemmas, indexed with nearly 10,000 references as a dictionary of compliments and a guide to the study of the tender science. London, Cassell, Petter and Galpin, 1867. xxv, 789pp.
Preface is signed J H.

519 LUCY, Sean
Love poems of the Irish, [compiled] by Sean Lucy. Cork, Mercier Press, 1967. 182pp.

520 THE LUTE OF LOVE
decorated by C Lovat Fraser. London, Selwyn and Blount, [1920]. 66pp, illus.
Poetry of the sixteenth and seventeenth centuries by familiar poets.

521 MABIE, Hamilton Wright
A book of English love songs, edited with an introduction by Hamilton Wright Mabie; and an accompaniment of decorative drawings by George Wharton. New York, Macmillan, 1897. xxv, 158pp, illus.

522 MacDOUGALL, Duncan and MacDOUGALL, August
The quaint comedy of love, wooing and mating: songs, lyrics, ballads and verses: an English, Scottish and Irish anthology, edited by Duncan and August MacDougall. London, Dent, 1907. xliv, 348pp.

523 MARTIN, Michael Rheta
The world's love poetry, edited by Michael Rheta Martin, illustrations
by Sheilah Beckett. New York, Bantam Books, 1960. viii, 370pp, illus.
An international anthology in translation covering poetry of all periods.
British poetry: pp 246-305. American poetry: pp 308-347.

524 MAYNARD, L
Latter-day love sonnets, selected and arranged by L Maynard. Boston,
Small, 1907. xiv, 111pp.
Limited edition: 725 copies.

525 O'DONNELL, Jessie F
Love poems of three centuries, 1590-1890, compiled by Jessie F
O'Donnell. New York, London, Putnam, 1890. 2 vols.

526 PALMER, John Williamson
The poetry of compliment and courtship, selected and arranged by John
Williamson Palmer. Boston, Ticknor and Fields, 1868. xx, 219pp.
Poetry of the sixteenth, seventeenth and nineteenth centuries. Some French,
Italian and Greek items in translation.

527 PARKER, Derek and PARKER, Julia
The compleat lover, by Derek and Julia Parker. London, Mitchell Beaz-
ley, 1972. 256pp, illus (some col).
A scrap-book on love, mostly written by Derek and Julia Parker. Contains
however three anthology sections: Falling in love: pp 97-112; Making love:
pp 161-176; The amorous muse: pp 209-220. Each contains poetry and
prose from the sixteenth to twentieth century. Illustrations consist of contemporary photographs and reproductions of paintings.

528 PARKER, T H and TESKEY, F J
The urge to mate, compiled by T H Parker and F J Teskey. London,
Blackie, 1970. 58pp, illus. (Themes to Explore Series.)
Headings: Bird, beast and fish; Brief encounter; Expressions of love; Wilt
though take?; A child is born.
Twentieth century poetry. Intended for school use.

529 PATTERSON, Lindsay
A rock against the wind: black love poems; an anthology, edited and
with an introduction by Lindsay Patterson. New York, Dodd & Mead,
1973. 172pp.

530 QUENNELL, Nancy
A lover's progress: seventeenth century lyrics, selected by Nancy Quennell. London, The Golden Cockerel Press, 1938. 84pp.
Limited edition: 215 numbered copies printed on Caslon Old Face type on
hand-made paper.

531 RANSOME, Arthur
The book of love: essays, poems, maxims and prose passages arranged by
Arthur Ransome. London, T C and E C Jack. [1910]. xix, 458pp.

Extracts from the Bible to the nineteenth century. pp xv-xvii: within the introduction a poetic evocation of the making of anthologies.

532 RAY, Robin
   Time for lovers: a personal anthology, [compiled] by Robin Ray.
London, Weidenfeld and Nicholson, 1975. 130pp.
Headings: Spring; summer; autumn; winter.
Poetry and prose of all periods. Covers all aspects of love.

533 RENDALL, Vernon
   The way of a man with a maid: an anthology of courtship and wooing,
compiled by Vernon Rendall. London, Methuen, 1936. xxiii, 419pp.
Poetry and prose of all periods, with an emphasis on the nineteenth century.

534 ROCHE, Pete
   Love, love, love: the new love poetry, edited with an introduction by
Pete Roche. London, Corgi Books, 1967. 127pp.

535 SAMUDA, Mike
   Love and marriage: an anthology, compiled by Mike Samuda. Exeter,
A Wheaton, 1976. 80pp, illus. (Dimensions series.)
Headings: Beginnings and developments; Looking back; Alone; Together
again; Matrimony; Achievement.
Twentieth century prose, drama and poetry.

536 SEDLEY, Stephen
   The seeds of love: a comprehensive anthology of folk songs of the
British Isles, compiled and edited by Stephen Sedley. London, Essex Music Ltd, in association with the English Folk Dance and Song Society,
1967. 261pp. Music.
Headings: Boy meets girl; Courting; Desire is a witch; Lost love; A step too
low; The cold clay; It's better to stay single; True love.

537 SIDGWICK, Frank
   Ballads and lyrics of love, edited with an introduction by Frank Sidgwick. London, Chatto and Windus, 1908. xvii, 180pp.
Includes thirty-eight ballads and songs taken from Percy's 'Reliques of
ancient English poetry'.

538 SMITH, John
   Modern love poems, selected by John Smith. London, Studio Vista,
1966. 47pp. (The Pocket Poets.)

539 SMITH, T R
   Poetica erotica: a collection of rare and curious amatory verse, edited
by T R Smith. New York, Crown, 1927. xxx, 770pp.
Poetry of all periods by well-known poets; includes also a large amount of
anonymous verse.

540 SOUTHGATE, Henry
   The bridal bouquet, culled in the garden of literature by Henry Southgate. London, Lockwood, 1873. 388pp, illus.

Headings: The meeting; Love; Lovers; Courtship; Beauty; Marriage; Husband and wife; Happy home.
Poetry and some prose. Mostly nineteenth century verse by unknown poets.

541 SOUTHGATE, Henry
The way to woo and win a wife illustrated by a series of choice extracts together with some original matter never before printed, [compiled] by Henry Southgate. London, William P Nimmo, 1976. 272pp.
Headings: Prefatory thoughts; First glance; Admiration; Declaration; Betrothed; Courtship; First kiss; Love letters of old; Wooing; Gifts; Wedding ring; Wedlock; Domestic hearth.
Mostly nineteenth century verse.

542 STALLWORTHY, Jon
The Penguin book of love poetry, edited with an introduction by Jon Stallworthy. London, Allen Lane, 1973. 399pp.
Headings: Intimations; Declarations; Persuasions; Celebrations; Aberrations; Separations; Desolations; Reverberations.
Poetry from the seventeenth to twentieth century, mostly by well-known poets.

543 STANFORD, Derek
The body of love: an anthology of erotic verse from Chaucer to Lawrence, edited and introduced by Derek Stanford. London, Anthony Blond, 1965. 236pp, plates. Plates are ink sketches.

544 TEASDALE, Sara
The answering voice: 100 love lyrics by women, selected by Sara Teasdale. Boston, Houghton Mifflin, 1917. xx, 85pp.
Poetry of the second half of the nineteenth century.

545 TRENT, L
Eros, anthology of modern love poems, edited by L Trent; illustrated by Herbert Fouts. New York, H Harrison. 1939. 525pp, illus, plates.

546 TYNAN, Katharine
Irish love songs, selected by Katharine Tynan. London, Fisher Unwin, 1892. 118pp.

547 UNTERMEYER, Louis
Love lyrics [edited] by Louis Untermeyer; illustrated by Antonio Frasconi. New York, Odyssey Press, [1965]. 44pp, illus.

548 UNTERMEYER, Louis
Love sonnets, selected and with notes by Louis Untermeyer; illustrated by Ben Shahn. New York, Odyssey Press, [1964]. 45pp, col illus.

549 UNTERMEYER, Louis
An uninhibited treasury of erotic poetry, edited with a running commentary by Louis Untermeyer. New York, Dial Press, 1963. xxiv, 588pp.

Covers all periods. pp 24-81: Classical poets; pp 359-409: ballads and folk songs; pp 477-480: a sampler of German love sayings. Twentieth century poetry (pp 485-578) is mostly American.

550 VANCE, Bruce
In and out of love: poems and images, arranged by Bruce Vance. London, Heinemann Educational; Toronto, Van Nostrand Reinhold, 1972. 119pp.
Poetry of the seventeenth, nineteenth and twentieth centuries.

551 VICTOR, Joan Berg
A time to love: love poems for today, edited and illustrated by Joan Berg Victor. New York, Crown, 1971. 111pp, illus.

552 WARDROPER, John
Love and drollery, [compiled] by John Wardroper. London, Routledge, and Kegan Paul, 1967. xxiii, 316pp.
Headings: Love pursued; Love experienced; Love mocked; The critical eye; The merry heart.
Notes and sources (often MSS): pp 237-305. Seventeenth century verse.

553 WATSON, William
Lyric love: an anthology, edited by William Watson. London, Macmillan, 1892. xxii, 238pp. (Golden Treasury Series.)
Headings: Love's tragedies; Romance of love; Love's philosophy; Love and nature; Chivalric love; Love's divine comedy; The wings of Eros; Love with many lyres.
Poetry of the sixteenth, seventeenth and nineteenth centuries by well-known poets. A number of ballad-type poems.

554 WILKINSON, Mary E
Love poems, compiled by Mary Elizabeth Wilkinson. Melbourne, Whitcombe and Tombs, 1920. (Gleanings from Australasian Poesie.)

555 WILSON, Kenneth G
An edition of some Middle English amatory lyric poems. PhD thesis, Michigan University, 1951.

556 YAFFE, H
An anthology of love and marriage, made and edited by H Yaffe. London, Faber, 1945. 341pp.
Traces the progress of love from its early days to late on in married life. Poetry and prose from the sixteenth to nineteenth century. Compiler aimed at choosing the less familiar. Includes some French pieces in translation.

See also: 18, 289, 297, 299, 308, 375, 418, 453, 663, 752b, 754, 790, 794, 991, 1593, 1733.

Studies and criticism

557 AGAJANIAN, Shakeh S
The Victorian sonnet of love and the tradition: a study of aesthetic morphology. PhD thesis, New York University, 1963.

558 BATES, Paul A
Elizabethan amorous pastorals. PhD thesis, Kansas University, 1955.

559 BROADBENT, J B
Poetic love, by J B Broadbent. London, Chatto and Windus, 1964. 310pp.
Chapters: Courtly love; Chaucer; Wyatt; Interregnum; Spenser's sonnets and secular hymns; Religious love poetry; Sidney; Shakespeare's sonnets; The fairy queen; Shakespeare's plays; Spenser and Donne: epithalamions; Donne; The metaphysical decadence; The rape of the lock; The sentimental decadence.

560 CANTELUPE, Eugene B
Representations of Venus in Italian Renaissance painting and English Renaissance poetry. PhD thesis, Washington University, 1959.

561 COLLINS, Michael John
Comedy in the love poetry of Sidney, Drayton, Shakespeare and Donne. PhD thesis, New York University, 1973.

562 FARLEY, Thomas Ernest Hilary
Love and death in Canadian poetry. MA thesis, Carleton University, 1963.

563 FINN, Sister Dorothy M
Love and marriage in Renaissance literature. PhD thesis, Columbia University, 1955.

564 GERVAIS, Claude
The Victorian love sonnet sequence. PhD thesis, Toronto University, 1970.

565 GOLDEN, Arline H
Victorian Renascene: the amatory sonnet sequence in the nineteenth century. PhD thesis, Indiana University, 1970.

566 GOLDMAN, Lloyd N
Attitudes toward the mistress in five Elizabethan sonnet sequences. PhD thesis, University of Illinois, 1964.

567 HATTO, A T
Eos: an enquiry into the theme of lovers' meetings and partings at dawn in poetry [by various authors] edited by Arthur T Hatto. The Hague, Mouton, 1965. 854pp, plates. References in footnotes. Part I: general survey (pp 17-64) by the editor. Part II: consideration of the theme in

literatures throughout the world; English literature by T J B Spencer
(pp 505-533).

568 KENT, Mariann S
Endless monuments for short time: studies in the love lyric. PhD thesis,
Yale University, 1970.

569 LEVER, J W
The Elizabethan love sonnet, by J W Lever. London, Methuen, 1956.
xii, 282pp. References in footnotes.
Chapters: The Petrarchan sonnet; Wyatt; Surrey; Sidney; Spenser; The
late Elizabethan sonnet; Shakespeare.

570 LEWIS, C S
The allegory of love: a study in medieval tradition, by C S Lewis. Ox-
ford, Clarendon Press, 1936. 378pp. References in footnotes.
Chapters: Courtly love; Allegory; The romance of the rose; Chaucer; Gower;
Thomas Usk; Allegory as the dominant form; The fairie queene.

571 McDOWELL, Dimmes A
Courtly love in the early English Renaissance, 1485-1557. PhD thesis.
Cornell University, 1953.

572 MERRILL, Rodney H
Formal elements in the late medieval courtly love lyric. PhD thesis,
Stanford University, 1970.

573 NOLL, Dolores Louise
The love universe in late medieval English and Scottish allegorical love
poetry. PhD thesis, University of Kentucky, 1965.

574 PARMISANO, S A
A study of the relationship between the attitudes towards love and marriage in late fourteenth and early fifteenth century English poetry and contemporary ecclesiastical teaching on these topics. PhD thesis, University of
Cambridge, 1969.

575 PEARSON, Lu Emily
Elizabethan love conventions, by Lu Emily Pearson. London, Allen and
Unwin, 1933. xi, 365pp. Bibliography.
Chapters: I—Petrarchism; Love conventions and the sonnets; Provencal
love conventions; Dante and Italian love conventions before Petrarch;
Chaucer and courtly love conventions; Petrarch and petrarchism; Love and
the ideal courtier; Wyatt as courtier and sonneteer; The Earl of Surrey,
petrarchan. II—Petrarchism in Elizabethan England; Sonneteering; Sir Philip
Sidney's analysis of love; The south wind; Fashionable sonneteers; Early
disintegrating influences; The form and cadence of Samuel Daniel's sonnets;
Spenser's Amoretti; Sonnets by Sir William Alexander, Earl of Stirling and
William Drummond of Hawthorndon; The changing moods of Michael Drayton's sonnets. III—Anti-Petrarchism; The reaction; John Donne's love
lyrics. IV—Shakespeare, petrarchist and anti-petrarchist.

576 RENNICK, R M
   The disguised lover theme and the ballad (in Southern Folklore Quarterly, Vol 23, December 1959, pp 215-232).

577 RICHMOND, H M
   The school of love: the evolution of the Stuart love lyric, by H M Richmond. Princeton, Princeton University Press, 1964. 337pp. Bibliography. References in footnotes.
   Chapters: The evolution of sensibility; The classic themes; The new style; The new attitude; An historical perspective (to 1700); A critical perspective (1700 to the present).

578 QUAINTANCE, Richard Edgecombe
   Passion and reason in Restoration love poetry. PhD, Yale University, 1962.

579 SAIZ, Prospero
   The persona in the early medieval love lyric. PhD thesis, Iowa University, 1971.

580 SALERNO, Nicholas Andrew
   Romantic love in Victorian poetry. PhD thesis, Stanford University, 1962.

581 SALOMON, Louis B
   The rebellious lover in English poetry. PhD thesis, Pennsylvania University, 1931.

582 SCHREIBER, Earl George
   The figure of Venus in late middle English poetry. PhD thesis, University of Illinois, 1969.

583 VOORT, Donnell van der
   Love and marriage in the medieval English romance. PhD thesis, Vanderbilt University, 1938.

584 WEDECK, H E
   Dictionary of erotic literature, by H E Wedeck. London, Peter Owen, 1963. 556pp, plates. Entries are under authors' names or titles; emphasis on the Classical writers, but extends to the twentieth century with a number of poems quoted in full. Full bibliographical details only rarely given.

585 WITTMAN, Richard Eugene
   Australian love poetry in the fourties. MA thesis, University of Melbourne, 1968.

See also: 264, 265, 284, 286, 287, 646, 784

MARRIAGE

586 BROWN, Ivor
   The book of marriage, selected with a foreword by Ivor Brown; decorated
by William Mclaren. London, Hamilton, 1963. 283pp, illus.
Headings: Wooing; The Wedding day; Later on; Opinion and advice.
Poetry and prose of all periods.

587 CARTER, Charles Frederick
   The wedding day in literature and art: a collection of the best descriptions of weddings from the works of the world's leading novelists and
poets, [compiled] by Charles Frederick Carter. New York, Dodd Mead,
[1900], xii, 294pp.
Reprinted: Detroit, Singing Tree Press, 1969.

588 CASE, Robert H
   English epithalamies, [compiled] by Robert H Case. London, John
Lane; Chicago, A C McClurg, 1898. lx, 198pp. (The Bodley Head An-
thologies.)
Sixteenth and seventeenth century pieces. Includes lists of omitted epitha-
lamia written before 1700 and epithalamia published since 1700.

589 CROSLAND, Margaret and LEDWARD, Patricia
   The happy yes: an anthology of marriage proposals grave and gay, compiled by Margaret Crosland and Patricia Ledward. London, Benn, 1949.
160pp. Poetry and prose from the seventeenth to twentieth century. Mod-
erately long passages from novels; poetry includes some nursery rhymes
and folk songs.

590 FURLONG, Agnes
   Man proposes: some proposals of marriage mostly from literature, collected by Agnes Furlong; illustrated by Olive M Simpson. London, Methuen,
1948. 186pp. Mostly prose extracts of the nineteenth and twentieth centuries.

591 GILMORE, J H
   Wedlock: selected from the best English and American poets, compiled
by J H Gilmore. Boston, H A Young, 1881. 110pp.

592 HESELTINE, G C
   A bouquet for a bride, gathered by G C Heseltine; and decorated by
William Littlewood. London, Hollis and Carter, 1951. 351pp, illus.
Headings: The wherefore and the why; Choosing; Wooing; The rubicon;
The rite; Royal Weddings; All manner of weddings; Mythical and mystical;
Blessings; And so to bed; To have and to hold; Ever after.
Poetry and prose from the sixteenth to the nineteenth century.

593 TUFTE, Virginia
   High wedlock then be honoured: wedding poems from nineteen countries
and twenty-five centuries, edited by Virginia Tufte. London, Macmillan,
1970. xxix, 288pp.

Part I: Greek and Roman, pp 5-57. Part II: Medieval to early Renaissance, pp 63-82. Part III: Renaissance to 1900. English pp 89-198; European pp 201-227; Oriental pp 229-230. Part IV: Twentieth century; Translations pp 233-248; English pp 252-288.

594 VIVIAN, Percival
   Poems of marriage, edited by Percival Vivian. London, Routledge, 1907. xi, 161pp. (The Golden Anthologies Series.)
Seventeenth and nineteenth century poetry.

Studies and criticism

595 McCOWN, G M
   The epithalamium in the English renaissance. PhD thesis, University of N Carolina, 1968.

596 TUFTE, Virginia
   The poetry of marriage: the epithalamium in Europe and its development in England. Berkeley, California University Press, 1970. ix, 341pp.

WOMEN

597 ARNOLD Roxane and CHANDLER, Olive
   Feminine singular: triumphs and tribulations of the single woman, an anthology chosen by the National Council for the Single Woman and Her Dependants, edited by Roxane Arnold and Olive Chandler. London, Femina Books, 1974. 190pp.
Headings: The Bible; Antiquity; The dark ages; The middle ages; Tudor times; Seventeenth and eighteenth century; The English governess; The educationists; The writers; The pioneers; The politicians; Victorians; Twentieth century.
Prose and poetry; mostly prose.

598 ASQUITH, Cynthia
   She walks in beauty: descriptions of feminine beauty in English prose and poetry, collected by Cynthia Asquith. London, Heinemann, 1934. xvi, 162pp.
Headings: Beauty in various vicissitudes; Her separate features are described; Portraits of individual characters.
Prose and poetry from the sixteenth to twentieth century.

599 CUNNINGTON, C Willett
   Women, by C Willett Cunnington. London, Burke, 1950. xvi, 259pp. (Pleasures of Life Series.)
Headings: Woman, a necessary evil; The damsel; Cupid's arrows; The perfect woman; The heroine; The rib; The mother; Ladies of easy virtue; Emancipation; Her dear of man; Jurymen's verdict.
Prose and poetry from the sixteenth to twentieth century connected by a running commentary.

600 CURRY, Jennifer
   The faces of woman, [compiled] by Jennifer Curry. London, Harrap,
1971. 208pp.
Headings: The ideal?; The private face—Childhood; Growing up; In love;
Sorrow in love; Courtship; Marriage; Motherhood; Woman alone; Bereavement; Growing old; Death. The public face—The worker; The rebel; The
social animal; The sinner; The saint.
Poetry and extracts from novels; mostly all twentieth century. Intended
for school use; project suggestions are given at the end of each section.

601 GUERMONPREZ, Paul
   Frailty thy name, selected by Paul Guermonprez; with illustrations by
Leo Meter. London, Allen and Unwin, 1948. 45pp, col illus.
Short extracts of prose and poetry by Classical and French, German and
English writers up to the nineteenth century. Only English writers repre-
sented are Thackeray and Byron.

602 LANG, Geoffrey
   Mirror to woman, compiled by Geoffrey Lang. London, Herbert
Jenkins, [1944]. 93pp.
Headings: Woman in love; Woman adorned; Woman and man; Woman
scorned; Woman's wit; Woman's virtues and failings; Mirror to woman.
Mostly short extracts of prose and poetry.

603 LUCAS, E V
   Her infinite variety: a feminine portrait gallery, edited by E V Lucas.
London, Methuen, 1908. xv, 371pp.
Headings: The buds; Virginal; The poets and the ideal; A west-country bevy;
The tender north; Wayside flowers; The heroines; Shakespeare's women;
Sir Walter's women; A special trio; Good company; The gentle; Mothers;
The wife perfect; Family friends; The adventurers; Thalis and Melpomene;
Addison and Steel's gallery; Dianas; The paragons; The blues; Characters;
Friends of the courtly; Saints; Immortal sisters; Aunts and grandmothers;
The tyrants; Dead ladies.
Poetry and prose from the seventeenth to nineteenth century.

604 PATERSON, Dorothy
   Woman: 'one of nature's agreeable blunders', compiled by Dorothy
Paterson. London, Spottiswoode & Ballantyne, 1947. 64pp.
Poetry of the seventeenth, nineteenth, and twentieth centuries.

605 SOUTHGATE, Henry
   What men have said about women: a collection of choice thoughts and
sentences, compiled and analytically arranged by Henry Southgate; with
illustrations by J D Watson. London, Routledge & Warne, 1865. xxvii,
320pp, illus.
Prose and poetry of the sixteenth to nineteenth century. A large number
of unfamiliar writers.

606 A VISION OF FAIR WOMEN
(tributes to beauty by poets and painters). London, John Bumpus, 1890. 136pp, plates (some col).
Mostly nineteenth century verse. Text reproduces handwriting of different styles.

607 WILLIAMS, Stephen
Women: an anthology for men, compiled by Stephen Williams. London, Hutchinson, 1942. 300pp.
Prose and poetry mostly of the nineteenth and twentieth centuries, apart from extracts from Shakespeare. Index of ladies' names.

Studies and criticism

608 BREWER, D S
The ideal of feminine beauty in medieval literature, especially Harley lyrics (BM Ms 2253), Chaucer, and some Elizabethans (in Modern Language Review, Vol 50, July 1955, pp 257-69).

609 DOHERTY, G
Role of the woman and the nature of relationship in Renaissance English literature, with special reference to Spenser, Donne, and Milton. PhD thesis, University of London, 1972.

610 MENON, K P K
Woman in English poetry from Milton to Wordsworth, by K P K Menon. Kerala, Kerala University, Institute of English, 1965. 285pp. References in footnotes. Covers Milton, Swift, Pope, Thomson, Crabbe, Wordsworth, Coleridge, Shelley, Byron, Keats.

611 ROGERS, Katharine M
The troublesome helpmate: a history of misogyny in literature, by Katharine M Rogers. Seattle, University of Washington Press, 1966. xvi, 288pp. References in footnotes.
Chapters: Eve, Xanthipe and Llodia; Medieval attitudes towards love and marriage; The court wanton; The bossy bourgeoise, and the insatiable strumpet: the Renaissance; St Paul with a difference: the puritans; Reason versus Folly and romantic illusion: the Restoration and the eighteenth century; The drooping lily: the nineteenth century; The fear of mom: the twentieth century; The reason why.
A general study of the theme with some references to poetry mainly before the nineteenth century.

612 THOMAS, Edward
Feminine influences on the poet, by Edward Thomas. London, Martin Secker. [1910]. 352pp, plates.
Chapters: The inspiration of poetry; Women and inspiration; Women as poets; Women, nature and poetry; Passion and poetry; Mothers of poets; Poets and friendly women; The tenth muse; Patronesses.

FRIENDSHIP

613 A BOOK OF FRIENDSHIP
London, Dent, 1923. 186pp. (The Bedside Series.)
Preface signed E R. Prose and poetry from the Bible to the nineteenth century. Extensive extracts from essays by Emerson, Montaigne, Samuel Johnson, Thoreau, Bishop Taylor and Plutarch.

614 CARPENTER, Edward
Ioläus: an anthology of friendship, compiled by Edward Carpenter. London, Swan Sonnenschein; Boston, C E Goodspeed, 1902. 190pp.
Second enlarged edition: London, G Allen, 1906. vi, 234pp.
Third enlarged edition: London, Allen and Unwin, 1915. vi, 234pp.

615 CROTHERS, Samuel McChord
The book of friendship, with an introduction by Samuel McChord Crothers; and with drawing by Wladyslaw T Benda. New York, Macmillan, 1910. xviii, 331pp.
Reprinted: Freeport, New York, Books for Libraries Press, 1969. (Granger Index Reprint Series.)

616 GROVER, Edwin Osgood
From friend to friend: a partnership in friendship, collected by Edwin Osgood Grover. Chicago, P E Volland, 1916. 64pp.

617 HILDITCH, Neville
In praise of friendship: an anthology of good wishes, compiled by Neville Hilditch. London, Frederick Muller, 1950. 62pp, illus.
Extracts of prose and poetry of all periods up to the nineteenth century.

618 HOWARD, John Raymond
Best poems on friendship, compiled by J R Howard. New York, Crowell, 1916. 246pp.

619 LEWIS, Edward and MYERS, Robert
To be a friend: sayings and verses celebrating the beauty of friendship, edited by Edward Lewis and Robert Myers; illustrated by Carol Jones. London, Roger Schlesinger, 1969. 61pp, illus.

620 MORRIS, Joseph and ADAMS, St Clair
The book of friendship verse, with selected prose passages and quotations collected and edited by Joseph Morris and St Clair Adams. New York, George Sully, [1924]. 369pp.

621 RANSOME, Arthur
The book of friendship: essays, poems, maxims and prose passages, arranged by Arthur Ransome. London, Edinburgh, T C and E C Jack, [1909]. xx, 478pp.
Ranges from the Bible to the nineteenth century.

622 RICE, Wallace and RICE, Frances
   The wealth of friendship, compiled by Wallace and Frances Rice; with a homily on friendship by the Rev F W Gunsaulus. London, Simpkin, Marshall, Hamilton & Kent, [1915]. 210pp.
Headings: Friendship's essentials; The stepping stone; The stumbling blocks; On being a friend; On being befriended; The advice of friends; Our friends the enemy; Friends and enemies; Men and women friends; Friendship of women; Friends and relations; Friendships that fail; In praise of friends; Benefits of friendship; Our friends are best; Friends that are gone; The great friendships.
Prose and poetry extracts, consisting of many short maxims and aphorisms, ranging from the Bible to the nineteenth century. Black borders, headings and authors' names in red.

623 SCHUTZ, Susan Polis
   The language of friendship, edited by Susan Polis Schutz; designed and illustrated by Stephen Schutz. Boulder (Colorado), Blue Mountain Arts, 1975. 63pp, illus.

624 WOODS, Ralph Louis
   A treasury of friendship: sentiment, philosophy, humour, inspiration, observations, counsel, analysis, idealism and friendship in action, gathered from memoirs, essays, letters, poetry, legend, fiction, epics, and history from ancient times to today. New York, D McKay, [1957]. 496pp.

Studies and criticism

625 MILLS, Laurens J
   The Renaissance development in England of the classical ideas about friendship. PhD thesis, Chicago University, 1925.

LONELINESS AND SOLITUDE

626 ADAMS, Anthony
   Loneliness and parting, edited by Anthony Adams. Oxford, Pergamon Press, 1968. 88pp. (Explorations series.)
Mostly prose of the twentieth century.

627 ALLAN, Philip Bertram Murray
   A little book of loneliness, for those who are wont to be alone, compiled by P B M Allan, London, Philip Allan, 1926. 240pp.
Headings: Its excellence; Contentment necessary; Town and country; Dawn; Nature's company; Evening; Night; Abodes of peace; The scholar; The hermit; The captive; The grave.
Poetry and prose, mostly of the seventeenth and nineteenth centuries.

628 JONES, Esmor
   Making contact, edited by Esmor Jones. Oxford, Pergamon Press, 1968. 59pp. (Explorations series.)

Mostly prose of the twentieth century, on 'the problems of establishing personal relationships and finding the balance between independence and reliance on others'.

629 PARKER, T H and TESKEY, F J
On being alone, edited by T H Parker and F J Teskey. Glasgow, Blackie, 1970. 58pp, illus. (Themes to Explore series.)
Headings: In desolate places; In a crowd; By choice; At night; In old age; With thoughts of God.
Twentieth century poetry, intended for schools.

Studies and criticism

630 GRUBER, Loren C
Isolation in Old English elegies and the Canterbury Tales: a contribution to the study of the continuity of English poetry. PhD thesis, Peabody University, 1972.

631 MARTIN, Abbott C
The love of solitude in eighteenth century poetry. (in South Atlantic Quarterly, Vol 29, January 1930, pp 48-59).

632 ROSTVIG, Maren-Sophie
The theme of retirement in seventeenth century English poetry. PhD thesis, University of California, Los Angeles, 1950.

633 WEAVER, Charles P
The hermit in English literature from the beginnings to 1660. PhD thesis, Peabody University, 1922.

SORROW, MELANCHOLY AND PESSIMISM

634 GEORGE, Daniel
A peck of troubles, or an anatomy of woe in which are collected by Daniel George many hundreds of examples of those chagrins and mortifications which have beset, still beset, and ever will beset the human race and overshadow its journey through the earthly paradise, the whole being conveniently displayed in an alphabetical arrangement for purposes of comparison, consolation and diversion. London, Jonathan Cape, 1936. 340pp. Prose extracts from the seventeenth to nineteenth century, taken mainly from letters and diaries.

635 KENNEDY, Charles W
Old English elegies, translated into alliterative verse with a critical introduction by Charles W Kennedy. Princeton, Princeton University Press, 1936. 104pp. Introduction: pp 1-41.
Contents: The wanderer; The seafarer; The ruin; Doer; The wife's lament; The husband's message; Beowulf (lines 2231-70).

636 MacPHAIL, Andrew
   The book of sorrow, [compiled] by Andrew MacPhail. London, Oxford
University press, 1916. xiii, 500pp.
Headings: Serenity; Rest; Oblivion; Inevitable; The sting of death; The grave's
triumph; The tyrant; Victory; The sadness of it; The pity of it; O come
quickly; Love and death; Farewell.
Poetry from the sixteenth to nineteenth century, mostly centering around
the theme of death.

637 SAGITTARIUS and GEORGE, Daniel
   The perpetual pessimist: an everlasting calendar of gloom and an almanac
of woe complete with reference section incorporating The Pessimist's Anthology of Old Wives Tales, [compiled by] Sagittarius and Daniel George;
decorations by John Glashar. London, Hutchinson, 1963. 128pp, illus.
Short prose and poetry quotations of all periods, including some foreign
writers in translation.

638 (BIBLIOGRAPHY) SENA, John F
   A bibliography of melancholy, 1600-1800, compiled by John F Sena.
London, The Nether Press, 1970. 70pp. (Nether Press Bibliographies,
Miscellaneous Series No 102.)
pp 23-43: list of individual poems on elegiac, funereal and melancholic
themes.

Studies and criticism

639 BRADFORD, Eugene Francis
   Anglo-Saxon melancholy. PhD thesis, Harvard University, 1927.

640 BRITTAIN, K C
   The sin of despair in English Renaissance literature. PhD thesis, University of California, Los Angeles, 1963.

641 GOODALE, Ralph H
   Pessimism in English poetry and fiction, 1847-1900. PhD thesis, Chicago
University, 1928.

642 GOODCHILD, Donald
   The literature and philosophy of melancholy at the end of the Renaissance.
PhD thesis, Princeton University, 1926.

643 HUGHES, T R
   The melancholy element in English poetry from Widsith to Chaucer. MA
thesis, University of Wales, 1928.

644 MYERS, Lena J
   Typical pessimistic attitudes in English literature 1800-1895. PhD thesis,
University of Illinois, 1926.

645 SENA, John F
The English malady: the idea of melancholy from 1700 to 1760. PhD thesis, Princeton University, 1967.

646 SICKELS, Eleanor M
The gloomy egoist: moods and themes of melancholy from Gray to Keats, by Eleanor M Sickels. New York, Columbia University Press, 1932. x, 456pp. Notes and references. (Columbia University Studies in English and Comparative Literature.)
Chapters: Compounded of many simples; Invocation to melancholy; Sic transit gloria mundi; King Death (pp 130-181); Blighted roses (love poetry); The sounding cataract; The soul of a poet.

647 SIEGEL, Paul N
Studies in Elizabethan melancholy. PhD thesis, Harvard University, 1941.

648 SNYDER, Susan B
The paradox of despair: studies of the despair theme in medieval and Renaissance literature. PhD thesis, Columbia University, 1963.

649 SPARKS, Lyle W
A study of romantic melancholy. PhD thesis, Indiana University, 1973.

650 STEMPEL, Daniel
Studies in nineteenth century pessimism. PhD thesis, Harvard University, 1949.

651 WHEATER, A A
Melancholy in eighteenth century literature. PhD thesis, Nottingham University, 1958.

DISASTERS AND DANGERS

652 ATLAS ASSURANCE COMPANY
On risk: a miscellany on the subject of risks and danger. London, Atlas Insurance Company, 1958. 48pp, plates.
Headings: Generality; Facts: earth, air, fire, water; Fancies: literary, utilitarian, ingenuous, paradoxical.
Poetry and prose. Mostly prose.

653 HARRIS, Marjorie Chadwick
Aberfan: a book of memorial verse written by children, edited, compiled and designed by Marjorie Chadwick Harris. Ilfracombe (Devon), Arthur H Stockwell, 1967. 140pp.
Poems written by children aged 7-19, submitted in response to the compiler's appeal for poems on the Aberfan mountain tip disaster.

654 ROLLINS, Hyder Edward
  The Pack of Autolycus: or strange and terrible news of ghosts, apparitions, monstrous births, showers of wheat, judgments of God, and other prodigious and fearful happenings as in broadside ballads of the years 1624-1693, edited by Hyder Edward Rollins. Cambridge (Mass), Harvard University Press, 1927. xvii, 269pp.

See also: 787, 1043

Shipwrecks: see Sea 1718-1779

CONSOLATION

655 ARMSTRONG, O V
  Comfort for those who mourn: Bible, poetry, prose, compiled by O V Armstrong. Nashville, Okesbury Press, 1930. 100pp.

656 GREGORY, Horace
  The triumph of life: poems of consolation for the English speaking world, edited and with an introduction by Horace Gregory. New York, The Viking Press, 1943. xxvii, 603pp. (The Viking Portable Library.)

657 PETERS, Madison Clinton
  Our children in heaven: a collection of consolatory poems, [compiled] by Madison C Peters. New York, Wilmore-Andrews, 1897. 94pp.

658 SIMS, Albert E
  A little book of comfort, compiled by Rev Albert E Sims. London, Harrap, 1911. 223pp. (The Choice Books series.)
  Headings: Bereavement; Chastening; Companionship; Darkness; Death; Immortality; Love; Patience; Peace; Perseverance; Providence; Resignation; Sorrows; Suffering; Trust.
  Poetry and prose, mostly of the nineteenth century, includes some extracts from the Bible.

659 SOMERVELL, R U
  Love and death: an anthology, compiled by R U Somervell. London, Methuen, 1934. xviii, 165pp.
  Headings: Prelude; Sorrow; Life; Love; Death. Extracts from the Bible and nineteenth and twentieth century writers.

PEACE

660 CLARK, Thomas Curtis and GARRISON, Winfred Ernest
  One hundred poems of peace: an anthology, compiled by Thomas Curtis Clark and Winfred Ernest Garrison. Chicago, Willet & Clark, 1934. 90pp.
  English and American poetry of the nineteenth and twentieth centuries.

661 EYRE, Frank
   The quiet spirit: an anthology of poems old and new, compiled by
Frank Eyre; drawings by Lynton Lamb. London, Oxford University Press,
1946. ix, 146pp, illus.
Headings: Verse and the quiet mind; The green shade; Night and sleep; The
final quiet.
Poetry of the seventeenth, nineteenth and twentieth centuries, by mostly
familiar poets.

662 GLASIER, J Bruce
   The minstrelsy of peace: a collection of notable verse in the English
tongue relating to peace and war, ranging from the fifteenth century to the
present day, collected with notes and an introductory essay on poetry and
war and peace in English poetry by J Bruce Glasier. Manchester, London,
National Labour Press, 1920. xlvi, 177pp.

663 GOUDGE, Elizabeth
   A book of peace: an anthology, [compiled] by Elizabeth Goudge. London, Michael Joseph, 1967. 3llpp.
Headings: Peaceful scenes; Serene people; Their peaceful work; Peaceful
creatures; Peaceful sights and sounds; Children and lovers.
Poetry and some prose, mostly of the nineteenth and twentieth centuries
by familiar and unfamiliar writers.

664 LEONARD, R M
   The poetry of peace, selected by R M Leonard. London, Oxford Univer-
sity Press, 1918. 128pp. Notes.
Poetry from the seventeenth to nineteenth century.

665 STANLEY, Arthur
   The seven stars of peace: an anthology for the times, selected and ar-
ranged by Arthur Stanley. London, Dent, 1940. xiii, 238pp.
Headings: Knowledge; Faith; Brotherhood; Joy; Gentleness; Liberty; Cour-
age.
Mostly prose extracts of all periods from the Bible to the twentieth century.

666 ZIM, Jacob
   My shalom, my peace: paintings and poems by Jewish and Arab children
edited and designed by Jacob Zim; selection of poems by Uriel Ofek, translation of poems by Dov Vardi. London, New English Library, 1975. 96pp,
col illus.
First published in Hebrew: Hashalom sheli, by the American Israel Publishing Company, 1974.

See also: War 1195-1363

CUSTOMS AND MANNERS

FOOD

667 ADAMS, Anthony and JONES, Esmor
 Inner and outer, [compiled] by Anthony Adams and Esmor Jones.
London, Nelson, 1974. 64pp, illus. (Nelson's Humanities Scheme, English
2.)
Headings: Food for life; Food for fun; Coverings; People and peacocks;
Food and clothes as metaphor.
Twentieth century prose and poetry. Intended for schools.

668 AGREE, Rose H
 How to eat a poem and other morsels: food poems for children, selected
by Rose H Agree; illustrated by Peggy Wilson. New York, Pantheon Books,
1967. 87pp, illus.
Headings: From soup to nuts; Snacks; Tutti-frutti; Mind your manners.
Twentieth century American and English poems, rhymes and limericks.

669 HILL, Brian
 The greedy book: a feast for the eyes, compiled by Brian Hill; with a
foreword by Compton Mackenzie, illustrated by Peter Forster. London,
Hart-Davies, 1966. 298pp, illus.
Headings: Behind the scenes; The breakfast hour; Luncheon is served; Cups
that cheer; The dinner gong; Supper time; A few snacks; Feasts and friv-
olities; Atrocious meals; Short commons; Travellers tales; A mixed grill.
Prose and poetry of all periods.

670 HUNT, Peter
 Eating and drinking: an anthology for epicures, compiled by Peter Hunt;
introduction by Andre L Simon. London, Ebury Press, 1966. 317pp, illus.
Headings: Hints for epicures; To indulge or not to indulge; Grapes and
bottles; Genial hosts, gracious guests; Food for thought; Dinner is served;
Eating out; Food fit for kings; Cooks and cookery; Eating in foreign parts;
Desert island dishes; Meals to forget; Another man's poison; Food and fan-
tasy.
Prose and poetry mostly of the nineteenth and twentieth centuries.

671 MACKAY, Robert
 An anthology of the potato, by Robert Mackay. Dublin, Allen Figgis,
for the Irish Potato Marketing Board, 1961. 92pp.

Mostly Irish ballads and songs connected with potato growing and the potato as food. Limited edition: 500 copies.

672 QUENNELL, Nancy
The epicure's anthology, collected by Nancy Quennell; with an essay on the epicure and the epicurean by A J A Symons and decorations by Osbert Lancaster. London, Golden Cockerel Press, 1936. 187pp, illus.
Headings: Banqueting delights; Gastronomic oddities; Gastronomic incidents.
Covers all periods. Mostly prose.

673 RAY, Cyril
The poetry of the table, (in 'The gourmet's companion', edited by Cyril Ray. London, Eyre & Spottiswoode, 1963. pp 441-399).

674 WOLFE, Linda
The literary gourmet: the pleasure of reading about wonderful food in scenes from great literature . . . [compiled] by Linda Wolfe. New York, Random House, [1962]. 387pp, illus.

See also: 289, 299, 327, 418, 1259

Studies and criticism

675 BATTISCOMBE, Georgina
English picnics, by Georgina Battiscombe. London, Harvill Press, 1949. 212pp.
Contains: The poets' picnic (pp 138-156), and picnics in fiction (pp 157-189).

DRINK AND DRINKING

676 BICKERDYKE, John
The curiosities of ale and beer: an entertaining history, illustrated with over fifty quaint cuts, by John Bickerdyke, in part collected by the late J G Fennell, now largely augmented . . . by the author and . . . J M D. London, Field and Tuer, [1886]. xii, 449pp, illus.
Contains a large number of verse extracts.
Reprinted: London, Spring Books, 1965.

677 CAMPBELL, Marie
Liquor ballads from the Kentucky mountains (in Southern Folklore Quarterly, Vol 2, September 1938, pp 157-64).

678 HOEY, Richard
Anthology of alcohol, [compiled] by Richard Hoey. London, Palantype Organisation, [1968]. 62pp.

679 JUNIPER, William
The true drunkard's delight: being an attempt in a collection of brave and witty things from English verse and prose to set forth in gratitude for Bacchus' bounty the whole art and philosophy of drinking . . . , all carefully collected together and in part written by William Juniper. London, Unicorn Press, 1933. xv, 375pp.
Headings: The philosophy of drinking; The law of drinking; The choice spirits' chaplet; In exaltation of ale and beer; In praise of wine; In commendation of spirits; Drinking customs; Gentlemen, I give you . . . (toasts and toasting); Notable drunkards; Wit and wine both together; Drinking slang; Drinking and the law; Doctor Bacchus; Inns and taverns; William Juniper's nightcaps; Tee-tee-totalism; Some lively deaths; Hic jacet.
Seventeenth and eighteenth century prose and verse.

680 (BIBLIOGRAPHY) MOTT, Margaret M
Songs about drinking (in Notes, July 1949, pp 379-418). A bibliography of American songs, covering—alcoholic: general, beer, ale and stout, wine. Non-alcoholic: chocolate, cider, coffee, milk, tea, water. Songs about not drinking: temperance, prohibition. Songs involving narcotics: Marihuana, opium and derivatives, tobacco.

681 MARCHANT, W T
In praise of ale: or songs, ballads, epigrams and epigrams relating to beer, malt and hops . . . collected and arranged by W T Marchant. London, George Redway, 1888. 632pp.

682 MAYNARD, Theodore
A tankard of alc: an anthology of drinking songs, compiled and edited by Theodore Maynard. London, Erskine Macdonald, [1920]. 188pp.
Songs and verse of the seventeenth and eighteenth centuries.

683 MORTLOCK, Geoffrey and WILLIAMS, Stephen
The flowing bowl: a book of blithe spirits and blue devil; a selection from the best things written through the ages on drinks, drinking and drinkers by poets, novelists, essayists, dramatists, drunkards, social reformers and teetotallers, made by Geoffrey Mortlake and Stephen Williams. London, Hutchinson, 1947. 259pp.

684 ROGERS, Cameron
Full and by: being a collection of verses by persons of quality in praise of drinking, compiled and edited by Cameron Rogers; illustrated by Edward A Wilson; with prefaces by Don Marquis and Christopher Morley. New York, Doubleday & Page, 1925. xxx, 153pp, illus.

685 SHAY, Frank
My pious friends and drunken companions: songs and ballads of conviviality, collected by Frank Shay; magnificently illuminated by John Held, jr. New York, Macmillan, [1927]. 192pp, illus. Music.

686 SHAY, Frank
  More pious friends and drunken companions: songs and ballads of conviviality, collected by Frank Shay; magnificently illuminated by John Held,
jr.; musical arrangement for any degree of inebrity by Helen Ramsey. New
York, Macaulay, [1928]. 190pp, illus. Music.

687 SIMON, André
  Drink, by André Simon. London, Burke, 1948. 272pp, col illus. (The
Pleasures of Life Series.)
Headings: In the beginning; Dionysus in Hellas; Bacchus in Imperial Rome;
Wine and the Elizabethans; Champagne; Wine today; The challenge of the
still; John Barleycorn; Cider; Inns and taverns.
A general cultural history of drink and drinking with numerous extracts of
prose and poetry of all periods.

See also: 398, 418

Studies and criticism

688 EWING, George Wilmeth
  Some verse of the temperance movement. PhD thesis, University of
Texas, 1962.

SMOKING

689 HAMILTON, Walter
  A lytell parcel of poems and parodyes, containing divers conceited
ballades and pithie sayinges, all newly collected and emprinted by Walter
Hamilton. London, Reeves & Turner, 1889. 180pp, illus.
Headings: Early poems in praise of tobacco; Poems on the pipe; Poems on
the cigar; Poems on the cigarette; Poems on snuff; Parodies relating to
smoking; Ballades on smoking.
Cover has the title: 'Poems and parodies in praise of tabacco'. Mostly nineteenth century prose and verse. Limited edition: 501 copies.

690 HUTCHINSON, William G
  Lyra nicotiana: poems and verses concerning tobacco, edited with an
introduction by William G Hutchinson. London, Walter Scott, [1898].
xlii, 262pp, port.
Headings: Seventeenth century smokers; Eighteenth century smokers;
Nineteenth century smokers.
Portrait is of the compiler.

691 PARTINGTON, Wilfred
  Smoke rings and roundelays: blendings from prose and verse since
Raleigh's time, compiled by Wilfred Partington; with woodcuts by Norman
Jones. London, John Castle, 1924. xvi, 320pp, illus.
Headings: In the beginning; Tobacco; Pipe songs and fancies; Woman and

the weed; Some great pipemen and others; Cigars; Cigarettes; Snuff; Matters
of choice; Virtues of the leaf; Parodies and imitations; On the varieties of
pipes; Tobacco and books; Dinner—and after; Smoke pictures; The philosophy of smoke.

692 SIMS, Albert E
   The witching weed, compiled by Albert E Sims. London, Harrap,
[1912]. 207pp. (The Choice Books Series.)
Headings: The poetry of smoking; The prose of smoking; The pleasures; In
praise of smoking; The prudence of smoking; Some proverbs on smoking.
Mostly nineteenth century prose and verse.

693 THE SMOKERS GARLAND
   Parts I, II, and III. Liverpool, at the office of Copes Tobacco Plant,
1890. 159pp.
Mostly nineteenth century verse. The collection was issued in three parts
with continuous pagination.

Studies and criticism

694 DICKSON, Sarah A
   Panacea or precious bane: tobacco in sixteenth century literature. PhD,
New York University, 1954.

COSTUME

695 FAIRHOLT, Frederick W
   Satirical songs and poems on costume from the thirteenth to the nineteenth century, edited by Frederick W Fairholt. London, Percy Society,
1849. iv, 267pp. (Percy Society Vol 27.)
Items taken from contemporary books and periodicals. Includes 'A ballad
of the beard'.

See also: 667

Studies and criticism

696 EAGLESON, Harvey
   Costume in the Middle English metrical romances (in PMLA, Vol 47,
June 1932, pp 339-45).

HOLIDAYS AND SPECIAL DAYS

General

697 ADAMS, Florence Ann and McCARRICK, Elizabeth
   Highdays and holidays, [compiled] by Florence Ann Adams and Elizabeth McCarrick; decorated by Emma L Brock. New York, Dutton, [1927].
337pp, illus.

698 COLE, William
Poems for seasons and celebration, edited by William Cole; illustrated by Johannes Troyer. Cleveland, World Publishing Company, [1961]. 191pp, illus.

699 CLARK, Thomas Curtis
Poems for special days and occasions, compiled by Thomas Curtis Clark. New York, R R Smith, 1930. 166pp.
Covers: New Year's day; Lincoln's birthday; Washington's birthday; Lent and Easter; Memorial Day; Flag day; Independence day; Labor day; Armistice day; Thanksgiving day; Christmas.

700 CLARK, Thomas Curtis and CLARK, Robert Earle
Poems for the great days, compiled by Thomas Curtis Clark and Robert Earle Clark. Nashville, Abingdon-Cokesbury Press, [1948]. 245pp.

701 DEMING, Norma H and BEMIS, Katharine F
Poems for everyday the schools celebrate, edited by Norma H Deming and Katharine F Bemis. New York, Noble, 1922. 349pp.

702 DICKSON, Margarette Ball
Modern poems for special days, selected and edited by Margarette Ball Dickson. New York, Dean, 1928. 180pp.

703 HARRINGTON, Mildred P and others
Our holiday in poetry, compiled by Mildred P Harrington and Josephine H Thomas, and a committee of the Carnegie Library School Association. New York, Wilson, 1929. 480pp.

704 HAZELTINE, Alice I and SMITH, Elva S
The year around: poems for children, selected by Alice I Hazeltine and Elva S Smith; decorations by P Hutchinson. New York, Abingdon Press, 1956. 192pp, illus.
Poems for each month and season of the year, and for: St Patrick's day, April Fools day, Easter, Mothers' day, Memorial day, Flag day, Independence day, Labor day, Columbus day, Halloween, Book week, Thanksgiving day; Christmas day, New Year's day, Lincoln's birthday, St Valentine's day, Washington's birthday.

705 SEABURG, Carl
Great occasions: readings for the celebration of birth, coming-of-age, marriage and death, compiled by Carl Seaburg. Boston, Beacon, 1968. xii, 462pp.

706 SECHRIST, Elizabeth Hough
Poems for red letter days, compiled by Elizabeth Hough Sechrist; illustrated by Guy Fry. Philadelphia, Macrae Smith, [1951]. 349pp, illus.

Birthdays

707 BREWTON, Sara and BREWTON, John E
Birthday candles burning bright: a treasury of birthday poetry, selected
by Sara and John E Brewton; decorations by Vera Bock. New York, Macmillan, 1960. 199pp, illus.
Headings: To be a birthday child; Two of us, two of us; When I was christened;
christened; So let thy birthdays come to thee: birthdays before seven; So
let thy birthdays come to thee: seven through thirteen; Cakes and candles;
Surprises, surprises! Growing up; Youth and age; Birthdays through adult
eyes; The birthday of the Lord.
Twentieth century poetry, mostly about children. Intended for children.

Halloween

708 HOPKINS, Lee Bennet
Hey-how for Halloween! [compiled] by Lee Bennet Hopkins; illustrated
by Janet McCaffeny. New York, Harcourt Brace Jovanovich, [1974]. 31pp,
illus.

709 SCHAUFFLER, Robert Haven
Holloween: its origin, spirit, celebration and significance as related in
prose and verse, compiled by Robert Haven Schauffler. New York, Dodd &
Mead, 1933. xxii, 391pp. (Our American Holidays series.)

November 5th

710 NOVEMBER 5th RHYMES
(in Notes and Queries, 14th series, clix, 1930, pp 294, 338, 356.)

See also: Easter 233-237; Christmas 202-232; 467 St Valentine's day

MAGIC AND THE SUPERNATURAL

GENERAL

711 CAUSLEY, Charles
The Puffin book of magic verse, chosen and introduced by Charles Causley; illustrated by Barbara Swiderska. Harmondsworth (Middx), Puffin Books, 1974. 239pp, illus.
A wide-ranging anthology, ranging from the songs of primitive societies and Anglo-Saxon verses to the twentieth century.

712 HADFIELD, John
A chamber of horrors, unlocked by John Hadfield: an anthology of the macabre in words and pictures. London, Studio Vista, 1965. 320pp, illus.
Headings: The bells of hell; Seeds of destruction; Love and death; Unquiet minds; Apparitions; The dance of death.
Prose and poetry mostly of the nineteenth and twentieth centuries.

713 IRESON, Barbara
Shadows and spells, edited by Barbara Ireson; illustrated by Gill Simmonds. London, Faber, 1969. 111pp, illus.
Headings: Who's that knocking on the window?; Each to his bed; What ghosts would walk; For every man that ye droon, I droon twa; Hey! High! low in his grave; The hag is astride.
Mostly twentieth century poetry.

714 JACOBS, Leland Blair
Poetry of witches, elves and goblins, compiled by Leland Blair Jacobs; drawings by Frank Aloise. Champaign, (Ill), Garrard, 1970. 63pp, illus.
Intended for children.

715 JONES, Rhodri
Imagination, edited by Rhodri Jones. London, Heinemann Educational, 1969. 71pp.
Headings: Supernatural; Night and dream; Wonder and terrors of the mind.
Twentieth century verse. Intended for school use.

716 MANLEY, Seon and LEWIS, Gogo
A gathering of ghosts: a treasury, edited by Seon Manley and Gogo Lewis. New York, Funk and Wagnalls, 1970. 217pp.
Poetry and prose. Intended for children.

717 MASON, Edward Tuckerman
  Songs of fairy land, compiled by Edward Tuckerman Mason; with illustrations after designs by Maud Humphrey. New York, Putnam, 1889. xiv, 252pp, illus.

718 MOORE, Lilian and WEBSTER, Lawrence
  Catch your breath: a book of shivery poems, selected by Lilian Moore and Lawrence Webster; illustrated by Graham Wilson. Champaign (Ill), Garrard, 1973. 64pp, illus.
Poems about unusual or frightening things; includes poems on Halloween, witches and creepy creatures.

719 NOYES, Alfred
  The magic casement: a book of faery poems, giving glimpses of the world beyond the casement, selected and arranged with an introduction and notes by Alfred Noyes; illustrated by Stephen Reid. London, Chapman & Hall, [1908]. xx, 391, illus.
Headings: The fairy life; Witches' cauldrons and blasted heaths; Come unto these yellow sands; Flower-fairies; Enchanted woods; Airy mountain and rushy glen; The faery voyager; Last echoes.
Mostly long poems and ballads from the sixteenth to twentieth century.

720 ROHDE, Eleanour Sinclair
  The fairy-lover's days: an anthology and diary, compiled by Eleanour Sinclair Rohde. London, The Medici Society, 1930. [116]pp, col front.
Prose and poetry extracts from the seventeenth, nineteenth and twentieth centuries, for each day of the year.

721 SAUNDERS, Dennis
  Hist whist: poems of magic and mystery and ghosts, collected by Dennis Saunders; illustrated by Kathy Wyatt. London, Evans, 1975. 94pp, illus.
Headings: 'Bearded, cloaked and cowled they go'; Strange visitors; Bewitched; Restless spirits; Odd bods; Awesome beasts.
Some sixteenth and seventeenth century poetry, but mostly twentieth century.

722 TESKEY, F J and PARKER, T H
  The supernatural, [compiled] by T H Parker and F J Teskey. Glasgow, London, Blackie, 1970. 58pp. (Themes to Explore Series.)
Headings: The ghost walks; Witches and wizards; What is to be?
Twentieth century poetry. Intended for school use.

723 WAITE, Arthur Edward
  Elfin music: an anthology of English fairy poetry, selected and arranged with an introduction by Arthur Edward Waite. London, Walter Scott, 1888. xxxv, 173pp.
Headings: The fairy family; Travels in fairyland; Men and fairies; Miscellaneous; Epilogue.
Mostly nineteenth century poetry by unknown poets.

724 WESTWOOD, Jennifer
  The Isle of Gramarye: an anthology of the poetry of magic, [compiled]
by Jennifer Westwood. London, Hart-Davis, 1970. 93pp, illus.
Headings: Of enchanters; Of enchantresses; The making of enchantments;
The waking dead.
Thirty-two poems by well-known poets of the nineteenth and twentieth
century.

See also: 1593, 1723

Studies and criticism

725 BRIGGS, K M
  The anatomy of Puck: an examination of fairy beliefs among Shakes-
peare's contemporaries and successors, by K M Briggs. London, Routledge
& Kegan Paul 1959. xi, 284pp. Bibliography (pp 262-276).

726 BRIGGS, K M
  The fairies in tradition and literature, by K M Briggs. London, Routledge & Kegan Paul, 1967. x, 261pp, plates. Bibliography (pp 241-250).
Chapter 18: The poets—eighteenth century. Chapter 19: The poets—nineteenth century and after.

727 DELATTRE, Floris
  English fairy poetry: from the origins to the seventeenth century, by
Floris Delattre. London, Henry Frowde; Paris, Didier, [1912]. 235pp.
Bibliography.
Chapters: Elves, fairies and fays; Early fairy poetry; Elizabethan fairies;
A Midsummer Night's Dream; Post-Shakespearean fairies; From Drayton to
Herrick.

728 HARCOURT-SMITH, G M H
  The treatment of the supernatural in English literature from Shakespeare
to Coleridge together with some consideration of the subject in its relation
to the metaphysical and mystical side of literature. MA thesis, London University, 1907.

729 McALINDON, T E
  The treatment of the supernatural in Middle English legend and romance,
1200-1400. PhD thesis, Cambridge University, 1961.

730 RAMSEY, John Stevens
  Magic and festivity in English Renaissance poetry. PhD thesis, University
of Maryland, 1971.

731 SENIOR, John
  The occult in nineteenth century symbolist literature. PhD thesis,
Columbia University, 1957.

732 SPACKS, Patricia Meyer
  The insistence of horror: aspects of the supernatural in eighteenth century poetry, [by] Patricia Meyer Spacks. Cambridge (Mass), Harvard University Press, 1962. 244pp. Bibliographies (primary and secondary sources).
Notes and references.

THE INDIVIDUAL AND SOCIETY

SLAVERY

733 (BIBLIOGRAPHY) HOGG, Peter C
The African slave trade and its suppression: a classified and annotated bibliography of books, pamphlets and periodical articles, [compiled] by Peter C Hogg. London, Frank Cass, 1973. 409pp.
Pp 324-341: imaginative literature, covering a number of individual poems and anthologies of the first half of the nineteenth century.

734 SYPHER, Feltus W
The anti-slavery movement to 1800 in English literature, exclusive of the periodical. PhD thesis, Harvard University, 1937.

735 TURNER, Lorenzo
Anti-slavery sentiment in American literature prior to 1865 (in Journal of Negro History, Vol 14, October 1929, pp 371-492).

See also: 402

PROTEST AND REVOLT

736 BEAUCHAMP, Joan
Poems of revolt: a twentieth century anthology, chosen by Joan Beauchamp. London, The Labour Publishing Company, 1924. 105pp.
Poems of general protest against life, work and war by mostly familiar poets of the twentieth century.

737 GRAHAM, Marcus
Anthology of revolutionary poetry, compiled and edited by Marcus Graham; with an introduction by Ralph Cheyney and Lucia Trent. New York, Active Press, 1975. 360pp.

738 LOWENFELS, Walter
Writing on the wall: 108 American poems of protest, [compiled] by Walter Lowenfels. Garden City, New York, Doubleday, 1969. 189pp.

739 WRIGHT, Robin
   Poems of protest, edited by Robin Wright. London, Studio Vista, 1966. 48pp. (Pocket Poets Series.)

FREEDOM

740 BENET, William Rose and COUSINS, Norman
   The poetry of freedom, edited by William Rose Benet and Norman Cousins. New York, Random House, 1945. xxxiv, 820pp. (The Modern Library of the World's Best Books Series.)

741 FEINBERG, Barry
   Poets to the people: South African freedom poets, edited by Barry Feinberg; foreword by Hugh Macdiarmid. London, Allen and Unwin, 1974. 83pp.

742 IVENS, Michael and DUNSTAN, Reginald
   Freedom quotes, edited by Michael Ivens and Reginald Dunstan. London, Aims for Freedom and Enterprise, 1976. 48pp.
Headings: Speaking of freedom; A house on the hill; Power—as friend and enemy; A bundle of contradictions; Destroyers, despotism and dangers; Rights of man; Education; The individual; Liberty and the free society; The state; Law; Enterprise and economics; Fighting for freedom; The unfree; Taxation.
A wide-ranging collection of quotations and short extracts from novelists, poets, philosophers, politicians and economists.

743 LAWRENCE, R
   Voice of freedom, edited by R Lawrence. New York, Haven Press, 1942. 596pp.

744 LINDSAY, Jack and RICKWOOD, Edgell
   A handbook of freedom: a record of English democracy through twelve centuries, chosen by Jack Lindsay and Edgell Rickwood. London, Lawrence & Wishart, 1939. xxiii, 408pp.
Headings: Against feudal oppression, 700-1381; For the land, law and freedom of belief, 1400-1600; Towards political democracy; Wealth accumulates and men decay; A revolutionary era, 1700-1825; The tide of Chartism, 1825-1860; Imperialist expansion versus international democracy, 1850-1914; For peace and social justice, 1914-1918.
Wide ranging collection consisting of poetry and prose extracts from histories, biographies, letters, etc.

745 MULGAN, John
Poems of freedom, edited by John Mulgan; with an introduction by W H Auden. London, Gollancz, 1936. 192pp.
Poetry mostly of the eighteenth, nineteenth and twentieth centuries.

746 REYNOLDS, George Fullmer and CONNORS, Donald S
   Freedom speaks: ideals of democracy in poetry and prose, selected by
George F Reynolds and Donald S Connors; sponsored by the College
English Association, New York, Ronald Press, 1943. xvi, 270pp.

747 RICHMOND, Bruce L
   The pattern of freedom in prose and verse, chosen by Bruce L Richmond.
London, Faber, 1940. 266pp.
Headings: Freedom; The free people; The free mind; Patriotism and service;
Rumours, slanders and fears; The oppressor's wrong; Good faith; The herd;
Refugees; Warfare and warriors; Peace; The choice of life.
Covers the classical writers and the sixteenth to twentieth centuries.

748 WEDGWOOD, Josiah C and NEVINS, Allan
   Forever freedom: being an anthology in prose and verse from England
and America, by Josiah C Wedgwood and Allan Nevins. Harmondsworth
(Middx), Penguin, 1940. 222pp.
Wide ranging anthology from the Bible to the twentieth century. Consists
of poetry, quotations and extracts from histories.

LAW

749 CROKE, J Greenbag
   Lyrics of the law: a recital of songs and verses pertinent to the law and
the legal profession, selected from various sources by J Greenbag Croke.
San Francisco, Sumner Whitney, 1884. 312pp. Notes.
Headings: Cupids court; The law; The profession; The practice; The reports.

750 CROKE, J Greenbag
   Poems of the law, collected by J Greenbag Croke. San Francisco, Sumner Whitney, 1885. 311pp. Notes.
Contains: 'General average' by William Allen Butler; 'Ye delectable ballad'
from Punch; 'Jacob homnium's hoss' by William M Thackeray; 'A Roman
lawyer in Jerusalem' by W W Strong; 'The conveyancer's guide'–anon; 'The
pleader's guide', attributed to James Anstey.

751 PARKER, T H and TESKEY, F J
   Law and order, compiled by T H Parker and F J Teskey. Glasgow,
Blackie, 1970. 58pp. (Themes to Explore Series.)
Headings: The law of the land; Rough justice; The law of nature; A matter
for protest; And God said.
Twentieth century poetry. Intended for school use.

752a WARREN, Ina Russelle
   The lawyer's alcove: poems by the lawyer, for the lawyer, about the
lawyer, edited by Ina Russelle Warren; introduction by Chauncey M Depen.
New York, Doubleday, 1900. 270pp, plates.

CRIME

752b BURT, Olive Woolley
American murder ballads and their stories, collected and edited by Olive Woolley Burt. New York, Oxford University Press, 1958. 272pp. Music. Headings: Friends and relations; Jealousy; Unrequited love and madness; The profit motive; For the love of God; A matter of pigment; Law at any price; A way of life; Any excuse will serve.

753 CALTHROP, Kenyon
Crime and punishment, edited by Kenyon Calthrop. Oxford, Pergamon, 1968. 112pp. (Explorations Series.) Bibliography (further reading). Poetry and prose; mostly prose of the twentieth century.

754 GOODMAN, Jonathan
Bloody versicles: the rhymes of crime, [compiled] by Jonathan Goodman. Newton Abbot (Devon), David & Charles, 1971. 224pp, illus. Headings: Murder; Adultery; Attempted suicide; Bigamy; Fraudulent conversion; Incest; Delinquency; Larceny; Perjury; Prostitution; Treason; Poetic justice; A medico-legal expert.
Verse and ballads of the nineteenth and twentieth centuries.

755 MARSHBURN, Joseph H and VELIE, Alan R
Blood and knavery: a collection of English Renaissance pamphlets and ballads of crime and sin, compiled by J H Marshburn and Alan R Velie. Rutherford, (New Jersey), Farleigh Dickinson University Press, 1973. 215pp.

See also: 421, 1139, 1733

PRISON

756 ABRAMOWITZ, Isidore
The great prisoners: the first anthology of literature written in prison, selected and edited by Isidore Abramowitz, with an analytical introduction to the time and place and circumstances of each prisoner's imprisonment, a general preface to the whole and a select bibliography. New York, Dutton, 1946, 879pp. Bibliography.
Reprinted: Freeport, New York, Books for Libraries, 1972. (Essay Index Reprint series.)

757 BRANDRETH, Gyles
Created in captivity, by Gyles Brandreth. London, Hodder and Stoughton, 1972. 186pp, plates.
A study on creativity in general in prisons. pp 135-186: 'Behold a dungeon' an anthology of prose and poetry written in prison. Plates are reproductions of prisoners' art work.

758 NORRIS, Faith G and SPRINGER, Sharon J
  Men in exile: an anthology of creative writing by inmates of the Oregon
State Penitentiary, edited by Faith G Norris and Sharon J Springer. Cor-
vallis, Oregon State University Press, [1973]. 247pp, illus.

759 PARKER, Tony
  The man inside: an anthology of writing and conversational comment by
men in prison, edited by Tony Parker; illustrations by Ken Ward. London,
Michael Joseph, 1973. 159pp, illus.
Mostly short descriptive pieces in prose and poetry.

760 STOCK, A G and REYNOLDS, Reginald
  Prison anthology, edited by A G Stock and Reginald Reynolds, with
nine illustrations. London, Jarrolds, 1938. 292pp, illus.
Headings: On prisoners and prisons; General criticism; Fact; Fiction; De-
fiance; Dock and scaffold; Domestic; Religion; The consolation of philosophy; Complaint; Miscellany.
Prose and poetry of all periods. Introduction: pp 15-34.

761 VOLAVKOVA, Hans
  I never saw another butterfly: children's drawings and poems from
Theresienstadt Concentration Camp, 1942-1944, edited by Hans Volavkova;
translated into English by Jeanne Nemcova. London, Neville Spearman,
1965. 86pp, illus. Biographical notes.
Poems and drawings by Czech children. The whole collection of drawings
and poems is housed in the State Jewish Museum, Prague.

See also: 772

Studies and criticism

762 KETLEY, Peter Michael
  The penal press in England and Wales: a study submitted in partial
fulfillment of the requirements for the degree of Master of Arts in the Post-
graduate School of Librarianship and Information Science at the University
of Sheffield, by Peter Michael Ketley. 1972. 88pp. Bibliography.
A general study, based on the results of a questionnaire, dealing with attitudes to the prison magazine or newspaper. Appendix (pp 76-9) lists
prison journals published in England and Wales, July 1972, giving title,
year of founding, size, frequency and circulation. (Copy of thesis in library
of the Home Office, Romney House, Marsham St, London.)

WORK

GENERAL

763 BOLD, Alan
 The Penguin book of socialist verse, edited with an introduction by Alan
Bold. Harmondsworth (Middx), Penguin Books, 1970. 550pp.
An international anthology covering poetry of the nineteenth and twentieth
centuries.

764 CLARK, Thomas Curtis
 Poems of justice, [compiled] by Thomas Curtis Clark. Chicago, New
York, Willett, Clark & Colby, 1929. xii, 306pp.
Covers social problems, work and the working classes.

765 DALLAS, Karl
 One hundred songs of toil, compiled and edited by Karl Dallas with
guitar chords. London, Wolfe, 1974. 253pp. Music.

766 DAWNEY, Michael
 The iron man: English occupational songs, edited by Michael Dawney.
London, Stainer & Bell in association with Leeds University and the English
Folk Dance and Song Society, 1974. 44pp. Music.
Songs all recorded from oral sources within the last few years.

767 FONER, Philip S
 American labor songs of the nineteenth century, compiled by Philip S
Foner. Urbana, University of Illinois Press, 1975. 356pp. Bibliography.
Headings: Colonial, revolutionary and early national period; The era of
Jacksonian democracy, 1823-40; The pre-war decades 1840-60; Foreign
born and black workers; The civil war and post civil war era 1861-72; The
long depression, 1873-79; The knights of labor; The early American feder-
ation of labor; The miners; The eight hour day and the navy market affair;
Boycotts, strikes and unemployment demonstrations, 1880-1900; Labor
parties, labor-farmers' alliance, coalition and labor-populism, 1880-97;
Socialism.

768 FOWKE, Edith and GLAZER, Joe
 Songs of work and protest, [compiled] by Edith Fowke and Joe Glazer;
music arrangements by Kenneth Bray. New York, Dover Publications,
1973. 209pp. Music.

Headings: Solidarity forever; On the line; Down in a coal mine; Hard times in the mill; Take this hammer; Men of the soil; Blow ye winds in the morning; Hard traveling; The rich man and the poor man; O freedom! These things shall be!

First published by the Labor Education Division of Roosevelt University under the title 'Songs of work and freedom', 1960.

769 GATES, Thomas
South Texas Negro work songs: collected and uncollected (in Publications of the Texas Folk-Lore Society No 5, 1926, pp 154-80).

770 GREENWAY, John
American folk songs of protest, by John Greenway. Philadelphia, University of Pennsylvania Press, 1953. x, 348pp. Music. Bibliography. (pp 329-338: songbooks and song collections containing songs of social and economic protest). Discography (pp 311-327).
Headings: Historical survey; Negro songs of protest; The songs of the textile workers; The songs of the miners; The migratory workers; Songs of the farmers; A labor miscellany.

771 INDUSTRIAL WORKERS OF THE WORLD
IWW songs: songs of the works. 27th ed, Chicago, IWW, 1939. 64pp, illus.

772 JACKSON, Bruce
Wake up dead man: Afro-American work songs from Texas prisons, collected and edited by Bruce Jackson. Cambridge (Mass), Harvard University Press, 1972. 326pp. Music.

773 JONES, Esmor
Work and leisure, edited by Esmor Jones. Oxford, Pergamon Press, 1968. 143pp. (Explorations series.) Bibliography (further reading). Filmography.
Mostly twentieth century prose extracts.

774 JONES, Rhodri
Men at work, edited by Rhodri Jones. London, Heinemann Educational, 1972. 78pp.
Headings: Diversity; Attitudes and conditions; On the sidelines.
Twentieth century poetry. Intended for schools.

775 MacCOLL, Ewan
The shuttle and cage: industrial folk-ballads, edited by Ewan MacColl. London, Workers' Music Association, 1954. 30pp. Music.
Folksongs of weavers, colliers, railwaymen, etc.

776 MARLAND, Michael
The experience of work: an anthology of prose, verse, drama and picture, compiled by Michael Marland. Harlow (Essex), Longman, 1973. 228pp, illus. (Longman Imprint Books.) Bibliography, discography, filmography.
Twentieth century writings, by known and unknown authors.

777 PALMER, Roy
   Poverty knock: a picture of industrial life in the nineteenth century
through songs, ballads and contemporary accounts, selected and edited by
Roy Palmer. London, Cambridge University Press, 1974. 64pp, illus.
Headings: I—Factory life: the dreary old drive; II—Pit life: down among the
coals.

778 PARKER, T H and TESKEY, F J
   And so to work, edited by T H Parker and F J Teskey. Glasgow, Blackie,
1970. 58pp, illus. (Themes to Explore series.)
Headings: And so to work; A variety of jobs; Men and machines; Home
from work.
Twentieth century poetry. Intended for schools.

779 SONGS OF THE WORKERS
   Dublin, The Socialist Party of Ireland, 1975. 41pp, illus.
English, American and Irish songs and ballads of the late nineteenth century
and the twentieth century.

780 WILSON, Richard
   Literature and labour: an anthology of effort, edited by Richard Wilson.
London, Dent; New York, Dutton, 1922. 256pp.
Mostly nineteenth century prose and poetry. Prose extracts which include
some philosophical items, are quite substantial.

781 WOOLDRIDGE, Dorothy
   The poetry of toil: an anthology of poems, compiled by Dorothy Wooldridge. London, Faber and Gwyer, 1926. xvi, 202pp.
Headings: Creation; Men; Machines; Description; Idleness; Content; Discontent.
Poetry of the seventeenth, nineteenth and early twentieth centuries, concerned mainly with work in the countryside; mostly known poets.

See also: 398, 415, 418, 420, 421, 663, 1053, 1466

Studies and criticism

782 CAMP, Charles Wellner
   The artisan in Elizabethan literature, by Charles Wellner Camp. New
York, Columbia University Press, 1924. 170pp.

783 HURST, Gerald B
   Songs of labour (in Nineteenth Century, 1923, pp 421-6).
A brief survey of some socialist verse.

784 ODUM, Howard W and JOHNSON, Guy B
   Negro workaday songs, by Howard W Odum and Guy B Johnson. Uni-
versity of N Carolina Press; London, Oxford University Press, 1926. 278pp.
Bibliography.
Chapters: The blues, workaday sorrow songs; Songs of jail, chain gang, and
policemen; Songs of construction camps and gangs; Just songs to help with

work; Man's song of woman; Woman's song of man; Folk minstrel types;
Workaday religious songs; The annals and blues of left wing Gordon; John
Henry: epic of the Negro working man; Types of Negro melodies.
A study with numerous examples.

785 TERRY, R C
The working class in some novels and poems of the period 1823-1850.
MA thesis, University of Bristol, 1963.

786 VICINUS, Martha
The industrial muse: a study of neneteenth century British working
class literature, by Martha Vicinus. London, Croom Helm, 1974. x, 357pp,
plates. Bibliography.
Chapters: Street ballads and broadsides: the foundations of a class culture;
Literature as propaganda: the coal miners' unions, 1825-1845; Chartist
poetry and fiction: the development of a class-based literature; Literature
as a vocation: the self-educated poets; An appropriate voice: dialect literature of the industrial north; The music hall: from a class to a mass entertainment.

COAL MINING

787 ADAMS, James Taylor
Death in the dark: a collection of factual ballads of American mine
disasters, compiled by James Taylor Adams; with a foreword and background
stories by James Taylor Adams. Big Laurel (Va), Adam Mullins Press, 1941.
119pp.

788 DAWNEY, Michael
Doon the wagon way: mining songs from the North of England, edited
by Michael Dawney. London, Stainer and Bell, in association with the
Leeds University Institute of Dialect and Folk-Life Studies and the English
Folk Dance and Song Society, 1973. 40pp, illus. Music. Glossary.
Most of the songs were collected by field workers of the Institute.

789 CHICANOT, E L
Rhymes of the miner: an anthology of Canadian mining verse, compiled
and edited by E L Chicanot; illustrations by G A Culbertson. Gardenvale,
Quebec, Federal Publications, 1969. 222pp, illus. Biographical notes.
Note on cover: 'reprinted 1969 by Canadiana House with acknowledge-
ments to the former editor and publisher whom it has not been possible to
trace; originally published circa 1937'.

790 KORSON, George
Coaldust on the fiddle: songs and stories of the bituminous industry,
[compiled] by George Korson. Philadelphia, University of Pennsylvania
Press, 1943. xvi, 460pp. Bibliography.
Headings: Part I Minstrelsy of the coal camps—Bituminous folklore; The
coal camp; Bread and the company store; Love, courtship and the miner's

wife; Miners at play. Part II Folklore of the coal miners—Singing in the
mines; Types of miners: The check weighman; Whoo, mule!; Miners' pets;
Craft superstition and legends; The luck of the mine; Mine disasters. Part
III The Union in song and story—Singers on the picket line; The struggle
for a better life; The Coal Creek Rebellion; 'Remember Virden!'; The Lud-
low massacre; Strike songs and ballads.

791 KORSON, George and LEMON, Melvin
  The miner sings: a collection of folk songs and ballads of the anthracite
miner, transcriptions and music arranged by Melvin Lemon, introduction
and editorial notes by George Korson. New York, Fischer, 1936. 42pp.
Music.

792 KORSON, George
  Minstrels of the mine patch: songs and stories of the anthracite industry,
by George Korson. Philadelphia, University of Pennsylvania Press; London,
Oxford University Press, 1938. xii, 332pp. Bibliography. Glossary.
Headings: Part I Ballads—The mine patch; Miners in good humour; Boy
colliers; Slavs as miners; Superstitions and legends; Injury and death; The
strike; The Molly Maguires; A miscellany. Part II—Stories.
Glossary of anthracite technical and colloquial words and phrases.

793 KORSON, George
  Songs and ballads of the anthracite miners: a seam of folklore which once
ran through life in the coal fields of Pennsylvania, gathered and edited by
George Korson. New York, Grafton Press, 1927. xxvii, 196pp.
Material in this volume included in the above work.

794 LLOYD, A L
  Come all ye bold miners: ballads and songs of the coalfields, compiled by
A L Lloyd. London, Lawrence & Wishart, 1952. 144pp. Music.
Headings: The miner at work; The miner at play; Love and the miner; Boy
miners and old miners; The perils of mining; Coalfield conditions and the
struggle for a better life; A miner's miscellany.

GOLD MINING

795 DWYER, Richard A and LINGENFELTER, Richard E
  The songs of the gold rush, edited with an introduction by Richard A
Dwyer and Richard E Lingenfelter; music edited with guitar arrangements
by David Cohen. Berkeley, University of California Press, 1965. 200pp.
Music.
Headings: Ho! for California; Coming round the horn; Crossing the plains;
Seeing the elephant; When I went off to prospect; An honest miner; A life
by the cabin fire; Life in California; California bloomer; California humbugs;
The unhappy miner; I'm sad and lonely here; Then hurrah for home! Cali-
fornia as it is and was.

FARMING

796 FREEMAN, James W
Prose and poetry of the live stock industry of the United States, with outlines of the origin and ancient history of our live stock animals, prepared by authority of the National Live Stock Association. Denver, Kansas City, Franklin Hudson, 1905. 757pp.
This original edition is very rare. It was issued only to the members of the Association; each volume had the name of the member stamped in gold on the cover.
Reprinted with a new introduction by Ramon F Adams. New York, Antiquarian Press, 1959. Limited edition of 500 copies.

797 JENKINS, Alan C
The prodigal earth, compiled by Alan C Jenkins. Glasgow, Blackie, 1976. 247pp.
Prose, poetry and first hand accounts of changing attitudes, customs, and outlooks in farming.

798 PALMER, Roy
The painful plough: a portrait of the agricultural labourer in the nineteenth century from folk songs and ballads and contemporary accounts, selected and edited by Roy Palmer. London, Cambridge University Press, 1973. 64pp, illus. Music.

799 WOODHOUSE, A E
New Zealand farm and station verse, collected by A E Woodhouse; with an introduction by L J Wild. Christchurch, Whitcombe & Tombs, 1950. 202pp, illus, plates (sketches and paintings). Biographical notes.

See also: 1014, 1634.

Studies and criticism

800 EMERY, Clark
The poet and the plough (in Agricultural History, Vol 16, January 1942, pp 9-15). References in footnotes.
On eighteenth century didactic agricultural poems. Deals in particular with Robert Dodsley's 'Agriculture' (1753).

801 JOHNSTONE, Paul H
Turnips and romanticism (in Agricultural History, Vol 12, July 1938, pp 224-255).
A general discussion of the 'agricultural enthusiasm' in the eighteenth century. pp 233-244 ('Apollo and the turnip patch') deal with poetry in particular. A summary of the author's doctoral dissertation with the same title, University of Minnesota, 1938.

COWBOYS

802 CARR, Robert Van
   Cowboy lyrics, [compiled] by Robert Van Carr. Chicago, W B Conkey, 1908. 182pp.

803 LOMAX, John Avery
   Cowboy songs and other frontier ballads, collected by John A Lomax; with an introduction by Barrett Wendell. New York, Sturgis & Walton, 1910. xxvi, 326pp. Music.
      2nd ed: 1916. xiii, 414pp.
      3rd ed: 1938. xxxviii, 431pp.

804 LOMAX, John Avery
   Songs of the cattle trail and the cow camp, [compiled] by John A Lomax; foreword by William Lyon Phelps. New York, Macmillan, 1919. xi, 189pp.

805 THORP, N Howard
   Songs of the cowboys, compiled by N Howard Thorp; with an introduction by Alice Corbin Henderson. Boston, Houghton Mifflin, 1921. xxii, 184pp.

EDUCATION

SCHOOL

General

806 EWART, Gavin
Forty years on: an anthology of school songs, compiled by Gavin Ewart.
London, Sidgwick and Jackson, 1969. 254pp, illus.
Illustrations are reproductions from Boys' Illustrated News (1881-82) and
the 1871 edition of Thomas Hughes' 'Tom Brown's school-days'. Com-
piled in collaboration with the schools concerned. Some items in Latin.

807 FOSTER, John L
School: an anthology, compiled by John L Foster. Exeter, A Wheaton,
1976. 82pp, illus. (Dimensions series.)
Headings: Making a start; The school day; Teachers and pupils; Special
occasions; What is school for?
Mostly twentieth century prose and drama.

808 HOLDER, C S
An anthology of school: being a selection of English poems on school,
schoolboys and schoolmasters, chosen and edited with notes and an introduction by C S Holder. London, John Lane The Bodley Head, 1928. xix,
275pp.
Headings: School life—public school songs, schools little and big, some
visitors, holidays, coming and going; The old boys, retrospect; Schoolmasters—the poets' masters; Real men; The boys—white, black, pied;
Lessons; Place aux demoiselles; Education; Prayer; The lighter side of
schools.
Index of schools covered.
Poetry from the eighteenth to twentieth century.

809 JONES, Rhodri
Work and play, edited by Rhodri Jones; photographs by John Krish.
London, Heinemann Educational 1971. 56pp, illus. (Prelude series for
younger readers.)
The first thirteen pieces are twentieth century poems about school life.

See also: 306, 990, 1398, 1433, 1454

Studies and criticism

810 DANBURY, J H
The concept and evolution of the dunce in English poetry, 1660-1743.
PhD thesis, London University, 1966.

Eton

811 PARKER, Eric
Floreat: an Eton anthology, by Eric Parker. London, Nisbet, 1923.
333pp.
Headings: The founder; Statutes; Provosts and head masters; Alumni; Customs; Montem; College; Chapel; The playing fields; The river; The fourth of June; Cricket; Lords; The wall; The field; Fives; The beagles; The corps; Manners; Societies; Masters; My dame; Poemas; Schoolfellows; Visitors; In school; Out of school; Holidays; Characters; The letter box; Fagging; Shops; Eton as she is not; Pro patria; In praise; Looking backward; Vale.
. . . 'an attempt to mirror the life of Eton as it has been lived from the Founder's day to our own' . . . A very comprehensive anthology covering poems, extracts from diaries, novels, letters, descriptive works, etc.

Harrow

812 WARNER, George Townsend
Harrow in prose and verse, edited by George Townsend Warner; with twenty-five plates in colour reproduced from sketches by Arthur Garratt, and from portraits in the Vaughan Library and in the National Portrait Gallery. London, Hodder and Stoughton, [1914]. xvi, 208pp, col plates.
Harrow in prose: pp 74-158; Harrow in verse: pp 167-207.

UNIVERSITY

General

813 (BIBLIOGRAPHY) SILVER, H and TEAGUE, S J
The history of British universities, 1800-1969, excluding Oxford and Cambridge: a bibliography by H Silver and S J Teague. London, Society for Research into Higher Education, 1970. 264pp.
Lists the student magazines produced by the colleges and universities since their founding.

Oxford

814 BALL, Oona H
The Oxford garland: an anthology of prose and verse in praise of Oxford, chosen by Oona H Ball. London, Sidgwick and Jackson, 1909. 96pp.
Nineteenth and early twentieth century pieces, some in French.

815 CANZIANI, Estella
   Oxford in brush and pen, compiled and illustrated by Estella Canziani.
London, Frederick Muller, 1949. 203pp, plates.
Section One— Wisdom, Charity, Humour; Friendship; First and later im-
pressions; Wanderings and musings; Today and yesterday. Section Two—
Christchurch; Some characters; St Frideswyde; Corpus Christi; Legends,
saints and scholars; The Mallard hunt; An ancient chapel and Russian bap-
tism. Section Three—A ghost story and ghostly writings. Section Four—
Music; Beating the bounds; University College; St Michael's; St Mary's and
its preachers; More saints and scholars; Newman; The Oxford Movement;
Kingsley; Brasenose; The Mitre; Shakespeare and a ceremony. Section Five
—Birds, beasts and flowers; Some personalities, eccentrics and lovers of
animals. Section Six—Balliol; Oxford by Moonlight; Trinity at night; The
pre-Raphaelites at Oxford; Artists and their jokes; The museum. Section
Seven—The Boar's Head; Queen's New College; Other customs and traditions;
The seasons at Oxford. Section Eight—Shotover; Headington; Queen Eliza-
beth's visit; A country shop and its visitors; Folk dancing. Section Nine—
More impressions; Modern life; American and English farewells; Brother
sun.
Prose and poetry; mostly twentieth century pieces.

816 FIRTH, J B
   The minstrelsy of Isis: an anthology of poems relating to Oxford and all
phases of Oxford life, selected and arranged by J B Firth. London, Chapman and Hall, 1908. xxvi, 397pp, plates.
Headings: Oxford; Oxford in retrospect; Sonnets; Oxford life (pp 153-201);
The Isis and Cherwell; Magdalen College; Bodley and the Bodleian; Occasional poems; Satirical and polemical; Oxford ale and ale houses.
Poetry from the seventeenth to nineteenth century. Plates are reproductions
of engravings.

817 HORDER, Thomas Jeeves
   In praise of Oxford: an anthology for friends, compiled by Lord Horder.
London, Frederick Muller, 1955. 55pp, illus.
Poetry and prose extracts.

818 KNIGHT, William
   The glamour of Oxford: descriptive passages in verse and prose by various writers, chosen and edited by William Knight. Oxford, Blackwell, 1911.
263pp.
Poetry and prose from sixteenth to nineteenth century, arranged chronologically; . . . 'a record of the appreciation, the gratitude, and in some cases
the benediction of its alumni and other visitors'.

819 LEWIS, C Day and FENBY, Charles
   Anatomy of Oxford, compiled by C Day Lewis and Charles Fenby. Lon-
don, Cape, 1938. 318pp.
Headings: The place; the seniors; The juniors.
Mostly prose.

820 SECCOMBE, Thomas and SCOTT, H Spencer
  The praise of Oxford: an anthology in prose and verse, compiled by
Thomas Seccombe and H Spencer Scott. London, Constable, 1910. 794pp.
2 vols.
Vol I—History and topography; Prehistoric Oxford; University origins;
Medieval Oxford; Renaissance and Reformation; Oxford during the troubles;
Ye antique towers; Some visitors to Oxford; Dreaming spires and fretted
pinacles; Old streets and lanes; Collegia quedam; Isle and cheer; Gardens of
Oxford; Oxford moods; Home of lost causes; New movements; Vol II—
Life and manners: In praise of Oxford; The road to Oxford; Terms and
vacation; Freshmen and their ways; Beer and battles; Penalties and proctors;
Oxford at work; Oxford clubs and libraries; Mimes and pastimes; Cap and
bells; Town and gown; Foreign impressions; Oxford's rivals; Academical
costumes; Personalia academica; Colleges: life and customs; Oxoniana: odds
and ends; Pietas oxoniensis.
Prose and poetry; more prose than poetry. Chronologically wide ranging,
covering all periods.

Cambridge

821 HORDER, Mervyn
  In praise of Cambridge: an anthology for friends, compiled by Mervyn
Horder. London, Frederick Muller, 1952. 56pp, illus.

822 KELLETT, E E
  A book of Cambridge verse, edited by E E Kellett. Cambridge, University
Press, 1911. xvi, 440pp, plates (ports).
Notes: pp 397-433. Chronological arrangement from the sixteenth to nine-
teenth century.

823 WATERLOW, Sydney
  In praise of Cambridge: an anthology in prose and verse, selected and
edited by Sydney Waterlow. London, Constable, 1912. x, 221pp.
Headings: The candid friend; Cambridge versus Oxford; Legendary; The
poets at Cambridge; Some great men; The university carrier; Mr Samuel
Pepys and Cambridge; Descriptive; The river; The environs; Men and manners;
The lighter side; The studious life; Sturbridge fair; College plays; Dress;
Glimpses of history; Distinguished visitors; Youth and friendship; The ro-
mantic view; Reminiscent; Vale.
Poetry and prose from the sixteenth to nineteenth century.

824 WHIBLEY, Charles
  In cap and gown: three centuries of Cambridge wit, edited with an intro-
duction by Charles Whibley. London, Heinemann, 1889. xxix, 354pp.
Satirical, occasional verse.

Harvard

825 AUBIN, Robert Arnold
    Harvard heroics: a collection of eighteenth century verse descriptions of Harvard College, compiled by Robert Arnold Aubin. Cambridge (Mass), Harvard University Press, 1934. 29pp.

HUMAN SETTLEMENTS

CITY AND TOWN

826 ADOFF, Arnold
   City in all directions: an anthology of modern poems, [compiled] by
Arnold Adoff; drawings by Donald Carrick. New York, Macmillan, 1969.
xv, 128pp.

827 BARTLETT, Alice Hunt
   The anthology of cities, edited by Alice Hunt Bartlett. London, Erskine
Macdonald, 1927. 246pp.
Part I: The poetry of cities and cities in poetry (pp 13-46). Part II: A col-
lection of poems on cities, chiefly original, arranged in alphabetical order
(pp 49-246).
Most of the poems were selected from entries in the Poetry Review's city
sonnet contest. A very wide range of cities of the world is covered.

828 GREEVER, Garland and BACHELOR, Joseph M
   The soul of the city: an urban anthology, compiled by Garland Greever
and Joseph M Bachelor. Boston, Houghton Mifflin, 1923. xxix, 364pp.
Twentieth century English and American poetry. Pp 363-4: selected list of
urban verse (collections by individual poets).

829 HOPKINS, Lee Bennett
   The city spreads its wings, [compiled] by Lee Bennett Hopkins; illustrations by Moneta Barnett. New York, F Watts, 1970. 46pp, col illus.
Twenty-one short, simple poems by well-known writers about various aspects of the city. Intended for children.

830 HOPKINS, Lee Bennett
   City talk, [compiled] by Lee Bennett Hopkins; photographs by Roy
Arenella. New York, Knopf, [1970]. 46pp, illus.
A collection of poems by children about their experiences in the city from
season to season.

831 JONES, Rhodri
   Town and country, edited by Rhodri Jones. London, Heinemann Edu-
cational, 1972. 68pp, illus. (Heinemann Themes Series.)
Headings: Town life; Country life; Change (demolition, development, etc)
Twentieth century poetry.

123

832 LARRICK, Nancy
I heard a scream in the street: poems by young people in the city, [compiled] by Nancy Larrick; illustrated with photos by students. New York, Evans, 1970. 141pp, illus.
A selection of seventy-seven poems written by children and young people from various cities of the USA and first published in schoool newspapers and community magazines. Illustrations are prize-winning photographs from the annual Scholastic Magazine—Eastman Kodak Contest.

833 LARRICK, Nancy
On city streets: an anthology of poetry, selected by Nancy Larrick; illustrated with photos by David Sagarin. New York, Evans, 1968. 158pp, illus.

834 SUSSAMS, T W
A book of town verse, chosen by T W Sussams; illustrated by M W Hawes. London, Oxford University Press, 1947. 62pp, illus. (Chameleon Books, 27.)
Headings: Round the town; Trains; The industrial scene; At home; People of the town.
Twentieth century verse, mostly of a 'poetic' nature.

835 WOOD, L S and BURROWS, H L
The town in literature, compiled by L S Wood and H L Burrows. London, Nelson, 1925. 256pp.
Poetry and prose from the seventeenth to twentieth century.

See also: 996, 1002, 1392, 1593, 1595, 1628, 1674.

Studies and criticism

836 CONNOR, J A
Some studies in the use of urban imagery in modern English poetry in the Victorian period. MA thesis, University of Manchester, 1967.

837 DOUBLEDAY, James Frank
The ruined city in Old English poetry. PhD, University of Illinois at Urbana, 1967.

838 FRANCIS, Wynne
Urban images in Canadian poetry. MA thesis, McGill University, 1963.

839 LOCKE, T J
The city in American poetry, 1880-1970. Thesis, Auckland University, 1973.

840 O'TOOLE, Bridget
Study of urban themes in English poetry of the nineteenth century with special reference to the 1890s and just after. Thesis, Ulster University, 197?
Listed in: Research in progress in English and historical studies of the British Isles, edited by S T Bindoff and James T Boulton. London, St James Press, 1971. 109pp.

841 WILLIAMS, Charles
The image of the city in English verse (in Dublin Review, No 414, July 1940, pp 39-51).

THE VILLAGE

Studies and criticism

842 PATTON, Julia
The English village: a literary study, 1750-1850, by Julia Patton. New York, Macmillan, 1919. x, 235pp.
Chapters: Introductory: the point of view; From the medieval village to the modern; The changing village and the national life; The village established in literature, 1770-1800; The village in poetry, 1800-1850; The village in prose: 1800-1850; Conclusion: looking forward.

See also: 1392

HOUSING

843 PATTEN, Brian and KRETT, Pat
The house that Jack built: poems for 'Shelter', edited by Brian Patten and Pat Krett. London, Allen and Unwin, 1973. 80pp.
Twentieth century poetry which gives 'some idea of the multiple deprivation suffered by those living in slum communities and the curbed potential of their lives'.

GYPSIES

844 SAMPSON, John
The wind on the heath: a gypsy anthology, chosen by John Sampson; with a frontispiece in colour by Augustus John and fourteen designs by John Garside. London, Chatto & Windus, 1930. 362pp, illus. Notes (pp 331-357).
Headings: The dark race; The romantic life; Field and sky; Gypsies and gentiles; Gypsy children; Stunt and strife; Black arts; A gypsy bestiary; Egipte speche; Scholar gypsies; Envoy.
An anthology 'of the gypsy spirit', consisting of prose and poetry. Glossary of Romany words.

TRANSPORT

GENERAL

845 HOPKINS, Lee Bennett
    Poetry on wheels, compiled by Lee Bennett Hopkins; illustrated by Liol
Weil. Champaign (Ill), Garrard, 1974. 64pp, col illus.
A collection of poems about cars, buses, trucks, trains, subways, building
machinery, boats, airplanes and rocket ships. Intended for children.

846 (BIBLIOGRAPHY) GROSVENOR LIBRARY, Buffalo
    Transportation in American popular song (in Grosvenor Library Bulletin,
Vol 27, No 3, June 1945, pp 61-106).
A bibliography of items in the Grosvenor Library. Songs of the nineteenth
and early twentieth centuries, covering automobiles, airplanes and airships,
balloons, bicycles, carriages, caravans, railroads (6pp), imaginary trains,
subway trains, roller-skates, ships, barges, canoes, ferries, gondolas, imaginary ships, rowboats, rowing machines, sailing vessels, steamships (4pp),
sleighs, and trolley cars.

See also: 1596, 1597

RAILWAYS

847 BOTKIN, Benjamin Albert and HARLOW, Alvin F
    A treasury of railroad folklore: the stories, tall tales, traditions, ballads
and songs of the American railroad men, edited by Benjamin Albert Botkin
and Alvin F Harlow. New York, Crown, 1953. 530pp.

848 DONOVAN, F P
    The railroad in literature: a brief survey of railroad fiction, poetry, songs,
biography, essays, travel and drama in the English language. Boston, Rail-
way and Locomotive Historical Society, 1940. 130pp.

849 HOPKINS, Kenneth
    The poetry of railways: an anthology selected and introduced by Kenneth
Hopkins. London, Leslie Frewin, 1966. 270pp.
Headings: Rolling stock; Mainly railwaymen; People and the permanent way;

Stations—arrivals and departures; Travellers and commuters; Trainscapes and journeys; Epilogue.
Twentieth century poetry.

850 LEGG, Stuart
    The railway book: an anthology edited by Stuart Legg. London, Hart-Davis, 1952. 256pp. Notes (pp 249-254).
Headings: The ringing grooves of change; Up trains, down trains; Rails around the world; A chapter of accidents; Trains of thought; Trains of triumph, trains of fate; The communication cord; Journeys in fact and fancy; Poets' corner; The grand old days; Journeys end.
Mostly prose.

851 McLAGAN, William
    Steam lines: railway poems from the steam age on, collected by William McLagan. Gartocharn (Dumbartonshire), Famedram, [1973]. 77pp.

852 SHERWIN, Sterling and McCLINTOCK, Harry K
    Railroad songs of yesterday, [compiled] by Sterling Sherwin and Harry K McClintock. New York, Shapiro & Bernstein, 1943. 48pp.

Studies and criticism

853 PEART, D A
    Literature and the railway in the nineteenth and twentieth century. MA thesis, University of Liverpool, 1963.

854 PORCELLO, Patricia Lucille Berger
    The railroad in American literature: poetry, folk song and the novel. PhD thesis, University of Michigan, 1968.

AEROPLANES

855 BRYDEN, H G
    Wings: an anthology of flight, edited by H G Bryden. London, Faber, 1942. 320pp.
Headings: Flight in legend and myth; Prophecies and premonitions; Balloons; Airships; The growing of the wings; In full flight; Landscapes and skyscapes; Night flight; Men and machines; Peril and prayer; War (pp 257-288); Dunkirk and the Battle of Britain; Wings of peace.
Poetry and prose by mostly unfamiliar writers of the twentieth century.

856 DE LA BERE, R
    Icarus: an anthology of the poetry of flight, compiled by R De La Bère. London, Macmillan, 1938. 192pp, plates.

857 JACKSON, C H Ward-
   Airman's song book: being an anthology of squadron concert party, training and camp songs and song-parodies, written by and for officers, airmen and airwomen mainly of the Royal Air Force, collected and edited with an introduction and explanatory notes by C H Ward-Jackson; music edited by Leighton Lucas and decorations by Biro; the whole set out in chronological order to present a historical picture of the RAF through its own songs. London, Sylvan Press, 1945. xiv, 190pp.
   2nd revised edition: Edinburgh, London, William Blackwood, 1967. xxi, 265pp.

858 LANDAUER, Bella C
   Some aeronautical music from the collection of Bella C Landauer. Paris, privately printed, 1933. Limited edition: 100 copies.
Consists of twenty-three unpaginated facsimiles of the covers of sheet songs and piano pieces connected with flying and ballooning, mostly the latter, of English, American and German origin. (Copy seen in the Library of the Royal Aeronautical Society, London.)

859 MURRAY, Stella Wolfe
   The poetry of flight: an anthology, edited by Stella Wolfe Murray. London, Heath Cranton, 1925. 144pp.
Headings: Winged man of the old world; Winged man of the new world; Winged woman.

860 RODMAN, Selden
   The poetry of flight, edited by Selden Rodman, New York, Duell, Sloan, & Pearce, [1941]. xii, 190pp.

See also: 1329, 1337, 1549

Studies and criticism

861 DILLON, Richard T
   The sound of wings: aviation in twentieth century literature. PhD thesis, California University, 1970.

See also: 1329, 1337, 1349

THE ARTS

GENERAL

862 LEONARD, R M
   Poems on the arts, selected by R M Leonard. London, Oxford University Press, 1914. 128pp. Notes. (Oxford Garlands.)
Poems from the sixteenth to nineteenth century, mostly by well-known poets. Covers: music (pp 5-64); architecture, sculpture and painting (pp 82-120).

See also: 289, 323, 998

Studies and criticism

863 ARMSTRONG, I M
   The theme of art in Victorian poetry. PhD thesis, Leicester University, 1963.

ARCHITECTURE

864 FROM KING BOGGEN'S HALL TO NOTHING AT ALL:
   a collection of improbable houses and unusual places found in traditional rhymes and limericks, illustrated by Blair Lent. Boston, Little 1967. 44pp.

865 TANNER, Lawrence E
   In praise of Westminster Abbey, compiled by Lawrence E Tanner. London, Frederick Muller, 1950. 64pp.
Poetry and prose extracts; mostly prose.

See also: 289, 1002

Studies and criticism

866 HIBBARD, G R
   The country house poem of the seventeenth century (in Journal of the Warburg and Courtauld Institutes, Vol 19, 1956, pp 159-74).

867 SOFIELD, David R
   English building poems, 1600-1680. PhD thesis, Stanford University, 1971.

868 STRATHAM, H Heathcote
Architecture among the poets, by H Heathcote Stratham, with illustrations by the author. London, Batsford, 1908. 143pp, illus.
A study with many extracts of poets' attitudes to architecture and build-
ings, and their use of architectural imagery.

CRAFTS

869 BAILY, James T
A crafts anthology, selected by James T Baily; edited by Leslie Baily,
with vignettes by A E Goodall. London, Cassell, 1953. xii, 172pp, illus.
Poetry and prose of all periods, but with an emphasis on the twentieth century. Covers crafts like jewellery, steel-work, carpentry, thatching, ship-
building, pottery, stone masonry, carving, shoe making, etc.

See also: 782

SCULPTURE

Studies and criticism

870 LARRABEE, Stephan A
English bards and Grecian marbles: the relationship between sculpture
and poetry especially in the romantic period, by Stephan A Larrabee. New
York, Columbia University Press, 1943. xi, 312pp. Bibliography. Refer-
ences in footnotes.
Headings: Poets and sculpture; The early poets; The seventeenth century;
The eighteenth century; Blake; Wordsworth and Coleridge; Byron; Shelley;
Keats; Landor and Hunt; The lesser poets. List of critical terms.

PAINTING

871 LOWELL, Carrie Thompson
Art lover's treasury: famous pictures described in poems; forty-eight
reproductions of famous pictures accompanied by poems by noted writers,
with text by Carrie Thompson Lowell. Boston, D Estes, [1905]. xv,
281pp, plates.

See also: 155

MUSIC

872 BISHOP, John
Music and sweet poetry: a verse anthology compiled by John Bishop;
drawings by Edmond X Kapp. London, Baker, 1968. 195pp, illus.

Headings: Music's power—homage to St Cecilia; Music in and out of doors;
In the concert hall; In quires and places where they sing; Church music;
Opera nights; The instruments of joy; Composers and their music; Fancies
and fantasies; Wit, humour and righteous indignation.
Contains a substantial amount of twentieth century poetry. Unlike the fol-
lowing items covers all aspects of music and music-making, not merely the
romantic aspects.
Paperback edition: London, Simon Publications, 1973.

873 D'ESTERRE-KEELING, Eleonare
The music of the poets: a musician's birthday book, edited by Eleonare
d'Esterre-Keeling. London, Walter Scott, 1889. 351pp.
Short extracts and quotations about music for each day of the year, with
blank pages opposite.
Second edition, completely revised: 1897. 356pp.

874 HOWARD, Esme J
Music in the poets: an anthology by Esme J Howard; with an introduction
by I J Paderewski. New York, Brentanos, [1927]. 190pp.
Headings: Music; Music of praise; Love's inspiration; Song; Musical instruments; Music of nature and the elements; Song of the birds.
Poetry of the sixteenth, seventeenth, and nineteenth centuries by well-
known poets.

875 KOELLE, L L Carmela
Music in song from Chaucer to Tennyson: being a selection of extracts,
descriptive of the power, influence and effects of music, compiled by L L
Carmela Koelle. London, Griffith & Faran, 1883. 128pp.
Poetry and prose.

876 MacDOUGALL, Duncan and MacDOUGALL, August
The bond of music: an anthology edited by Duncan and August Mac-
Dougall. London, Truslove and Hanson, 1907. 179pp.
Mostly nineteenth century poetry.

877 MURFEY, Etha Josephean
Tempo rubato: an anthology of poems on music, compiled by Etha
Josephean Murfey. Lakeland (Florida), Poetry Caravan Press, 1942. 56pp.

878 PALMER, John
In praise of music: an anthology for friends, compiled by John Palmer.
London, Frederick Muller, 1951. 64pp, illus.
Prose and poetry extracts.

879 PLOTZ, Helen
Untune the sky: poems of music and dance, compiled by Helen Plotz;
illustrated with wood engravings by Clare Leighton. New York, Crowell,
1957. 162pp, illus.

880 SAYLE, Charles
In praise of music: an anthology prepared by Charles Sayle. London, Elliot Stock, 1897. 307pp. Poetry and prose of all periods in English, French, German Latin and Greek.
A rare example of a multi-lingual anthology.

881 WOLLASTON, George Hyde
The poet's symphony: being a collection of verses written by those who have loved music, arranged for the present time by George Hyde Wollaston. Bristol, J W Arrowsmith; London, Simpkin & Marshall, 1913. 271pp.
Notes (pp 243-258).
Headings: Preludio; Intermezzo I; Adagio; Intermezzo II; Pastorale; Scherzo; Intermezzo III; Finale.
Mostly nineteenth century poetry.

882 ZIMMERMAN, Franklin B
Poets in praise of Purcell (in Musical Times, October 1959, pp 526-528).

See also: 289, 299, 323, 398, 1593

Studies and criticism

883 HOLLANDER, John
The untuning of the sky: ideas of music in English poetry, 1500-1700, by John Hollander. Princeton, Princeton University Press, 1961. xii, 467pp, plates. Bibliography.
Chapters: 'From heav'nly harmony'; 'The diapason closing full in man'; The musical subject in humanist poetry; 'What passions cannot music raise and quell?'; 'The sacred organ's praise'; The sky untuned: the trivialization of universal harmony.

884 HUTTON, James
Some English poems in praise of music (in English Miscellany, Vol 2, 1951, pp 1-63).
Covers poetry of the sixteenth and seventeenth centuries.

885 NAYLOR, E W
The poets and music, by E W Naylor. London, J M Dent, 1928. xii, 180pp, plates.
Chapters: Robert Browning; Rudyard Kipling, Tennyson, Coleridge and others; John Milton; Three poet-parsons: George Herbert, Robert Herrick, Thomas Traherne; William Shakespeare; Spenser, Skelton, Chaucer and others.

886 FRYE, Northrop
Music in poetry (in University of Toronto Quarterly, January, 1942, pp 167-79).

887 RUSSELL, Earl Louis
Music in eighteenth century English literature: reflections of thought on music in poetry, 1660-1800. PhD thesis, Case Western Reserve University, 1959.

888 WIMBERLEY, Lowry Charles
Minstrelsy, music and the dance in the English, and Scottish popular ballads, by Lowry Charles Wimberley. Lincoln, University of Nebraska, 1921. 63pp. (Studies in Language, Literature and Criticism No 4.)
Bibliography; references in footnotes. A study on the references to fiddlers, pipers and dancing in ballad poetry.

DANCE AND BALLET

889 CLARKE, Grace
In praise of ballet: an anthology of enjoyment, compiled by Grace Clarke. London, Frederick Muller, 1952. 56pp, illus.
Prose and poetry extracts of the seventeenth, nineteenth, and twentieth centuries.

890 DICKSON, Edward R
Poems of the dance: an anthology 1500BC-1920AD, chosen and edited by Edward R Dickson, with pictoral photographs by him; introduction by Louis Untermeyer. New York, Alfred A Knopf, 1921. 263pp, illus.
Mostly unfamiliar poets.

891 THE LIGHT FANTASTIC:
a short programme of dances. London, Boston, The Medici Society, [1929]. 80pp.
Prose and poetry extracts from the sixteenth to nineteenth century.

Studies and criticism

892 McKINNEY, Barbara Joan
Images of dancing in sixteenth century English poetry. PhD thesis, University of Minnesota, 1974.

POETRY AND POETS

893 ADAMS, Estelle Davenport
The poets' praise from Homer to Swinburne, collected and arranged with notes by Estelle Davenport Adams. London, Elliot Stock, 1894. xi, 407pp. pp 3-47 poets in general; pp 50-377 individual poets.

894 BEBBINGTON, W G
The judgement of peers: an anthology of poems about poets, compiled by W G Bebbington. London, Staples Press, 1949. 139pp.

Headings: Elegy and homage; Occasional poems; The poet.
Covers poems on poets from Homer to the twentieth century.

895 PETERSON, Houston and LYNCH, William S
    Poet to poet: a treasury of golden criticism, edited by Houston Peterson
and William S Lynch. New York, Prentice-Hall, 1945. xxviii, 368pp.
Covers poems on poets from Homer to the early twentieth century.

896 SNEATH, Anna
    Poet's song of poet, compiled by Anna Sneath. Boston, R G Badger,
[1912]. 250pp, front, ports.

897 STRACHEY, Richard
    Poets on poets, edited by Mrs Richard Strachey. London, Kegan Paul,
Trench & Trübner, 1894. 324pp. Notes (pp 305-316).

See also: 315, 413

Studies and criticism

898 ATKINS, Elizabeth
    The poet's poet: being essays on the character and mission of the poet as
interpreted in English verse of the last one hundred and fifty years, by
Elizabeth Atkins. Boston, Marshall Jones, 1922. xiv, 361pp.
Chapters: The ego-centric circle; The mortal coil; The poet as lover; The
spark from heaven; The poet's morality; The poet's religion; The pragma-
tism; A sober afterthought.
A study with many examples.

899 HAMILTON, Walter
    The poets laureate of England: being a history of the office of poet
laureate, biographical notices of its holders and a collection of the satires,
epigrams, and lampoons directed against them, by Walter Hamilton. London,
Elliot Stock, 1879. xxv, 308pp.

900 McMASTER, June Rosemary
    The poet as hero: the hero archetype in romantic poetry. PhD thesis,
University of Alberta (Canada), 1972.

901 SAGE, L
    Poems on poetry from Sidney to Milton. MA thesis, Manchester Univer-
sity, 1966.

Walter de la Mare

902 TRIBUTE TO WALTER DE LA MARE
    on his seventy-fifth birthday. Faber, 1948. 195pp, ports.
pp 105-132: poems for Walter de la Mare, mostly dealing with his work and
personality, by sixteen poets, including John Masefield, T S Eliot, C Day
Lewis, and S Sassoon.

Dylan Thomas

903 FIRMAGE, George J
A garland for Dylan Thomas, gathered and with a preface by George
Firmage. London, Vision Press, 1963. 152pp, plates. Biographical notes.
'A gathering of eighty-four poems by seventy-eight poets selected from
almost one hundred and fifty written in tribute to Thomas over the past ten
years.'

THEATRE

904 TREWIN, J C
In praise of the theatre: an anthology of enjoyment, compiled by J C
Trewin. London, Frederick Muller, 1952. 60pp, illus.
Prose and poetry extracts; mostly prose from the seventeenth to twentieth
century.

See also: 323, 348

William Shakespeare

905 CLARKE, Waldo
In praise of Shakespeare: an anthology for friends, compiled by Waldo
Clarke. London, Frederick Muller, 1949, illus. 55pp.
Mostly prose extracts. Poems by Ben Jonson, William Basse, John Milton,
and Mathew Arnold.

906 FORSHAW, Charles F
At Shakespeare's shrine: a poetical anthology, edited by Charles F Forshaw; with 'Plays partly written by Shakespeare' by Richard Garnett. London, Elliot Stock, 1904. xvi, 380pp.
A number of the verses were especially composed for the anthology, others
taken from collections of broadsides and ballads.

907 HUGHES, C E
The praise of Shakespeare: an English anthology, compiled by C E
Hughes; with a preface by Sidney Lee. London, Methuen, 1904. xvi, 342pp.
Poetry and prose, 1596-1902.

908 POEMS ON SHAKESPEARE:
a list of references to individual poems (in 'A Shakespeare bibliography';
the catalogue of the Birmingham Shakespeare library, Birmingham Public
Libraries. London, Mansell, 1971. pp 874-882. Part I: accessions pre-
1932. Part II: accessions post 1931, pp 1523-1537.)
Sonnets on Shakespeare: ibid. Part I, pp 1017-8.
Tercentenary, 1864, celebratory poems. ibid. Part I, pp 1072-1075.

SPORT

GENERAL

909 FOSTER, John L
  The experience of sport, edited by John Foster. Harlow (Essex), Longmans, 1975. viii, 200pp, illus. (Longman Imprint Books.)
Contains poems, articles, extracts from novels, short stories and a selection of photographs. Covers a wide variety of sport. Intended for young people.

910 GRAYSON, C
  Sportsman's hornbook, edited by C Grayson; decorated by Ernest Smythe. New York, Random House, 1933. xiii, 169pp, illus.
Limited edition: 500 copies.

911 JACOBS, Allan D and JACOBS, Leland B
  Sport and games in verses and rhyme, [compiled] by Allan D Jacobs and Leland B Jacobs; illustrated by George Delara. Champaign (Ill), Garrard, 1975. 64pp, illus.
Intended for children.

912 KNUDSON, R and EBERT, P K
  Sports poetry, edited by R Knudson and P K Ebert. New York, Dell, 1971. 181pp. (Laurel Leaf Library.)

913 LEONARD, R M
  Poems on sport, edited by R M Leonard. London, Oxford University Press, 1914. 128pp. Notes. (Oxford Garlands.)
Covers: hunting (pp 6-42), horse-racing, angling, archery, cricket, tennis, golf, skating, cycling, swimming and rowing.
Poetry from the seventeenth to the nineteenth century. Mostly by well-known poets.

914 MORRISON, Lillian
  Sprints and distances: sports in poetry and the poetry in sport, compiled by Lillian Morrison; illustrated by Clare and John Ross. New York, Thomas Y Crowell, 1965. ix, 211pp, illus.
Headings: The games; Races and contests; Pleasures of the country; The joys of locomotion; Instruction in the art; The road all runners come; Into lucid air.

Covers: baseball, boating, boxing, falconry, fencing, fishing, football, rugby, golf, horse-racing, hunting, hurling, ice-skating, kite-flying, riding, skiing, squash rackets, swimming, tennis, track and field, walking, climbing, wrestling.
Mostly twentieth century American and English poetry and verse.

915 (BIBLIOGRAPHY) MOTT, Margaret M
Sports and recreations in American popular songs: a bibliography of songs sheets, compiled by Margaret M Mott (in Notes, Second Series Vol 7, September 1950, pp 522-561, and Vol 8, December, 1951. pp 33-62).
First part covers: baseball, football, swimming. Second part covers: archery, basketball, bicycling, bowling, boxing, fencing, golf, gymnastics, hockey, lacrosse, mountain climbing, ping pong, tennis, track, walking, wrestling, yachting.

916 OSBORN, E B
Anthology of sporting verse, selected with a preface by E B Osborn. London, Collins, 1930. 288pp.
Poetry from the sixteenth to the twentieth century, mostly by unknown poets.

917 PALMER, Roy and RAVEN, Jon
The rigs of the fair: popular songs and pastimes in the nineteenth century through songs, ballads and contemporary accounts, selected and edited by Roy Palmer and Jon Raven. London, Cambridge University Press, 1976. 64pp, illus. Music. (Resources of Music Series.)
Headings: Fairs and wakes; Wife selling; Bull baiting and bull running; Cock-fighting; Prize fighting; Wrestling; Foot-racing; Hunting; Boat racing; Football; Piceon racing.

918 PARKER, Eric
The Lonsdale anthology of sporting prose and verse, edited and with an introduction by Eric Parker. London, Seeley & Service, 1932. 376pp, illus. (The Lonsdale Library Volume XII.)
Headings: Angling; Shooting; Big game; Stalking; Hunting; Riding and driving; Racing; Pig sticking; Cricket; Football; Fives; Tennis; Billiards; Golf; Winter sports; Skating; Athletics; Fencing; Rowing; Boxing; Archery; Mountaineering; Yachting; Swimming; Various.
Poetry and prose of the nineteenth and twentieth centuries.

919 PECK, Hedley
The poetry of sport, selected and edited by Hedley Peck; with a chapter on classical allusions to sport by Andrew Lang, and a special preface to the Badminton Library by A E T Watson; illustrated by A Thornburn, Lucien Davis, C E Brock and others. London, Longmans, 1896. 419pp, illus.

920 PORTER, Henry van Arsdale
Athletic anthology: a collection of poems and short prose articles, compiled by Henry van Arsdale Porter. De Kalb (Ill), the author, 1930. 79pp, illus.

921 PORTER, Henry van Arsdale
H v's athletic anthology, by H v Porter. Danville, (Ill). Interstate, 1939.
247pp, illus.
Part I: poems and excerpts from the writing of H v Porter; Part II: excerpts
from the scrapbook of H v Porter (some published in anthology 920).

922 RICE, W de G C
Athlete's garland: a collection of verse of sport and pastime, compiled
by W de G C Rice. Chicago, McClurg, 1905. 245pp.

923 SKULL, John
Sport and leisure, edited by John Skull. London, Heinemann Educational,
1970. 72pp, illus. (Heinemann themes.)
Headings: Contests and conflict; In, on and by the water; In the open air;
Good times; Dissenting voices.
Twentieth century poetry. Intended for school use.

924 TOMLINSON, William Weaver
Songs and ballads of sport and pastime, edited by William Weaver Tomlinson. London, Walter Scott, [1897]; xxiv, 294pp, front. Notes. Biographical
notes. (The Canterbury Poets, No 76.)
Nineteenth century verse, covering: fox-hunting, boar-hunting, stag-hunting,
lion-hunting, coursing, fishing, horse-racing, shooting, archery, boating,
cricket, curling, golf, skating, swimming, cycling, football, tennis, bowling,
fives, hockey, sleighing, foot-racing, wrestling and throwing the bar.
Frontispiece is 'The galloping squire' by T E Macklin.

925 WOOD, L S and BURROWS, H L
Sports and pastimes in English literature, compiled and edited by L S
Wood and H L Burrows London, Edinburgh, Nelson, 1925. xxi, 256pp.
Biographical notes. (The Teaching of English Series.)
Poetry and prose extracts.

See also: 299, 398, 418, 985, 997, 998, 990, 1139, 1146, 1452, 1454,
1616, 1714.

ARCHERY

926 HARE, Kenneth
The archer's chronicle and greenwood chronicle, [compiled] by Kenneth
Hare. London, Williams and Norgate, 1929. 244pp, illus.
Poetry and prose extracts from the sixteenth to twentieth century.

927 (BIBLIOGRAPHY) LAKE, Fred and WRIGHT, Hal
Bibliography of archery. Manchester, Simon Archery Foundation,
1975. 501pp.
Twenty items by individual poets are listed in this bibliography of archery.

928 STOCKTON, Edwin L
Archery in the ballads (in The Society of Archer-Antiquaries Journal, Vol 5, Part 2, December 1962, pp 40-4).

BALLOONING See 858

BASEBALL

929 DICHTER, Harry
Baseball in music and song: a series in facsimile of scarce sheet music. Philadelphia, Musical Americana, 1954. 14 facsims in portfolio.

930 GROBANI, Anton
Baseball drama, verse, ballads (in 'Guide to baseball literature', edited by Anton Grobani. Detroit, Gale Research, 1975, pp 181-184).
Lists twenty-eight items, all by individual writers of the twentieth century.

931 LYMAN, Edward Branch
Baseball fanthology: hits, skits of the game, compiled by Edward Lyman. New York, the compiler, 1924. 34pp.

CHESS

932 HARWOOD, Graeme
Caissa's web: the chess bedside book, selected and compiled by Graeme Harwood. London, Latimer New Dimensions, 1975. 167pp, plates, illus.
Includes extracts of poetry, drama, history; proverbs; paintings and cartoons.
Covers all periods.

933 KNIGHT, Norman and GUY, Will
King, queen and knight: a chess anthology, compiled by Norman Knight and Will Guy. London, Batsford, 1975. 256pp, illus.
Headings: In praise of chess; In damnation of chess; Chess and poetry (pp 7-20); Chess and drama; Chess and the novel; Chess in essays and philosophy; —in biography and autobiography; —in history and historical fiction; —in fantasy; —in captivity; Travelers tales; Chess and love; —and war; —and life; —and religion; Chess quarrels; The humour of chess; Chess man and chess board; Chess and mathematics and science; Chess in proverbs.
Covers all periods.

CRICKET

934 AYE, John
In praise of cricket: an anthology for all lovers of cricket, compiled by John Aye. London, Frederick Muller, 1946. 63pp, illus.
Mostly prose extracts.

935 BRODRIBB, Gerald
The book of cricket verse: an anthology edited by Gerald Brodribb. London, Hart-Davis, 1953. 215pp. Notes.
Headings: The season opens; Personalities; In praise of cricket; Great occasions; Colts; A few extras; Some longer poems; Some incidental references.
Poetry mostly of the nineteenth and twentieth centuries.

936 FREWIN, Leslie
The poetry of cricket: an anthology, edited by Leslie Frewin. London, Macdonald, 1964. xxxiv, 531pp, illus.
Headings: Book I—The spirit of the game; First over; All round the wicket; On batsmen and batting; On bowlers and bowling; On fields, fielders and fielding; On umpires and scoring; Aids and accessories. Book II—Lords; Time for Grace; Giants! The Hambledon men; Romantic days; In praise of cricket; Close of play. Book III—Narrative poems.
The material here is an almost exact duplicate of that in the anthology by Brodribb.

937 LOOKER, Samuel J
Cricket: a little book for lovers of the game, edited with a foreword by Samuel J Looker. London, Simpkin, Marshall, Hamilton & Kent, 1925. xxix, 255pp, illus. (Beechwood Books.)
Headings: Hambledon men; The charm of cricket; Cricket in the past; Giants of the past; Lords; Batting; Bowling; The poetry of cricket; The game in cricket; Ranji; England v Australia; In other climes; Miscellanea.
Prose and poetry from the eighteenth to twentieth century.

938a PARKER, Eric
Between the wickets: an anthology of cricket, compiled by Eric Parker. London, Philip Allan, 1926. 308pp.
Headings: Dedicatory; Beginnings; Bats; In praise; The boy; The Hambledon Club; Batsmen; Bowlers; Fieldsmen; Single wickets; Summer days; Counties; Lords; Oxford v Cambridge; Eton v Harrow; England and Australia; Umpires; Hits; Characters; The old days; The village; Spectators; Meals; Songs; The arm-chair; The press; In other climes; Yarns; Odds and ends; The luck of it; I remember; In memoriam; Vale.
Poetry and prose of the nineteenth and twentieth centuries.

FISHING

938b AUSTIN, A B
An angler's anthology, collected by A B Austin; illustrated from drypoints by Norman Wilkinson. London, Country Life, 1930. 168pp, illus.
Headings: Praise and dispraise; Days of youth; Men and manners; Angling ways and means; Fishes; Rivers and lakes; Sights and sounds; The end of life.

939 BUCHAN, John
Musa piscatrix, [compiled] by John Buchan. London, John Lane; Chicago, A C McClurg, 1896. 103pp, plates. Notes. (The Bodley Anthologies.)
Poetry and prose from the seventeenth to nineteenth century, including twelve items by Thomas Tod Stoddart. Index of rivers mentioned.

940 HAYNES, William and HARRISON, Joseph Leroy
Fisherman's verse, chosen by William Haynes and Joseph Leroy Harrison: with an introduction by Henry van Dyke. New York, Duffield, 1919. xxxiv, 312pp.
American and English poetry of the nineteenth and twentieth centuries.
pp 303-306: pseudonyms of angling authors.

941 LOOKER, Samuel J
Float and fly: a little book for anglers, edited with a foreword by Samuel J Looker; and a frontispiece by Claud Lovat Fraser. London, Daniel O'Connor, 1922. xxiv, 230pp, ports (on end-papers). (Beechwood Books.)
Headings: 'Brothers of the angle'; Fisherman's joy; 'By still, silent streams'; Where leap the trout; 'The father of angling' (ie Izak Walton); The voice of the mountains; The heart's desire; Angling is an art; Three critics of angling; Fishing-lore; Some humours; Philosophers, poets and playwrights; Fishing in many lands; 'Profit and pleasure'.
Poetry and prose from the seventeenth to twentieth century.

942 MORRIS, Joseph and ADAMS, St Clair
Songs of the fishermen, collected by Joseph Morris and St Clair Adams. Cincinnatti, Stewart Kidd, [1922]. 330pp.

943 PARKER, Eric
An angler's garland of fields, rivers and other country contentments, compiled by Eric Parker. London, Philip Allan, 1920. 320pp.
Headings: To the reader; Beginnings; The boy; The holiday; Morning; The months; Brothers of the angle; The philosophy of it; Difficulties; Red letter days; The chalkstream; The mountain; Rivers; Flies and tackle; Baits and recipes; Along the bank; The mill; Evening; The inn; The kitchen; The bookshelf; Night; The veterans; Golden rules; Yarns; Fisherman's weather.
Prose and verse.

944 WILLOCK, Colin
In praise of fishing: an anthology for addicts, compiled by Colin Willock. London, Frederick Muller, 1954. 63pp, illus.
Prose extracts and poetry from the seventeenth to twentieth century.

945 WESTWOOD, T and SATCHELL, T
A collection of citations touching on angling and fishing from old English authors, dramatists and poets (in 'Bibliotheca piscatoria: a catalogue of books on angling, the fishes and fish culture . . . ' by T Westwood and T Satchell. London, W Satchell, 1883. pp 354-368).

Contains also details of a number of collections pre 1875 and individual poems.

See also: 1718

Studies and criticism

946 HALL, Henry
    Idylls of fishermen: a history of the literary species. PhD thesis, Columbia University, 1912.

GOLF

947 EVANS, Webster and SCOTT, Tom
    In praise of golf: an anthology for all lovers of the game, compiled by Webster Evans and Tom Scott. London, Frederick Muller, 1950. 63pp.
Prose and poetry of the nineteenth and twentieth centuries; mostly prose.

948 LOOKER, Samuel J
    On the green: An antohology for golfers, edited with a foreword by Samuel J Looker; and a frontispiece by Claud Lovat Fraser. London, Daniel O'Connor 1922. xix, 237pp, front, ports (on end-papers). (Beechwood Books.)
Headings: The fascination of golf; Past glories; The ladies game; Some humours; Two novelists; Playing the game; Some giants; The poets of golf; Some tragedies; The caddie; Records and jottings.
Poetry and prose of the nineteenth and twentieth centuries.

949 WEST, Henry Litchfield
    Lyrics of the links, compiled by Henry Litchfield West; illustrated by George M Richards. New York. Macmillan, 1921. 180pp.
Twentieth century verse, taken mostly from magazines.

HUNTING

950 BIRKETT, Lady Dorothy Nina
    Hunting lays and hunting ways: an anthology of the chase, collected and recollected by Lady Birkett. London, John Lane The Bodley Head, 1924. xv, 166pp.

951 FOTHERGILL, George A
    Twenty sporting designs, with selections from the poets, [compiled] by George A Fothergill. Edinburgh, printed by Neill & Co for the author, 1911 xii, 110pp, illus.
Limited edition: 300 copies. pp 1-36: the designs—engravings and paintings by George A Fothergill, mostly decorating the poems. pp 37-110: selection from the poets, sixteenth to twentieth century, with critical and biographical notes. (pp 103-5: coaching rhymes). pp 107-110: list of subscribers.

952 GRAHAM, Reginald
Poems of the chase, collected and recollected by Sir Reginald Graham.
London, Arthur L Humphreys, 1912. 136pp.
Mostly nineteenth century verse, all by unknown writers.

953 LOOKER, Samuel J
The chase, an anthology of hunting, edited with a foreword by Samuel
J Looker; and a frontispiece by Claud Lovat Fraser. London, Daniel O'Connor, 1922. xvi, 241pp, front. (Beechwood Books.)
Headings: The hunt in literature; Notable runs in fact and fiction; Hunting-
lore; The fox; The hare; The horse; The hounds; Writers on hunting; The
poetry of hunting; Wise saws and modern instances; Giants of the past; Personalities; Humour in the chase; Tally-ho! Here and there; Whale hunting.
Poetry and prose from the seventeenth to twentieth century.

954 NORTHCOTT, Richard
Hunting jingles, collected by Richard Northcott. London, The Press
Printers, 1920. 54pp, illus, ports. Music.
Mostly nineteenth century verse.

955 SOMERVILLE, E and ROSE, Martin
Notes of the horn: hunting verse, old and new, collected by E Somerville
and Martin Ross; with illustrations by Ben Marshall, Stubbs, Sartorius, Alken,
etc. London, Peter Davies, 1934. xii, 95pp, plates.
Songs, verse and traditional ballads.

956 THE SOUND OF THE HORN:
a booklet about hunting. London, The Medici Society, 1929. 81pp.
Verse from the sixteenth to nineteenth century.

Studies and criticism

957 CHAPMAN, Paul H
Foxhunting in nineteenth century English literature. PhD thesis, Ohio
State University, 1951.

MOUNTAINEERING See: Mountains, hills and mountaineering 1786-1793

RIDING and HORSES

958 BIEGEL, Peter
Booted and spurred: an anthology of riding, edited and illustrated by
Peter Biegel. London, Adam and Charles Black, 1949. 159pp, illus.
Headings: Buying a horse; Learning to ride; Famous riders; Famous rides in
fact and fiction; Riding to hounds; Race riding; Steeplechasing; Flat racing;
Cavalry riding; Polo; Pigsticking; Riding for ladies.
Prose and poetry of the nineteenth and twentieth century; more prose than
poetry.

959 CLYDE, Ethel
   Horse sense in poetry, prose and song, edited by Ethel Clyde. New York, Your Mind Publishers, 1948. 53pp, Music.

960 EMBERS, F J
   Famous horse-back rides in English poetry: an anthology of narrative poems, edited by F J Embers. Pretoria, Union Booksellers, 1949. 169pp.

961 FROTHINGHAM, Robert
   Songs of the horses: an anthology, selected and arranged by Robert Frothingham. Boston, Houghton Mifflin, 1920. xiv, 231pp.

962 LONGFELLOW, Annie A
   In the saddle: a collection of poems of horseback riding, compiled by Annie A Longfellow. Boston, Houghton Mifflin, 1882. iv, 185pp.

963 MURPHY, Genevieve
   The horse lover's treasury: an illustrated anthology of verse and prose, compiled and edited by Genevieve Murphy. London, Souvenir Press, 1963. ix, 320pp, illus.
   Headings: The horseman's fantasy; It takes all kinds; The art of riding; Adventures on horseback; The training period; Treks in many lands; Hounds gentlemen please; Some words of praise; Up and over; Horse sense; They're off; Fun and games; A change of owner; The judge's choice; Sing, riding's a joy.
   Mostly twentieth century poetry and prose.

964 PULLEIN-THOMPSON, Josephine
   Horses and their owners, [compiled] by Josephine Pullein-Thompson. London, Nelson, 1970. 208pp, illus.
   Contains fifteen pieces of poetry about riding.

965 WALKER, Stella A
   In praise of horses: an anthology for friends, compiled by Stella Walker. London, Frederick Muller, 1953. 64pp, illus.

966 WALKER, Stella A
   Long live the horse: an anthology, compiled by Stella A Walker. London, Country Life, 1955. 156pp.
   Headings: Prologue; A harrass of horses; Horsemen and horsewomen; Horsemanship; In the hunting field; The sport; The horses; The field; Racing and chasing; The horse in harness; Buying and selling; The horse in battle; The Englishman's horse; Horse lore; Questions of colour; Decline and fall; Epilogue.
   Poetry and prose extracts from novels, biographies, diaries and letters from the sixteenth to twentieth century.

967 WILLIAMS, Dorian
   The horseman's companion, edited by Dorian Williams. London, Eyre and Spottiswoode, 1967. 566pp, plates.

Headings: The horse in history and legend; Equestrian lore; Famous horses and horsemen; Great races; Horse and hound; The horse in fiction; The horse in verse (pp 521-565).
Only the last section contains poetry. Covers the nineteenth and twentieth centuries.

SHOOTING

968 PARKER, Eric
   Game pie: an anthology of shooting, compiled by Eric Parker. London, Philip Allan. 1925. 303pp.
Headings: The boy; Guns; Powder and shot; Kit and gear; The holiday; Companions; Fellow sportsmen; Dogs; The moor; The twelfth; The first; The forest; Grouse; Blackgame; Partridges; Pheasants; Snipe; Woodcock; Duck; Hares; Rabbits; Geese and swan; Various; The rookery; Enemies and friends; Red-letter days; Gamekeepers; Poachers; Meals; The inn; The kitchen; The bookshelf; Recipes; Golden rules; Yarns; Weather; The deer stalker; The wildfowler; The philosophy of it.
Prose and poetry mostly of the nineteenth and twentieth centuries. More prose than poetry.

TOPOGRAPHY AND GENERAL DESCRIPTION

TRAVEL

969 ADAMS, Anthony and JONES, Esmor
Place to place, [compiled] by Anthony Adams and Esmor Jones. London,
Nelson, 1975. 64pp, illus. (Nelson's Humanities Scheme, English 3.)
Headings: And see the world; Travelling people; Forced to go; A new home;
Barriers; Eldorado.
Twentieth century poetry and prose. Intended for schools.

970 DUBOIS, Mary R J
Poems for travellers, compiled by Mary R J Dubois. London, Bell; New
York, Henry Holt, 1909. xvi, 496pp.
Covers: France, Germany, Austria, Switzerland, Italy and Greece.
Mainly nineteenth century poetry by known and unknown poets; includes
some foreign and classical authors in translation.

971 EMMONS, Frederick E
Traveler's book of verse, edited by Frederick E Emmons. New York,
Holt, [1928]; xviii, 406pp, plates.
Italy: pp 173-387.

972 GRAHAM, Stephen
The tramp's anthology, edited by Stephen Graham. London, Peter
Davies, 1928. xix, 215pp.
Poetry and prose mostly of the nineteenth and twentieth centuries on wan-
dering and nature.

973 HORAN, Kenneth O'Donnell
Parnassus en route: an anthology of poems about places, not people, on
the European continent, compiled by Kenneth O'Donnell Horan. New
York, Macmillan, 1929. xx, 265pp.
Reprinted: Freeport, New York, Books for Libraries, 1972. (Granger
Index Reprint series.)

974 HUMPHREY, Lucy H
The poetic old world: a little book for tourists, compiled by Lucy H
Humphrey. London, Bell; New York, Henry Holt, 1909. xxiii, 513pp.
Covers: England, Ireland, Scotland, Holland, Belgium, Germany, France

146

Switzerland, Italy, Sicily, Spain and Greece.
Mostly nineteenth century poetry by well-known poets; includes some
foreign and classical poets in translation.

975 LEONARD, R M

Poems on travel, selected by R M Leonard. London, Oxford University
Press, 1914. 128pp. Notes. (Oxford Garlands.)
Poems about travelling in general and individual countries.

976 LOCKLEY, R M

In praise of islands: an anthology for friends, compiled by R M Lockley.
London, Frederick Muller, [1957]. 47pp, illus.
Prose and poetry extracts of the nineteenth and twentieth centuries on
islands in general and specific islands.

977 MacDONALD, Hugh

On foot: an anthology selected by Hugh MacDonald. London, Oxford
University Press, 1942. 320pp.
Contents: Miscellaneous, including a few urban walks; Lake District, Wales
and Scotland; The Alps.
Prose and poetry from the sixteenth to twentieth century; emphasis on the
nineteenth century.

978 SONGS OF HOME AND OTHER LANDS:

a selection of poems for the geography lesson. Bath, New York, Pitman,
[1909]. 96pp.
Headings: Songs of Great Britain; Songs of Europe; Songs of Empire; Songs
of other lands (America and Africa); Songs of the river and the sea.
Well-known nineteenth century poets.

979 STANLEY, Arthur

The golden road: an anthology of travel, selected and arranged by Arthur
Stanley; illustrated by Phyllis Bray. London, Dent, 1938. xii, 623pp, illus.
Headings: The ancient ways; Pilgrimage; All aboard; All abroad; Tales of
Araby; Terra incognita; Light luggage; The grand tour; Lesser journeys; The
footpath way; Visitors' book; The modern traveller.
Poetry and prose from the classical writers to the twentieth century. In-
cludes many unknown writers. Mostly prose.

980 THOMAS, M G Lloyd

Traveller's verse, chosen by M G Lloyd Thomas; with original lithographs
by Edward Bawden. London, Frederick Muller, 1946. 120pp, plates. Notes.
(New Excursions into English Poetry series.)
Poetry from the sixteenth to twentieth century, covering a wide range of
places. Mostly well-known poets.

See also: 827, 285

Studies and criticism

981 BLACKSTONE, Bernard
The lost travellers: a romantic theme with variations, by Bernard Blackstone. London, Longmans, 1962. xi, 292pp. References in footnotes.
Chapters: Strangers and pilgrims; The land of dreams; Caverns measureless
to man; The traveller unknown (Blake); The secondary founts (Wordsworth);
The little boy lost (Coleridge); The pilgrim of eternity (Byron); The herd
abandoned (Shelley); The journey homeward; An analysis of various travel
patterns in early nineteenth century verse.

982 GREENFIELD, Stanley B
The exile-wanderer in Anglo-Saxon poetry. PhD thesis, Berkeley, University of California, 1950.

983 STOKER, Ray C
Geographical lore in the Middle English metrical romances. PhD thesis,
Stanford University, 1929.

GREAT BRITAIN

984 BETJEMAN, John and TAYLOR, Geoffrey
English, Scottish and Welsh landscape, 1700-1860, chosen by John
Betjeman and Geoffrey Taylor; with original lithographs by John Piper.
London, Frederick Muller, 1944. 121pp, col plates. (New Excursions into
English Poetry Series.)
Includes much poetry by unknown clergymen of the eighteenth and nine-
teenth centuries.

985 HADFIELD, John
A book of Britain: an anthology of words and pictures, compiled by
John Hadfield. London, Hulton Press, 1956. 255pp, plates.
Headings: Seascape; Landscape; Figures in a landscape; Detail; Sporting
print; Flower piece; Street scene; Envoi.
Prose and poetry.

986 HILDITCH, Neville
In praise of the British: an anthology for the present times, compiled by
Neville Hilditch. London, Frederick Muller, 1949. 63pp, illus.
Prose and poetry extracts from Shakespeare and the eighteenth to twenti-
eth century, on the British character and way of life.

987 SEARLE, Lindley
Britain in verse and sketch, compiled and illustrated by Lindley Searle.
London, Staples Press, 1945. 112pp, illus.
Covers places in England, Wales and Scotland. Poetry of the nineteenth and
twentieth centuries. Includes thirteen poems by H D Rawnsley.

See also: 977, 1151

Studies and criticism

988 SNYDER, Edward Douglas
The wild Irish: a study of some English satires against the Irish, Scots and Welsh (in Modern Philology, xvii, January 1920, pp 687-725).

England

989 BRONSON, Bertrand Harris
That immortal garland, [compiled by Bertrand Harris Bronson]. London, Faber, 1943. 260pp.
Headings: Native soil; Victories and heroes; National character and ideals; Self-dedicatory; Hortatory; Consolatory; Invocatory; Thanksgiving; Prophecy.
Poetry from the sixteenth to twentieth century by well-known poets.

990 BROWN, Ivor
A book of England, edited by Ivor Brown, with 110 photographs from The Times. London, Glasgow, Collins, 1958. 511pp, plates.
Headings: History; London; Customs; Places; Gardens, flowers and trees; Going to the play; Colleges and school; Seas and sailors; Sport; Character and comedy; First and last things.
Poetry and prose from the seventeenth to twentieth century.

991 BURKE, Thomas
The charm of England: an anthology compiled and edited by Thomas Burke. London, Truslove and Hanson, [1914]. 179pp.
Headings: The English town and countryside; The English girl and woman; Love and marriage in England; The English home and garden; English customs and festivals; England and the champion.
Mostly nineteenth century poetry and prose.

992 BUTLER, Audrey
The old country: a book of love and praise of England, edited by Audrey Butler. London, Dent; New York, Dutton, 1965. xiv, 192pp, plates (some col).
Based on the collection by E Rhys (qv) with the same title. Retains the 'enduring elements' of this volume, and adds material to cover the twentieth century.

993 HAMILTON, G Rostrevor and ARLOTT, John
Landmarks: a book of topographical verse for England and Wales, chosen by G Rostrevor Hamilton and John Arlott. London, Cambridge University Press, 1943. xiii, 236pp.
Headings: London; Out of London; The home counties and the south country; The west country; The border counties and Wales; The north country; The east country; The midlands.
Poetry from the seventeenth to twentieth century: covers particular towns, villages and landscapes.

994 LONGFELLOW, Henry W
England, edited by Henry W Longfellow. Boston, Houghton & Osgood, 1877, 1881. 2 vols. xiii, 250pp; xi, 280pp. (Poetry of Places Series.)

995 LONGFELLOW, Henry W
England and Wales, edited by Henry W Longfellow. Boston, Houghton & Osgood, 1876. ix, 266pp. (Poetry of Places series.)

996 MAWSON, Christian
Portrait of England: an anthology by Christian Mawson. Harmondsworth, Penguin Books, 1942. 222pp.
Headings: The country; The people; A free society; In adversity; Battle; St George and the dragon; Pax britannica.
Prose and poetry by known and unknown writers from the seventeenth to twentieth century.

997 MORTIMER, John D
An anthology of the home counties, by John D Mortimer; with an introduction by John Betjeman. London, Methuen, 1947. 256pp, plates.
Headings: The seasons; The English scene; Forest and downland; Rivers; Palaces, churches and houses; Gardens and parks; Agriculture and country life; Economic life; Fairs and markets; Sports; Social life; Travel; Good living; Customs and eccentrics; Songs and ballads; Historical and biographical; Epitaphs and inscriptions; Country, town and village; Love and family life.
Counties covered: Berks, Bucks, Herts, Essex, Middx, Surrey and Sussex.
Poetry and prose from the seventeenth to nineteenth century.

998 [NICOLSON, Harold]
England: an anthology; with an introduction by Harold Nicolson. London, Macmillan, for the English Association, 1944. xxiv, 296pp. Notes.
Headings: Countryside; Town; Sport; War; Reflection; Humour; Poets; Painting, architecture, sculpture; Music; Character.
Poetry from the sixteenth to twentieth century by mostly well-known poets.

999 RHYS, E
The old country: a book of love and praise of England, edited by E Rhys. London, Dent, 1917. 319pp.

1000 SIMMONS, Jack
Journeys in England: an anthology, edited by Jack Simmons. London, Oldhams Press, 1951. 288pp.
Mostly prose, some poetry, recording some of the journeys that have been made in England.
Second edition: Newton Abbot (Devon), David and Charles, 1969. 288pp.

1001 THOMAS, Edward
This England: an anthology from her writers, compiled by Edward Thomas London, Oxford University Press, 1915. xii, 177pp.
Headings: This England; Merry England; Her sweet three corners; London;

Abroad and home again; Great ones; The vital commoners.
Prose and poetry from the sixteenth to nineteenth century.

Studies and criticism

1002 AUBIN, Robert Arnold
Topographical poetry in eighteenth century England, by Robert Arnold
Aubin. New York, Modern Language Association of America, 1936. 419pp.
Bibliographies.
Chapters: Pelion on Ossa; Groves of Eden; Cloud-capped towers; Old lands
and new; Murmuring waters; The travellers.
The bibliographies list individual poems, published separately or in collec-
tions, giving library locations if outside Harvard University. Subjects
covered: hill poems, sea poems, mine (and cave) poems, estate poems, town
poems, building poems, region poems, river poems, journey poems.

1003 MACKAY, J J
The sentiment of place in English poetry from 1700-1780. MA thesis,
University of London, 1937.

1004 ORUCH, Jack Bernard
Topography in the prose and poetry of the English Renaissance, 1540-
1640. PhD thesis, Indian University, 1964.

Counties and districts

1005 COUNTRY LIKE THIS
A book of the Vale of Aylesbury, with a preface by Sir A Bryant. Aylesbury, Friends of the Vale of Aylesbury, 1972. 160pp, illus, maps on end
papers.

The Local History Collection of the Buckinghamshire Country Library at
Aylesbury has a card index to poems about the county.

1006 HAWKEY, Muriel
A Cornish chorus: a collection of prose and verse, edited by Muriel
Hawkey; with a preface by J C Trewin. London, Westaway Books, 1948.
144pp, plates.

1007 ROWSE, A L
A Cornish anthology, chosen by A L Rowse. London, Macmillan, 1968.
300pp.
Headings: Prologue; Places; People; History and events; Travellers and travelling; Occupations and callings; Folklore, charms and inscriptions; Birds,
beasts, flowers, gardens; Customs and beliefs; Victoriana.
Prose and poetry from the seventeenth to twentieth century. More prose
than poetry.

1008 THOMAS, Donald Michael
The granite kingdom: poems of Cornwall: an anthology, edited by D M
Thomas. Truro (Cornwall), D Bradford Barton, 1970. 112pp, illus. Notes.

Headings: Legends; Coast and sea; Inland Cornwall; Flowers, birds and beasts; People; Songs and ballads.
Includes a significant amount of twentieth century poetry.

1009 JERROLD, Walter and JERROLD, Clare
   Cumberland in prose and verse: an anthology, [compiled] by Walter and Clare Jerrold. London, Elkin Mathews and Marrot, 1930. xvi, 155pp. Notes. (The Country Anthologies series.)

1010 MOULT, Thomas
   Derbyshire in prose and verse: an anthology, [compiled] by Thomas Moult. London, Elkin Mathews and Marrot, 1929. xiii, 150pp, map. Glossary. Notes. (The County Anthologies series.)

1011 HILDITCH, Neville
   In praise of Devon: an anthology for friends, compiled by Neville Hilditch. London, Frederick Muller, 1952. 57pp, illus.
Poetry and prose extracts.

1012 GOLDSWORTHY, Margaret
   The Dorset bedside anthology, collected and arranged by Margaret Goldsworthy; introduction by Ralph Wightman. Bognor Regis, Arundel Press, 1951. ix, 339pp.
Includes about fifty poems, but not all relate directly to Dorset.

1013 ALLAN, Victor
   East Anglian enchantment: an anthology, compiled by Victor Allan. Ipswich, East Anglian Magazine Ltd, 1947. 127pp.
Headings: The spell of the land; The spirit of the people; Of things past; The heritage.
Poetry and prose. Poetry is not always related directly to East Anglia.

1014 GOODWYN, E A and BAXTER, J C
   East Anglian verse, chosen and edited by E A Goodwyn and J C Baxter. Ipswich, The Boydell Press, 1974. 131pp. Notes.
. . . 'largely poetry of the village . . . poetry about farming, poverty, people at their work and at their leisure . . . fundamentally an agricultural poetry . . .'

1015 HUTCHINGS, Richard J
   An island of poetry: an illustrated anthology of Isle of Wight poetry, compiled by Richard J Hutchings. Shanklin (Isle of Wight), G G Saunders, 1970. 40pp, illus.
Mostly nineteenth century poetry all connected with the island.

1016 CHURCH, Richard
   The little kingdom: a Kentish collection, [compiled] by Richard Church; illustrated by John Ward. London, Hutchinson, 1964. 300pp, illus.
Part 1: The story (the history of Kent as affected by national events); Part 2: Persons and places.
Poetry and prose from the sixteenth to twentieth century, with some commentary.

1017 VAYNES, Julia H L de
    The Kentish garland, edited by Julia H L de Vaynes; with additional
notes and pictorial illustrations copied from the rare originals by J W Ebsworth. Hereford, Stephen Austin, 1881. 2 vols. 950pp, illus.
Vol I: The country in general; Vol II: On persons and places.

1018 WALKER, S A
    In praise of Kent: an anthology for friends, compiled by S A Walker.
London, Frederick Muller, 1952. 58pp, illus.
Poetry and prose extracts.

1019 ABRAHAM, Ashley P
    Poems of Lakeland: an anthology, compiled by Mrs Ashley P Abraham;
with a foreword by Hugh Walpole, a frontispiece in colour and twelve full
page illustrations. London, Warne, 1934. 179pp, illus.

1020 SANDILANDS, G S
    In praise of the lakes: an anthology for friends, compiled by G S Sandi-
lands. London, Frederick Muller, 1953. 64pp, illus.
Poetry and prose extracts.

1021 SANDILANDS, G S
    The lakes: an anthology of Lakeland life and landscape [compiled] by
G S Sandilands; illustrated by E W Tristram. London, Frederick Muller,
1947. 203pp, col illus.
Poetry and prose covering the different areas of the district.

1022 CASE, R H
    Lancashire in prose and verse: an anthology [compiled] by R H Case.
London, Elkin Mathews and Marrot, 1930. xvi, 167pp, map. Glossary.
Notes. (County Anthologies series.)

1023 YATES, May
    A Lancashire anthology, compiled and edited with short biographical
notices of the authors by May Yates. Liverpool, University Press; London,
Hodder & Stoughton, 1923. 344pp.
Mainly urban and industrial dialect poems.

1024 WADE, Barrie
    Lines and levels: an anthology of poems with a Lincolnshire setting, edited
by Barrie Wade; illustrated by David Paton. Lincoln, The Lincolnshire Association for the Arts, 1972. 63pp, illus.
Twentieth century poetry.

1025 HIKINS, Sylvia
    Roll the union on; Mersyside poems, stories, songs and street rhymes
from 1775 to the present day, edited by Sylvia Hikins, Liverpool, Toulouse
Press, 1973. 128pp.

1026 POPE, T Michael
Middlesex in prose and verse: an anthology by T Michael Pope. London, Elkin Mathews and Marrot, 1930. xv, 141pp. Notes. (County Anthologies series.)

1027 FENNELL, Caroline
A Norfolk anthology, compiled by Caroline Fennell. Ipswich, Boydell Press, 1972. 224pp.
Wide-ranging anthology of prose and poetry.

1028 HALLIWELL, J O
The Norfolk anthology: a collection of poems, ballads and rare tracts relating to the county of Norfolk, collected by J O Halliwell. London, 1852. 212pp.
Limited edition: 80 copies.

1029 SNAPE, Anne
Anthology of Oxfordshire poetry, [compiled] by A Snape. [c 1965]. [110]pp.
Typescript of an incompleted anthology located in the Local History Collection, City of Oxford Public Library.

1030 PARKER, Eric
Surrey anthology, [compiled by] Eric Parker. London, Museum Press, 1952. 248pp, illus.
Mostly prose extracts. Running commentary.

1031 COOK, C F
Another book of Sussex verse, edited by C F Cook. Hove, Combridges, 1928. xvi, 237pp, illus.
Mostly nineteenth and early twentieth century poetry.

1032 COOK, C F
The book of Sussex verse, edited by C F Cook; foreword by Arthur F Bell. Hove, Combridges, 1914. 224pp. Biographical notes.
Headings: Sussex; West Sussex; Brighton and neighbourhood; Downland; East Sussex; Some old Sussex songs.
Mostly nineteenth century poetry.

1033 GOLDSWORTHY, Margaret
The Sussex bedside anthology, collected and arranged by Margaret Goldsworthy; with an introduction by Mervyn D Francis. Bognor Regis, Arundel Press, 1950. xix, 620pp.
Poetry and prose; more prose than poetry.

1034 HILDITCII, Neville
In praise of Sussex: an anthology for friends, compiled by Neville Hilditch. London, Frederick Muller, 1950. 64pp, illus.
Nineteenth and twentieth century prose and poetry extracts.

1035 TAYLOR, James
The Sussex garland: a collection of ballads, sonnets, tales, elegies, songs, epitaphs, etc illustrative of the county of Sussex, with notices historical, biographical and descriptive, [compiled] by James Taylor. Printed for the editor, 1851. xii, 376pp.

1036 WORTH, Richard Nicholas
West Country garland, selected from the writings of the poets of Devon and Cornwall from the fifteenth to nineteenth century, with folk songs and traditional verse edited by Richard Nicholas Worth. London, Houlston, 1875. xvi, 176pp.

1037 HALLIWELL, James Orchard
The Yorkshire anthology: a collection of ancient and modern ballads, poems and songs relating to the county of Yorkshire, collected by James Orchard Halliwell. London, 1851. viii, 404pp.
Limited edition: 110 copies.

1038 SLINGSBY, Eleanor
In praise of Yorkshire: an anthology for friends, compiled by Eleanor Slingsby. London, Frederick Muller, 1951. 64pp, illus.
Prose and poetry extracts.

1039 WILSON, George Francis
Yorkshire in prose and verse: an anthology, by G F Wilson. London, Elkin Mathews and Marrot, 1929. xix, 147pp. Notes. (The County Anthologies series.)

English towns

1040 WHITBY, Charles
The Bath anthology of prose and verse, compiled and edited by Charles Whitby, with five illustrations. London, Folk Press, 1928. 153pp, illus.
Covers all periods in the town's history to the present day. Poetry and prose extracts (from diaries, accounts, etc).

1041 MARTIN, Edward
600 years of Bristol poetry, compiled by Edward Martin. Bristol, Arts and Leisure Committee of the City and County of Bristol, 1973. 88pp.

Cambridge See: 821-827

1042 BING, F G
The book of Canterbury verse: an illustrated anthology, compiled and edited by F G Bing. Canterbury, Gibbs, 1932. xxv, 243pp, plates.

1043 AUBIN, Robert Arnold
London in flames; London in glory: poems on the fire and rebuilding of London, 1666-1709, edited by Robert Arnold Aubin. New Brunswick, Rutgers University Press, 1943. 383pp. Notes (pp 305-374).

1044 BISHOP, John and BROADBENT, Virginia
London, between the lines: a verse anthology, compiled by John Bishop
and Virginia Broadbent; cover design and illustrations by Diana de Vere
Cole. London, Simon Publications, 1973. 176pp, illus.
Headings: London town; Dreams and nightmares; Londoners; Streets, parks
and markets; All seasons; Churches and cathedrals; Pleasures and pastimes;
The river; All round St Pauls.
Poetry from the eighteenth to twentieth century, with an emphasis on the
twentieth.

1045 JAMES, Norman G Brett
A London anthology, edited by Norman G Brett James. London, Harraps,
1928. 299pp. (Harraps Modern English series.)
Prose and poetry from the Middle Ages to the nineteenth century. More
prose than poetry.

1046 BROWN, Ivor
A book of London, edited by Ivor Brown; with fifty-four photographs
from the Times. London, Glasgow, Collins, 1961. 352pp, plates. (Collins
National Anthologies series.)
Headings: London observations; For and against; History; Characters; Green
islands; Shops; Riverside; Streets; At plays and play; Inns and lodging.
Poetry and prose. Poetry is mostly of the eighteenth and seventeenth cen-
turies.

1047 HENLEY, W E
A London garland, selected from five centuries of English verse by W E
Henley; with pictures by members of the Society of Illustrators. London,
New York, Macmillan, 1895. 203pp, illus.

1048 HILDITCH, Neville
In praise of London: an anthology for friends, compiled by Neville Hil-
ditch. London, Frederick Muller, 1944. 58pp.
Poetry and prose extracts.

1049 HYATT, Alfred H
The charm of London: an anthology, compiled by Alfred H Hyatt.
London, Chatto and Windus, 1907. 372pp.
Headings: The Londoner's farewell; The Londoner returns; In London
streets; The East End; The West End; Some London phases; The seasons in
London; River, bridge and tower; A few London memories; The praise of
London; The play's the thing; Rus in urbe; The fringe of the town.
Poetry and prose, mostly of the nineteenth century.

1050 JONES, Esmor
Paved with gold: a scrapbook of London life, [compiled by] Esmor
Jones. Glasgow, London, Blackie, 1975. 88pp, illus.
Poetry and prose from the eighteenth to twentieth century. Mostly prose
taken from novels, accounts, diaries, etc.

1051 A LONDON OMNIBUS
   London, Chatto & Windus, 1927. 138pp, front, plates.
Mostly prose extracts from the seventeenth to twentieth century.

1052 LOW, D M
   London is London: a selection of prose and verse, made by D M Low;
illustrated by Edward Bawden. London, Chatto & Windus, 1949. 300pp,
illus.
Poetry and prose mostly of the seventeenth and eighteenth centuries.

1053 MACKAY, Charles
   A collection of songs and ballads relative to the London prentices and
trades and to the affairs of London generally during the fourteenth, fif-
teenth and sixteenth centuries, edited with notes and introduction by
Charles Mackay. London, Percy Society, 1841. viii, 157pp. (Percy Society
Publications Vol l.)

1054 MELVILLE, Helen and MELVILLE, Lewis
   London's lure: an anthology in prose and verse, [compiled] by Helen and
Lewis Melville. London, Bell, 1909. 328pp.
Headings: Town and country; Dawn; Night; Hyde Park and Kensington
Gardens; Piccadilly and Mayfair; St James St and Pall Mall; Westminster
Abbey and St Paul's Cathedral; The Strand, Covent Garden and the Inns of
Court; Mean streets; The city; The river and riverside; Rain, smoke and fog;
Some literary men in London; Impressions; Ballads and songs; Miscellaneous;
L'envoi.
Prose and poetry mostly of the nineteenth century.

1055 WHITTEN, Wilfred
   London in song, compiled by Wilfred Whitten. London, Grant Richards,
[1898]; xvi, 354pp. Notes (pp 323-352).
Headings: London town; London river; London city.
Poetry by known and unknown poets of the seventeenth to nineteenth cen-
tury.

See also: 865, 990, 993, 1001, 1398, 1454, 1784

Oxford See: 814-820

Studies and criticism

1056 CLARK, Jeanne G
   London in English literature, 1880-1955. PhD thesis, Columbia University, 1957.

Wales

1057 FRASER, Maxwell
   In praise of Wales: an anthology for friends, compiled by Maxwell Fraser.
London, Frederick Muller, 1950. 63pp, plates.
Prose and poetry extracts, mostly of the nineteenth and twentieth centuries.

1058 LLOYD, D M and LLOYD, E M
A book of Wales, edited by D M and E M Lloyd. London, Glasgow, Collins, 1953. 384pp, plates.
Headings: Places; History—literary and general; Pastoral and industrial; People, great and small; Humour, romance and sentiment; Customs, beliefs and reflection on life; Poems, songs and ballads; Religious and philosophical. Poetry and prose from the Middle Ages to the twentieth century.

See also: 995

1059 MONMOUTHSHIRE POETRY
an anthology of poetry relating to the county, or written by writers associated with Monmouthshire. Newport, R H Johns, [1949]. 148pp.

Studies and criticism

1060 HUGHES, W J
Wales and the Welsh in English literature from the beginnings of the sixteenth to the beginnings of the nineteenth century. MA thesis, University of Wales , 1919.

Scotland

1061 DOUGLAS, Ronald Macdonald
The Scots book: a miscellany of poems, folklore, prose and letters with many facts some well-known and some less known about Scotland and her people, compiled and in part written by Ronald Macdonald Douglas; thirty-one illustrations by Douglas Percy Blis and Betty Aylmer. London, Alexander Maclehose, 1935. xxiv, 367pp, illus.
Poetry (mostly ballads or historical): pp 3-94.

1062 FINDLAY, Henry J
A book of Scotland, arranged by Henry J Findlay. London, Glasgow, Collins, 1934. 255pp.
Enlarged edition by G F Maine. 1950. 384pp, plates.
Headings: Places; History; Pastoral; People, great and small; Humour and sentiment; Customs; Hospitality; Poems, songs and ballads; Religious and mystical.
Poetry and prose, mostly from the eighteenth to twentieth century.

1063 HILDITCH, Neville
In praise of Scotland: an anthology for friends, compiled by Neville Hilditch. London, Frederick Muller, 1946. 61pp, illus.
Poetry and prose extracts.

1064 KERMACK, W R
The Scottish bedside book: an anthology of prose and verse in Scots and English, compiled by W R Kermack. Edinburgh, London, W & A K Johnston, 1949. 128pp.

Headings: Characters; Humour; Enchantment; Witches and warlocks; Bygone beliefs and customs; War; The highlands; Parting and exile; Burns and Scott (criticism); Love and loyalty.
Mainly eighteenth and nineteenth century writings.

1065 LINDSAY, Maurice
    Scotland: an anthology, compiled by Maurice Lindsay. London, Robert Hale; New York, St Martin's Press, 1974. 479pp.
Headings: Places; History; People; A sheaf o ballants; Creatures; Pursuits and pastimes; Mysticism; Humour; The Scot's character.
Poetry and prose from the eighteenth to twentieth century.

1066 LONGFELLOW, Henry W
    Scotland, edited by Henry W Longfellow. Boston, Osgood and Houghton, 1876, 1881. 2 vols. x, 246pp, xi, 266pp. (Poetry of Places series.)

Scottish localities

1067 MASSON, Rosaline
    In praise of Edinburgh: an anthology in prose and verse, selected and edited by Rosaline Masson. London, Constable, 1912. 308pp.
More prose than verse. Covers all periods.

1068 QUIGLEY, Hugh
    Lanarkshire in prose and verse: an anthology, [compiled] by Hugh Quigley. London, Elkin Mathews and Marrot, 1929. xviii, 148pp. Notes. Glossary of Scottish terms. (The County Anthologies series.)
Headings: The Clyde; Lanarkshire and the southern uplands; Glasgow.

1069 HUMBLE, B H
    The songs of Skye: an anthology, edited by B H Humble; with an introduction by the Rev Lauchlan Maclean Watt. Stirling, Ereas Mackay, 1934. 176pp, folding plates. Bibliography. Notes.
Headings: The road to Skye; Legend and romance through the ages; Longing for Skye; Mountains and moorland; The Canadian boat song; The Skye bards.
Poetry of the nineteenth and twentieth centuries.
    A 'second edition', 1944, contains only one further poem.

IRELAND

1070 DOUGLAS, Ronald Macdonald
    The Irish book: a miscellany of facts and fancies, folklore and fragments, poems and prose to do with Ireland and her people, compiled and in part written by Ronald Macdonald Douglas. Dublin, Cork, Talbott Press, 1936. xxvi, 393pp.
Poetry: pp 3-49.

1071 FLOOD, J M
   Irene: a selection of prose and poetry relating to Ireland, compiled by
J M Flood. Dublin, Talbot Press, 1929. 208pp. Biographical notes.

1072 HILDITCH, Neville
   In praise of Ireland: an anthology for friends, compiled by Neville Hil-
ditch. London, Frederick Muller, 1951. 64pp, illus.
Prose and poetry extracts.

1073 O'CONNOR, Frank
   A book of Ireland, edited by Frank O'Connor. London, Glasgow,
Collins, 1959. 384pp, plates.
Headings: History; Pastoral and town life; Humour, romance and sentiment;
Customs and beliefs; Poems, songs and ballads; Religious and philosophical.
Poetry and prose, mostly of the nineteenth and twentieth centuries.

SCANDINAVIA

1074 LONGFELLOW, Henry W
   Denmark, Iceland, Norway, Sweden, edited by Henry W Longfellow.
Boston, Osgood & Houghton, 1880. vii, 268pp. (Poetry of Places series.)

GERMANY

1075 LONGFELLOW, Henry W
   Germany, edited by Henry W Longfellow. Boston, Osgood & Houghton,
1877. viii, 254pp. (Poetry of Places series.)

FRANCE

1076 HYATT, Alfred H
   The charm of Paris: an anthology, compiled by Alfred H Hyatt. London,
Chatto and Windus, 1908. 406pp.
Headings: The charm of Paris; In praise of Paris. The streets of Paris; Some
Parisian phases; Bohemian Paris; A few Parisian portraits; The seasons in
Paris; Portraits of places; The romance of Paris; Paris of the past.
Poetry and prose of the nineteenth century; includes some French items in
translation.

1077 LONGFELLOW, Henry W
   France, edited by Henry W Longfellow. Boston, Osgood and Houghton,
1880. vii, 265pp. (Poetry of Places series.)

1078 LONGFELLOW, Henry W
   France and Savoy, edited by Henry W Longfellow. Boston, Osgood and
Houghton, 1880. vii, 266pp. (Poetry of Places series.)

SWITZERLAND

1079 EBERLI, Henry
Switzerland poetical and pictorial: a collection of poems by English and American poets, compiled by Henry Eberli. Zurich, Institut Orell Fussl, 1893. 537pp, illus. Notes.
Headings: Poetical and historical; Poems on the Alps; Mont Blanc; The lake of Geneva; The Valais; The Italian lakes, the Grisons and the Rhine; Berne; St Gothard; Lakes of Lucerne and Zurich; Guides, herdsmen, hunters; Flora; Sunrise, sunset, winter; Ranz des Vaches, alpine horn, etc.
Engravings by J Weber; red borders. Mostly nineteenth century poetry.

1080 JAMES, Norman G Brett
The charm of Switzerland: an anthology, compiled by Norman G Brett James. London, Methuen, 1910. 304pp.
Headings: Mountains, old mountaineers; Swiss freedom; Narrative passages; Lucerne and neighbourhood; The Oberland; Geneva and its lake; Geneva to Chamonix; Mont Blanc and Chamonix; The Valais; Passes; Miscellaneous.
Prose and poetry of the nineteenth century.

1081 LONGFELLOW, Henry W
Switzerland and Austria, edited by Henry W Longfellow. Boston, Houghton & Osgood, 1877. ix, 264pp. (Poetry of Places Series.)

1082 LUNN, Arnold
Switzerland in English prose and poetry, edited by Arnold Lunn. London, Eyre & Spottiswoode, 1947. xxiii, 261pp. Biographical notes. (The New Alpine Library Series.)
Prose and poetry, mainly prose, covering all periods.

See also: Mountains 1791-1793

ITALY

1083 LONGFELLOW, Henry W
Italy, edited by Henry W Longfellow. Boston, Osgood and Houghton. 3 vols. (Poetry of Places series.)
Vol I: 1877. ix, 278pp. Contains twenty-one poems on Florence, ten on Milan and thirteen on Naples; Vol II: 1877. vii, 262pp. Contains ten poems on Ravena; Rome (pp 87-252); Vol III: 1877. viii, 256pp. Contains thirteen poems on Sorrento, forty-three on Venice.

1084 PHELPS, Ruth Shepard
Skies Italian: a little breviary for travellers in Italy, chosen and arranged by Ruth Shepard Phelps. London, Methuen, 1910. 368pp.
Headings: The approach; The north; The Ligurian shore; The Lombard plain; Venetia; Emilia and the marches; In Tuscany; Umbria; The Roman campagna; The south; Meditations; Adieu!
Nineteenth century poetry by mostly well-known poets.

1085 SCHAUFFLER, Robert Haven
Through Italy with the poets, compiled by Robert Haven Schauffler.
New York, Moffat & Yard, 1908. xviii, 429pp.
Includes some foreign poetry in translation.

1086 STANLEY, Arthur
Under Italian skies: an anthology, selected and arranged by Arthur
Stanley. London, Gollancz, 1950. 272pp.
Headings: Ancient ways; Medieval interlude; Renaissance; Grand tour; Romantic visitors; Modern times.
Poetry and prose by known and unknown writers. More prose than poetry.

1087 WOLLASTON, George Hyde
The Englishman in Italy: being a collection of verses written by some of
those who have loved Italy, arranged by George Hyde Wollaston. Oxford,
Clarendon Press, 1909. 316pp. Notes (pp 285-303).
Mostly nineteenth century poetry.

See also: 971

Venice

1088 HYATT, Alfred H
The charm of Venice: an anthology, compiled by Alfred H Hyatt. London, Chatto and Windus, 1908. ix, 388pp.
Headings: The charm of Venice; Venice from the sea; The sea spell; Gondola
and gondolier; Island and lagoon; Canal and bridge; Some Venetian phases;
Architecture and art; A Venetian day; The seasons in Venice; Venice of the
past; The romance of Venice.
Nineteenth century prose and poetry by known and unknown writers.

1089 VENICE REDISCOVERED
A loan exhibition in aid of the 'Venice in Peril' fund, 8th November-15th
December, 1972. London, Wildenstein, 1972. 62pp, plates.
pp 21-43: Venice through literary eyes; an anthology of extracts of prose
and poetry, mostly of the nineteenth century.

Studies and criticism

1090 BRAND, C P
Italy and the English romantics: the italianate fashion in early nineteenth
century England, by C P Brand. London, Cambridge University Press,
1957. xi, 285pp, plates. Bibliographies.
Chapters: Travel and language; Literature—the interest in Italian literature
and its influence in England; The arts and landscape (pp 165-173: the
appeal of the Italian scene— some poetry); History, politics and religion
(some poetry).
Bibliographies list works published in the first fifty years of the nineteenth
century in England, dealing with Italian literature, antiquities and history,
and art and architecture.

1091 LLOYD, D M W
    The idea of Italy in English literature from 1770-1900. BLitt thesis,
Oxford University, 1954.

1092 MARSHALL, Roderick
    Italy in English literature: origins of the romantic interest in Italy, by
Roderick Marshall. New York, Columbia University Press, 1934. xii,
432pp. (Columbia University Studies in English and comparative Literature,
No 116.)

1093 WHITE, Robert L
    Some passionate pilgrims: the image of Italy in American romanticism.
PhD thesis, University of Minnesota, 1960.

SPAIN

1094 FONTRODONA, E Pujals
    Spain and Spanish themes in modern English poetry, 1900-56. PhD
thesis, University of London, 1957.

1095 LONGFELLOW, Henry W
    Spain, edited by Henry W Longfellow. Boston, Osgood and Houghton,
1877. ix, 256pp. (Poetry of Places series.)

1096 LONGFELLOW, Henry W
    Spain, Portugal, Belgium, Holland, edited by Henry W Longfellow.
Boston, Osgood and Houghton, 1877. viii, 274pp. (Poetry of Places series.)

GREECE

1097 LONGFELLOW, Henry W
    Greece and Turkey, edited by Henry W Longfellow. Boston, Osgood and
Houghton, 1878. 271pp. (Poetry of Places Series.)

1098 M, H S
    The Englishman in Greece, being a collection of the verse of many English
poets [compiled by H S M] ; with an introduction by Sir Rennell Rodd.
Oxford, Clarendon Press, 1910. 328pp.

Studies and criticism

1099 MORRISON, A
    Greek poems by English poets. PhD thesis, Birmingham University,
1961.

1100 PIERCE, Frederick E
    The Hellenic current in English nineteenth century poetry (in Journal
of English and Germanic Philology, XVI, 1917, pp 103-135).
On the evocation of Greek landscape, life and myth.

1101 SPENCER, T J
The prelude to philhellenism: a study of contemporary Greece in English literature before the time of Byron. PhD thesis, London University, 1953.

1102 STERN, Bernard Herbert
The rise of romantic hellenism in English literature, 1732-1786, by Bernard Herbert Stern. Menasta (Wisconsin), George Banta, 1940. 182pp. Bibliography, (pp 169-180). References in footnotes.
Chapter 5: Romantic hellenism in English poetry—considers the work of Thomson, Gray, Collins, Mason and the Wartons.

RUSSIA

1103 PARTRIDGE, M
Slavonic themes in English poetry of the nineteenth century (in Slavonic and East European Review, 1963, pp 420-441). References in footnotes.

MIDDLE EAST

1104 LONGFELLOW, Henry W
Asia, edited by Henry W Longfellow. Boston, Osgood and Houghton, 1878. vii, 260pp. (Poetry of Places series.)
Covers: Asia Minor, Mesopotamia; Arabia; Turkestan, Afghanistan.

See also: 1345

Persia   *Studies and criticism*

1105 JAVADI-TABRIZI, H
The idea of Persia and Persian literature in English literature, with special reference to the nineteenth century. PhD thesis, Cambridge University, 1964.

1106 SURATGAR, M L K
Traces of Persian influence upon English literature during the fifteenth and sixteenth centuries, PhD thesis, London University, 1939.

THE ORIENT

1107 LONGFELLOW, Henry W
Asia, edited by Henry W Longfellow. Boston, Osgood and Houghton, 1878. vii, 249pp. (Poetry of Places series.)
Covers Persia and India.

Studies and criticism

1108 AHMAD, M
Oriental influences in English poetry of the romantic period. PhD thesis, Birmingham University, 1959.

1109 BROUGHTON, E S
Orientalism in English poetry. MA thesis, University of London, 1919.

1110 HADDAWY, Husain F
English arabesque: the oriental mode in eighteenth century English literature. PhD thesis, Cornell University, 1962.

1111 HUSAIN, I
The oriental elements in English poetry (1784-1859). PhD thesis, Edinburgh University, 1934.

1112 ULLAH, F S
Orientalism in the romantics. PhD thesis, Edinburgh University, 1953.

1113 VARMA, S P
True and false orientalism with special reference to Hinduism and India in English poetry. PhD thesis, London University, 1926.

India

1114 DUNN, Theodore Douglas
India in song: eastern themes in English verse by British and Indian poets, selected and arranged by Theodore Douglas Dunn. Bombay, Madras, Oxford University Press, 1918. 96pp. Biographical notes. Notes.

1115 PANDEY, B N
A book of India, edited by B N Pandey. London, Glasgow, Collins, 1965. 384pp, plates. Chronology.
Headings: History; Places; Pastoral; People great and small; Humour and sentiment; Manners and customs; Amusements and festivals; Poems, songs and tales; Religions and beliefs.
Poetry and prose by English and Indian writers of all periods.

See also: 1322

China Studies and criticism

1116 CH'IEN, C S
China in the English literature of the eighteenth century. BLitt thesis, Oxford University, 1937.

1117 NORTH, William R
Chinese themes in American verse. PhD thesis, Pennsylvania University, 1934.

1118 YU, S P
  China as treated by English and French writers in the first half of the
eighteenth century. BLitt thesis, Oxford University, 1932.

AFRICA

1119 LONGFELLOW, Henry W
  Africa, edited by Henry W Longfellow. Boston, Osgood and Houghton,
1878. vii, 253pp. (Poetry of Places series.)

See also: 310; Slavery 733-735

Studies and criticism

1120 BRAITHWAITE, R H E
  The negro in English Literature, 1756-1841. MA thesis, University of
London, 1956.

1121 DAMON, S Foster
  The negro in early American songsters (in Papers of the Bibliographical
Society of America, Vol 28, 1934, pp 132-63).

1122 HOPSON, James O
  Attitudes toward the negroes as an expression of English Romanticism.
PhD thesis, Pittsburgh University, 1948.

1123 JOHNSON, Lemuel A
  The devil, the gargoyle and the buffoon: the negro as metaphor in Western literature, by Lemuel A Johnson. Port Washington, London, Kennikat
Press National University Publications, 1971. 185pp.
pp 33-65: the English metaphor.

1124 JONES, J
  The 'distress'd' negro in English magazine verse, 1749-1832 (in University
of Texas Studies in English, Vol 17, July 1937, pp 88-106).

1125

1126 WALI, Obiajunwa
  The negro in English literature with special reference to the eighteenth
and early nineteenth centuries. PhD thesis, Northwestern University, 1967.

AUSTRALASIA

1127 LONGFELLOW, Henry W
  Oceanica, Australasia, Polynesia and miscellaneous seas and islands, edited
by Henry W Longfellow. Boston, Osgood and Houghton, 1879. vii, 288pp.
(Poetry of Places series.)
Australia: pp 37-54; Polar regions: pp 128-147; The Ocean: pp 185-259).

Australia

1128 ANDERSON, Hugh
   Colonial ballads, [compiled by] Hugh Anderson; with illustrations by
Ronald G Edwards. Ferntree Gully, Rams Skull Press, 1955. 155pp, illus.
Music.

1129 FLYNN, M M and GROOM, J
   This land: an anthology of Australian poetry for young people, [com-
piled by] M M Flynn and J Groom; illustrated by R Wenban. Rushcutters
Bay (New South Wales), Pergamon Press (Aust), 1968. vi, 202pp, illus.
Headings: The dream time; The awakening; Convicts and bushrangers; Days
of the soil; The roaring days; People and background; The sea; Living things;
War; Something to think about.
Running commentary.

1130 GAY, Florence
   In praise of Australia: an anthology in prose and verse, compiled by
Florence Gay. London, Constable, 1912. 250pp.
Headings: Rude sketches of Australia's story; The blackman; The white man
and his environment.
More prose than poetry.

1131 HANSEN, Ian V
   The call of the gums: an anthology of Australian verse, selected by Ian
V Hansen. London, Edward Arnold, 1962. 180pp.
Headings: Bush songs and ballads; Not very serious; The people of the land;
In time of war; Visionary; The landscape and the mood; The sense of history.

1132 INGLETON, Geoffrey Chapman
   True patriots all; or news from early Australia as told in a collection of
broadsides garnered and decorated by Geoffrey Chapman Ingleton. Sydney,
Angus and Robertson, 1952. vii, 280pp, illus. Notes (pp 259-276).
Mostly prose narratives; some verse, on murders, piracies, shipwrecks, trans-
portations, convicts, etc.

1133 MOORE, Tom Inglis
   A book of Australia, edited by T Inglis Moore. London, Glasgow, Collins,
1961. 320pp, plates.
Headings: Places; History; Pastoral; People, great and small; Humour and
sentiment; Customs and sports; Poems, songs and ballads; Traditions and
beliefs.
Poetry and prose.

1134 PATERSON, A B
   The old bush songs, composed in the bushranging, digging and overland-
ing days, edited by A B Paterson. Melbourne, E W Cole, 1905. xvi, 135pp.
   The American National Union Catalogue lists other editions up to a
seventh edition, 1930. 185pp.
   Revised and enlarged edition by Douglas Stewart and Nancy Keesing.
Sydney, London, Angus and Robertson, 1957. xxvii, 289pp. Bibliography.

Headings: Convicts and bushrangers; Immigrants and new chums; The goldfields; The stockmen of Australia; The stringyback cockatoo; A cry from
the north; Shanties; On the wallaby; The springtime it brings on the shearing.

1135 SLADEN, Douglas B W
   Australian ballads and rhymes: poems inspired by life and scenery in
Australia and New Zealand, selected and edited by Douglas B W Sladen.
London, Walter Scott, 1888. xxxiv, 301pp. Notes (pp 265-276).
pp 277-301: a study of Henry Kendall as a bush poet.

1136 STEWART, Douglas and KEESING, Nancy
   Australian bush ballads, edited by Douglas Stewart and Nancy Keesing.
Sydney, London, Angus and Robertson, 1955. xxx, 423pp. Bibliography
(verse collections and anthologies).
Headings: Bushrangers; The goldfields; Black; Perishes, etc; Shanties; Horses
and horsemen; The teams shearing; Swaggies; Tall stories and take-downs;
People and places; The Irish; Bush yarns; Old days, old ways; The light-
horse.

1137 WANNAN, Bill
   The Australian: yarns, ballads, legends and traditions of the Australian
people, gathered together by Bill Wannan. Melbourne, Australasian Book
Society, 1954. 288pp.
Covers rhymes and verse about the Australians and Australian life.

1138 WANNAN, Bill
   The heather in the South: lore, literature and balladry of the Scots in
Australia, edited by Bill Wannan. Melbourne, London, Lansdown Press,
1966. xv, 189pp, illus.
Part III: ballads old and new (pp 167-189).

1139 WANNAN, Bill
   The wearing of the green: the lore, literature, legend and balladry of the
Irish in Australia, edited by Bill Wannan. Melbourne, London, Lansdown
Press, 1966. xviii, 328pp.
Part III—Songs and ballads: Transportation and other convict songs and bal-
lads; Emigrant songs and ballads; Outlaw songs and ballads; Sporting songs
and ballads.

Studies and criticism

1140 LANSBURY, Coral
   Arcady in Australia: the evocation of Australia in nineteenth century
English literature, by Coral Lansbury. Melbourne, Melbourne University
Press, 1970. 202pp. Bibliography (pp 182-193). Notes.
Chapters: Botany Bay: convicts and kangaroos; The golden age; Younger
sons and yeoman farmers; S Sidney discovers Arcady; The Caxtons; The
Micawbers; Charles Reade strikes gold; Distant friends; The convict re-
deemed; The bush.

1141 RYE, L H
   South Australian verse: verse connected with South Australia: a survey
and appreciation together with a bibliography, complete up to December
31st, 1934. MA thesis, Queensland University, 1936.

New Zealand

1142 REID, John Cowie
   A book of New Zealand, edited by J C Reid, with fifty-four photographs.
London, Glasgow, Collins, 1964. 351pp, plates, map on endpapers. Chron-
ology.
Headings: History; Places; The land; People, great and small; The Maori;
Humour and sentiment; Amusements and sports; Poems, songs and ballads;
Traditions, customs and beliefs.
Prose and poetry.

See also: 799

POLAR REGIONS

1143 HOBBS, William H
   Literature and especially poetry on polar expeditions (in Poetry Review,
1937, March-April, pp 141-4).

See also: 1127

ALASKA

1144 POEMS ON ALASKA
   The land of the midnight sun, descriptive, personal, humorous, by authors
residing in the territory. Sitka (Alaska), Alaska print, [1891]. 68pp, illus.

CANADA

1145 FOWKE, Edith and MILLS, Alan
   Canada's story in song, [compiled] by Edith Fowke and Alan Mills;
piano accompaniments by Helmut Blume. Toronto, W J Cage, [1969];
230pp, illus. Music. Bibliography, discography, filmography.
Headings: Before the white man; The discovery of Canada; Voyageurs and
missionaries; The coming of the English; Wars against the United States;
The rebellion of 1837-8; The country grows; The opening of the West; Cowboys and homesteaders; Sailors and fishermen; Lumberjacks; Miners and
prospectors; Modern times.

1146 LIGHTHALL, William Douw
  Canadian poems and lays: selections of native verse, reflecting the
seasons, legends, and life of the dominion, arranged and edited by William
Douw Lighthall. London, Walter Scott, [1893]; xxxii, 276pp. (The
Canterbury Poets.)
Headings: The imperial spirit; The new nationality; The Indian; The voy-
ageur and habitant; Settlement life; Sports and free life (canoeing, fishing,
skating); The spirit of Canadian history; Places; History.

1147 SAMSON, Solomon
  A glimpse of Newfoundland (as it was and as it is) in poetry and pictures,
all edited and arranged and set with pictures appropriate to the poems by
Solomon Samson. Poole (Dorset), J Looker, 1960. xv, 80pp, illus.

1148 TOYE, William
  A book of Canada, edited by William Toye, with fifty photographs.
London, Glasgow, Collins, 1962. 416pp, plates.
Headings: the passage of the years: People; Places; Man and nature: east to
west; Man and nature: the far north; Work and play; Faiths and follies.
Mostly prose.

Studies and criticism

1149a KILGALLIN, Anthony R
  Toronto in prose and poetry. Phil M thesis, Toronto University, 1966.

UNITED STATES OF AMERICA

1149b AISON, Gerta
  American states anthology, edited by Gerta Aison. New York, Galleon
Press, 1935. 2 vols.
A compilation of contemporary American poetry classified by states.

1150 (BIBLIOGRAPHY) HUDDLESTONE, Eugene L
  Topographical poetry in America: a checklist, 1783-1812, by Eugene L
Huddlestone (in Bulletin of Bibliography, 1966, pp 8-13, 35, 39).
Headings: Hill poems; Estate poems; Town poems; River poems; Natural
phenomena poems; Travel poems.

1151 LAMB, G F
  United States and United Kingdom: comparisons, contrasts and simi-
larities in English and American life and literature: an anthology, edited by
G F Lamb. London, Harrap, 1944. 248pp.

1152 LONGFELLOW, Henry W
  America: New England, edited by Henry W Longfellow. Boston, Osgood
& Houghton, 1881. 2 vols. (Poetry of Places series.)
Vol I:vii, 270pp. Includes fourteen poems on Boston, and thirteen on Cam-
bridge, Mass. Vol II: vii, 288pp.

1153 LONGFELLOW, Henry W
  America: middle states, edited by Henry W Longfellow. Boston, Osgood
& Houghton, 1877. viii, 278pp. (Poetry of Places series.)
Includes ten poems on the River Hudson, thirteen on New York City, and
ten on the Niagara.

1154 LONGFELLOW, Henry W
  America: western states, edited by Henry W Longfellow. Boston, Osgood
& Houghton, 1879. vvi, 254pp. (Poetry of Places series.)

1155 LONGFELLOW, Henry W
  America: southern states, edited by Henry W Longfellow. Boston, Osgood
& Houghton, 1879. viii, 268pp. (Poetry of Places series.)

1156 LONGFELLOW, Henry W
  America: British America, Danish America, Mexico, Central America,
South America, West Indies, edited by Henry W Longfellow. Boston, Osgood
& Houghton, 1879. viii, 271pp. (Poetry of Places series.)
pp 227-269: West Indies.

See also: 1780

Studies and criticism

1157 BARNES, Richard Gordon
  The effect of the New World on English poetry 1600-1625. PhD thesis,
Claremont Graduate School, 1960.

1158 BRYANT, William
  Concepts of America and Americans by the English romantic poets,
1790-1850. PhD thesis, Vanderbilt University, 1942.

Individual states and towns

1159 COMBS, Josiah Henry
  All that's Kentucky: an anthology, edited by Josiah Henry Combs.
Louisville, John P Morton, 1915. xxiv, 285pp.

1160 BERBRICH, Joan D
  Sounds and sweet airs: the poetry of Long Island, edited by Joan D
Berbrich. Port Washington, New York, Friedman, 1970. xii, 179pp.

1161 ARMSTRONG, Hamilton Fish
  The book of New York verse, edited by Hamilton Fish Armstrong. New
York, Putnams, 1917. 450pp, illus.

1162 GORDON, John
  New York: the city as seen by masters of art and literature, edited by
John Gordon and L Rust Hills. New York, Shorecrest, 1965. 403pp, illus.

1163 DAVIDSON, Levette Jay
Poems of the Old West: a Rocky Mountain anthology edited by Levette
Jay Davidson. Denver, University of Denver Press, 1951. 240pp.
Reprinted: New York, Books for Libraries Press, 1968.

1164 COATES, Walter John
Vermont in heart and song: tributes to the state from her early singers,
compiled by Walter John Coates. North Montpelier (Vt), printed as one of
'ye alle tyme gifte bookes', 1926. 44pp.
Limited edition: 500 copies.

1165 COATES, Walter John and TUPPER, Frederick
Vermont verse: an anthology, edited by Walter John Coates and Frederick Tupper. Brattleboro, Stephen Daye Press, 1931. 256pp, illus.

WEST INDIES See: 1156

PATRIOTISM

ENGLISH PATRIOTISM

1166 AUCHMUTY, Arthur Compton
  Poems of English heroism from Brunanburh to Lucknow, from Athelstan
to Albert, collected and arranged with notes historical and illustrative by
Arthur Compton Auchmuty. London, Kegan Paul & Trench, 1882. ix,
152pp.
Mostly well-known poets of the nineteenth century.

1167 BELL, G K A
  Poems of patriotism, edited by G K A Bell. London, Routledge; New
York, Dutton, [1907]. vii, 248pp. (The Golden Anthologies series.)

1168 CORFIELD, Mary Hay
  The loyal heart: an anthology on monarchy and country for the year
of the silver jubilee of his Majesty the King, May 1935 to April 1936, compiled by Mary Hay Corfield. London, Elliot Stock, 1935. 111pp.
Headings: Loyalty; The soul of England; Glory of the gardens; Seeking the
beautiful; The glamour of Scotland; All saints tide—they that serve in the
church; The friendship in homes; Christmastide; New year; Voices of spring;
Freedom—the call of the sea; Eastertide—service and deeds of bravery for
the Empire.
Prose and poetry of the nineteenth and twentieth centuries.

1169 HALLIDAY, Wilfrid J
  Pro patria: a book of patriotic verse, compiled by Wilfrid J Halliday.
London, Dent, 1915. 220pp. Notes.
Mainly well-known nineteenth century poets; poetry on valour on the field
of battle, love of one's country and the nobility of sacrifice.

1170 KNIGHT, William Angus
  Pro patria et regina: being poems from nineteenth century writers in
Great Britain and America, issued in aid of Her Majesty Queen Alexandra's
fund for soldiers and sailors, [compiled] by William Angus Knight. Glasgow,
J Maclehose, 1901. xxi, 163pp.

1171 LEONARD, R M
  Patriotic poems, selected by R M Leonard. London, Oxford University
Press, 1914. 128pp. Notes. (Oxford Garlands series.)

1172 SALT, L Goodwin
   English patriotic poetry, selected and edited by L Goodwin Salt. London,
Cambridge University Press, 1911. lx, 160pp. Notes (pp 91-160).
Poetry from the sixteenth to the nineteenth century.

1173 SALT, R P and WALLAS, Katharine T
   The call of the homeland: a collection of English verse, selected and arranged by R P Scott and Katharine T Wallas. London, Blackie [1908];
426pp.
Headings: Echoes from history; echoes from history—some ideals of the
nineteenth century; Britain overseas; The sea; The changing year; English
countryside; Home; Exile; Compatriots; The call to serve; The call to happiness.
Known and less well known poets, mostly of the nineteenth century.

1174 STANLEY, Arthur
   Patriotic song: a book of English verse; being an anthology of the patriotic poetry of the British Empire from the defeat of the Spanish Armada
till the death of Queen Victoria, selected and arranged by Arthur Stanley;
with an introduction by the Reverend J E C Welldon. London, C A Pearson,
1901. xxvii, 363pp. Notes.
Headings: England; Wales; Scotland; Jacobite songs; Ireland; Canada; India;
South Africa; Australia; New Zealand.
Poetry from the sixteenth to nineteenth century; includes some unknown
poets.

1175 WEDMORE, F and WEDMORE, M
   Poems of the love and pride of England, edited by F and M Wedmore.
London, Ward Lock, 1897. xvi, 291pp. Notes. Familiar poets of the nine-
teenth century.

Studies and criticism

1176 DOBREE, Bonomy
   The theme of patriotism in the poetry of the early eighteenth century,
by Bonomy Dobrée. London, Geoffrey Cumberlege, 1949. 19pp.
The Wharton Lecture on English Poetry, British Academy, 1949.

1177 PIERCE, John Roland
   English nationalistic poetry, 1485-1558. PhD thesis, Ohio State University, 1959.

1178 PRZEGONIA-KRYNSKI, S L
   Patriotism in English poetry, 1702-1832. BLitt thesis, Oxford University,
1947.

IRISH PATRIOTISM

Studies and criticism

1179 LOFTUS, Richard J
Nationalism in modern Anglo-Irish poetry, [by] Richard J Loftus. Madison, Milwaukee, University of Wisconsin Press, 1964. 363pp. Bibliography (pp 334-346). Notes (pp 287-333).
Chapters: For Houlihan's daughter; The Irish heritage; W B Yeats: the national ideals; W B Yeats: the holy land of Ireland; AE (George W Russell): the land of promise; Pearse, Macdonagh and Plunkett: the Messianic ideal; Padraic Colum: the peasant nation; James Stephens: the nation of love; F R Higgins: the gold and honey country; Austin Clarke: Ireland of the black church; Conclusion.

AMERICAN PATRIOTISM

1180 DOREN, Carl van
The patriotic anthology, introduced by Carl van Doren. Garden City, New York, Doubleday & Doran, 1941. xxvii, 527pp.

1181 GATHANY, Jesse Madison
American patriotism in prose and verse, 1771-1918, selected and edited by Jesse Madison Gathany. New York, Macmillan, 1919. xiv, 305pp, front. (Macmillan's Pocket American and English Classics series.)

1182 HOWARD, John R
Poems of heroism in American life, edited by John R Howard. New York, Crowell, [1922]. xviii, 353pp.

1183 MATTHEWS, James Brander
Poems of American patriotism, chosen by James Brander Matthews. New York, Scribners, 1882. xiii, 285pp.
Revised and enlarged edition: illustrated by N C Wyeth. 1922. xviii, 222pp, col plates.

1184 NEGLEY, Harry Elliott
Poems with a punch for patriotic people, [compiled] by Harry Elliott Negley. Indianapolis, the compiler, 1918. 116pp.

1185 PAGET, R L
Poems of American patriotism, 1776-1898, selected by R L Paget. Boston, L C Page, 1898. xiv, 414pp.
Second edition: 1898. xvi, 421pp.
Third edition: 1926. xiv, 393pp, plates, ports.
Reprinted: New York, Books for Libraries, 1970.

1186 WOOD, Dorothy Carrico
This nation: the spirit of America in songs, speeches, poems and documents, [compiled] by Dorothy Carrico Wood; illustrated by J W McDaniel. Cleveland, World Publishing, [1967]. 175pp, illus.
Intended for children.

HISTORY

GENERAL

1187 BOWLIN, William R
A book of historical poems, compiled and edited by William Bowlin.
Chicago, A Whitman, 1939. ix, 158pp, illus.
English and American poetry.

1188 FORD, James Lauren and FORD, Mary K
Every day in the year: a poetical epitome of the world's history, edited
by James L Ford and Mary K Ford. New York, Dodd & Mead, 1902. ix,
443pp.
Reprinted: Detroit, Gale, 1969.

1189 FORD, Henry Allen
Poems of history by famous poets of all ages relating to most notable
nations, eras, events and characters of the past from the time of Adam to
the year 1883, chosen and annotated by Henry Allen Ford. Detroit, M W
Ellsworth, 1883. viii, 469pp, illus, plates.

1190 HINE, Al
From other lands: poetry that makes history live, [compiled] by Al
Hine. Philadelphia, Lippincott, 1969. 281pp.
113 short poems and excerpts from longer poems, mainly by British poets
commemorating heroic deeds and personalities significant in the history of
Western civilization from the siege of Troy to the Vietnam War.

1191 McGRADY, S H
Musa historica: an anthology of poems of world history, selected and
edited by S H McGrady. London, Herbert Russell, [1926]. 120pp.

See also: 315, 413; Protest and revolt 736-739; Freedom 740-748

Antiquity

1192 ASHTON, Dore
Poets and the past: an anthology of poems and objects of art of the pre-
Columbian past, edited by Dore Ashton; photographs by Lee Boltin. New
York, Andre Emmerich Gallery, 1959. 66pp, illus.
Twentieth century poems reflecting on various aspects of antiquity.

Eighteenth century

1193 (BIBLIOGRAPHY) ROGAL, Samuel J
  Poems occasioned by the War of the Spanish Succession, 1701-1714 (in
Bulletin of Bibliography, Vol 29 January-March 1972, pp 7-9).

Twentieth century   *Studies and criticism*

1194 BOWRA, Cecil Maurice
  Poetry and politics, 1900-1960, by C M Bowra. London, Cambridge
University Press, 1966. 157pp. References and notes.
Chapters: The change of attitude; Prophets and seers; The private vision;
Conflicts and uncertainties.
Covers English, German, French, Italian, Spanish, and Greek poetry.

WAR

General

1195 ADAMS, Anthony
  War, edited by Anthony Adams. Oxford, Pergamon, 1968. 113pp.
(Explorations series.)
Poetry and prose, mostly of the twentieth century, by well-known authors.

1196 ADLER, Kurt
  Songs of many wars, from the sixteenth century to the twentieth, selec-
ted and arranged by Kurt Adler. New York, Howell & Soskin, 1943. 221pp,
Music.

1197 BALLADS OF FAMOUS FIGHTS
  illustrated in colour by W H C Groome, Archibald Webb and Dudley
Tennant. London, Henry Frowde, Hodder & Stoughton, 1910. 79pp,
plates.
Fifteen items on famous battles by nineteenth century poets.

1198 BOLD, Alan
  The martial muse: seven centuries of war poetry, selected and edited with
an introduction and notes by Alan Bold. Exeter, A Wheaton, 1976. 227pp.
Bibliography. Biographical notes. Notes. (Wheaton Studies in Literature.)
Poetry by well-known poets from the Middle Ages to the twentieth century,
with an emphasis on the twentieth. Introduction: pp 13-56.

1199 BUSH, Eric Wheler
  Salute the soldier: an anthology of quotations, poems and prose, edited
by Captain Eric Wheler Bush. London, Allen and Unwin, 1966. xxxviii,
435pp.
Headings: Prelude to arms; Great captains (Cromwell, Marlborough, Mal-
paquet, Clive, Wolfe, Abercomby, Wellington). The peninsular war, 1808-
1814; Waterloo and afterwards; A hundred years, 1814-1914; The great war,

1914-1918; The great war, 1914-1918 overseas; The second world war–the
battle of France; –the Middle East; –the onslaught of Japan; Last post.
Each section is prefixed with a series of short quotations. Some poetry, but
mostly prose extracts from histories, accounts and diaries.

1200 BUTLER, Harold E
  War songs of Britain, selected by Harold E Butler. London, Archibald
Constable, 1903. 239pp. Notes.
Nineteenth century poetry on war and battles by well-known poets.

1201 CLARK, Leonard
  Sound of battle, edited by Leonard Clark; illustrated by Ewart Oakeshott.
Oxford, Pergamon, 1969. xiii, 137pp, illus. (The Pergamon English Library.)

1202 COLLINS, V H
  Poems of war and battle, selected by V H Collins. Oxford, Clarendon
Press, 1914. 192pp.
Nineteenth century poetry on battles by well-known poets.

1203 CROMIC, Robert
  Where steel winds blow: poets on war, a collection, edited by Robert
Cromic. New York, David McKay, 1968. xxvii, 188pp.
Twentieth century American and English poetry, mostly anti-war; includes
some Chinese poems in translation.

1204 DALLAS, Karl
  The cruel wars: one hundred soldiers songs from Agincourt to Ulster, compiled by Karl Dallas. London, Wolfe, 1972. 272pp. Music.

1205 (BIBLIOGRAPHY) DENISOFF, R Serge
  Songs of protest, war and peace: a bibliography and discography, compiled by R Serge Denisoff. Santa Barbara (California); Oxford, Clio Press,
1973. 76pp. (War and Peace Bibliography series.)
Contains: books (pp 3-10), periodicals (pp 11-32), songbooks; Selected
propaganda songs in Communist party publications (1932-1949); Songs of
war and peace: sing out (1950-1964); Selected songs of war and peace:
Broadside (NYC) (1962-1972); Selected discography of American protest
songs; Selected discography of patriotic country and western songs; Country
music and patriotic songs; Literature on the radical right's attack upon protest songs.

1206 DICKINSON, Patric
  Soldiers' verse: verses chosen by Patric Dickinson; with original litho-
graphy by William Scott. London, Frederic Muller, 1945. viii, 119pp, col
illus. (New Excursions into English Poetry series.)
Twentieth and some nineteenth century poetry.

1207 DOLPH, Edward Arthur
  'Sound off!': soldier songs from the Revolution to World War II, edited
by Edward Arthur Dolph; music arranged by Philip Egner, illustrated by
Lawrence Schick. New York, Farrer & Rinehart, 1942. xiii, 621pp, illus.

1208 EAGER, Alexander
    Songs of the sword and the soldier, collected and edited by Alexander
Eager. London, Sands, 1901. xii, 281pp.
Headings: The praise of the sword; The glory of the banner; The summons
to war; Doughty deeds; Hope in defeat and death on the field of honour;
Gallant lost causes; The soldier's life; The praise of a man's fatherland.
Mainly nineteenth century poetry, of a patriotic nature; includes some
German pieces in translation.

1209 EBERHART, Richard and RODMAN, Selden
    War and the poet: an anthology of poetry expressing man's attitude to
war from the ancient times to the present, edited by Richard Eberhart and
Selden Rodman. New York, Devin-Adair, 1945. xxiv, 240pp. Biographical
notes.
A multilingual anthology in translation; covers all periods but has an emphasis on the nineteenth and twentieth centuries.

1210 FAWSIDE, John
    The flag of England: ballads of the brave and poems of patriotism, selec-
ted by John Fawside. London, Eveleigh Nash, 1914. 218pp. Notes.
Poetry from the seventeenth to nineteenth century, mostly by well-known
poets, on battles, war, freedom, etc.

1211 FERGUSON, John
    War and the creative arts: an anthology edited by John Ferguson.
London, Macmillan in association with the Open University Press, 1972.
380pp, plates (some col).
Prose and poetry covering wars from the eighteenth to twentieth century
with an emphasis on the two World Wars. Includes some twentieth century
material by foreign writers in translation. Notes on the text and illustrations:
pp 360-372. Plates are reproductions of works of art. Designed as a companion to the Open University course A301: War and Society.

1212 FOSTER, A E Manning
    Lord God of battles: a war anthology, compiled by A E Manning Foster.
London, Cape & Fenwick, 1914. 78pp.
Mainly nineteenth century poetry by well-known poets.

1213 GEORGE, Daniel
    All in a maze: a collection of poetry and prose, chronologically arranged
by Daniel George with some assistance from Rose Macaulay. London,
Collins, 1938. 488pp.
A wide ranging anthology covering all periods. Includes prose extracts from
speeches, newspapers, letters and diaries. The compiler's aim was to 'illustrate . . . the continual clash between man's sense of the horror, folly and
waste . . . and the recurrent fits of madness in which he plunges into it with
noble, savage and often pious cries'.

1214 GOODCHILD, George
England, my England: a war anthology, [compiled] by George Good-child. London, 1914. 223pp.
Headings: Poems inspired by the present war; Historical (pp 37-188); Patriotic and miscellaneous.
Poetry from the seventeenth to nineteenth century, by mostly well-known poets.

1215 HARDIE, John
Verses of valour: an anthology of shorter war poems of sea, land, air, selected and arranged by John L Hardie. Glasgow, Art and Educational Publishers, 1943. xv, 128pp, illus. Notes.
Poetry from the seventeenth to twentieth century, by mostly well-known poets.

1216 JONES, Donald Lewis
War poetry: an anthology, edited with an introduction and commentaries by D L Jones. Oxford, Pergamon, 1968. xi, 142pp. (Pergamon Oxford English series.)
Poetry by well-known poets from the seventeenth to twentieth century. Commentaries on each poem.

1217 KNIGHT, W A
Pro patria et rege: poems on war—its characteristics and results, selected in aid of the Belgian relief fund from British and American sources by Professor Knight with an explanatory preface dedicated to Lord Roberts.
London, J Bennett (the Century Press), 1915. xxix, 218pp.
Poetry of the nineteenth and twentieth centuries.
Second series: xxviii, 204pp. [1915]. Contains less familiar poets.

1218 LING, Peter
Gentlemen at arms: portraits of soldiers in fact and fiction in peace and war: an anthology of prose and poetry, chosen, introduced and with a foreword by Peter Ling. London, Peter Owen, 1969. 248pp, plates.
Headings: Alexander to Marlborough; Culloden to the workhouse; The last hundred years.
Prose and poetry from the seventeenth to twentieth century; mostly prose extracts from novels, plays, letters and memoirs.

1219 [LUCAS, E V]
Remember Louvain—a little book of liberty and war. London, Methuen, 1914. vii, 86pp. Preface is signed E V L.
Headings: Liberty; The call to arms; Our sea; Great hearts; Great deeds; Home; The toll; After.
Poetry mostly of the nineteenth century by well-known poets.

1220 MacLEAY, John
War songs and ballads of martial life, selected with an introductory note, by John MacLeay. London, Walter Scott, [1900]. xxix, 226pp, port (of Lord Roberts). (Canterbury Poets series.)

Headings: National: Patriotic; War and battle; The call to arms; Soldiers and soldiering; Love; After the battle.
Poetry of the seventeenth to nineteenth century, mostly of the nineteenth, by Scott, Burns and others.

1221 OMMANNEY, E C
  True to the flag: soldiers poems, compiled by E C Ommanney. London, Routledge; New York, Dutton, 1904. xvi, 196pp.
Nineteenth century poetry, mostly by well-known poets, on heroism, patriotism and battle.

1222 PARKER, T H and TESKEY, F J
  Five faces of war, edited by T H Parker and F J Teskey. Glasgow, Blackie, 1970. 58pp, illus.
Headings: Reflections on war; Children and war; Women and war; The fighting man dies; The future?
Twentieth century prose and poetry. Intended for school use.

1223 RUTTER, Owen
  We happy few: an anthology by Owen Rutter; with eleven engravings by John O'Connor. London, Golden Cockerel Press, 1946. 150pp, illus.
Headings: Britain at war; Britain at sea; Britain in the air.
Poetry and prose extracts (letters, speeches, etc) from the seventeenth to twentieth century. Limited edition: 750 copies.

1224 SHEPPARD, E W
  Red coat: an anthology of the British soldier, by E W Sheppard. London, Batchworth Press, 1952. xiii, 245pp, plates.
Mostly prose extracts; pp 92-8: 'the soldier in poetry and song'.

1225 STANLEY, Arthur
  Britain at war: an anthology selected and arranged by Arthur Stanley. London, Eyre & Spottiswoode, 1943. vii, 335pp.
Headings: Lilies of France; Scottish interlude; Galleons of Spain; Puritans and cavaliers; Malbrook s'en va-t-en guerre; Romantic war; War in the age of reason; Our struggle with Napoleon; The course of empire; Our own times.
Poetry and prose from the fifteenth to twentieth century. Compiler claims that the majority of the items have not, to his knowledge, been included in any previous anthology.

1226 SYMONS, Julian
  An anthology of war poetry, compiled by Julian Symons. Harmondsworth (Middx), Penguin, 1942. xv, 189pp, port (of the compiler).
Poetry from the sixteenth to twentieth century, arranged chronologically.

1227 STONE, Christopher
  War songs, selected by Christopher Stone; with an introduction by Sir Ian Hamilton. Oxford, Clarendon Press, 1908. xviii, 188pp. Notes (pp 174-185).
Songs and ballads from the Middle Ages to the nineteenth century. Much

of the anonymous material is derived from broadside collections in the
Bodleian and British Museum libraries.

1228 WILLIAMS, Oscar
The war poets: an anthology of the war poetry of the twentieth century,
edited with an introduction by Oscar Williams. New York, John Day, 1945.
485pp, ports. Biographical notes.
American and English poetry of the two world wars. pp 12-30: comments
by the poets on war poetry.

1229 WINSTOCK, Lewis
Songs and music of the redcoats: a history of the war music of the British
army 1642-1902, [by] Lewis Winstock. London, Leo Cooper, 1970. viii,
298pp. Bibliography. Music.
Headings: The civil wars 1642-1655; Lilliburlero and the war of the Spanish
succession 1688-1713; The Jacobite risings 1715 and 1745; The seven years
war 1756-1763; The American war of independence 1775-1783, and the
war of 1812; The French wars 1793-1815; The Crimean war 1854-1856;
The Indian mutiny 1857-1858; Egypt and the Sudan 1882-1898; The little
wars of the nineteenth century; The South African war 1899-1902.
Covers the songs and music that were an integral part of the military events.
Many examples with a running commentary.

See also: 418, 421, 662, 998

Studies and criticism

1230 ACKERMAN, Robert W
Armour and weapons in the Middle English romances (in Research Studies
of the State College of Washington, Vol 7 June 1939, pp 104-118). References in footnotes.

1231 BANERJEE, A
Spirit above wars: a study of the English poetry of the two world wars,
by A Banerjee. London, Macmillan, 1976. 240pp. Bibliography (pp 213-
224).
Chapters: The pre-war poetic scene; Poets of the first world war: Brooke,
Grenfell, Sorley, Sassoon, Owen and Rosenberg; Poetry of the second world
war; Keith Douglas; Alun Lewis; Sidney Keyes.
Bibliography covers primary and secondary sources for the works of individual poets; lists also short contemporary articles on war poetry in general.

1232 BARTEL, Roland
Anti-war sentiment in the late eighteenth century. PhD thesis, Indiana
University, 1952.

1232a BROWN, Lilian Rowland
War poetry of women (in Nineteenth Century, Vol 81 February 1917,
pp 434-452).
Covers the work of unknown French and English poetesses from the sixteenth
to nineteenth century.

1233 CREWE, R O A
War and English poetry, by the Most Hon the Marquess of Crewe, K G.
London, English Association, 1917. 26pp. (English Association Pamphlet
no 38.)
A brief study of war poetry up to the first world war.

1234 JONES, R A
War and peace in English poetry, 1780-1830. MA thesis, University of
Wales, 1948.

1235 McDERMOTT, Francis Joseph
The impact of war on British poetry, 1830-1914. PhD thesis, Harvard
University, 1965.

1236 O'SHEA, M A
English poetry and war. MA thesis, National University of Ireland, 1931.

1237 PHIPPS, Frank
The image of war in America 1891-1917: a study of a literary theme and
its cultural origins and analogies. PhD thesis, Ohio State University, 1953.

1238 RAMSEY, Lee Carter
The theme of battle in Old English poetry. PhD thesis, Indiana University, 1965.

1239 RIES, Lawrence Robert
The response to violence in contemporary British poetry. PhD thesis,
Southern Illinois University, 1971.

1240 WARREN, Thomas Herbert
Poetry and war, by Sir Herbert Warren. London, Oxford University Press,
[1915]; 31pp. (Oxford Pamphlets series.)

First World War

1241 ANDREWS, Clarence Edmund
From the front: trench poetry selected by Lieutenant C E Andrews with
an introduction by the editor. New York, London, D Appleton, 1918.
xxviii, 220pp.
Poetry by unknown poets evoking all aspects of daily life at the trenches.

1242 (BIBLIOGRAPHY) BIRMINGHAM PUBLIC LIBRARY
Catalogue of the war poetry collection. (Birmingham), 1921. vii, 60pp.
Covers mainly English works by individual authors, but includes some
foreign material, some anthologies and criticism.

1243 BLACK, E L
1914-1918 in poetry: an anthology, selected and edited by E L Black.
London, University of London Press, 1970. 157pp. Biographical notes.
Notes (pp 128-140).
Headings: Early visions; Puzzled questioning; Realism on the western front;
The pity of it; Bitter satire; Comments from remoter points in place and time.

Well-known poets. Each section has a substantial introduction. Intended
for upper forms of schools and students in colleges of education.

1244 BRAITHWAITE, William Stanley
Victory! celebrated by thirty-eight American poets, brought together by
William Stanley Braithwaite; with an introduction by Theodore Roosevelt.
Boston, Small & Maynard, 1919. viii, 84pp.
Poems on patriotism, glory and universal peace and brotherhood. Poems
to Marshal Foch, Sir Douglas Haig, General Pershing, General Armando
Diaz, General Leonard Wood and Cardinal Mercier.

1245 BRERETON, Frederick
An anthology of war poems, compiled by Frederick Brereton; introduc-
tion by Edmund Blunden. London, Collins, 1930. 191pp.
Known and unknown poets.

1246 BROOKE, Charles Frederick Tucker and CANBY, Henry Seidel
War aims and peace ideals: selections in prose and verse illustrating the
aspirations of the modern world, selected by Charles Frederick Tucker
Brooke and Henry Seidel Canby. New Haven, Yale University Press, 1919.
xi, 264pp.

1247 BROPHY, John and PARTRIDGE, Eric
Songs and slang of the British soldier, 1914-1918, edited by John Brophy
and Eric Partridge. London, Scholartis Press, 1930. 200pp.
Songs—I: predominatly sung on the march (26 items); II: songs sung on the
march, but more often in billets and estaminets (16 items); III: chants and
songs, rarely if ever sung on the march (12 items). Glossary: pp 93-190.
Appendices: chants and sayings; bugle calls.
Second edition: London, Scholartis Press, 1930. 222pp. Postscript
(pp 203-222) gives a further ten songs and the glossary contains 100 further
words, with additional material in the appendices.
Third edition: London, Scholartis Press, 1931. 383pp. Additional songs,
chants and sayings. pp 231-238: music hall songs.
Fourth edition: The long trail: what the British soldier sang and said in
the Great War of 1914-1918. London, André Deutsch, 1965. 239pp, plates.
Bibliography.
Similar to the third edition, but some passages have been removed and re-
placed. Plates consist of photographs, cartoons and posters.

1248 CAWS, B W and WATTS, R F
What greater glory? a scrapbook of the first world war, compiled by
B W Caws and R F Watts. Glasgow, London, Blackie, 1974. 88pp, illus.
Music. Bibliography.
Prose and poetry. Illustrations include facsimiles of official forms and an-
nouncements, newspaper extracts and notices. Bibliography (pp 85-86)
lists further source material: autobiography and personal accounts, history,
fiction and poetry.

1249 CLARKE, George Herbert
   A treasury of war poetry: British and American poems of the world war 1914-1918, edited with introduction and notes by George Herbert Clarke. London, Hodder & Stoughton, 1917. 448pp.
Headings: England; Scotland; Ireland; Canada; Australasia; Belgium; France; America; Great Britain and America; Italy; Serbia; Greece and Romania; Liege; Ypres; Verdun; Oxford; Reflections; Incidents and aspects; Poets militant; Keeping the seas; The airmen; The wounded; The fallen; Women and the war; Peace; Known and unknown heroes.

1250 COLLECTION OF POEMS RELATING TO THE EUROPEAN WAR
   from newspapers, magazines, etc. 1914-1917. 5 vols. 72 pages in each vol.
A collection of cuttings from a wide range of local and national newspapers and magazines. The name Gladys Pehrson is embossed on the binding of the first volume. Location: War Poetry Collection, Birmingham Reference Library.

1251 COLLECTION OF POEMS RELATING TO THE EUROPEAN WAR
   1914-1918, from newspapers, magazines, etc. 36 vols. 98 pages in each vol.
Collection of cuttings from a wide range of newspapers and magazines. Location: War Poetry Collection, Birmingham Reference Library.

1252 CUNLIFFE, J W
   Poems of the great war, selected by J W Cunliffe on behalf of the Belgium Scholarship Committee. New York, Macmillan, 1916. xx, 297pp.
Consists of Australian, Canadian, Indian, British and American poetry.

1253 EATON, W D
   War in verse and prose, edited with introduction, notes and original matter by W D Eaton. Chicago, Denison, 1918. 199pp.

1254 ELLIOTT, H B
   Lest we forget: a war anthology, edited by H B Elliott; foreword by Baroness Orczy. London, Jarrold, 1915. 143pp, illus.
Poetry of a patriotic and elegiac nature taken mostly from newspapers and reviews.

1255 FORSHAW, Charles F
   One hundred of the best poems on the European war by poets of the empire, edited by Charles F Forshaw. London, Elliot Stock, 1915. 2 vols. 192pp; 170pp.

1256 FOXCROFT, Frank
   War verse, edited by Frank Foxcroft. New York, Crowell, 1918. xii, 303pp.
The American National Union Catalogue lists this edition and also a seventh edition: 1918. xv, 373pp.

1257 GARDNER, Brian
   Up the line to death: the war poets 1914-1918, an anthology, selected and arranged with an introduction and notes by Brian Gardner; foreword by Edmund Blunden. London, Methuen, 1964. xxv, 185pp. Biographical notes.
Headings: Happy is England now; Field manoeuvres; Tipperary days; To unknown lands; Home front; Death's kingdom; A bitter taste; Behind the lines: O Jesus, make it stop; At last, at last.
Mostly well-known poets.

1258 GARVIN, John W
   Canadian poems of the great war, chosen and edited by John W Garvin. Toronto, McClelland & Steward, 1918. 256pp. Biographical notes.
Includes 'The Shell' by A C Stewart.

1259 GIBBONS, Herbert Adams
   Songs from the trenches: the soul of the A E F: a collection of verses by American soldiers in France, brought together by Herbert Adams Gibbons from poems submitted in the prize competition of the New York Herald. New York, London, Harper, 1918. xv, 207pp.
Mostly light verse by unknown poets. Includes: 'The greasy army cooks', by James E Dimond, 'Chant of army cooks', by John T Winterich, and 'I love corned beef' by A P Bowen.

1260 GRETTON, M Sturge
   Calendar of the war, [compiled] by M Sturge Gretton [with appropriate readings, chiefly poetry]. London, Nisbet, [1919]. 122pp.

1261 HOLMAN, Carrie Ellen
   In the day of battle: poems of the great war, selected by Carrie Ellen Holman. Toronto, William Briggs, 1916. 116pp.
Consists of poetry previously published in magazines and reviews. Includes some Canadian poetry.

1262 HUSSEY, Maurice
   Poetry of the first world war: an anthology, selected and edited by Maurice Hussey. London, Longmans, 1967. xvi, 180pp. (Longmans English series.) Bibliography (further reading). Biographical notes:
Headings: Before marching (pre-war poems); Marching (pp 21-145); After marching.
Mostly well-known poets. Each section prefaced with a substantial introduction.

1263 JAQUET, E R
   These were the men: poems of the war 1914-1918, edited by E R Jaquet. London, Edinburgh, New York, Marshall Brothers, 1919. 100pp.
Mostly unknown poets. Poetry previously published in magazines and reviews.

1264 JONES, Edna D
Patriotic pieces from the great war, compiled by Edna D Jones. Philadelphia, Penn, 1918. 224pp.

1265 KANE, William Reno
Soldier's scrap book, full o' fighting songs and poems with pep, including homely parodies, gems of prose and poetry and familiar songs, original poems, songs and parodies, and the 'Corporal of our army' the prose masterpiece by George O Van Camp, [compiled] by William Reno Kane. Ridgewood (New Jersey), 1918. 111pp.

1266 LAIRD, J T
Other banners: an anthology of Australian literature of the first world war, selected and edited by J T Laird. Canberra, The Australian War Memorial and the Australian Government Publishing Service, 1971. x, 187pp. Headings: The bugles of England: early imperialistic sentiments; Dig, dig, dig until you are safe: Gallipoli (the event); Hail and farewell: Gallipoli—nationalistic and elegiac responses; The sun fairly scorched us: training in Egypt; The sky drizzles to rain: western front; Saddle and charge the magazine: desert warfare; Our heroes lost: disenchantment and pacifism; Now peace has come: return to civilian life; Blast the flaming war: seeing the lighter side; There is no glory: disenchantment and pacifism 1922-9.

1267 LEONARD, Sterling Andrus
Poems of the war and the peace, collected with a foreword and notes by Sterling Andrus Leonard. New York, Harcourt Brace, 1921. xvii, 162pp.

1268 LEVY, Edward Lawrence
Poetry relating to the great war: newspaper cuttings, 1914-19. 2 vols. 1073pp.
Covers wide range of newspapers. Location: War Poetry Collection, Birmingham Reference Library.

1269 LLOYD, Bertram
The paths to glory: a collection of poems written during the war 1914-19, edited by Bertram Lloyd. London, Allen and Unwin, 1919. 119pp.
An anti-war collection. Includes some French and German items in translation.

1270 LLOYD, Bertram
Poems written during the great war 1914-1918: an anthology, edited by Bertram Lloyd. London, Allen & Unwin, 1918. 111pp. Bibliography, (pp 110-111).
Poetry by mostly unfamiliar poets, mostly expressing sentiments of disgust and disillusionment.

1271 McALLISTER, C B
Selected poems for Armistice Day, edited by C B McAllister; illustrated by John Daniel Kreuttner. New York, Dean, 1928. v, 109pp, illus.

1272 [MacDONALD, Erskine]
A crown of Amaranth: being a collection of brave and gallant poems to the memory of the gentlemen who have given their lives for Great and Greater Britain, 1914-1918. London, Erskine MacDonald, 1915. 76pp, illus.
The editorial note is signed Erskine MacDonald and S Gertrude Ford.
Second edition: 1917. 84pp, illus.

1273 MACKLIN, Alys Eyre
The Lyceum book of war verse, edited by Alys Eyre Macklin. London, Erskine MacDonald, 1918. ix, 58pp.
Poetry by women. The editor was President of the Poetry Circle of the Lyceum Club 1913-1917.

1274 MOULT, Thomas
Cenotaph: a book of remembrance in poetry and prose for November the eleventh, compiled and edited by Thomas Moult; the frontispiece from a drawing by Joseph Pike. London, Cape, 1923. 223pp, front.

1275 NETTLEINGHAM, F T
Tommy's tunes: a comprehensive collection of soldiers' songs, marching melodies, rude rhymes and popular parodies, composed, collected and arranged on active service with the B E F by F T Nettleingham. London, Erskine MacDonald, 1917. 91pp. Music. Footnotes.

1276 NETTLEINGHAM, F T
More Tommy's tunes: a comprehensive collection of soldiers' songs, . . . arranged . . . by F T Nettleingham. London, Erskine MacDonald, 1918. 98pp. Music. Glossary, abbreviations.

1277 NICHOLS, Robert
Anthology of war poetry, 1914-1918, assembled by Robert Nichols. London, Nicholson & Watson, [1947]. 156pp.

1278 NILES, John Jacob
Singing soldiers, compiled by John J Niles; illustrated by Margaret T Williamson. New York, London, Scribner, 1927. 171pp, illus.
Reprinted: Detroit, Singing Tree Press, 1968.

1279 OSBORN, E B
The muse in arms: a collection of war poems for the most part written in the field of action by seamen, soldiers and flying men who are serving, or have served in the great war, edited with an introduction by E B Osborn. London, John Murray, 1917. xxxviii, 295pp.
Headings: The mother land; Before action; Battle pieces; The sea affair; War in the air; In memoriam; The future hope; The christian hope; School and college; Chivalry of sport; The ghostly company songs; Loving and living; Moods and memories.
Mostly unknown poets.

1280 PARSONS, I M
Men who march away: poems of the first world war, edited with an intro-
duction by I M Parsons. London, Chatto & Windus, 1965. 192pp. Biblio-
graphy.
Headings: Visions of glory; The bitter truth; No more jokes; The pity of war;
The wounded; The dead; Aftermath.
Mostly well-known poets, similar to those in 1262, but different poems chosen.

1281 SOLDIER POETS
songs of the fighting men. London, E Macdonald, 1917. 2 vols.
Preface is signed Galloway Kyle. Some poems reprinted from Poetry Review
and New Witness.

1282 SONGS AND SONNETS FOR ENGLAND IN WAR TIME
being a collection of lyrics by various authors inspired by the great war.
London, John Lane The Bodley Head, 1914. xiv, 96pp.

1283 SONGS OF THE SOLDIERS AND SAILORS, U S
Issued by the commissions on training camp activities of the Army and
Navy Departments. Washington, Government Printing Office, 1917. 62pp,
plates.

1284 THE TIMES
War poems, 1914-1915. 16pp. Issued with the Times, August 9th, 1915.

1285 TREVES, Frederick and GOODCHILD, George
Made in the trenches: composed entirely from articles and sketches con-
tributed by soldiers, edited by Sir Frederick Treves and George Goodchild.
London, Allen & Unwin, 1916. 240pp, illus.
Includes nineteen pieces of verse. Items selected from newspapers and
magazines. Limited edition: 150 copies.

1286 TROTTER, Jacqueline T
Valour and visions: poems of the war 1914-1918, arranged and edited by
Jacqueline T Trotter. London, Longmans, 1920. xii, 146pp. Notes.
Known and unknown poets. Poems, often of a poetic and nostalgic nature,
are grouped chronologically in five sections corresponding to the five years
of the war.

1287 TULLOCH, Donald
Songs and poems of the great war, [compiled] by Donald Tulloch.
Worcester (Mass), privately printed, 1915. 298pp.
Includes the national songs of the allies, in translation; and a list of British
Army regimental marches.

1288 THE VIGILANTES
Fifes and drums: a collection of poems of America at war. New York,
G H Doran, 1917. ix, 142pp. (The Vigilantes Books.)

1289 WALSH, Colin
Mud, songs and blighty: a scrapbook of the first world war, compiled by
Colin Walsh. London, Hutchinson, 1975. 176pp, illus.
Headings: I'll make a man of you; Good-bye-ee!; It's a long way to Tipperary; There's a long trail; Where are the lads of the villages tonight?; Take me
back to Old Blighty; Keep the home fires burning; The laddies who fight and
win.
Poetry, songs and prose passages. Illustrations include posters, letters, song
sheet covers and contemporary photographs.

1290 WETHERELL, James Elgin
The great war in verse and prose, selected and edited by James Elgin
Wetherell; with an introduction by H J Cody. Toronto, the Legislative
Assembly, 1919. 160pp.
'Recommended for use in schools'. Mainly patriotic items.

1291 WHEELER, W Reginald
Book of verse of the great war, edited by W Reginald Wheeler; with a
foreword by Charlton M Lewis. New Haven, Yale University Press, 1917.
xxx, 184pp.
Mostly unfamiliar poets.

1292 YORK, Dorothea
Mud and stars: an anthology of world war songs and poetry. New York,
Holt, 1931. xxv, 301pp. Bibliography. Music.
Headings—I American: Enlistment and camp songs; The sea and the navy;
France; Marching songs and trench ballads; War; Aftermath; The Russian
campaign. II British: England and the Empire; Canada; Australian.
Bibliography (pp 287-296) lists individual songs with publishers.

1293 ZIV, Frederic W
The valiant muse: an anthology of poems by poets killed in the world
war, edited by Frederic W Ziv. New York, G P Putnam, 1936. 160pp.
Mostly unknown poets.

Field-Marshal Lord Kitchener

1294 FORSHAW, Charles F
Poems in memory of the late Field-marshal Lord Kitchener, edited by
Charles F Forshaw. Bradford, Institute of British Poetry, 1916. vi, 252pp.

Studies and criticism

1295 ADCOCK, A St John
For remembrance: soldier poets who have fallen in the war, by A St
John Adcock. London, Hodder & Stoughton, 1918. 246pp, ports. Bio-
graphical notes.
Includes some little known poets.
Revised and enlarged edition: 1920. 312pp.

1296 BERGONZI, B

Heroes of twilight: a study of the literature of the great war, by B Bergonzi. London, Constable, 1965. 235pp. Bibliography. Notes.
Chapters: Between Hotspur and Falstaff: reflections on the literature of war; Brooke, Grenfell, Sorley; Graves, Blunden, Read and others. Sassoon; Rosenberg and Owen; Civilian responses; Retrospect I: autobiography; Retrospect II: fiction; Remythologizing.
Chronology of publications: 1914-1964.

1297 BLUNDEN, Edmund

War poets 1914-1918, by Edmund Blunden. London, Longmans, for the British Council, 1958. 43pp, ports. Bibliography. (Writers and their Work series, no 100.)
Chapters: Older war poetry; Rubert Brooke and others; Siegfried Sassoon; Mainly Wilfred Owen.

1298 BOWRA, Cecil Maurice

Poetry and the first world war, by Sir Maurice Bowra. The Taylorian lecture 1961. Oxford, Clarendon Press, 1961. 35pp.
Covers English, French, German, Italian and Russian poetry.

1299 (BIBLIOGRAPHY) CARROLL, J M E

A checklist of British poetry of the first world war. PhD thesis, University of Texas, 1970.
Copy in library of the Imperial War Museum, London.

1300 DAVIES, M R

British poetry 1914-1918: changing attitudes to the Great War as expressed through its poetry. MA thesis, University of Wales, 1969.

1301 FORSYTH, Alexander

The poetics of war, 1914-1918. PhD thesis, University of Edinburgh, 1971.

1302 FUSSELL, Paul

The Great War and modern memory, by Paul Fussell. New York, London, Oxford University Press, 1975. 363pp, illus, ports. References.
Chapters: A satire of circumstance; The troglodyte world; Adversary proceeding; Myth, rituals and romance; Oh what a literary war; Theatre of war; Arcadian recourses; Soldier boys; Persistence and memory.
Covers the British experience at the western front 1914-1918 and the way this experience has been remembered and mythologised. Draws on the work of well-known poets, on diaries and letters, music hall and popular lore.

1303 GREGSON, J M

Poetry of the first World War, by J M Gregson. London, Edward Arnold, 1976. 72pp. Bibliography. (Studies in English Literature no 64.)
Chapters: Rupert Brooke and the initial reaction; Charles Sorley and the first hints of realism; Siegfried Sassoon: disillusion and anger; Wilfred Owen and the wider vision of war; Isaac Rosenberg: odd man out.

1304 HART, James A
  American poetry of the first world war (1914-1920): a survey and a checklist. PhD thesis, Duke University, 1965.

1305 HEALEY, E W
  Poetry of the Great War. MA thesis, National University of Ireland, 1939.

1306 JOHNSTONE, John H
  English poetry of the first world war: a study in the evolution of lyric and narrative form, by John H Johnstone. Princeton (New Jersy), Princeton University Press, 1964. xvi, 354pp. Bibliography.
  Chapters: The early poets: Rupert Brooke, Robert Nichols, Charles Sorley; Realism and satire: Siegfried Sassoon; Undertones: Edmund Blunden; Poetry and pity: Wilfred Owen, Isaac Rosenberg; The 'higher reality': Herbert Read; The heroic vision: David Jones.

1307 LOGUE, Leona Whitworth
  Recent war lyrics: a study of war concepts in modern lyrics, by Leona Whitworth Logue; with an introduction by Robert Morss Lovett. New York, Grafton Press, 1928. 65pp. Bibliography.
  Limited edition: 500 copies.

1308 MOORE, T Sturge
  Some soldier poets, by T Sturge Moore. London, Grant Richards, [1919]. 147pp.
  Chapters on Grenfell, Brooke, Nichols, Sassoon, Graves, Sorley, Francis Ledwidge, Edward Thomas, F W Harvey, Richard Aldington and Alan Seeger.

1309 (BIBLIOGRAPHY) MORRISON, Hugh Alexander
  Guide to the poetry of the world war, compiled by Hugh Alexander Morrison. Washington, 1921. 376pp.
  Contents; author list; title list. Includes European poetry which has appeared in translation. Typescript in the Library of Congress.

1310 PANAHI, M H
  A critical study of the poetry of war 1914-1918. MA thesis, Exeter University, 1964.

1311 SILKIN, Jon
  Out of battle: the poetry of the great war, by Jon Silkin. London, Oxford University Press, 1972. x, 366pp. Bibliography (pp 352-356).
  Chapters on: Hardy, Kipling, Brooke, Sorley, Edward Thomas, Blunden, Ivor Guerney, Sassoon, Herbert Read, Richard Aldington, Ford Maddox Ford, Owen, Rosenberg, David Jones.

1312 SPEAR, Hilda D
  Poetry and the first world war. PhD thesis, Leicester University, 1972.

1313 WIDDOWSON, P J
Illusion and disillusion in the English poetry and painting of the first
world war. PhD thesis, Nottingham University, 1968.

Spanish Civil War   Studies and criticism

1314 FORD, Hugh Douglas
British poetry of the Spanish civil war. PhD thesis, University of Pennsylvania, 1961.

1315 MUSTE, J M
Say that we saw Spain die: literary consequences of the Spanish civil war,
by J M Muste. Seattle, University of Washington Press, 1966. xi, 208pp.

1316 ROSENTHAL, Marilyn
Poetry of the Spanish civil war. PhD thesis, New York University,
1972.

Second World War

1317 BECKWITH, E G C
Selections from 'The quill': a collection of prose, verse and sketches by
officers prisoner-of-war in Germany, 1940-1945, edited by Captain E G C
Beckwith. London, Country Life, 1947. 264pp, illus (some col).

1318 BLYTHE, Ronald
Components of the scene: stories poems and essays of the second world
war, introduced and edited by Ronald Blythe. Harmondsworth (Middx),
Penguin, 1966. 398pp. Biographical notes.
Headings: The city; The sky; The sea; Declarations; The patient khaki beast;
Confessions and conclusions; The dark.
Mostly well-known authors.

1319 CAWS, B W and WATTS, R F
The earthquake hour: a scrapbook of the second world war, compiled by
B W Caws and R F Watts. Glasgow, Blackie, 1976. 88pp, illus, ports. Mu-
sic.
Prose and poetry.

1320 CLARKE, George Herbert
The new treasury of war poetry: poems of the second world war, edited
with an introduction and notes by George Herbert Clarke. Boston, Hough-
ton Mifflin, [1945]. xxxiv, 285pp.
Headings: America; England and America; England; France; Russia; Norway;
Czechoslovakia; Greece; Poland; Canada; South Africa; Dunkirk; Raids and
ruins; Keeping the seas; The flyers; The fallen; The dictators. The conquered;
Incidents and aspects; Reflections; Women and the war; Peace.
Covers a considerable amount of poetry by unknown poets.

1321 CUNARD, Nancy
Poems for France, written by British poets on France since the war, collected by Nancy Cunard, with autobiographical notes of the authors. London, La France Libre, 1944. 95pp.
Poems, mostly by unknown English poets, taken from journals, reviews and anthologies, mainly concerned with France during the second world war.

1322 CURREY, R N and GIBSON, R V
Poems from India by members of the forces, chosen by R N Currey and R V Gibson. London, Oxford University Press, 1946. xx, 166pp. Biographical notes.
Headings: Indian scene; Nostalgia; Ex India; Troops; War.

1323 GARDNER, Brian
The terrible rain: the war poets 1939-1945: an anthology, selected and arranged with an introduction and notes by Brian Gardner. London, Methuen, 1966. xxv, 227pp. Biographical notes.
Headings: Yes, we are going to suffer; Take your gun; The new learning; When no allies are left; The blazing fire; Johnny the bright star; One more day of war; The desert; The cruel sea; Home front; Beneath the German sky; Brief encounter; After several years; The jungle; Into Europe; Victory.
Poetry covering all aspects of the war by familiar and unfamiliar poets.

1324 HAMBLETT, Charles
I burn for England: an anthology of the poetry of World War II, selected and introduced by Charles Hamblett. London, Leslie Frewin, 1966. 403pp.
Covers the work of 142 mostly unfamiliar poets.

1325 HAMILTON, Ian
The poetry of war 1939-1945, edited by Ian Hamilton. London, Ross, 1965. x, 173pp, plates (including ports).
Reprinted in paperback: London, New English Library, 1972.

1326 KING, Amabel Reeves
Voices of victory: representative poetry of Canada in wartime, compiled by Amabel Reeves King. Toronto, Macmillan, 1942. xii, 97pp.

1327 LEDWARD, Patricia and STRANG, Colin
Poems of this war by younger poets, edited by Patricia Ledward and Colin Strang; with an introduction by Edmund Blunden. London, Cambridge University Press, 1942. xii, 99pp.
Headings: 'We saw doom patterned in the ordinary sky'; 'Line after line, we wheel to enter battle'; 'After the sirens sound'; In Memoriam; Songs in wartime; Love and friendship; In the midst of death is life.
Mostly unknown poets.
Reissued: 1947, with the title: Retrospect 1939-42.

1328 MUDIE, Ian
Poets at war: an anthology of verse by Australian servicemen, compiled by Ian Mudie. Melbourne, Georgian House 1944. 154pp. (A Jindyworobak Publication.)

1329

1330 PAGE, Martin
For gawdsake don't take me: songs, ballads, verses, monologues, etc of
the call-up years, 1939-1945, edited by Martin Page; illustrated by Bill
Tidy. London, Hart-Davis, 1976. 187pp, illus.
Heading: You, you and you; A day in the life of a squadron; Our fun; Wartime experiences; The gremlins in Husky; Love, lust and the like; Our ribald
ditties; The concert party; Sod's operas; Bolshies; Korea: when the ice is on
the rice; Odds and sods; The home front; Envoi.

1331 PAGE, Martin
Kiss me goodnight Sergeant Major: the songs and ballads of World War
II, edited by Martin Page; illustrated by Bill Tidy, introduction by Spike
Milligan. London, Hart-Davis, 1973. 192pp, illus.
Headings: I don't want to go to war; We had a sergeant major; The Nazi
gang; The literary life; Land of heat and sweaty socks; Patriotic poetesses;
Allies; Frightfully GHQ; A soldier came on leave one day; Wearing Khaki
bloomers; The paras; Flying; In the prison camps; Invasion; The forgotten
army.

1332 PALMER, Edgar A
G I songs, written, composed or collected by 'The men in Service', edited
by Edgar A Palmer; illustrated by A Loederer and Kurt Werth. New York,
Sheridan House, 1944. 253pp, illus. Music.

1333 POEMS FROM ITALY
Verses written by members of the Eighth Army in Sicily and Italy, July
1943—March 1944. London, Harrap, 1945. 92pp.
Foreword by Lieutenant General Sir Oliver Leese (formerly Commander of
the Eighth Army) and an introduction by Siegfried Sassoon. Poems submitted in poetry competitions organised in the Eighth Army by the Army
Educational Corps.

1334 POEMS FROM THE DESERT
Verses by members of the Eighth Army; with a foreword by General Sir
Bernard Montgomery. London, Harrap, 1944. 45pp.
Limited edition: 110 copies. Twenty-seven poems, twenty-six of which
were considered the best entries in a poetry competition organised by the
Eight Army's education officer.

1335 POEMS OF THE FORCES
The Fortune forces' anthology. London, Fortune Press, [1949]. 152pp.
Poetry by unknown poets, mostly relating to war experience.

1336 POSSELT, Eric
Give out!: songs of, by and for men in service, edited by Eric Posselt;
illustrated by Dave Breger, G Frank, Fritz Kredel and others. New York,
Arrowhead Press, [1943]. 128pp, illus. Music.

1337 PUDNEY, John and TREECE, Henry
Air force poetry, edited by John Pudney and Henry Treece. London, John Lane The Bodley Head, 1944. 90pp.
Poems on bombing, flying and war in general by pilots and aircraftsmen.

1338 REVEILLE
War poems by members of our armed forces, selected by Daniel Henderson, John Kieran and Grantland Rice. New York, A S Barnes, 1943. xviii, 254pp.

1339 ROSCOE, Theodora and WERE, Mary Winter
Poems by contemporary women, compiled by Theodora Roscoe and Mary Winter Were; with a foreword by P H B Lyon. London, Hutchinson, 1944. 76pp.
Poems mostly relating to wartime experiences, by unknown poetesses.

1340 RHYS, Keidrych
More poems from the forces: a collection of verses by serving members of the navy, army and air force, edited by Keidrych Rhys. London, Routledge, 1943. 324pp.

1341 RHYS, Keidrych
Poems from the forces: a collection of verses by serving members of the navy, army and air force, edited with an introduction by Keidrych Rhys. London, Routledge, 1941. xxiv, 140pp.

1342 SACKVILLE-WEST, V
Poems from the Land Army: an anthology of verse by members of the Women's Land Army, [selected with an] introduction by V Sackville-West. London, [n d]. 56pp.

1343 SUNDAY TIMES
War poems from the Sunday Times: a selection from the poetry by various contributors which has appeared in the Sunday Times since the beginning of the war. Printed for private circulation, 1945. 94pp.
Mostly unknown poets.

1344 TAMBIMUTTA, M J
Poetry in wartime: an anthology edited by M J Tambimutta. London, Faber, 1942. 191pp.
Mostly well-known poets.

1345 WALLER, John and MAUNY, Eric de
Middle East anthology, edited by John Waller and Eric de Mauny London, Lindsay Drummond, 1946. 170pp.
Prose and poetry describing Middle East experiences during the second world war.

1346 WOLLMAN, Maurice
Poems of the war years: an anthology, compiled by Maurice Wollman. London, Macmillan, 1948. 275pp.
Mostly well-known poets.

Second edition: 1950. xlvii, 326pp. Biographical notes. Notes (pp 277-323). (The Scholar's Library series.)

See also: 761, 855

Studies and criticism

1347 ANDREWS, Charles Rolland
A thematic guide to selected American poetry about the second world war. PhD thesis, Case Western Reserve University, 1967.

1348 BROWN, William Richard
American soldier poets of the second world war. PhD, University of Michigan, 1965.

1349 CURREY, R N
Poetry of the 1939-1945 war, by R N Currey. London, Longmans, for the British Council and the National Book League, 1960. 48pp, plates (ports). Bibliography. (Writers and their Work series, no 127.)
Chapters: Poets of the 1939-45 war; First world war: Brooke, Sassoon and Owen; Between the wars; Second world war: Sidney Keyes, Alun Lewis, Keith Douglas, Roy Fuller, Charles Causley, Roy Campbell and others; A new type of war; A moral problem.
Bibliography covers collections by individual poets, anthologies and some critical studies.

1350 DAVIDSON, Mildrid
The poetry is in the pity, by Mildrid Davidson. London, Chatto & Windus. 1972. 166pp.
Chapters: Up to 1918; The 1930 poets; The Spanish Civil War; Auden and Campbell; 1939: the older generation of poets; 1939: the middle generation of poets; 1939: the younger generation of poets; The communal sense in second world war poetry.
Appendix: reviewers on the poetry.

1351 FEIN, Richard Jacob
Major American poetry of World War II: a critical study. PhD, New York University, 1960.

1352 GOODE, Stephen H
British war poetry of the second world war. PhD thesis, University of Pennsylvania, 1956.

1353 MORGAN, H L
English poetry and the second world war. MA thesis, University of Wales, 1950.

1354 RAJIVA, Stanley F
The appearance of choice: a critical examination of themes and attitudes in English poetry of the second world war. PhD thesis, Wisconsin University, 1967.

1355 SCANNELL, Vernon
  Not without glory: poets of the second world war, by Vernon Scannell.
London, Woburn Press, 1976. 240pp. Bibliography.
Chapters: Setting the scene; Keith Douglas; Alun Lewis; Sidney Keyes; Roy
Fuller; Alan Ross and Charles Causley; Henry Reed and others; American
poets and the second world war.

1356 SCOTT, A H
  English poetry of the second world war. MLitt thesis, Aberdeen University, 1968.

The Vietnam War

1357 CASS, Shirley and others
  We took their orders and are dead: an anti-war anthology, edited by
Shirley Cass, Ros Cheney, David Malouf and Michael Wilding. Sydney
(Australia), Yure Smith, 1971. 256pp.
Prose and poetry by Australian writers, referring mostly to the Vietnam war
and Australia's involvement in it.

1358 COTHRAN, K
  In my hand: songs for the Vietnam war. Atlanta, Atlanta Committee to
End the War, 1966.

1359 DANE, Barbara and SILBER, Irwin
  The Vietnam songbook, compiled and edited by Barbara Dane and Irwin
Silber. New York, The Guardian, distributed by the Monthly Review Press,
[1969]. 223pp, illus. Music.

1360 DI PRIMA, Diane
  War poems, [compiled] by Diane Di Prima. New York, Poets Press,
1968. 86pp.

1361 LOWENFELS, Walter
  Where is Vietnam? American poets respond: an anthology of contemporary poems edited by Walter Lowenfels; with the assistance of Nan Bray-
mer. New York, Anchor Books, 1967. xx, 160pp.

1362 BLY, Robert and RAY, David
  A poetry reading against the Vietnam War: collection edited by Robert
Bly and David Ray. Madison (Minnesota), The Sixties Press, 1966. 63pp.
Poems and prose pieces chosen and read by various poets at the poetry
readings against the Vietnam War held at various campuses and public halls
during Spring 1966.

Studies and criticism

1363 MERSMANN, James F
  Out of the vortex: a study of poets and poetry against the Vietnam War.
PhD thesis, University of Kansas, 1972.

Arab-Israel War See: 666

ENGLISH HISTORY

General

1364 ASHRAF, Mary
   Political verse and song, edited by Mary Ashraf. London, Lawrence and Wishart, 1975. 440pp.
Poetry from the fourteenth to twentieth century, 'attacking or ridiculing statesmen and monarchs and voicing the sentiments, protests and revolts of the common people'.

1365 BARTON, John
   The hollow crown: an entertainment by and about the kings and queens of England: music, poetry, speeches, letters and other writings from the chronicles, from plays and in the monarch's own words, also music concerning them and by them, devised by John Barton. London, Samuel French and Harrap, 1962. 76pp.
Programme first presented by the Royal Shakespeare Theatre at the Aldwych Theatre, London, 19th March, 1961.

1366 BATES, Katharine Lee and COMAN, Katharine
   English history told by English poets: a reader for school use, compiled by Katharine Lee Bates and Katharine Coman. New York, Macmillan, 1902. xv, 452pp.

1367 A BOOK OF HISTORICAL POETRY
   London, Edward Arnold, 1913. 128pp.
Nineteenth century poetry, mostly by well-known poets, covering English history from the Roman invasion to the middle of the nineteenth century.

1368 CROSSLAND, John R
   Historical poetry, compiled and edited by John R Crossland. London, Glasgow, Collins, 1942. 191pp. Notes. (Laurel and Gold series.)
Poetry from the seventeenth to twentieth centuries covering events from the eleventh to the nineteenth. Well known poets.

1369 DRINKWATER, John
   A pageant of English life presented by her poets, with a running commentary by John Drinkwater. London, Thornton Butterworth, 1934. 221pp.
Headings: From Piers Plowman to the first Stuart; From cavalier and roundhead to the close of the seventeenth century; From Anne to Victoria.
Covers historical, political and social events. Known and some unknown poets.

1370 FIRTH, C H
   English history in English poetry from the French revolution to the death of Queen Victoria, [compiled] by C H Firth. London, Horace Marshall, [1911]. lxi, 240pp. Notes (pp 220-240).

Headings: The French revolution; The peace of Amiens (all Wordsworth); The war 1803-1815; England 1815-1820; Italy and Greece; Political and social reforms; Ireland 1798-1848; National movements; At home and abroad 1852-1901.
Mostly well-known poets of the nineteenth century.

1371 GILKES, Martin
Tribute to England: an anthology, [compiled] by Martin Gilkes. London, Hutchinson [1933]. 255pp.
Headings: Invocation; Before the Norman conquest; After the conquest; Plantagenet; Tudor; Elizabethan; Cavalier and puritan; The restoration and the eighteenth century; The era of Napoleon; The Victorian era; The South African war and after; The great war 1914-18.
Mostly poetry of a patriotic nature.

1372 HASLAM, Anthony
Anthology of empire, compiled by Anthony Haslam. London, Grayson & Grayson, 1932. 493pp.
Headings: 'God save the King'; 'This precious stone set in a silver sea'; 'Buy my English posies'; 'Richest, royalest seed'; 'Sun that never sets'; 'Once more unto the breach'; 'Down to the sea in ships'; 'Here's a health unto his majesty'.
Poetry and some short prose extracts from the middle ages to the twentieth century, by known and unknown writers.

1373 LANG, John and LANG, Jean
Poetry of empire: nineteen centuries of British history, selected and edited by John and Jean Lang; with sixteen drawings in colour by W Rainey. London, T C and E C Jack, [1910]; xx, 406pp, plates. (Romance of Empire series.)
Poetry from the Middle Ages (four items by Lawrence Minot) to the nineteenth century; emphasis on the nineteenth century; twenty-five anon items.

1374 MILMAN, Arthur
English and Scotch historical ballads, edited with introduction and glossary for the use of schools by Arthur Milman. London, Longmans & Green, 1871. 260pp. Glossary and notes (pp 229-260).

1375 NICKLIN, J A
Poems of English history, 61-1714 A D, edited by J A Nicklin. London, Adam and Charles Black, 1901. 146pp.
Headings: Bodicea to Richard II; Henry IV to Mary; Elizabeth to Anne.

1376 PALMER, Roy
A touch on the times: songs of social change, 1770-1914, illustrated with old photographs, edited by Roy Palmer. Harmondsworth (Middx), Penguin Educational, 1974. 352pp, illus.
Headings: The times are altered; Stirrings on Saturday night; On Monday morning I married a wife; Time to remember the poor; The world turned upside down.
Ballads and songs reflecting social change.

1377 PERKINS, D L J
  History and poetry: a book of verses bearing upon British history, selected and edited by D L J Perkins. London, Edinburgh, Nelson, 1926. 224pp. (The Teaching of English series.)

1378 PERTWEE, Ernest
  English history in verse, edited by Ernest Pertwee; with a preface by A T Pollard. London, Routledge; New York, Dutton, 1906. 407pp. (The New Universal Library.)
Mostly well known poets of the nineteenth century. Includes some extracts from Shakespeare plays.

1379 PETERS, D J and TOWERS, B E
  The poetry of history: an anthology of historical verse, selected and edited by D J Peters and B E Towers. London, Macmillan, 1960. xxvii (introduction), 227pp. Notes (pp 183-227).
Covers history from the Middle Ages up to the present century. Substantial amount of twentieth century verse. Includes items on social conditions and progress.

1380 SIDGWICK, F
  Ballads and poems illustrating English history, edited by F Sidgwick. Cambridge, University Press, 1907. vii, 211pp. (Pitt Press series.)

1381 THOMSON, Clara Linklater
  Carmina Britanniae: a selection of poems and ballads illustrative of English history, arranged by C L Thomson. London, Horace Marshall, [1901]; xii, 251pp.
Covers history from AD 61-1854.

1382 WINDSOR, M E and TURRAL, J
  Lyra historica: poems of British history, AD 61-1910, selected by M E Windsor and J Turral; with a preface by J C Smith. Oxford, Clarendon Press, 1911. 96pp. Notes.

1383 WRIGHT, David
  The Penguin book of everyday verse: social and documentary poetry 1250-1916, edited by David Wright. Harmondsworth (Middx), Penguin, 1976. 542pp.

1384 YONGE, Charlotte M
  Historical ballads, edited and annotated by Charlotte M Yonge, arranged to meet the new code of 1882, Schedule II, English. London, National Society's Depository, 1885. 3 parts. 119pp; 254pp; 286pp.
Mostly well-known poets of the nineteenth century.

See also: 996, 1016, 1053; Patriotism 1166-1178

Studies and criticism

1385 BAINTON, E
The modern democratic movement as reflected in the English poets. MA thesis, University of Birmingham, 1911.

1386 DAVIES, G L
The democratic spirit in English poetry up to the time of the French Revolution. MA thesis, University of Wales, 1929.

1387 EDWARDS, Thomas R
Imagination and power: a study of poetry of public themes, by Thomas R Edwards. London, Chatto and Windus, 1971. 232pp. References and notes.
Chapters: The disappearance of heroic man; The shepherd and the commissar; From satire to solitude; The modern poet and the public world.

1388 PREVITE-ORTON, C W
Political satire in English poetry, by C W Previte-Orton. London, Cambridge University Press, 1910. 244pp.
Chapters: Political satire in the middle ages; Satire under the despots—development of modern verse; The development of party satire; The satiric age; The days of Fox and Pitt; Moore, Praed and the modern mockery in rhyme; The elevated satire of the nineteenth century.

Thirteenth century

1389 WRIGHT, Thomas
The political songs of England from the reign of John to that of Edward II, edited and translated by Thomas Wright. London, The Camden Society, 1839. xi, 408pp. Notes (pp 347-408).
Items are in Latin, French, Anglo-Norman and English (13).
Revised edition: by Edmund Goldsmid. Edinburgh, privately printed, 1884. (Bibliotheca Curiosa.)

Fourteenth century   Studies and criticism

1390 BARNIE, John E
English attitudes to the hundred years war 1337-1399. PhD thesis, Birmingham University, 1971.

1391 BRUCE, Herbert
The fourteenth century, by Herbert Bruce. London, Bell for the Historical Association, 1914. 66pp. (English History in Contemporary Poetry series, vol 1.) References in footnotes.
A study with numerous examples.

Fourteenth and fifteenth centuries

1392 BENNETT, Herbert Stanley
England from Chaucer to Caxton, [compiled] by H S Bennett. London, Methuen, 1928. 246pp. (English Life in English Literature series.)

Headings: Home life; Village life; Town life; Church life; Foreign life.
Prose and poetry from The Paston letters, Langland, Chaucer, Mandeville,
Wyclif, etc.

1393 ROBBINS, Rossell Hope
Historical poems of the fourteenth and fifteenth centuries, edited by
Rossell Hope Robbins. New York, Columbia University Press, 1959. xlvii,
440pp. Glossary. Notes (pp 248-391).
Headings: An outline of dynastic history; Poems from Harley MSS 2253;
War poems by Lawrence Minot from Cotton MS Galba E IX; Poems from
Digby MS 102; Popular struggles: the great revolt, later discontent; Popular
ballads; Politics in song; Commemoration of kings; Political prophecies;
The first utopia; The wicked age; Critics of the Lollards; Critics of the friars;
England's commerce; The falls of princes; The red rose of Lancaster; The
white rose of York; The will for peace.

1394 WRIGHT, Thomas
Political poems and songs relating to English history, composed during
the period from the accession of Edward III to that of Richard III, edited
by Thomas Wright. London, Longman, Green, Longman & Roberts, 1859,
1861. 2 vols. civ, 462pp; lxxii, 357pp. (Chronological Memorials of
Great Britain and Ireland during the Middle Ages series.) Glossaries. References in footnotes.

Fifteenth century   Studies and criticism

1395 KINGSFORD, Charles Lethbridge
Lancaster and York, 1399-1485, by Charles Lethbridge Kingsford. Lon-
don, Bell for the Historical Association, 1913. 48pp. (English History in
Contemporary Poetry series, Vol 2.) References in footnotes.
A study with numerous examples.

1396 SCATTERGOOD, V J
Politics and poetry in the fifteenth century, 1399-1485, by V J Scattergood. London, Blandford Press, 1971. 415pp, plates, ports. Bibliography.
Chapters: Political verse in medieval England; Nationalism and foreign
affairs; Domestic affairs, 1399-1422, 1422-1455, 1455-1485; Religion and
the clergy; English society: the theoretical basis; English society: some
aspects of social change; English society: verses of protest and revolt.

The Middle Ages   Studies and criticism

1397 LYONS, Thomas Raphael
Middle English political poetry: the poet's call for stability. PhD thesis,
Washington University, 1972.

1398a O'SULLIVAN, M M
The treatment of political themes in medieval English verse, with special
reference to BM Cotton Roll II, 23. Thesis, London University, 1972.

Sixteenth century

1398b HARRISON, George B
England in Shakespeare's day, [compiled] by George B Harrison. London,
Methuen, 1928. xii, 234pp. (English Life in English Literature series.)
Headings: The court; The service of the state; Education and youth; Travel
and trade; London life; Country life; Matters of religion; Men of letters;
Moods and manners.
Prose and poetry by known and less well known writers.

Studies and criticism

1399 FINK, Zera S
Anti-foreign sentiment in Tudor and early Stuart literature. PhD thesis,
Northwestern University, 1931.

1400 FRAZER, N L
The Tudor monarchy, 1485-1588, by N L Frazer. London, Bell for the
Historical Association, 1914. 52pp. (English History in Contemporary
Poetry series, Vol 3.) References in footnotes.
A study with numerous examples.

1401 McALEER, John J
Ballads on the Spanish Armada (in Texas Studies in Literature and
Language, 1963, pp 602-12). References in footnotes.

1402 McQUIEN, Paul
Sir Francis Drake in English and Spanish literature of the sixteenth and
seventeenth century. PhD thesis, Texas Technological University, 1973.

Queen Elizabeth I

1403 BRADBOOK, M C
The Queen's garland: verses made by her subjects for Elizabeth I, Queen
of England, now collected in honour of Her Majesty Queen Elizabeth II,
compiled by M C Bradbook. London, Oxford University Press, for the
Royal Society of Literature, 1953. 74pp.
Headings: Urania, the heavenly muse: two songs by Queen Elizabeth; Glori-
ana, the royal Queen and Empress; Belphoebe, the virtuous and beautiful
Lady; Diana, goddess of woods and springs, also called Cynthia, as goddess
of the moon and seas; Flora, the lady of May and Queen of the shepherds;
Sweet Bessy: local and popular verse; Astraea, the heavenly maid.
Items by well known poets of the late sixteenth century.

1404 GLOVER, Alan
Gloriana's glass: Queen Elizabeth reflected in verses and dedications
addressed to her, reports concerning her, and her own words, written and
spoken, compiled by Alan Glover; with wood engravings by Joan Hassall.
London, Nonesuch Press, [1953]. 153pp, illus, port. Notes.
Contents: The coronation; Speeches of the queen; Letters of the queen;
'Lovely and loving'; A progress—'the honourable entertainment given to the

Queenes Majestie in Progresse, at Elvetham in Hampshire, by the right Honorable Earl of Hertford in 1591; Poems and dedications (pp 97-129); New Year's gifts to the queen, 1561-2; The queen's prayer after a progress, 1574. Poems by well-known poets of the late sixteenth century.

Studies and criticism

1405 BAZERMAN, Charles
Verse occasioned by the death of Queen Elizabeth I and the accession of King James I. PhD thesis, Brandeis University, 1971.

1406 PURDY, Mary M
Literary treatment of the proposed marriage of Queen Elizabeth I. PhD thesis, Pittsburgh University, 1928.

1407 WILSON, Elkin C
England's Eliza: a study of the idealization of Queen Elizabeth in the poetry of her age, by Elkin C Wilson. Cambridge (Mass), Harvard University Press, 1939. xii, 479pp, col front, plates, ports. (Harvard Studies in English, XX.)
pp 413-458: a short title list of books and MSS dedicated, inscribed or presented to Queen Elizabeth I.

Seventeenth century

1408 GOLDSMID, Edmund Marsden
Some political satires of the seventeenth century, selected from the writings of the Earl of Rochester, Sir John Denham and Andrew Marvel by Edmund Goldsmid. Edinburgh, privately printed, 1885. 2 vols. (Bibliotheca Curiosa.)

Studies and criticism

1409 HEARNSHAW, F J C
Court and parliament, 1588 to 1688, by F J C Hearnshaw. London, Bell for the Historical Association, 1913. 47pp. (English History in Contemporary Poetry series.) References in footnotes.
A study with numerous examples.

1410 HUGHES, Peter Albert Martin
The monarch's and the muse's seat: Stuart kingship and poetry of the royal estate. PhD thesis, Yale University, 1965.

1411 NEVO, Ruth
The dial of virtue: a study of poems on affairs of state in the seventeenth century, by Ruth Nevo. Princeton, Princeton University Press, 1963. 283pp. Bibliography.

1412 RIVERS, Isabel
The poetry of conservatism, 1600-1745: a study of poets and public affairs from Jonson to Pope, by Isabel Rivers. Cambridge, Rivers Press,

1973. 279pp. Bibliography. Chronology. Notes.
Chapters: Public poetry—its context; Ben Jonson—the nature of aristocracy; Poets and revolution (Milton and Marvel); John Dryden: the recreation of monarchy; Alexander Pope: the decline of a public myth.

1413 WEDGWOOD, C V
Poetry and politics under the Stuarts, by C V Wedgwood. London, Cambridge University Press, 1960. vii, 220pp. Notes and references.
Chapters: Court and country; The halcyon days; Poets at war; The vanquished and the victors; Satire and eulogy; Conclusion.

James I

1414 FIRTH, C H
Ballad history of the reign of James I (in Transactions of the Royal Historical Society, third series, Vol 5, 1911, pp 21-61). References in footnotes.

Henry, Prince of Wales

1415 (BIBLIOGRAPHY) EDMOND, John Philip
Elegies and other tracts issued on the death of Henry, Prince of Wales, 1612. (in Paper of the Edinburgh Bibliographical Society, Vol 6, 1906, pp 141-58).
Lists 44 items with library locations.

1416 WILSON, Elkin Calhoun
Prince Henry and English literature, by Elkin Calhoun Wilson. Ithaca, New York, Cornell University Press, 1946. xi, 187pp, illus. References in footnotes.
A study of contemporary prose and poetry descriptions of the Prince.

George Villiers, Duke of Buckingham

1417 FAIRHOLT, Frederick William
Poems and songs relating to George Villiers, Duke of Buckingham and his assassination August 23, 1628, edited with introduction and notes by Frederick W Fairholt. London, Percy Society, 1850. xxxi, 78pp. (Percy Society Vol 29.)

Charles I

1418 FIRTH, C H
[Ballad history of] The reign of Charles I (in Transactions of the Royal Historical Society, third series, Vol 6, 1912, pp 19-65). References in footnotes.

The Commonwealth and Protectorate

1419 MACKAY, Charles
The cavalier songs and ballads of England, 1642-1684, edited by Charles Mackay. London, Griffin Bohn, 1863. vii, 310pp.

1420 ROLLINS, Hyder Edwards
Cavalier and puritan ballads and broadsides illustrating the period of the great rebellion 1640-1660, edited with an introduction and notes by Hyder Edwards Rollins. New York, New York University Press, 1923. xv, 532pp.

1421 THE RUMP
or, an exact collection of the choycest poems and songs relating to the late times, by the most emminent wits from 1639 to 1661, printed for Henry Brome . . . and Henry Marsh. Reprinted 1874. 2 vols.
First published 1662.
Index and notes by H F Brooks: in Oxford Bibliographical Proceedings and Papers, 1939, pp 281-304).

1422 WRIGHT, Thomas
Political ballads published in England during the Commonwealth, edited by Thomas Wright. London, Percy Society, 1841. 270pp. (Percy Society Vol 3.)
Items taken from the 'King's Pamphlets' collection in the British Museum library.

Studies and criticism

1423 BENNETT, L C
A study of the influence of politics on poetry during the years 1640 to 1660. MA thesis, London University, 1924.

1424 CRUTTNELL, Patrick
The war's and fortune's son (in Essays in Criticism, Vol 2, January 1952, pp 24-37).
Seventeenth century poets and Cromwell, and a new attitude to the warlike hero.

1425 DUBINSKI, Roman Rudolph
Royalist political poetry, 1640-1660. PhD thesis, University of Toronto, 1969.

1426 JUDKINS, David Cummins
Studies in seventeenth century political poetry of the English civil war. PhD thesis, Michigan State University, 1970.

1427 SWARTCHILD, William G
The character of a roundhead: theme and rhetoric in anti-puritan verse satire from 1639 through Hudibras. PhD thesis, Columbia University, 1966.

Charles II and the Restoration

1428 (BIBLIOGRAPHY) ALDEN, John
The muses mourn: a checklist of verse occasioned by the death of Charles II, by John Alden. Charlottesville, University of Virginia, Bibliographical Society, 1958. 61pp.
Lists 68 items with library locations.

1429 WILLIAMS, Weldon M
   The early political satire of the restoration. PhD thesis, Washington University, 1940.

The Stuarts, 1660-1714

1430 EBSWORTH, Joseph Woodfall
   The Bagford ballads illustrating the last years of the Stuarts with introduction and notes by Joseph Woodfall Ebsworth, with copies of all the original woodcuts. Hertford, printed for the Ballad Society, 1878. 2 vols, illus.

1431 LORD, George de F
   Poems on affairs of state: Augustan satirical poetry, 1660-1714, edited by George de F Lord. New Haven, Yale University Press, 1963-1795. 7 vols, plates (some ports). Notes.
   Anthology of poems on affairs of state [a selection from the above seven volumes] edited by G de F Lord. New Haven, Yale University Press, 1975. xxxii, 800pp, illus.

1432 VOWLES, Richard B
   Poems on affairs of state, 1689: a critical edition. PhD thesis, Yale University, 1950.

Eighteenth century

1433 GEORGE, Mary Dorothy
   England in Johnson's day, [compiled] by Mary Dorothy George. London, Methuen, 1928. xvi, 235pp. (English Life in English Literature series.)
   Headings: The English scene; Religion, the church and the clergy; Education; Women's education; Authors, publishers and patrons; Life and letters; Life and politics; The Court; Men and manners; Prejudices, follies and fashions; The theatre; Travelling; Gardening; Spas and watering places; The seaside sport.
   Mostly prose extracts, by well-known authors.

1434 McALEER, John J
   Ballads and songs loyal to the Hanoverian succession, 1703-1761, selected with an introduction by John J McAleer. University of California, William Andrews Clark Memorial Library, 1962. 37pp. Music. Notes. (The Augustan Reprint Society Publication no 96.)

Studies and criticism

1435 MOORE, C A
   Whig panegyric verse, 1700-1760: a phase of sentimentalism (in Publications of the Modern Language Association, 1926, pp 362-401).

1436 (BIBLIOGRAPHY) MOORE, Maurice A
   English political poetry, 1714-1760: an annotated bibliography with a critical introduction. PhD thesis, University of N Carolina, 1956.

1437 THOMSON, C L

The eighteenth century, by C L Thomson. London, Bell for the Historical Association, 1914. 68pp. (English Literature in Contemporary Poetry series.) References in footnotes.
A study with numerous examples.

See also: 316, 1193

Jacobite rebellion

1438 BOULTON, Harold

Prince Charlie in song: a short selection of Jacobite songs dealing with the prince's career in historical sequence from his landing in Eriska on 23rd July 1745 till his death in Rome 1788, [compiled] by Sir Harold Boulton. London, Geoffrey Bles, 1933. 56pp, plates.
Plates are of glasses and goblets of the period engraved with the prince's portrait.

1439 EDMONDS, Charles

Poetry of the anti-jacobin: comprising the celebrated, political and satirical poems by the Rt Hons G Canning, John Hookham Frere, W Pitt, The Marquis Wellesley, G Ellis, W Gifford, The Earl of Carlisle and others, edited with explanatory notes, etc, [compiled] by Charles Edmonds.

Third edition, considerably enlarged with six illustrations and a folio plate by James Gillray. London, Sampson Low, Marston, Searle and Rivington, 1890. xxviii, 341pp, plates.
Poems which appeared in the 'Anti-Jacobin, or Weekly Examiner', 1797-1798.

Earlier editions: London, G Willis, 1852. 220pp. London, G Willis, 1854. xvi, 248pp, plates.

1440 GROSART, Alexander B

English Jacobite ballads, songs and satires, etc from the MSS at Towneley Hall, Lancashire, edited with introduction, notes and illustrations by the Rev Alexander B Grosart. Printed for private circulation, 1877. 200pp. Limited edition: 100 copies.

1441 MACKAY, Charles

The Jacobite songs and ballads of Scotland from 1688 to 1746 with an appendix of modern Jacobite songs, edited by Charles Mackay. London, Glasgow, Richard Griffin, 1861. xvi, 348pp. Notes.
Based on the 'Jacobite minstrelsy', 1829.

1442 MacQUOID, G S

Jacobite songs and ballads, edited with notes and introductory note by G S MacQuoid. London, Walter Scott, 1887. 361pp. Notes (pp 279-358). Genealogical table. (The Canterbury Poets.)
Based mainly on the 'Jacobite minstrelsy', 1829.

1443 RICE-OXLEY, L
Poetry of the Anti-Jacobin, edited with introduction and notes by L Rice-Oxley. Oxford, Blackwell, 1924. xxvi, 192pp. (Percy Reprints no 8.)
A reprint taken from the first edition, 1799, of 'The poetry of the Anti-Jacobin'.

See also: 1477

Studies and criticism

1444 SNYDER, Franklin B
The Jacobite lyrics. PhD thesis, Harvard University, 1909.

Sir Robert Walpole

1445 LARGMANN, Malcom G
The political image of Sir Robert Walpole created by literary satire in the opposition press, 1721-1742. PhD thesis, New York University, 1965.

1446 PERCIVAL, Milton
Political ballads illustrating the administration of Sir Robert Walpole, edited by Milton Percival. Oxford, Clarendon Press, 1916. lviii, 211pp. Notes (Oxford Historical and Literary Studies no 8.)
Appendix (pp 183-200): list of political ballads issued during the administration of Sir Robert Walpole but not printed in the collection.

The war with France

1447 KLINGBERG, Frank J and HUSTVEDT, Sigurd B
The warning drum: the British home front faces Napoleon: broadsheets of 1803, edited by Frank J Klingberg and Sigurd B Hustvedt. Berkeley, Los Angeles, University of California Press, 1944. vii, 287pp. (Publications of the William Andrews Clark Memorial Library.) Bibliography. Notes (pp 221-260).
Prose and verse broadsides; based on a collection acquired by the Clark Memorial Library.) University of California in 1930. pp 263-280: guide to persons, places and societies.

Studies and criticism

1448 BENNETT, Betty T
British poetry and the war with France, 1793-1815. PhD thesis, New York University, 1970.

1449 ROBINSON, Forest E
The peninsular war in the political evolution of five English Romantic poets. PhD thesis, Colorado University, 1965.

1450 WICHERT, Robert A
Napoleon and the English romantic poets. PhD thesis, Cornell University, 1948.

Nineteenth century

1451 ADAMS, W Davenport
Songs of society—from Anne to Victoria, edited with notes and intro-
duction by W Davenport Adams. London, Pickering, 1880. xviii, 234pp.
Notes.
'The poetry of fashionable life'; mostly unknown poets.

1452 ADAMS, Anthony and LEACH, Robert
Talent, wonder and delight: a scrapbook of Victorian entertainment,
[compiled] by Anthony Adams and Robert Leach. Glasgow, Blackie,
1976. 88pp, illus. Music. Bibliography (further source material).
Headings: At home; Clubs and pubs; Shows and showmen; The seaside;
Sport.
Contemporary verse and prose; mostly prose.

1453 ALDRIDGE, P R and ALDRIDGE, J P
Building Jerusalem: a scrapbook of Britain during the industrial revolution, [compiled] by P R and J P Aldridge. Glasgow, Blackie, 1976. 88pp,
illus. Music. Bibliography (further source material). List of museums of
special interest.
Poetry and prose written mostly during the first four decades of the nineteenth century, dealing with social conditions and life in general; known
and unknown writers. Illustrations are caricatures, paintings and engravings.

1454 KING, R W
England from Wordsworth to Dickens, [compiled] by R W King. Lon-
don, Methuen, 1928. xv, 240pp. (English Life in English Literature series.)
Headings: National characteristics; The French revolution and the wars; The
industrial revolution; Statesmen: parliament; Religion, the church, dissent;
The countryside, travel, the sea; Sports and pastimes; Manners and customs;
Town life, London; The theatre, players and playgoers; Books, writers and
readers; Education: school and university; Domestic life, dress, fashions.
Prose and poetry, by mostly well-known writers.

1455 PENNELL, H Cholmondeley
Muses of Mayfair: selection from verse de société, [compiled] by H
Cholmondeley Pennell. London, Chatto & Windus, 1874. xv, 382pp.
pp 359-381: translations from the French and German by Ethel Grey.
Poems of fashionable life.

Studies and criticism

1456 DAVIS, Arthur K
The political thought of Victorian poets. BLitt thesis, Oxford University,
1923.

1457 DAVIS, Arthur K
The political thought of Victorian poets. PhD thesis, Virginia University,
1924.

1458 HUGHES, Bertram L
   The social protests in early Victorian poetry. PhD thesis, Cornell University, 1936.

1459 RAMAGE, Ethel
   Chartism in English literature, 1839-1876. PhD thesis, Wisconsin University, 1939.

1460 WOODRING, Carl
   Politics in English romantic poetry, [by] Carl Woodring; Cambridge (Mass), Harvard University Press, 1970. xvi, 385pp, illus. References and notes.
Chapters: The climate; Varieties of romantic experience; Wordsworth; Byron; Shelley.

The Prince Regent

1461 STUART, Dorothy Margaret
   The prince regent and the poets (in Transactions of the Royal Society of Literature, 1955, pp 109-128).

Queen Victoria

1462 FORSHAW, Charles F
   Poetical tributes to the memory of Her Most Gracious Majesty Queen Victoria, edited by Charles F Forshaw; with a foreword by Mackenzie Bell. London, Swan Sonnenschein, 1901. 312pp, port.
Poetry by unknown poets taken mostly from newspapers and journals.

1463 HAMMERTON, J A
   The passing of Victoria: the poet's tribute, containing poems by Thomas Hardy, W E Henley, A C Benson, Sir Lewis Morris, Flora Annie Steel, Violet Fane, etc. edited by J A Hammerton. London, Horace Marshall, 1901. 192pp. Notes (pp 178-192).

The Marquess of Salisbury

1464 FORSHAW, Charles F
   Poetical tributes to the memory of the late Most Hon the Marquess of Salisbury, K G, edited by Charles F Forshaw. London, Swan Sonnenschein, 1904. 123pp.

Twentieth century

King Edward VII

1465 FORSHAW, Charles F
   Poetical tributes to the glorious and blessed memory of His Late Majesty King Edward VII, edited by Charles F Forshaw. London, Elliot Stock, 1910. 316pp.

Inter-war years

1466 HARD HITTING SONGS FOR HARD HIT PEOPLE
New York, Oak Publications, 1976. 368pp, illus.
Over 150 folk songs dealing with the Depression and the Labour movement.

1467 JACKSON, Lionel
Fit for heroes: a scrapbook of Britain between the wars, [compiled by]
Lionel Jackson. Glasgow, Blackie, 1975. 86pp, illus. Music. Bibliography
(further reading and references).
Poetry and prose dealing with political and social matters, by mostly well-
known writers. Illustrations consist of contemporary photographs, cartoons,
posters and facsims of newspaper advertisements and articles.

See also: 309

Studies and criticism

1468 LOESER, Diana
The songs of the peace movement in Great Britain from 1945-1960.
Thesis, Humboldt University, Berlin, 1972.

SCOTTISH HISTORY

1469 BRONDER, Maurice
Scottish and border battles and ballads, [compiled] by Maurice Bronder.
London, Seeley Service, 1975. 300pp. Music. Bibliography.
Covers Scottish battles 1263-1746.

1470 BROUGHAM, Eleanor M
News out of Scotland: being a miscellaneous collection of verse and
prose, sacred and profane, from the fourteenth to the eighteenth century,
compiled and annotated by Eleanor M Brougham. London, Heinemann,
1926. 284pp.

1471 MacKENZIE, Agnes Mure
Scottish pageant, edited by Agnes Mure Mackenzie. Edinburgh, London,
Oliver and Boyd, for the Saltire Society, 1946. 4 vols. 261pp; 330pp;
371pp; 401pp.
Prose and poetry covering Scottish history 55BC-1802.

1472 SCOTTISH HISTORICAL BALLADS AND POEMS
London, Nelson, [1909]. vi, 100pp. (Short Studies in English Litera-
ture series No 15.) Biographical notes. Notes.
Twenty-seven items, mostly of the nineteenth century.

See also: 1374

Studies and criticism

1473 FIRTH, C H
Ballads illustrating the relations of England and Scotland during the seventeenth century (in Scottish History Review, Vol 6, January 1909, pp 113-28).

1474 FIRTH, C H
Ballads on the Bishops's War 1638-42 (in Scottish History Review, Vol 3, April 1906, pp 257-73).

IRISH HISTORY

1475 AFTERMATH OF EASTER WEEK
Dublin, published for the benefit of the Irish National Aid and Volunteers' Dependents Fund, September, 1917. 28pp.
Fifteen anonymous items; authors' names pencilled in on BM copy.

1476 BROWN, Mary J
Historical ballad poetry of Ireland, arranged by M J Brown; with an introduction by Stephen J Brown. Dublin, Belfast, The Educational Company of Ireland, 1912. 206pp, plates. Notes.
Enlarged edition: edited by Stephen J Brown. Dublin and Cork, The Talbot Press, 1927. xvii, 380pp.

1477 CROKER, Thomas Crofton
The historical songs of Ireland illustrative of the revolutionary struggle between James II and William III, edited with introductions and notes by T Crofton Croker. London, Percy Society, 1841. vii, 139pp. (Percy Society, Vol 1.)
Thirteen ballads.

1478 DAIKEN, Leslie H
Goodbye twilight: songs of the struggle in Ireland, compiled by Leslie H Daiken; woodcuts by Harry A Kernoff. London, Lawrence and Wishart, 1926. xviii, 104pp, illus. Notes.
Twentieth century Irish poetry.

1479 FITZHENRY, Edna C
Nineteen-sixteen: an anthology, compiled by Edna C Fitzhenry. Dublin, Browne & Nolan; London, Harrap, 1935. 112pp.
Headings: Prelude; Battle; Requiem.
Poetry by Thomas Macdonaugh, Padraic Perse, Dermot O'Byrne, and Francis Ledwidge.

1480 GALVIN, Patrick
Irish songs of resistance, [compiled] by Patrick Galvin. London, Workers' Music Association, [1955]; 102pp. Music.
Ballads of Irish history from the earliest times to 1923. Historical commentary.

1481 KELLY, Richard J
   Popular and patriotic poetry, [compiled by Richard J Kelly]. Dublin,
Catholic Truth Society of Ireland, [1911]. 214pp.
Issued in six parts. Poetry mostly concerned with Irish historical themes.

1482 SPARLING, H Halliday
   Irish minstrelsy: being a selection of Irish songs, lyrics and ballads, orig-
inal and translated, edited with notes and introduction by H Halliday Sparl-
ing. London, Walter Scott, 1887. xv, 368pp. Biographical notes. (The
Canterbury Poets series.)
Irish historical themes.

1483 ZIMMERMANN, Georges-Denis
   Songs of Irish rebellion: political street ballads and rebel songs 1780-
1900, by Georges-Denis Zimmermann. Dublin, Allen Figgis, 1967. 341pp.
Bibliography. Music. References in footnotes.
Part I (pp 15-116): study and historical survey. Parts II and III: songs and
ballads. Bibliography covers: primary sources—broadside ballads, song books
and anthologies, nationalist newspapers (1780-1916); secondary sources—
books and articles on songs and ballad-singers and studies of historical or
literary problems.

See also: 1179

AMERICAN HISTORY

General

1484 BREWTON, Sarah Westbrook and BREWTON, John Edmund
   America forever new: a book of poems, compiled by Sarah Westbrook
Brewton and John Edmund Brewton; drawings by Ann Grifalconi. New
York, Crowell, 1968. 269pp, illus.
Intended for children.

1485 DUDDEN, Arthur Power
   Pardon us, Mr President!: American humor on politics, edited and intro-
duced by Arthur Power Dudden. South Brunswick, New York, A S Barnes;
London, Thomas Yoseloff, 1975. 613pp, illus.
Prose and verse satirising American politics and politicians from colonial
times to Watergate. Mostly prose.

1486 EGGLESTON, George Cary
   American war ballads and lyrics: a collection of songs and ballads of the
colonial wars, the revolution, the war of 1812-1815, the war with Mexico
and the civil war, edited by George Cary Eggleston. New York, Putnam,
1889. 2 vols, illus. vii, 226pp; viii, 278pp. (Nickerbocker Nuggets series.)

1487 GINIGER, Kenneth Seeman
America, America, America: prose and poetry about the land, the people and the promise, selected by Kenneth Seeman Giniger. New York, Franklin Watts, 1957. 231pp, illus.
Headings: Pilgrims and strangers; Times that tried men's souls; A dream of the West; A time of testing; A land and its people; Land of promise.

1488 HOLLAND, Robert Sargent
Historic poems and ballads, described by Robert Sargent Holland. Philadelphia, George W Jacobs, [1912]. 297pp, front, plates.

1489 HUBBELL, Jay B
American life in literature, edited by Jay B Hubbell. New York, Harper, 1936. 2 vols. Bibliography (pp 825-839).
Traces the history of America in prose and poetry from the colonial period to the twentieth century.

1490 SCOLLARD, Clinton
Ballads of American bravery, edited with notes by Clinton Scollard. New York, Boston, Silvert & Burdett, [1900], x, 230pp. (The Silver Series of English and American Classics.)

1491 SCOLLARD, Clinton and RICE, Wallace
Ballads of valor and victory: being short stories in song from the annals of America, [compiled] by Clinton Scollard, and Wallace Rice. New York, Chicago, Fleming H Revell, 1903. 145pp.

1492 SCOTT, John Anthony
The ballad of America: the history of the United States in song and story, [compiled] by John Anthony Scott. New York, Bantam Books, 1966. xi, 404pp, illus. Bibliography (pp 381-387).

1493 SOUTH, John Corbly
Story of our country in poetry and song, [compiled] by John Corbly Scott. Chicago, Flannagan, 1902. 182pp, front, plates.

1494 STEVENSON, Burton E
Great Americans as seen by the poets: an anthology, selected and arranged by Burton E Stevenson. Philadelphia, Lippincott, 1933. xvi, 494pp.

1495 STEVENSON, Burton E
My country: poems of history for young Americans, selected and edited by Burton E Stevenson. Boston, New York, Houghton Mifflin, 1932. xx, 428pp.

1496 STEVENSON, Burton E
Poems of American history, collected and edited by Burton E Stevenson. Boston, New York, Houghton Mifflin, 1908. xxx, 704pp.
Revised edition: 1922. xxxi, 720pp.
Reprinted: New York, Books for libraries, 1970.

See also: 421, 767; Holidays and special days 697-704; Patriotism 1180-1186

Studies and criticism

1497 GRIFFITH, John W
Studies in American narrative historical poetry. PhD thesis, Oregon University, 1969.

The colonial period and earlier

1498 BISBEE, Marvin Davis
Songs of the pilgrims, edited by Marvin Davis Bisbee; with an introduction by the Rev H M Dexter. Boston, Chicago, Congregational Sunday School and Publishing Society, 1887. 217pp.

1499 FIRTH, C H
An American garland: ballads relating to America, 1563-1759, edited with introduction and notes by C H Firth. Oxford, Blackwell, 1915. xlvii, 91pp.

1500 SPOONER, Z H
Poems of the pilgrims, selected by Mrs Z H Spooner. Boston, A Williams, 1881. 99pp, plates.

Studies and criticism

1501 STEARNS, Bertha M
The Columbus theme in American poetry. (in Americana, Vol 33 1939, pp 7-14.)

Eighteenth century

The Revolution and Declaration of Independence

1502 BRAND, Oscar
Songs of '76: a folksinger's history of the revolution, [compiled] by Oscar Brand. New York, M Evans, 1972. xiv, 178pp, illus. Music.
Over sixty songs providing eyewitness reports of events; collected from MSS, newspapers, etc.

1503 HEARTMAN, Charles Frederick
The cradle of the United States, 1765-1789: contemporary broadsides, pamphlets and a few books pertaining to the history of the Stamp Act, the Boston massacre and other pre-revolutionary troubles, the war for independence and the adoption of the federal constitution . . . , historically and sometimes sentimentally described by the owner Charles Frederick Heartman. Perth Amboy (New Jersey), 1922-3. 2 vols.

1504 MOORE, Frank
Songs and ballads of the American revolution, with notes and illustrations by Frank Moore. New York, D Appleton, 1855. xii, 394pp, front, illus.

1505 PRESCOTT, Frederick C and NELSON, John H
Prose and poetry of the revolution (1765-1789), edited by Frederick C Prescott and John H Nelson. New York, Crowell, [1925]. xxii, 266pp, front (port), illus (facsims).

1506 SCHAUFFLER, R H
Independence day: its celebration, spirit and significance as related in prose and verse, edited by R H Schauffler. New York, Moffat & Yard, 1912. 318pp.

1507 SILBER, Irwin
Songs of independence, compiled and edited with historical notes by Irwin Silber. Harrisburg (Pa), Stackpole Books, 1973. 249pp. Bibliography. Discography.

1508 STONE, William L
Ballads and poems relating to the Burgoyne campaign, annotated by William L Stone. Albany (NY), Joel Munsell, 1893. 359pp. (Munsell's Historical series no 20.)

Studies and criticism

1509 GRANGER, Bruce Ingham
Political satire in the American revolution, 1763-1783, by Bruce Ingham Granger. Ithaca, Cornell University Press, 1960. ix, 314pp. Bibliography.

1510 MODLIN, Charles E
Political satire in America 1789-1801. PhD thesis, Tennessee University, 1969.

1511 MINER, Louie M
Our rude fathers: American political verse, 1783-1788, by Louie M Miner. Cedar Rapids (Iowa), The Torch Press, 1937. vii, 274pp.

1512 PATTERSON, Samuel White
The spirit of the American revolution as revealed in the poetry of the period: a study of American patriotic verse from 1760 to 1783, by Samuel White Patterson. Boston, Richard G Badger, 1915. 233pp, front, ports. Bibliography (pp 219-226).

1513 ROTH, George L
Verse and satire and the new republic 1790-1820. PhD thesis, Princeton University, 1949.

1514 WERNER, Dorothy Leeds
The idea of union in American verse 1776-1876, by Dorothy Leeds Werner. University of Pennsylvania Press, 1932. 180pp. Bibliography.

George Washington

1515 CARNEGIE LIBRARY SCHOOL ASSOCIATION
Washington and Lincoln in poetry: poems chosen by a committee of the Carnegie Library School Association. New York, Wilson, 1927. 71pp (one side only).

1516 SCHAUFFLER, Robert Haven
Washington's birthday: its history, observance, spirit and significance as related in prose and verse, with a selection from Washington's speeches and writing, edited by Robert Haven Schauffler. New York, Moffat & Yard, 1910. xxvi, 328pp. (Our American Holidays series.)

Nineteenth century

Civil War 1861-1866

1517 MASON, Emily V
The Southern poems of the war, collected and arranged by Miss E V Mason. Baltimore, J Murphy, 1867. 456pp.

1518 BROWNE, Francis F
Bugle-echoes: a collection of poems of the civil war, Northern and Southern, edited by Francis F Browne. New York, White, Stokes & Alleb, 1886. x, 336pp.

1519 DAVIDSON, Nora Fontaine M
Cullings from the confederacy: a collection of Southern poems original and others popular during the war between the states and incidents and facts worth recalling, 1862-1866, including the doggerel of the camp as well as a tender tribute to the dead, compiled by Nora Fontaine Davidson. Washington, R H Darby, 1903. 163pp, ports.

1520 CAPPS, Claudius Meade
The blue and gray: the best poems of the civil war, edited by Claudius Meade Capps. Boston, Bruce Humphries; Toronto, Ryerson Press, [1943]. 281pp.

1521 MOORE, Frank
The civil war in song and story: 1860-1865, collected and arranged by Frank Moore. New York, P F Collier, 1889. 500pp.

1522 MOORE, Frank
Personal and political ballads, arranged and edited by Frank Moore. New York, Putnam, 1864. 368pp.
'a selection from the best political and personal ballads that have appeared since the commencement of the present Rebellion'.

1523 STEINMETZ, Lee
The poetry of the American civil war, edited by Lee Steinmetz. East Lansing, Michigan State University Press, 1960. xii, 264pp. Bibliography (pp 257-264).

1524 WAR SONGS OF THE BLUE AND GRAY
as sung by the brave soldiers of the Union and Confederate Armies in camp, on the march, and in garrison; with a preface by Prof Henry L Williams. New York, Hurst, 1905. 215pp.

1525 WELLMAN, Marly Wade
The rebel songster: songs the confederates sang, with commentary and illustrations by Marly Wade Wellman; music scores by France Wellman. Charlotte (NC), Heritage Printers, 1959. 53pp.

1526 [WHARTON, Henry Marvin]
War songs and poems of the Southern Confederacy, 1861-1865, collected and retold with personal reminiscences of the war by H M W. Philadelphia, 1904. 421pp.

1527 WHITE, Richard Grant
Poetry, lyrical, narrative and satirical of the civil war, selected and edited by Richard Grant White. New York, American News Company, 1866. xxii, 334pp.

Studies and criticism

1528 AARON, Daniel
The unwritten war: American writers and the civil war, by Daniel Aaron. New York, Knopf, 1973. London, Oxford University Press, 1975. xvi, 387pp.

1529 ELLINGER, Esther Parker
The southern war poetry of the civil war. PhD thesis, University of Pennsylvania, 1918.

1530 FOWKE, Edith
American civil war songs in Canada (in Midwest Folklore, XIII, pp 33-42).

1531 HITT, Ralph E
Controversial poetry of the civil war period 1830-1878. PhD thesis, Vanderbilt University, 1955.

Abraham Lincoln

1532 BETTS, William W
Lincoln and the poets, edited by William W Betts. Pittsburgh, University of Pittsburgh Press, 1965. 140pp.

1533 NEIDELMAN, Edna H
America's Lincoln, from the hearts of many poets, compiled by Edna H Neidelman. New York, Pageant Press, 1966. 135pp.

1534 POETICAL TRIBUTES
to the memory of Abraham Lincoln. Philadelphia, Lippincott, 1865. xii, 306pp.

1535 WILLIAMS, A Dallas
   The praise of Lincoln: an anthology, collected and arranged by A Dallas
Williams. Indianapolis, Bobbs-Merrill, [1911]. 243pp.

See also: 1515

James Garfield

1536 THE POETS' TRIBUTE TO GARFIELD
   a collection of many memorial poems with portrait and biography. Cambridge (Mass), M King, 1882. 168pp.

War with Spain, 1898

1537 WITHERBEE, Sidney A
   Spanish-American war songs: a complete collection of newspaper verse
during the recent war with Spain, compiled by Sidney A Witherbee. Detroit,
the compiler, 1898. iii, 984pp.

Twentieth century

1538 BLY, Robert
   Forty poems touching on recent American history, compiled by Robert
Bly. Boston, Beacon, 1970. 105pp.
Includes some items in German and Spanish with English translations.

1539 DENISOFF, R Serge
   Great days are coming: folk music and the American left, by R Serge
Denisoff. Urbana, University of Illinois Press, 1971. 219pp. Bibliography
(pp 198-211).

John F Kennedy

1540 GLIKES, Erwin A and SCHWABER, Paul
   Of poetry and power: poems occasioned by the Presidency and by the
death of John F Kennedy, edited by Erwin A Glikes and Paul Schwaber.
New York, Basic Books, [1964]; xiv, 155pp.

FRENCH HISTORY

The French Revolution   Studies and criticism

1541 BROWN, Esther E
   The French revolution and the American man of letters, by Esther E
Brown. Columbia, University of Missouri Press, 1951. 171pp. Bibliography
(mainly historical works). (University of Missouri Studies vol xxiv no 1.)
Chapters: Representative men; Revolutionary doctrines; Action and reaction;
Propaganda pro and con; The summing up.
Six representative writers analysed: Thomas Jefferson, John Adams, Joel
Barlow, Noah Webster, Timothy Dwight, and Philip Freneau.

1542 HANCOCK, Albert Elmer
The French revolution and the English poets: a study in historical criticism, by Albert Elmer Hancock. New York, Henry Holt, 1899. xvi, 194pp.
Chapters: Part I (pp 3-30) The principles of the French revolution; Part II
The romantic movement—Shelley, Byron, Wordsworth, Coleridge.

World War Two See:1321

ITALIAN HISTORY

1543 TREVELYAN, George Macaulay
English songs of Italian freedom, chosen and arranged with an introduction by George Macaulay Trevelyan. London, Longman & Green, 1911.
xxxvi, 221pp. Notes.
Well-known nineteenth century poets.

SOUTH AFRICAN HISTORY

1544 PETRIE, A
Poems of South African history, AD 1497-1910, selected and edited by
A Petrie. Cape Town, London, Oxford University Press, [1919]. xi, 138pp.
Notes.
Unknown nineteenth century poets.

See also: 741

SCIENCE AND THE NATURAL WORLD

GENERAL

1545 EASTWOOD, W
   A book of science verse: the poetic relations of science and technology, selected by W Eastwood. London, Macmillan, 1961. xvi, 279pp.
A comprehensive collection covering all aspects of technology, invention, astronomy, etc. Appendix (pp 247-279): 'some views on the relations of science and poetry'.

1546 MACKAY, Alan L
   The harvest of a quiet eye: a selection of scientific quotations, collected by Alan L Mackay; edited by Maurice Ebison with a foreword by Sir Peter Medawar. London, Institute of Physics, 1977. xii, 192pp, illus.
Quotations on science taken from scientists and philosophers, writers and poets, clerics and politicians of all periods and nationalities, including proverbs and graffiti.

1547 McCOLLEY, Grant
   Literature and science: an anthology from American and English literatures, 1600-1900, selected and edited by Grant McColley. Chicago, Packard, 1940. xii, 528pp.

1548

1549 SHORTRIDGE, Virginia
   Songs of science: an anthology chosen by Virginia Shortridge. Boston, Marshall Jones, 1930. xxiv, 245pp.
Headings: Prelude (science in general); Philosophy; Healing (medicine and doctors); Triumphs of science; On wings of the wind (flying and aeroplanes); Habitations of men; Science and art.
Mostly nineteenth and twentieth century poetry.

1550 WEBER, Robert Lemmerman
   A random walk in science an anthology, compiled by R L Weber; edited by E Mendoza with a foreword by William Cooper. London, Institute of Physics, 1973. xvi, 206pp.

Studies and criticism

1551 BUSH, Douglas
   Science and English poetry: a historical sketch, 1590-1950, by Douglas
Bush. New York, Oxford University Press, 1950. viii, 166pp.
Chapters: The Elizabethans—the medieval heritage; The new science and
the seventeenth century poets; Newtonianism, rationalism and sentimentalism; The romantic revolt against rationalism; Evolution and the Victorian
poets; Modern science and modern poetry.
Not many poetry examples given. First given as the Patten Lectures, 1949,
at Indiana University.

1552 CRUM, Ralph B
   Scientific thought in poetry, by Ralph B Crum. New York, Columbia
University Press, 1931. 246pp. Bibliography. (Columbia University Studies
in English).
Chapters: Science and poetry; Pre-Newtonian science and poetry: Lucretius;
Poetry and the new science; Poetry solemnly surveys the Newtonian world
machine; Poetry champions evolution; Poetry smiles at a growing world:
Erasmus Darwin; Nature red in tooth and claw: Tennyson's problem; The
poet's dilemma: reason or mysticism; In conclusion: John Davidson.

1553 EMERY, Clark Mixon
   Science and eighteenth century poetry. PhD thesis, University of Washington, 1940.

1554 FORREST-THOMPSON, V E M
   Poetry as knowledge: the use of science as knowledge. PhD thesis, University of Cambridge, 1972.

1555 FOSTER, Stephen M
   Ambiguous gifts: the impress of science on contemporary Anglo-American
poetry. PhD thesis, University of Washington, 1965.

1556 JONES, William Powell
   The rhetoric of science: a study of scientific ideas and imagery in eighteenth century English poetry, by William Powell Jones. London, Routledge
and Kegan Paul, 1966. xi, 243pp.

1557 HOSKINS, H H
   Science on Parnassus: some eighteenth century instructional poets, by
H H Hoskins. Groningen, J B Wolters, 1949. 17pp.
Originally given as an inaugural lecture at the University of Groningen, April
5th, 1949.

1558 NEILSON, G E
   The influence of scientific speculation on imaginative literature in the
seventeenth century. MA thesis, University of Bristol, 1923.

1559 NICOLSON, Marjorie
The breaking of the circle: studies in the effect of the 'new science' upon seventeenth century poetry. New York, Columbia University Press; London, Oxford University Press, 1960. 216pp.
Many poetry extracts.

1560 (BIBLIOGRAPHY) NICOLSON, Marjorie
Resource letter SL-1 on science and literature (in American Journal of Physics, Vol 33, March 1965, pp 175-183).
A particularly useful annotated bibliography on the impact of science on literary culture.

1561 RATTANSI, P M
The literary attack on science in the late seventeenth and eighteenth centuries. PhD thesis, London University, 1960.

1562 ROSS, L L
The effect of the advance in scientific knowledge upon seventeenth century literature. MA thesis, University of Birmingham, 1912.

1563 WAGGONER, Hyatt H
Science and modern American poetry. PhD thesis, Ohio State University, 1942.

EVOLUTION

Studies and criticism

1564 CONNER, Frederick William
Cosmic optimism: a study of the interpretation of evolution by American poets from Emerson to Robinson. PhD thesis, University of Pennsylvania, 1944.

1565 DODGE, Stewart Charles
The use of evolutionary theory by American poets, 1900-1950. PhD thesis, University of Illinois, 1958.

1566 HARRISON, J E
The idea of evolution in eighteenth and nineteenth century poetry.
MLitt thesis, University of Durham, 1968.

1567 POTTER, George R
The idea of evolution in the English poets from 1744-1832. PhD thesis, Harvard University, 1922.

1568 ROPPEN, Georg
Evolution and poetic belief: a study in some Victorian and modern writers, by Georg Roppen. Oslo, University Press; Oxford, Blackwell, 1956. xi, 474pp. Bibliography. (Oslo Studies in English no 5—Publications of the British Institute in the University of Oslo).

Chapters: The background; Evolution in the platonic tradition: Alfred
Tennyson, Robert Browning; Evolution as a cult of life and man: Algernon
Charles Swinburne, George Meredith; Darwin and Hardy's universe; Butler's
more living faith; Two evolutionary utopias: George Bernard Shaw; Homo
Sapiens in a modern utopia: H G Wells; Shaw and Wells: summary and com-
parison.

1569 STEVENSON, Lionel
   Darwin among the poets. Chicago, Chicago University Press, 1932. vii,
357pp.
Originally a PhD thesis, University of California, 1925.

THE PHYSICAL SCIENCES

Astronomy

1570 CLARK, Cumberland
   Astronomy in the poets, by Cumberland Clark. Bournemouth, Sydenham;
London, Simkin, Marshall, Hamilton & Kent. [1922]. 116pp.
Extracts of poetry with running commentary. pp 1-60: Astronomy in
Shakespeare; pp 61-81: The astronomy of Paradise Lost; pp 82-116: Astron-
omy in some other poets (mainly Tennyson).

1571 CREMER, John Dorland
   Scrap-book of the sky: word pictures by the world's nature poets, delin-
eating the wonders of the heavens, dawn, sunrise, sunset, twilight and night,
storms, the rainbow, sun, moon and stars and all the clouds, compiled by
John Dorland Cremer. Boston, Badger, 1926. 382pp.

1572 JACOBS, Leland Blair
   Poetry for space enthusiasts, selected by Leland Blair Jacobs; drawings
by Frank Aloise. Champaign (Ill), Garrard, 1971. 164pp, illus.
Poetry about the sky, moon, astronauts, rockets, etc. Intended for children.

1573 PARKER, T H and TESKEY, F J
   Pathway to the stars, [compiled by] T H Parker and F J Teskey. London,
Glasgow, Blackie, 1970. 58pp, illus. (Themes to Explore series).
Headings: The wonder and the mystery; Off the ground; Into space.
Twentieth century poetry; Intended for school use.

1574 ROHDE, Eleanour Sinclair
   The star lover's days, compiled by Eleanour Sinclair Rohde. London,
The Medici Society, 1929. [116] pp.
Mostly nineteenth century prose and poetry extracts concerning the sun,
moon and stars. Some biblical extracts.

1575 VAS DIAS, Robert
   Inside outer space: new poems of the space age, compiled by Robert Vas
Dias. Garden City, New York, Anchor Books, 1970. xxxix, 398pp.

Studies and criticism

1576 EIDSON, Donald Ray
The sun as symbol and type of Christ in English non-dramatic poetry from the Anglo-Saxon period through the Victorian period. PhD thesis, University of Missouri, Columbia, 1969.

1577 GROVER, F
Poetry and astronomy (in Scientific Monthly, Vol 44, June 1937, pp 519-529).

1578 HILLEGAS, Mark R
The cosmic voyage and the doctrine of inhabited worlds in nineteenth century English literature. PhD thesis, Columbia University, 1957.

1579 McCOLLEY, William G
The Copernican theory in English poetry from heresy to orthodoxy, 1543-1840. PhD thesis, Northwestern University, 1928.

1580 MEADOWS, A J
The high firmament: a survey of astronomy in English literature, by A J Meadows. Leicester, Leicester University Press, 1969. x, 207pp. References.
Period covered is roughly 1400 to 1900. A number of poetry extracts are included.

1581 NICOLSON, Marjorie
The 'new astronomy' and English literary imagination (in Studies in Philology, XXXII, 1935, pp 428-462).

1582 NICOLSON, Marjorie
The telescope and imagination (in Modern Philology, XXII, 1935, pp 233-260).
Both this and 1581 are concerned with the impact of astronomical discoveries on seventeenth century poets.

1583 NICOLSON, Marjorie
A world in the moon: a study of the changing attitude towards the moon in the seventeenth and eighteenth centuries. Northampton (Mass), Smith College, 1936. 72pp. (Smith College Studies in Modern Languages, Vol XVII, No 2, January, 1936).
Numerous extracts of poetry of the period.

1584 RIVERS, James C
Astronomy and physics in British and American poetry 1920-1960. PhD thesis, University of S Carolina, 1967.

Chronology

Time (including clocks, sundials, and sundial mottoes)

1585 FOX, C A O
An anthology of clocks and watches, selected and edited by C A O Fox. Swansea, the compiler, 1947. 68pp, plates.
Mostly verse extracts from the sixteenth to nineteenth century on all types of clocks, clock-makers and time.

1586 GATTY, Margaret Scott
A book of sun-dials, collected by Mrs Alfred Gatty. London, Bell & Daldy, 1872. xvi, 155pp, illus.
Second edition: 1889. vii, 519pp.
Third edition: 1890. viii, 578pp.
Fourth edition, enlarged and re edited by II K F Eden and E Lloyd. xvii, 529pp.

1587 THE HOUSE, THE GARDEN AND THE STEEPLE
a collection of old mottoes. London, Arthur L Humphreys, 1906. 88pp.
Mottoes, including some rhyming ones, taken from old houses, sundials and bells.

1588 HYATT, Alfred H
A book of sundial mottoes, compiled by Alfred H Hyatt. London, Philip Wellby; New York, Scott-Thaw, 1903. xii, 123pp.
pp 117-123: in praise of sundials—includes two verse extracts by Marvell and Shakespeare.

1589 RAWLINGS, Alfred
The book of old sundials and their mottoes, [compiled] by Alfred Rawlings; eight illustrations in colour by Alfred Rawlings and thirty-six drawings of some famous dials by Warrington Hogg. London, T N Foulis, [1914]. 104pp, plates (some col).
Introductory essay by Launcelot Cross.

See also: 1948

Studies and criticism

1590 NEWBOLT, Henry
Poetry and time (in Transactions of the Royal Society of Literature, second series, 1919, pp 177-202).

1591 NEWMAN, Franklin B
The concept of time in Elizabethan poetry. PhD thesis, Harvard Universith, 1947.

1592 STAINTON, Albert P
The time motif in the medieval lyric. PhD thesis, Rutgers University, 1971.

Night

1593 DEVERSON, H J
   Journey into night: an anthology, compiled by H J Deverson. London,
Leslie Frewin, 1966. xii, 316pp, illus (photographs).
Headings: Night is for beginnings, −for star-gazing, −for pleasure, −for
adventure, −for the city, −for loving, −for owls, −for music, −for beds,
−for sleep, −for the sleepless, −for dream, −for ghosts and witches, −for
conflict; −for crime, −for endings.
Prose and poetry from the sixteenth to twentieth century.

See also: 627, 629, 661

Studies and criticism

1594 DONNELLY, Jerome James
   The concept of night, its use and metamorphosis in the poetry of the
eighteenth century. PhD thesis, University of Michigan, 1966.

Physics

Machines

1595 McNEIL, Horace J
   Poems for a machine age, selected and edited by Horace J McNeil with
the editorial collaboration of Clarence Stratton. New York, London,
McGraw-Hill, 1941. xix, 568pp. Notes (pp 483-523).
A general collection of twentieth century American poetry which 'attempts
to relate to the modern reader and his own experience of modern life.'
Modern civilization (poems on machines): pp 3-45. The city: pp 49-113.

1596 WARBURG, Jeremy
   The industrial muse: the industrial revolution in English poetry: an
anthology, compiled with an introduction and comment by Jeremy Warburg;
and decorated by Roy Morgan. London, Oxford University Press, 1958.
xxxv, 174pp.
Notes and references: pp 157-169. Poems on the machine in general and
various types of transport. Nineteenth and twentieth century poetry.

See also: Transport 845-861

Studies and criticism

1597 GINESTIER, Paul
   The poet and the machine, by Paul Ginestier; translated from the French
by Martin B Friedman. Chapel Hill, University of N Carolina Press; London,
Oxford University Press, 1961. viii, 183pp.
Chapters: Outline for a method of literary aesthetics; Homo faber and
poetry; The poetry of the re-shaping of the universe; The dynamism of the

conquest of fluid space and its poetry; The black magic of the modern
world; The poetry of the machine: value, meaning and influence.
Covers English and French twentieth century poetry.

1598 KOVACEVICH, Ivanka
    The mechanical muse: the impact of technical inventions in eighteenth
century neo-classical poetry (in Huntington Library Quarterly Vol 28,
May 1965, pp 263-81).

1599 SUSSMAN, Herbert L
    The response to machine technology in Victorian literature. PhD thesis,
Harvard University, 1963.

Optics

1600 NICOLSON, Marjorie Hope
    Newton demands the Muse: Newtons 'Opticks' and the eighteenth cen-
tury poets, by Marjorie Hope Nicolson. Princeton, Princeton University
Press, 1946. xi, 178pp.
Chapters: The popular reception of the Opticks; Colour and light in the
descriptive poets; The physics of light in the scientific poets; Optics and
vision; Aesthetic implications of the Opticks; Metaphysical implications of
the Opticks; Epilogue: The poetic damnation of Newton.
A study with many extracts of contemporary poetry.

Geology

1601 DEAN, Dennis Richard
    Geology and English literature: crosscurrents 1770-1830. PhD thesis,
University of Wisconsin, 1968.

1602 HEATHER, P J
    Custom and belief connected with precious stones, as shown in the
Middle English verse of the fourteenth century. PhD thesis, London University, 1931.

1602a HEATHER, P J
    Precious stones in the Middle English verse of the fourteenth century (in
Folklore Vol 42, September 1931, pp 217-264).

Meteorology

1603 INWARDS, Richard
    Weather lore: a collection of provers, sayings and rules concerning the
weather, compiled and arranged by Richard Inwards. London, W Tweedie,
1869. 91pp.
    Second edition: 1893. xii, 190pp. Bibliography.
    Third edition: 1898. xii, 233pp. Bibliography.
    Fourth edition: Weather lore: the unique bedside book, taken from the
world's literature and the age-old wisdom of farmers, mariners, bird watchers,

concerning flowers, plants, trees, butterflies, birds, animals, fish, tides, clouds, rainbows, stars, mock suns, mock moons, haloes, edited, revised and amplified for the Royal Meteorological Society by E L Hawke. London, New York, Rider, 1950. 251pp, plates. Bibliography (pp 231-236).

1604 JONES, Rhodri
Weathers, edited by Rhodri Jones; photographs by John Krish. London, Heinemann Educational, 1971. 48pp, illus. (Preludes series.)
Mostly twentieth century verse about the wind, rain, sun, snow, etc. Intended for children.

1605 RIMBAULT, E F
Old ballads illustrating the great frost of 1683-1684 and the fair on the River Thames, edited by E F Rimbault. London, Percy Society, 1844. xxx, 38pp (in Percy Society Publications, Vol 9).

1606 SWAINSON, Charles
A handbook of weather folklore: being a collection of proverbial sayings in various languages relating to the weather with explanatory, illustrating notes, by the Rev Charles Swainson. Edinburgh, London, Blackwood, 1873. x, 275pp.

NATURE AND THE COUNTRYSIDE

General

1607 BARING, Maurice
English landscape: an anthology, compiled by Maurice Baring. London, Oxford University Press, 1916. 122pp.
Mostly nineteenth century verse, concerning nature in general.

1608 BARRELL, John and BULL, John
The Penguin book of English pastoral verse, introduced and edited by John Barrell and John Bull. London, Allen Lane, 1975. 539pp.
Headings: The Elizabethan pastoral; The pastoral drama; The seventeenth century pastoral: The Augustan pastoral; Whigs and Post Augustans; Some versions of anti-pastoral; Romantics and Victorians.

1609 BELL, Adrian
The open air: an anthology of English country life, [compiled] by Adrian Bell. London, Faber, 1936. 368pp.
Mostly prose.

1610 BELL, G K A
Poems of nature, edited by G K A Bell. London, Routledge; New York, Dutton, [1906]. 234pp. (The Golden Anthologies series.)
Mostly well-known nineteenth century poetry.

1611 BRYAN, G S
Poems of country life: a modern anthology, [compiled] by George S Bryan. New York, Sturgis and Walton, 1912. xix, 349pp.

1612 BURROUGHS, John
  A book of songs of nature, compiled by J Burroughs. Garden City, Garden City Publishing Co. 1929. x, 359pp.

1613 CHAMBERS, Edmund K
  English pastorals, selected and with an introduction by Edmund K Chambers. London, Blackie, 1895. xxlviii, 275pp.
Sixteenth and seventeenth century poetry.

1614 CHANGING YEAR
  being poems and pictures of life and nature, illustrated by A Barraud. Boston, Frank Dadd; London, Cassell, [1882]. 192pp, illus.

1615 CLARK, Leonard
  The poetry of nature, selected by Leonard Clark. London, Hart-Davis, 1965. 144pp.
American and English poetry from the sixteenth to twentieth century.

1616 DEAKIN, Bartram
  Nothing of the town: a countryman's anthology, collected by Bartram Deakin. London, Frederick Muller, 1947. 248pp, plates.
Headings: The farm and the garden; Field sports; The countryside; The angler and the running stream; Country folk; Games; Man's best friend; Prose and poetry of the nineteenth and twentieth centuries, mostly by well-known writers.

1617 EDWARDS, B L
  I am gone into the fields: an anthology, edited by B L Edwards. London, Benn, 1929. 156pp.
Poetry and prose, mostly by nineteenth century writers.

1618 EDWARDS, B L
  Study to be quiet: an English nature anthology, edited by B L Edwards; with an introduction by Ernest Rhys. London, Benn, 1928. 175pp.
Poetry and prose, mostly by familiar nineteenth century writers.

1619 FILLMORE, C G
  Dear home in England: an anthology of poetry, compiled by C G Fillmore. London, Frederick Muller, 1959. 152pp.
Mostly general nature poetry by mainly well-known poets from the seventeenth to twentieth century. Emphasis on the nineteenth century.

1620 FRENCH, C N
  A countryman's day book: an anthology of countryside lore, compiled and arranged by C N French. London, Dent, 1929. 254pp, illus.
Quotations for each day of the year: sayings, rhyming proverbs, extracts of prose and poetry. Illustrations are from medieval sources.

1621 GEORGE, Hereford B and HADOW, W H
  Poems of English country life, selected and edited with an introduction and notes by Hereford B George and W H Hadow. Oxford, Clarendon Press, 1902. 112pp.

Mostly well-known nineteenth century poetry on nature as it may be seen in England. Some poems on country pursuits.

1622 GOLDMARK, Pauline and HOPKINS, Mary
The gypsy trail: an anthology for campers, compiled by Pauline Goldmark and Mary Hopkins. Vol 1: New York, M Kennerley, 1914. Vol 2: New York, Doubleday, 1930. xxi, 326pp.
Headings (Vol 2): The call of the open; Spring; Sursum Corda; Camp; Sunrise and morning; Woods and trees; Bird notes; Earth folk; Inland waters; The sea; The wind; The hills; The road to Elfland; Greek echoes; Comradeship; Evening; Night; Autumn; Winter.
Mainly early twentieth century poetry, by American and English poets; some German, French, Spanish and Italian. The second volume is similar to the first but contains more recent verse.

1623 GOSSET, Adelaide L J
Shepherd songs of Elizabethan England—workaday shepherds, holiday shepherds, shepherds passionate: a pastoral garland, [compiled] by Adelaide L J Gosset. London, Constable, 1912. xviii, 139pp.
Compiler acknowledges debt to A H Bullen's anthologies.

1624 GRIGSON, Geoffrey
Country poems, selected by Geoffrey Grigson. London, Edward Hutton, 1959. 48pp. (The Pocket Poets.)
Covers poetry from the medieval period to the twentieth century, dealing with nature in its general amd more specific aspects. Mostly little known pieces.

1625 GROVER, E O
Nature lovers knapsack: an anthology of poems, compiled for lovers of the open road by E O Grover. New York, Crowell, 1927. xxii, 279pp.
Enlarged edition: 1947. xxv, 294pp.

1626 H, R and I, N
Anthology of birds, beasts, insects and plants, edited by R H and N I. London, Kings College School, Art Society Press, 1966. 78pp.

1627 HYATT, Alfred H
The footpath way: an anthology for those who travel by countryside, compiled by Alfred H Hyatt. Edinburgh, London, T N Foulis, 1906. 375pp.
Headings: The country life; Travellers and travelling; The open eye of Heaven; 'Neath waving branches; Country characters; Sights and sounds by the way; Birds and flowers; Gardens; Sea, river and stream; Winds of heaven; God's acre; The passing seasons; Rest at the inn; Under the stars. Night; Christmas and the new year.
Prose and poetry, mostly of the seventeenth and nineteenth centuries, mostly by well-known writers.

1628 INGLIS, Fred
   The scene: an anthology about the city and country, edited by Fred
Inglis; illustrated by Allen Fraser. London, Cambridge University Press,
1972. 199pp. Notes.
Headings: The presence of the past; Home sweet home; The picturesque
tradition; The wasteland and the long horizon.
Poetry and prose: mostly poetry of the nineteenth and twentieth centuries.

1629 JONES, Esmore
   The road to the country, edited by Esmore Jones. Oxford, Pergamon
Press, 1968. 78pp. (Explorations series.)
Poetry and prose, mostly of the twentieth century, exploring some atti-
tudes to the country and nature. Intended for schools.

1630 KERMODE, Frank
   English pastoral poetry from the beginnings to Marvell, edited by Frank
Kermode. London, Harrap, 1952. 256pp.
Notes: pp 239-256.

1631 LARCOM, Lucy
   Hillside and seaside in poetry: an anthology by Lucy Larcom. Boston,
James R Osgood, 1877. 303pp.
Nineteenth century American and English poetry describing mountains,
valleys, lakes, oceans, etc.

1632 LARCOM, Lucy
   Roadside poems for summer travellers, edited by Lucy Larcom. Boston,
James R Osgood, 1876. 263pp.
American and English general nature poems of the nineteenth and twenti-
eith century.

1633 LINSSEN, E F
   Nature interlude: a book of natural history quotations, compiled by
E F Linssen; with a foreword by Brian Vesey-FitzGerald. London, Williams
& Norgate, 1951. 256pp.
Headings: I—Pan; Animals; Arachnids—spiders and scorpions; Birds; Fishes;
Insects; Molluscs and others. II—Pastoral; Flowers; Fruit; Plants; Trees and
shrubs. III—Nature; Natural history; The infinitely small; Nomenclature;
Biological control.
Short prose and poetry extracts from the sixteenth to twentieth century.
Some French pieces in translation.

1634 LORD, Russell
   Voices from the field: a book of country songs by farming people, edited
by Russell Lord; with an introduction by Carl van Doren. Boston, Houghton
Mifflin, 1937. xxiii, 166pp.

1635 LOVEJOY, Mary I
   Nature in verse: a poetry reader for children, compiled by Mary I Lovejoy.
Boston, Silver & Burdett, 1898. xiv, 305pp.

1636 MARBLE, Annie Russell
Nature pictures by American poets, selected and edited by Annie Russell Marble. New York, Macmillan, 1899. xliii, 205pp.
Headings: Landscape vistas; Music of winds and storms; Sea, streams and tides; Bird notes and cricket chirrup; Flower songs; Calender of the seasons. All nineteenth century American poetry.

1637 MEYNELL, Viola
The poet's walk: a nature anthology, made by Viola Meynell. London, Cape, 1956. 448pp.
Headings: Nature and man—1; Spring; Morning; Summer; Autumn; Evening; Winter; Night; Nature and man—2;
Ranges from the seventeenth to the twentieth century.

1638 MOUGHTON, William J
The poetry of nature: an anthology of nature verse, in five volumes, garned by William J Moughton, and illustrated in colour by K Nixon. Birmingham, Davis and Moughton, 1934. 5 vols. col illus.
All aspects of nature; mostly twentieth century verse. For children and school use.

1639 RICHARDSON, John
In the garden of delight: a nature anthology in prose and verse by John Richardson. London, Harrap, 1912. 244pp.

1640 STANLEY, Arthur
The out-of-doors book: an anthology for the open air, selected and arranged by Arthur Stanley. London, Dent, 1933. 486pp, illus.
Headings: The road; Fun and frolic; The footpath way; Wheels and wings; The pleasant land; Living things; Under the bough; Trees, flowers and gardens; Sport and play; Hills and mountains; River, shore and sea; Good company.
Mainly nineteenth and twentieth century poetry and prose by known and unknown authors.

1641 STOWELL, Leonard
The call of the open: a nature anthology, compiled by Leonard Stowell. London, A and C Black, 1922. 226pp, col plates.
Headings: The happy vagabond; Songs and thoughts of the seasons; Poems of moods and places; From day break to night fall; Through the changing seasons; By sea and shore.
Mostly nineteenth century poetry, with some French and German pieces in translation. Originally published in two volumes, 1914, with the titles: 'Nature's moods' and 'The call of the open'.

1642 THOMAS, R S
The Batsford book of country verse, edited by R S Thomas. London, Batsford, 1961. 128pp, col illus.

1643 THOMAS, William Beach
   The squirrel's granary: a countryman's anthology [compiled] by Sir William Beach Thomas. London, Alexander and Maclehose, 1936. 386pp, illus.
Headings: Birds, beasts and insects; Flowers; Scenery—the sky, sea and shore; Time and Seasons—seasons, the months, night and day; Weather; England; Gardens; Natural philosophy; Some naturalists.
Poetry and prose. Wide ranging from the Bible to the twentieth century.

1644 WARREN, C Henry
   The good life: an anthology of the life and work of the countryside in prose and poetry, by C Henry Warren; drawings by Alexander Walker. London, Eyre and Spottiswoode, 1946. xviii, 259pp.
Part 1: Living in the country—its consolations and delights versus the town;
Part 2: Working in the country—the seasonal labour.
Poetry and prose; more prose than poetry—some of the extracts are relatively long. Nineteenth and twentieth centuries, with some traditional material.

1645 WILCOX, Alice Wilson
   Treasured nature lyrics, selected by Alice Wilson Cox. Boston, R G Badger, 1919. 79pp.

1646 WILKINSON, Mary E
   Nature poems, gathered by Mary E Wilkinson. Melbourne (Australia), Whitcombe and Tombs, [1921]; 128pp. (Gleanings from Australian verse.)

1647 WILLARD, Barbara
   Field and forest, edited by Barbara Willard, illustrated by Faith Jaques. London, Kestrel Books, 1975. 256pp, illus.
Headings: Living things; The seasons; The hunt; Enchantment.
Poetry and prose.

1648 WOODS, R L
   The glories of nature, edited by R L Woods. New York, World Publishing Company, 1971. 6 vols, col illus.
I Flowers; II Summertime; III Springtime; IV Rivers; V The sun; VI The sea;
Poetry and prose quotations.

See also: 289, 296, 751, 781; Farming 796-801, 990, 998, 1007, 1008, 1603, 1760, 1824

Studies and criticism

1649 BEACH, Joseph Warren
   The concept of nature in nineteenth century English poetry, by Joseph Warren Beach. New York, Macmillan, 1936. 618pp.
Chapters: Part I—The Romantic period; The forms of nature; The metaphysical concept of nature; Wordsworth's naturalism; Wordsworth and nature's teaching; Nature in Wordsworth: summary; Shelley's naturalism;

Shelley's Platonism; Goethe. Part 2—Transcendatalism; Carlyle; Coleridge, Emerson and naturalism; Emerson's nature poetry; Whitman. Part 3—The Victorians: Arnold; Tennyson; Browning; Swinburne; Meredith. Part 4— Disappearance of the concept of nature; Hardy; Victorian afterglow; The vanishing point. Notes and references: pp 561-612.

1650 BINYON, Laurence
Landscape in English art and poetry, by L Binyon. London, Cobden-Sanderson, 1931. xii, 295pp, plates, illus. Lectures delivered at the Imperial University of Tokyo, October 1929.

1651 BLADEN, Peter L
The attitude of Australian poets to nature: a selective examination of Australian poetry from the earliest days of settlement to the present. MA thesis, Melbourne University, 1961.

1652 BELBY, M L
The rise and development of the pastoral, with special reference to the English pastoral. MA thesis, University of Birmingham, 1906.

1653 BROOK, D E
Nature in English poetry from 1610 to 1660. MA thesis, University of Liverpool, 1936.

1654 BRYAN, John Thomas Ingram
The interpretation of nature in English poetry, by J T I Bryan. Tokyo, Kaitakusha Publishing Co, [1932]. 318pp.

1655 CHANNING, Michael Dennis
The presentation of nature in twentieth century American poetry. PhD thesis, University of Stanford, 1974.

1656 DEANE, C V
Aspects of eighteenth century nature poetry, by C V Deane. Oxford, Blackwell, 1935. 145pp.
Chapter 5: Part I—Personification and abstraction: stock imagery: poetic periphrases; The diction of the Scottish Chaucerians; Conventional expressions in the ballads; Virgil and his translators. Dryden and Warton; Theories of generalized form and diction in criticism of the classical period. Part II—Pictorial description and landscape art: Implications of Lessing's Laokoon; Principals of visual composition in eighteenth century poetry; The 'prospect' poem. Part III—Pope's 'Pastorals' and 'Windsor forest'; Ambrose Philips; John Philips (1676-1708), William Shenstone. Conclusion.

1657 DE HAAS, Cornelis Engelbertus
Nature and the country in English poetry of the first half of the eighteenth century, by C E de Haas. Amsterdam, H J Paris, 1928. 301pp.
Covers the poetry of John Pomfret and John Phillips, Ambrose Philips and Alexander Pope, John Gay, The Countess of Winchelsea, Thomas Parnell and John Hughes, John Dryer, James Thomson, David Mallet and

Richard Savage, William Pattison and Stephen Duck, William Somerville, Mark Akenside, William Shenstone.

1658 DENNIS, Carl Edward
The poetry of mind and nature: a study of the idea of nature in American transcendental poetry. PhD thesis, University of California, Berkeley, 1966. 360pp.

1659 DIBBLE, Brian
A theory of the pastoral and a study of American pastoral poetry. PhD thesis, University of Chicago, 1972.

1660 DOBREE, Bonomy
Nature poetry in the early nineteenth century (in Essays and Studies, 1965, pp 13-33).
A study with many extracts.

1661 DRISKILL, L L P
Cyclic structure of Renaissance pastoral poetry. PhD thesis, Rice University, 1970.

1662 ECONOMOU, George D
The goddess Natura in medieval literature. PhD thesis, Columbia Universith, 1967.

1663 EDWARDS, Margaret Fountain
American nature poetry and a sense of ecology. PhD thesis, Stanford University, 1971. 191pp.

1664 EMPSON, William
Some versions of pastoral, by William Empson. London, Chatto and Windus, 1935. 298pp.

1665 FEINGOLD, Richard
Nature and society: some aspects of bucolic tradition in the poetry of the later eighteenth century. PhD thesis, Columbia University, 1970. 237pp.

1666 FOERSTER, Norman
Nature in American literature: studies in the modern view of nature, by Norman Foerster. New York, Macmillan, 1923. xiii, 324pp.
Chapters on Bryant, Whittier, Emerson, Thoreau, Lowell, Whitman, Lanier, Muir, Burroughs. Name and subject index.

1667 FLORANCE, A W
Poetry and the rustic in the eighteenth century. MA thesis, University of Bristol. 1935.

1668 GAMMON, Donald B
The concept of nature in nineteenth century Canadian poetry, with special reference to Goldsmith, Sangster and Roberts. Thesis, University of Brunswick, 1948.

1669 GLOVER, Thomas
Nature in early Canadian poetry. PhD thesis, Montreal University, 1951.

1670 HAASE-DUBOSC, Danielle Helen
Lyric nature poetry in France and England in the first half of the seventeenth century. PhD thesis, Columbia University, 1969.

1671 HEATH-STUBBS, John
The pastoral, by John Heath-Stubbs. London, Oxford University Press, 1969. 86pp. Bibliography.
The pastoral from the Elizabethans to the twentieth century. Many lengthy quotations.

1672 HOWE, Evelyn M
Convention and revolt in the treatment of landscape in the early nineteenth century. PhD thesis, Wisconsin University, 1946.

1673 LERNER, Laurence
The uses of nostalgia: studies in pastoral poetry, by Laurence Lerner. London, Chatto and Windus, 1972. 248pp.
Chapters: Part I—A map of Arcadia: What pastoral is; On nostalgia; Arcadia and Utopia; Sex in Arcadia; Golden slumbers: the politics of pastoral; City troubles: pastoral and satire. Part II—Some Arcadians: Sir Caldiore's holiday (pastoral in 'The fairie queen'); Farewell, rewards and fairies (the world of 'Comus'); Pastoral versus Christianity (nature in Marvell); The loss of paradise (Milton's Eden); Olympus' faded hierarchy (antiquity in Keats and Nerval); The proper place of nostalgia (Arnold's pastoral impulse).

1674 LINDSAY, Jean S
A survey of the town-country and court-country theme in non-dramatic Elizabethan literature. PhD thesis, Cornell University, 1943.

1675 MacKENZIE, James Joseph
A new American nature poetry: Theodore Roethke, James Dickey, and James Wright. PhD thesis, University of Notre Dame, 1971.

1676 MACKIE, Alexander
Nature knowledge in modern poetry, being chapters on Tennyson, Wordsworth, Mathew Arnold and Lowell as exponents of nature study, by Alexander Mackie. London, Longmans, 1906. 132pp.
Chapters: Tennyson as botanist, as entomologist, as ornithologist, as geologist; Wordsworth as a nature poet, Wordsworth's birds; Mathew Arnold as naturalist, Mathew Arnold's birds; James Russell Lowell as naturalist, Lowell's birds.

1677 MOORMAN, Frederic W
The interpretation of nature in English poetry from Beowulf to Shakespeare, by Frederic W Moorman. Strasbourg, Karl J Trubner, 1905. xiii,

244pp. (Quellen und Forschungen zur Sprach—und Culturgeschichte der germanischen Volker, no 95.)
Chapters: Beowulf; Christian narrative poetry; Old English lyric and allegoric poetry; The age of transition; The verse-romance; Middle English historical and lyrical poetry; The Gawayne-poet; Chaucer; The English poets of the fifteenth century; The Scottish poets of the fifteenth and sixteenth centuries; The early Elizabethans; Spenser; The minor Elizabethans; The pre-Shakespeare drama; Shakespeare.

1678 PALGRAVE, Francis Turner
Landscape in poetry from Homer to Tennyson, with many illustrative examples, by Francis T Palgrave. London, Macmillan, 1897. 302pp.
Chapters: Landscape in the Greek epic; —in Greek lyrical, idyllic and epigrammatic poetry; —in Lucretius, Vergil and other Augustan poets; —in later Roman epics and the 'Elocutio novella'; in Hebrew poetry; —in early Italian poetry; —in Celtic and Gaelic poetry; —in Anglo-Saxon poetry; —in English mediaevel poetry; Chaucer and his successors; Landscape in Elizabethan poetry; Under the Stuart kings; Landscape poetry to the close of the eighteenth century; Landscape in recent poetry—Scott and Byron, Coleridge, Keats, Shelley; The landscape of Wordsworth, of Browning, Arnold, Barnes and Charles Tennyson; of Alfred Lord Tennyson.

1679 PEARSALL, Derek and SALTER, Elizabeth
Landscapes and seasons of the medieval world, [by] Derek Pearsall and Elizabeth Salter. London, Paul Elek, 1973. xv, 252pp, plates (some col). Notes and references.
Chapters: Classical traditions; The early middle ages; The landscape of paradise; The enclosed garden; The landscape of the seasons; Late medieval.
' . . . offers a series of approaches to the subject of medieval landscape, and some tentative notions about the interrelationships of art, literature, social life and the life of the intellect' . . Plates are reproductions of paintings and illuminations.

1680 PITMAN, M R
The description of landscape in poetry from Spenser to Milton. BLitt thesis, University of Oxford, 1964.

1681 POWER, P E C
The countryside and Anglo-Irish poets (1885-1947). PhD thesis, University of Ireland, 1970.

1682 RAMSEY, Clifford E
The scenic analogy: a study in seventeenth and eighteenth century landscape poetry. PhD thesis, Florida University, 1967.

1683 RAWNSLEY, W A
The place of natural history in English literature, 1789-1846. MA thesis, University of London, Kings College, 1938.

1684 SCHOCH, Margaret Aitken
   The evolution of Canadian nature poetry. Thesis, Bishops University,
1945.

1685 SCOULAR, Kitty W
   Natural magic: studies in the presentation of nature in English poetry
from Spenser to Marvell, by Kitty W Scoular. Oxford, Clarendon Press,
1965. 196pp, plates. References in footnotes.
Chapters and contents: I—Natural magic: From Henry Peacham, 'Thalias
bouquet' (1620); From John Hagthorpe 'Divine meditations and elegies'
(1622). II—Much in little: From Thomas Moufet, 'The silk-wormes and
their flies' (1599); From Thomas Cutwode 'Caltha poetarum' (1599); From
William Warner 'Albions England' (1592); Richard Lovelace 'The falcon';
Richard Lovelace 'The snayl'. III—Order in confusion: Andrew Marvell
'Upon Appleton House, to my Lord Fairfax'; Robert Southwell 'A vale of
teares'.
These are the most substantial examples and pieces, but there are other
shorter quotations.

1686 SIMPSON, G F
   English nature poetry of the eighteenth century. BLitt thesis, University of Oxford, 1925.

1687 SPENCER, Jeffry Burress
   Five poetic landscapes, 1650-1750: heroic and ideal landscape in English
poetry from Marvell to Thomson. PhD thesis, Northwestern University,
1971.

1688 STUART, Dorothy M
   Landscape in Augustan verse (in Essays and Studies, 1942, pp 73-87).

1689 TOLIVER, Harold E
   Pastoral forms and attitudes, by Harold E Toliver. Berkeley, University
of California Press, 1971. 391pp.
Chapters: Pastoral contrasts; Pastoral hierarchy and entelechy; Sidney's
knights and shepherds; Spenser: the Queen and the court singer; Shakespeare's inner plays and the social contract; Poetry as sacred conveyance in
Herbert and Marvell; Milton: platonic levels and Christian transformation;
The Augustan balance of nature and art; Industrial and romantic versions
of nature; Wordsworth's two natures; Keat's pastoral alchemy as therapy;
Hardy's novels of scene and manners; Steven's supreme fiction and its
printed fragments; Bellow's idyll of the tribe; Frost's enclosures and clear-
ings.

1690 TRUESDALE, Calvin William
   English pastoral verse from Spenser to Marvell. PhD thesis, University of
Washington, 1956.

1691 VEITCH, John
   The feeling for nature in Scottish poetry, by John Veitch. Edinburgh, London, William Blackwood, 1887. 2 vols: 353pp, 364pp.
A chronological survey ranging from the thirteenth to the nineteenth century with many examples.

1692 WATSON, John Richmond
   Picturesque landscape and English romantic poetry, by J R Watson. London, Hutchinson Educational, 1970. 210pp. Bibliography (pp 199-206). Chapters: Part I—The picturesque at work: The spreading scene: Thomson and Gilpin; The individual and experience: Gray and Walpole; Part II—The first romantics: Wordsworth's early poetry; 'Tintern abbey' and 'Resolution and independence'; 'The prelude' and after; 'The guide to the lakes'; Coleridge and the landscape of happiness; Scott and the landscape of poetic fiction; Part III—The later romantics: Keats and the pursuit of the sublime; Shelley and the restless traveller; Alpine and proud: Byron on the mountain tops; The romantic landscape: some directions.

1693 WHEELER, Harold P
   Studies in sixteenth century English literature of rustic life. PhD thesis, Illinois University, 1938.

1694 YEO, Margaret Elizabeth
   The living landscape: nature imagery in the poetry of Margaret Atwood and other modern Canadian lyric poets. MA thesis, Carleton University, 1969.

The seasons

1695 ADAMS, Oscar Fay
   Poet's year: original and selected poems embodying the spirit of the seasons, edited by Oscar Fay Adams. Boston, Lothrop, [1890]. 266pp, plates, illus.

1696 ADAMS, Oscar Fay
   Through the year with the poets, edited by Oscar Fay Adams. Boston, Lothrop, 1885-6. 12 vols.

1697 HADFIELD, Miles
   An English almanac, by Miles Hadfield; with over sixty illustrations by the author. London, Dent, 1950. 225pp, illus.
Various aspects of each month of the year are described, concluding with a section headed 'The poet', consisting of short extracts of poetry with brief commentary.

1698 LANE, Rhona Arbuthnot
   An anthology of the seasons, collected by Rhona Arbuthnot Lane; with an introduction by Guy Kendall. London, Frederick Muller, 1936. 294pp. Poetry of the sixteenth, seventeenth, and nineteenth centuries.

1699 SAUNDERS, Dennis
 Weather and seasons: poems, selected by Dennis Saunders; photographs by Terry Williams. London, Evans, 1974. 32pp, illus. (Poems and Pictures series).

1700 THE SEASONS IN POETRY AND ART
 all round the year, an illustrated anthology. London, Mowbray, 1931. 127pp, plates.
Mostly nineteenth century poetry.

1701 THE SEASONS OF THE YEAR
 London, Nelson, 1858. 96pp, illus.

1702 SHARPLEY, Ada
 The poet's year: an anthology, compiled by Ada Sharpley. London, Cambridge University Press, 1922. vii, 371pp.
Poems for each month of the year; chronologically wide ranging.

1703 WOODWARD, Ida
 The seasons with the poets: an anthology, arranged by Ida Woodward. London, Elkin Mathews, 1904. xv, 241pp.
Mostly nineteenth century poetry.

1704 LOVEJOY, Mary Isabella
 Poetry of the seasons, compiled by Mary Isabella Lovejoy. New York, Boston, Silver & Burdett, 1898. 336pp, illus.

1705 LOVEJOY, Mary Isabella and ADAMS, Elizabeth
 Pieces for every month of the year, compiled by Mary Isabella Lovejoy and Elizabeth Adams. New York, Noble, 1924. xiv, 303pp, illus.
 Enlarged edition: 1929. xiv, 32pp, col plates, illus.

1706 OLIVER, Martha Capps
 Round the year with the poets; a compilation of nature poems with twelve selected portraits, by Martha Capps Oliver. New York, R Tuck, 1900. 403pp, illus.

1707 THE POETRY OF EARTH
 a nature anthology. London, Harrap, [1909]. 216pp.
Sections are headed 'Of January', 'Of February', etc. for all the months of the year. Most of the extracts deal with nature or the seasons in general. Mostly nineteenth century pieces.

1708 POETRY OF THE YEAR
 passages from the poets descriptive of the seasons. Philadelphia, Hubbard, 1873. 128pp, front, plates. (The Parlour Treasury Gems of Poetry— vol 5 no 2.)

See also: 698, 764, 997

Spring

1709 IN PRAISE OF SPRING
   an anthology for friends. Hurstpierpoint (Sussex), Sunjoy Studios,
   [1935]. 56pp, illus (some col).
Mostly nineteenth and twentieth century poetry by well-known poets.

Summer

1710 JACOBS, Leland Blair
   Poems for summer, compiled by Leland Blair Jacobs. Champaign (Ill),
   Garrard, 1970. 64pp, illus.
55 poems about the various activities and pleasures of summer.

Autumn

1711 AN AUTUMN ANTHOLOGY
   Illustrations by Rigby Graham. Coalville (Leics), 1964. 18pp, illus.
Privately printed for an anonymous gentleman by the Cistercians of Mount
Saint Bernard Abbey Coalville, distributed by the Brewhouse Press.
Prose and poetry pieces: extracts from Rev Francis Kilvert's diary, from
James Thompson's 'The seasons', Penelope Holt's 'Thoughts on autumn',
Keats' ode, extracts from Gilbert White's 'Natural history of Selbourne',
and Shelley's 'Autumn, a dirge'.

1712 SEED TIME AND HARVEST
   London, Longmans, 1969. 30pp. (Longmans' Poetry Library, edited by
Leonard Clark.)
27 poems, mostly of the twentieth century.

Winter

1713 SITWELL, Edith
   A book of the winter, compiled by Edith Sitwell. London, Macmillan,
   1950. xiv, 86pp.
Chronologically wide ranging collection, including some French pieces in the
original and in translation; not all pieces are directly connected with the
winter.

1714 WOLFE, Humbert
   A winter miscellany, edited and compiled by Humbert Wolfe, to which
are added original poems by the editor; decorated by Frank Adams. London, Eyre and Spottiswoode; New York, The Viking Press, 1930. 351pp,
illus. Limited edition: 225 numbered and signed copies.
Headings: Countryman's winter; Traveller's winter; Soldiers' and sailors'
winter; Revellers' and fireside winter; Sportsman's winter; The poet's
winter; God and Mary's winter.
Extracts of poetry and prose; chronologically wide ranging.

Studies and criticism

1715 ENKVIST, Nils Erik
The seasons of the year: chapters on a motif from Beowulf to the
Shepherd's Calendar, by Nils Erik Enkvist. Copenhagen, Ejnar Munksgaards
Forlag; Helsinki, Academic Bookstore, 1957. vii, 219pp. Bibliography.
(Societas Scientiarum Fennica. Commentationes Humanarum Litterarum
vol XXII, no 4).
Chapters: The seasons in Old English poetry; The classical background; The
place of the seasons in some medieval traditions; The seasons in Middle
English lyrics and romances; Chaucer and Gower; Lydgate and the triumph
of rhetoric; The poetry of Scotland: rhetoric and realism; The pastoral.

1716 MARTIN, B K
Aspects of winter in Latin and Old English poetry (in Journal of English
and Germanic Philology—University of Illinois, vol 68 1969, pp 375-90.
References in footnotes).

1717 WILHELM, James J
The cruellest month: the spring motif in classical and medieval lyric
poetry. PhD thesis, Yale University, 1961.

The sea (including naval songs, ballads, and shanties)

1718 ABRAHAMS, Roger D
Deep the water, shallow the shore: three essays on shantying in the West
Indies, by Roger D Abrahams; music transcribed by Linda Sobin. Austin,
University of Texas Press for the American Folklore Society, 1974. 125pp.
(American Folklore Society Memoir series, vol 60.)
Chapters: Shantying in the West Indies; 'Row bully, row boy': Singing the
fishing on Nevis and Tobago; 'Solid fas' our captain out: blackfishing at
Barouallie.
Many examples with a running commentary.

1719 ADAMS, Estelle Davenport
Sea song and river rhyme from Chaucer to Tennyson, selected and ar-
ranged by Estelle Davenport Adams; with a new poem by Algernon Charles
Swinburne ['Award for the Navy'], with twelve etchings. London, George
Redway, 1887. xxxii, 324pp, plates.
Part 1: Sea song (pp 3-161); Part 2: River rhyme (pp 167-317).
Poetry from the seventeenth to nineteenth century, mainly nineteenth,
with much unfamiliar verse.

1720 ASHTON, John
Real sailor songs, collected and edited by John Ashton. London, The
Leadenhall Press; New York, Charles Scribner, 1891. 97 numbered items,
illus.
Headings: Sea fights; Press gang; Disaster; Love.
Ballads of the seventeenth, eighteenth and nineteenth centuries. Detailed
historical notes are given for each piece.

1721 BARNES, James
Ships and sailors: being a collection of songs of the sea as sung by the
men who sail it, edited and compiled by James Barnes; with numerous illus-
trations in colour and black and white by Rufus F Zogbaum. New York,
Frederick A Stokes, 1898. 124pp, col plates, illus. Music.
Headings: Modern navy songs (by James Barnes); Old sea songs; Patriotic
songs; Sea ballads.
Musical arrangements are included, 'by kind permission of Bryan, Taylor &
Co'. Most items are familiar.

1722 BARTLETT, Alice Hunt
The sea anthology, including one hundred original sonnets on the sea,
edited by Alice Hunt Bartlett; forewords by Admiral Mark Kerr and Rear-
Admiral Bradley A Fiske. London, Erskine Macdonald, 1924. 160pp.
Headings· The sea sonnets; Sea poems of the present, The sea in earlier
English poetry.
The results of a competition, organised by the compiler through the Poetry
Society, for the best sonnet on the sea.

1723 BENWELL, Gwen and WAUGH, Arthur
Sea enchantress: the tale of the mermaid and her kin, by Gwen Benwell
and Arthur Waugh; London, Hutchinson, 1961. 287pp.
Chapter 14: in literature (pp 234-259); examples in poetry and ballad.

1724 BRUCE, Charles
Poems, songs and ballads of the sea, and celebrated discoveries, battles,
shipwrecks and incidents illustrative of life on the ocean wave, compiled and
arranged by Charles Bruce. Edinburgh, William P Nimmo, 1874. xvi, 399pp.
Nineteenth century verse about life at sea.

1725 BUSH, Eric Wheler
The flowers of the sea: an anthology of quotations, poems and prose,
edited by Captain Eric Wheler Bush. London, Allen and Unwin, 1962. xxvi,
350pp.
Headings: The sea; Storm and shipwreck; Sweethearts and wives; Home
from sea; Sea shanties; The old navy; The English admirals; Trafalgar and
afterwards; World War I; World War II. Glossary of sea terms: pp 345-350.
Poetry and prose from the sixteenth to twentieth century. Poetry consists
mostly of ballads; prose of extracts from novels, biographies, histories,
accounts and letters.

1726 BY THE SEASHORE
a selection of poems by various authors; illustrated by B D Sigmund.
London, Hildesheimer and Faulkner; New York, George C Whitney, [1888].
[12] pp, illus.
Poems by Shelley, Wordsworth, Byron and Heine in translation. Each page
is illustrated and has ornamental writing.

1727 CLEMENTS, Rex
   Manavillins: a muster of sea-songs, as distinguished from shanties written
for the most part by seamen, and sung on board ship during the closing
years of the age of sail, 1890-1910, compiled by Rex Clements. London,
Heath Cranton, 1928. 120pp.
Headings: Introduction (pp 17-37; Historical ballads I; Historical ballads II;
Professional songs; Ditties sentimental and humorous.
Consists of 37 pieces with a running commentary; compiler believes that a
number have not been published before.

1728 COLCORD, Joanna C
   Roll and go: songs of American sailormen, compiled by Joanna C Colcord;
with an introduction by Lincoln Colcord. Indianapolis, Bobbs-Merrill,
1924. 118pp, plates.
Headings: Short-drag shanties; Halyard shanties; Windlass or capstan shanties;
Forecastle songs.
   Enlarged and revised edition: Songs of American sailormen. 1938. 212pp.
   Paperback edition of the above: New York, Oak Publications, 1964.

1729 COLE, William
   The sea, ships and sailors: poems, songs and shanties selected by William
Cole; with drawings by Robin Jacques. London, Hart-Davis, 1968. 236pp,
illus.
Headings: The moods of the sea; Of ships and men; The sillies; Songs and
shanties; Storms, wrecks and disasters; Under the sea; Sea stories.
Mostly nineteenth and twentieth century verse and ballads.

1730 CROSSLAND, J R
   Spendrift: an anthology of sea-poems, [compiled] by J R Crossland.
London, Collins, [1934]. 191pp. (Laurel and Gold series.)

1731 CUMMING, John and VINCE, Charles
   The lifeboat in verse: an anthology covering a hundred years, selected
with a commentary by Sir John Cumming and Charles Vince. London,
Hodder and Stoughton, for the Royal National Life-Boat Institution,
1938. 131pp.
Headings: The call of humanity; The life-boat service and its founder; The
life-boatman; The women; The launch; The rescue; Songs (with music for
two items). Commentary: pp 113-131.
Items consisting mainly of ballads, date from 1833-1937.

1732 DE SELINCOURT, Aubrey
   The book of the sea, edited by Aubrey de Selincourt. London, Eyre and
Spottiswoode, 1961. xxiv, 376pp, plates (oil paintings). Notes (pp 361-
367).
Headings: The face of the sea; Fair weather; Foul weather; Shipwreck; The
day's work; Strange adventures; Small stuff.
Prose and poetry of a wide range from the classical writers to the twentieth
century. Virtually no sailors' songs or shanties.

1733 DOERFLINGER, William Main
   Shantymen and shantyboys: songs of the sailor and lumberman, collected and compiled by William Main Doerflinger. New York, Macmillan,
1951. xxiii, 364pp, plates. Bibliography.
Headings: 'Bust or break or bend her': short-hand shanties; 'Up aloft that
yard must go': halyard shanties; 'Heave away': capstan, windlass and pump
shanties; The rise of shantying; Deep-water songs; Ballads of the fishing
barks; Forecastle songs of the West Indies trade; The shantyboy's life;
Satirists of the sawdust country; Ballads of bold adventure; Minstrelsy of
murder; The barks of the roses: romantic ballads and love songs.
The items were all recorded personally by the compiler with tape recorder
in America and Canada. Running commentary.

1734 FIRTH, C H
   Naval songs and ballads, selected and edited by C H Firth. London, The
Naval Records Society, 1908. cxxiii (introduction), 387pp. Notes (pp
339-364).
Ballads from the sixteenth to the nineteenth century, illustrating the history
of the British navy. Index of proper names and names of ships. Tunes are
mentioned.

1735 FROTHINGHAM, Robert
   Songs of the sea and sailors chanteys: an anthology, selected and arranged
by Robert Frothingham. Cambridge (Mass), Houghton Mifflin, 1924. xxii,
283pp. Music.
Mostly unfamiliar pieces.

1736 HADFIELD, E C R
   A book of the sea, chosen by E C R Hadfield; illustrated by Norman
Hepple. London, Oxford University Press, 1940. 80pp, illus. (Chameleon
Books, II.)
Mostly familiar pieces of the nineteenth and twentieth centuries with ballads
predominating.

1737 HALLIWELL, James Orchard
   Early naval ballads of England, collected and edited by James Orchard
Halliwell. London, The Percy Society, 1841. 144pp. (Percy Society vol
2).
Consists of 57 pieces; in all cases the printed or MSS sources are given.

1738 HARLOW, Frederick Pease
   Chanteying aboard American ships, by Frederick Pease Harlow. Massa-
chussetts, Barre Gazette, 1962. xiii, 250pp, illus. Music.

1739 HOPE, Ronald
   The Harrap book of sea verse, arranged and edited by Ronald Hope.
London, Harrap in co-operation with the Seafarers' Education Service,
1960. 208pp.

Headings: in cabined ships; The boundless blue; Sailors young and old; A reminiscence of the land; Voyagers thoughts; The briny world.
Poetry from the sixteenth to the twentieth century.

1740 HUGILL, Stan
    Shanties and sailors songs, by Stan Hugill; with drawings by the author.
London, Herbert Jenkins, 1969. x, 243pp, illus. Bibliography.
The historical background of the sea song and shanty: pp 1-66. How
shanties and other kinds of ship board songs were used: pp 67-110. Shanty
collectors, books and records: pp 111-121 (includes many of the works
listed here in addition to those of Sharp, Terry, Tozer and Whall, the collectors and arrangers). The songs: pp 122-232, with some music.
Unlike 1741, this book includes numerous examples of the non-working
sea-song.

1741 HUGILL, Stan
    Shanties from the seven seas: ship-board work-songs and songs used as
work-songs from the great days of sail, collected by Stan Hugill. London,
Routledge, and Kegan Paul; New York, E P Dutton, 1961. 609pp. Bibliography. Glossary.
Part I: Shanties telling of John's shore activities; Of the gals; Of booze and
limejuice; Shanghaiing; The lowlands family; The stormalong group; Mexico
and Rio; The Sacramento and California; Goodlys and hurrahs. Part 2:
Runaway choruses; Young things and their mammies; The Roll family;
Rolling rivers and rolling homes and rolling kings; Fishes; The blow family;
Pigs—human and otherwise; The Ranzo group. Part 3: The Hilo group; gals
with blue dresses and hogseye men; Johnnies of all kinds; The heaving
group and cheerily man items; Paddy Doyle and all his relations; Shanties
of railroad origin and banjoes; Good mornin' ladies all. Part 4: The Haul
family; Rosie and rosies; Susanna and polkas; Girls names; Transportation
and place names; Meni names and professions; Ships both famous and fic-
titious. Part 5: Pot-pourri of British, American, French, German and other
foreign shanties; Sweatin'-up and hand-over hand shanties; Go to sea no
more.
Material collected by the compiler during his many years at sea.

1742 HUNTINGTON, Gale
    Songs the whalers sang, compiled by Gale Huntington. Mass, Barre Pub-
lishing Co, 1964. 328pp, illus.
Eighteenth and nineteenth century whaling songs; includes shore folk-songs,
music hall and art songs in addition to 'real' whaling songs;

1743 LAWSON, Cecil
    Naval ballads and sea songs, selected and illustrated by Cecil C P Lawson;
with an introduction by Commander Charles N Robinson. London, Peter
Davies, 1933. xiii, 72pp, illus (some col).
32 ballads, mostly anon of the seventeenth to nineteenth centuries. 26
items are taken from the collections by Firth, Masefield, and Ashton (qv).

1744 LONGFELLOW, Samuel and HIGGINSON, Thomas Wentworth
Thalatta: a book for the sea-side, [compiled] by Samuel Longfellow and
Thomas Wentworth Higginson. Boston, Ticknor, Reed and Fields, 1853.
vii, 206pp.
Nineteenth century poetry, including some of American origin.

1745 LUCE, S B
Naval songs: a collection of original, traditional sea songs, selected and
compiled under the direction of Admiral S B Luce. New York, W A Pond,
1883. 171pp.
Second edition, revised and enlarged: 1908. ix, 230pp.

1746 MELVILLE, Helen and MELVILLE, Lewis
Full fathom five: a sea anthology in prose and verse [compiled] by
Helen and Lewis Melville. London, Bell, 1910. 263pp.
Headings: The call of the sea; On the shore; The departure; The lighthouse;
En voyage; In lighter vein; Sea songs; Legends and phantasies; The cruelty
of the sea; Rule Britannia; The return.

1747 NEESER, Robert W
American naval songs and ballads, edited by Robert W Neeser. New
Haven, Yale University Press; London, Oxford University Press, 1938. xvii,
373pp, plates. Bibliography.
Headings: The revolution; From 1797 to 1811; The war of 1812; Subsequent
to 1816.
Bibliography: pp 359-361; gives library locations and includes about 50 col-
lections pre 1880. Index of ships' names. Items are taken from collections
of broadsides in the American Antiquarian Society, Worcester (Mass), New
York and Boston public libraries and the Essex Institute, Salem (Mass).
Plates are reproductions of original broadsides.

1748 OMMANNEY, E C
True to the flag: sailors' poems, compiled by E C Ommanney. London,
Routledge, 1905. 239pp.
Covers: The ocean and nature—appeal to man; Naval incidents—brave deeds;
Poems on love, joy, sorrow, etc; Religious thoughts and aspirations.
Mostly familiar poetry.

1749 PATTERSON, J E
The sea's anthology, from the earliest times to the middle of the nineteenth century, edited with notes, introduction and an appendix by J E
Patterson. London, Heinemann, 1913. xxxvi, 379pp.
Headings: The ocean's self, man's love for it, its message and its call; Its
winds, tides, and water, its mystery, music and colours; Its creatures, its
myths and its treasures; Its men, its ships and its wrecks; Ballads, songs and
chanties (pp 119-233); Naval battles and ships of war; Pirates, slave-carrying
and smuggling; Humorous pieces.
Mostly familiar poets.

1750 PIPER, Myfanwy
   Sea poems, chosen by Myfanwy Piper; with original lithographs by Mona Moore. London, Frederick Muller, 1944. 120pp, col illus. (New Excursions into English Poetry series.)
A chronologically arranged anthology covering the seventeenth to twentieth centuries. Concentrates on the poetic aspects of the sea only.

1751 PROCTER BROS
   Fisherman's ballads and songs of the sea, compiled by Procter Brothers and respectfully dedicated to the hardy fishermen of Cape Ann. Gloucester (Mass), Procter Bros, 1874. 184pp, illus.

1752 RATCLIFFE, Dorothy Una
   The sea microcosm, edited by Dorothy Una Ratcliffe. Leeds, City Chambers, The Microcosm Office, [1929]. 99pp, illus.
Prose and poetry pieces by unknown English writers of the twentieth century; includes 'The Spanish lady', a one-act comedy by the editor (pp 46-60), and 'The poetry of the sea' by W J Halliday (pp 8-12).

1753 RAWLINGS, Alfred
   The sea anthology, selected and illustrated by Alfred Rawlings. London, Gay and Hancock, 1913. 171pp, plates.
Poetry mostly of the seventeenth to nineteenth centuries, but includes also some classical pieces in translation.

1754 RICKABY, Franz L
   Ballads and songs of the shanty-boy, collected and edited by Franz L Rickaby. Cambridge (Mass), Harvard University Press, 1926. xli, 244pp, front, plates. Music.

1755 RINDER, Frank
   Naval songs and other songs and ballads of sea life, selected with an introductory note by Frank Rinder. London, Walter Scott, [1899]. xxxi, 293pp. (The Canterbury Poets series).
Headings: Patriotic; Sea fights; Disaster; Afloat; Ashore; Piracy; Drink; Love.

1756 SAUNDERS, Dennis
   Sea and shore, poems selected by Dennis Saunders; photographs by Terry Williams. London, Evans, 1974. 32pp, illus. (Poems and Pictures series.)

1757 SCOTT, Sybil
   A book of the sea, selected and arranged by Lady Sybil Scott. Oxford, Clarendon Press, 1918. xxiv, 472pp.
Headings: Lyrics; Reflections and pictures; Stories of beauties and wonders; Sailors, their deeds and songs.
Poetry of the seventeenth to nineteenth centuries; includes some French and Italian in the original and some classical pieces in translation.

1758 SHARP, William
   Songs and poems of the sea, edited by Mrs William Sharp. London,
Walter Scott, 1888. xxiii, 471pp.
Pre-Victorian period: pp 13-148; Victorian period: pp 151-467.

1759 SHAY, Frank
   Iron men and wooden ships: deep sea shanties, edited by Frank Shay;
decorations and woodcuts by Edward A Wilson, introduction by William
McFee. New York, Doubleday & Page, 1924. xx, 154pp, plates (some col).
   English edition: Deep sea shanties: old sea songs. London, Heinemann,
1925. Limited edition of 200 copies.
   Enlarged and revised edition: American sea songs and chanteys from the
days of iron men and wooden ships, [compiled] by Frank Shay; illustrated
by Edward A Wilson, musical arrangements by Christopher Thomas. New
York, Norton, 1948. 217pp, illus, col plates. Music.
Headings: Chanteys; Forecastle songs; Wardroom ballads; Miscellaneous
songs and ballads.

1760 SHAY, Frank
   A little book of vagabond songs: poems of the hills and sea, compiled by
Frank Shay; with etchings by Philip Kappel. New York, London, Harper,
1931. 60pp, plates.
pp 31-60: 23 poems on the sea. The rest are about travelling, vagabondage,
and nature in general.

1761 SMITH, C Fox
   A book of shanties, [compiled] by C Fox Smith. London, Methuen,
1927. 93pp. Music.
Introduction: pp 7-15. Texts and music for 31 items; each shanty has a
commentary, in some cases giving sources and other versions.

1762 SMITH, C Fox
   A sea chest: an anthology of ships and sailormen, compiled by C Fox
Smith. London, Methuen, 1927. 216pp.
Headings: Introduction (pp 1-18); In praise of seafaring; The way of a ship;
Ships company; A group of passengers; Sea legends and weather signs;
Figureheads; Shipwrecks, piracy and other marine risks; A gallery of ships;
Sailortown; The building of a ship; A few yarns and some salt water wisdom;
Port after stormy seas; So long!
Poetry and prose ranging from the Bible to the nineteenth century.

1763 SMITH, Laura Alexander
   The music of the waters: a collection of the sailors chanties or working
songs of the sea, of all maritime nations. Boatmen, fishermen, and rowing
songs and water legends, by Laura Alexander Smith. London, Kegan Paul
& Trench, 1888. 360pp. Music.
An international collection with a running commentary.

1764 STONE, Christopher
   Sea songs and ballads, selected by Christopher Stone; with an introduction by Admiral Sir Cyprian Bridge. Oxford, Clarendon Press, 1906. xxiv,
213pp. Notes (pp 195-209).
Nearly all the songs were written before the battle of Trafalgar. Sources
are: volumes of the Ballad Society, the Roxburgh and Bagford ballads, and
the collections by Ashton and Halliwell (qv).

1765 SWALE, Ingram
   The voice of the sea, edited by Ingram Swale. London, Routledge,
[1907]. x, 163pp. (Wayfaring Books.)
Headings: England and the sea; The message of the sea; The immensity of
the sea; Morning and night on sea; Winds and waves of the seas; The murmuring sea; The world beneath the sea; By the sea-shore; Strange aspects of
the sea; The sea as symbol.
Mostly nineteenth century poetry, by well-known poets.

1766 U S NAVAL ACADEMY, ANNAPOLIS. THE TRIDENT SOCIETY
   The book of navy songs, collected and edited by the Trident Society of
the U S Naval Academy at Annapolis, Maryland; music arranged and harmon-
ized by Joseph W Crosley. Garden City, New York, Doubleday & Page,
1926. x, 200pp, front, illus, plates. Music.

1767 WARD, Anna L
   Surf and wave: the sea as sung by the poets, edited by Anna L Ward.
New York, Crowell, 1883. xii, 618pp, illus (by Miss Florentine H Hayden).
Headings: Sea breezes; Waves of the deep; Sea-spray; Surf-edges; Ocean-
soundings;
Mostly unknown nineteenth century poetry.

1768 WHITHEAD, Edward
   In praise of the sea: an anthology for friends, compiled by Edward White-
head. London, Frederick Muller, 1955. 64pp, plates.
Prose and poetry extracts.

1769 WILLIAMSON, W M
   The eternal sea: an anthology of sea poetry, edited by W M Williamson;
drawings by Gordon Grant. New York, Coward-McCann, 1946. x, 565pp,
illus.
Headings: The call of the sea; The building of the ship; Outward bound;
Stormy seas; Calm, sunny seas; 'Roll on, thou deep and dark blue ocean,
roll on!'; Nautica mystica; 'Love still has something of the sea'; Homeward
bound—making port; Sailor town; Sea wings; Fishermen; Naval songs and
ballads; 'Ah bl-o-ows!'; Pirates and buccaneers; Neptune's kingdom; Ghost
ships and phantoms; 'Spin a yarn, sailor'; Child of the sea; The voice of
the sea; Hail and farewell.
Mostly twentieth century American and English verse.

1770 WILSON, Richard
A book of ships and seamen, edited by Richard Wilson; with an introduction by 'Q'. London, Dent; New York, Dutton. 1921. 256pp.
Extracts range from the Bible and Shakespeare to the nineteenth century. Poetry and prose.

See also: 418, 421, 985, 990, 1002, 1008, 1127, 1648

Studies and criticism

1771 AUDEN, W H
The enchafed flood, or the romantic iconography of the sea, by W H Auden. London, Faber, 1951. 126pp.
Chapters: The sea and the desert; The stone and the shell; Ishmael—Don Quixote.
Contents originally given in lecture form during March 1949, under the auspices of the University of Virginia and the trustees of the Page-Barbour Lecture Foundation. ' . . . chapters are an attempt to understand the nature of romanticism through an examination of its treatment of a single theme, the sea . . .'

1772 BONE, David W
Capstan bars, by David W Bone; with 8 woodcuts by Freda Bone. Edinburgh, The Porpoise Press; London, Faber; New York, Harcourt Brace, 1931. 160pp, illus. Music. Glossary (pp 151-160).
Chapters: The calendar of chanties; Short hand chanties; Halyard chanties; Debt and credit; Capstan chanties; Out of the blue; Windlass and pump chanties; 'Leave 'er, John-nie, Leave 'er'; The Liverpool song.
An essay on the sea shanty with 24 pieces quoted as examples. The author wished to convey his own experience of these songs and their significance.

1773 BOURKE, John
The sea as a symbol in English poetry, by John Bourke. Eton (Bucks), Alden and Blackwell, 1954. 44pp. References in foot-notes.
Chapters: The sea as a symbol of freedom; The sea as a symbol of human life; The sea as a symbol of eternity.

1774 COVO, Jacqueline
The lake of darkness: marine imagery in relationship to themes of disruption in medieval poetry. PhD thesis, Brandeis University, 1967.

1775 DAVIES, W J F
The sea in Old English poetry. MA thesis, University of Wales, 1948.

1776 FOLSOM, John B
The sea as a shaping influence in the making of some late Elizabethan narrative poems. PhD thesis, University of California, Berkeley, 1961.

1777 KISSACK, R A
The sea in Anglo-Saxon and Middle English poetry (in Washington University Studies, Humanistic Series, xiii, 1926, pp 371-89).

1778 O'MAHONY, J F
   The sea in English poetry. MA thesis, National University of Ireland, 1942.

1779 TRENEER, Anne
   The sea in English literature from Beowulf to Donne, by Anne Treneer. Liverpool, Liverpool University Press; London, Hodder and Stoughton, 1926. xvii, 299pp.
Chapters: The sea in Old English literature; Glimpses of the sea in Middle English; Hakluyt; Miscellaneous prose; The sea in English poetry from Surrey to Donne; The sea in sixteenth century drama.

Rivers

1780 CARMER, Carl Lamson
   Songs of the rivers of America, edited by Carl Lamson Carmer; music arranged by Dr Albert Sirmay. New York, Farrer & Rinehart, 1942. xi, 196pp. Music.
Volume intended to provide song material for the multi-volume series 'The rivers of America', issued by the same publisher in the 1940s.

1781 PARKER, T H and TESKEY, F J
   Inland waterways, [compiled] by T H Parker and F J Teskey. Glasgow, Blackie, 1970. 58pp, illus. (Themes to Explore series).
Headings: Personal reflections; The further bank; Sacred waters; Under the surface.
Twentieth century poetry. Intended for school use.

1782 SANDILANDS, G S
   In praise of rivers: an anthology for friends, compiled by G S Sandilands. London, Frederick Muller, 1956. 64pp, illus.
Poetry and prose extracts from the seventeenth to twentieth century.

1783 WHEELER, Mary
   Steamboatin' days: folk songs of the river packet era, compiled by Mary Wheeler. Baton Rouge (La), Louisiana State University Press, 1944. x, 121pp, plates. Music.

See also: 938, 943, 997, 1002, 1150, 1648, 1719

River Thames

1784 IRWIN, John and HERBERT, Jocelyn
   Sweete Themmes: a chronicle in prose and verse, edited by John Irwin and Jocelyn Herbert; with a foreword by W J Brown. London, Max Parrish, 1951. 271pp, illus.
Headings: The river remembers (up to 1613); Carnival and pageant (1614-1713); The four Georges (1714-1836); The great and good (1937-1900); The tumultuous years (1901 to the present).
Prose and poetry mostly concerned with the Thames in and around London.

1785 MAXWELL, Gordon S
   The author's Thames: a literary ramble through the Thames valley by
Gordon S Maxwell; illustrated by Lucilla Maxwell. London, Cecil Palmer,
1924. 324pp, illus.
A descriptive study of the River Thames with numerous short poetry ex-
tracts.

See also: London 1043-1054

River Hudson See: 1153

Mountains, hills, and mountaineering

1786 BAKER, Ernest A and ROSS, Francis E
   The voice of the mountains, edited by Ernest A Baker and Francis E
Ross. London, Routledge, [1905]. 294pp.
Headings: The mountains; In the valley; The mountains of fancy; Man and
mountains; The mountains and Good; Many waters; Cloud pageantry; Storm;
The making of the mountains; The end of the mountains; Hills and fells of
England; Eryri; Albyn; The Isle of Mist; The alps of the Alps; The monarch;
Italy; The Pyrenees and Spain; Hellas and the Orient; The West; A mountain
wreath; Dawn; Sunset and dawn; The spirit of solitude; Vision of the heights.
Poetry and prose, mostly of the nineteenth century. Some foreign items in
translation.

1787 HIRST, John
   The songs of the mountaineers, collected and edited by John Hirst for
the Rucksack Club. [1922]; 124pp.
Songs (only the names of the airs are given) on climbing, walking, the open
air and comradeship.

1788 THE MOUNTAINS
   a collection of poems. Boston, Roberts, 1876. 198pp.
Nineteenth century English and American poets, known and unknown.

1789 STYLES, Showell
   The mountaineer's week-end book, by Showell Styles. London, Seeley
Service, [1951]. 396pp.
pp 335-396: a short anthology of mountain poems.

1790 YOUNG, Eleanor and YOUNG, Geoffrey Winthrop
   In praise of mountains: an anthology for friends, compiled by Eleanor
and Geoffrey Winthrop Young. London, Frederick Muller, 1948. 56pp.
Prose and poetry extracts.

See also: 1002, 1150

The Alps

1791 LUNN, Arnold
   The Englishman in the Alps: being a collection of English prose and
poetry relating to the Alps, edited by Arnold Lunn. London, Oxford

University Press, 1913. 294pp.
Poetry: pp 218-292; Prose: pp 1-216.

1792 McSPADDEN, Joseph Walker
The alps as seen by the poets, edited by J Walker McSpadden. New
York, Crowell, [1912]. 222pp, col plates.

1793 SPENDER, Harold
In praise of Switzerland: being the Alps in prose and verse [compiled]
by Harold Spender. London, Constable, 1912. 291pp.
Headings: The alps in admiration, in description, in adventure i) the pion-
eers, ii) the heroes, in tragedy, in comedy, in history, in fiction.
Mainly nineteenth century.

Studies and criticism

1794 BATES, Robert H
A study of the literature of the mountains and mountain climbing written in English. PhD thesis, Pennsylvania University, 1947.

1795 COLLETTE, Elizabeth
A study of the Alps in English literature. PhD thesis, New York, University, 1927.

1796 GRIGSON, Geoffrey
Hills [and their effect on poets] and poems (in Geographical Magazine,
1956, pp 388-96).

1797 ZINK, David
The beauty of the Alps: a study of the Victorian mountain aesthetic.
PhD thesis, Colorado University, 1962.

ANIMALS

General

1798 BARNES, Derek Gilpin
Lords of life: an anthology of animal poetry of the last fifty years,
chosen and edited with an introduction by Derek Gilpin Barnes; illustrated
by Kathleen Barnes. London, Rich and Cowan, [1946]. 175pp, illus.

1799 BERG, Leila
Four feet and two, and some with none: an anthology of animal verse,
compiled by Leila Berg; with illustrations by Shirley Burke and Marvin
Bileck. Harmondsworth (Middx), Penguin, 1960. 220pp, illus. (Puffin
book.)

1800 BOAS, Cecily
Birds and beasts in English literature, collected by Cecily Boas. London,
Edinburgh, Nelson, 1926. vii, 240pp.

Headings: Birds; Dogs; Cats; Sheep and cattle; Donkeys; Horses; Wild animals.
Each section has short introduction outlining treatment of the subject by writers. Prose and poetry; mostly well-known pieces.

1801 BODY, Alfred H
    Animals all: an anthology for schools, selected and edited by Alfred H Body; with animal decorations by J C Macdonald. Cambridge, University Press, 1940. 160pp, illus.
Headings: Friends of man; Birds; Beasts; Insects and vermin; Strange creatures; Animals and Man.
Prose and poetry from the seventeenth to the twentieth century. Pp 135-160: exercises.

1802 BREWTON, John Edmund
    Under the tent of the sky: a collection of poems about animals large and small; with drawings by Robert Lawson. New York, Macmillan, 1954. xvi, 205pp, illus.

1803 CLARKE, Frances Elizabeth
    Poetry's plea for animals: an anthology of justice and mercy for our kindred in fur and feathers, collected and edited by Frances Elizabeth Clarke; with an introduction by Edwin Markham, illustrated by W F Stecher. Boston, Lothrop, Lee & Shepard, [1922]. xxxiv, 426pp, illus.

1804 COLE, William
    The birds and beasts were there: animal poems, selected by William Cole; woodcuts by Helen Siegl. Cleveland, New York, The World Publishing Co, 1963. 320pp, illus.
Headings: Small animals of the woods and fields; Under the water and on the shore; slitherers, creepers and hardshells; Dogs, cats, horses and donkeys; The farmyard; Big beasts; Wild beasts; Buzzers, leapers and flyers; Birds; Animals all together; Impossible animals.
Contains much twentieth century American poetry.

1805 D'OYLEY, Elizabeth
    An anthology for animal lovers: of the love of beasts [compiled] by Elizabeth D'Oyley; with an introduction by John Galsworthy. London, Collins, 1927. 271pp.
Headings: Of beauty; Of friendship; Of fellowship; Of service; Of cruelty; Of piety; Of immortality; Of character; Here they speak for themselves; From the post bag.
Poetry and prose; biblical extracts and pieces from the seventeenth to the twentieth century. Some French and classical writers in translation and some extracts from Punch.

1806 FOUGASSE [Cyril Kenneth Bird]
    The neighbours: an animal anthology, compiled and illustrated by Fougasse. London, Methuen for U F A W (The Universities Federation for Animal Welfare), 1954. x, 117pp.

Prose and poetry from the seventeenth to the twentieth century, with an emphasis on the twentieth, and containing many less familiar pieces.

1807 GROVER, Edwin Osgood
Animal lover's knapsack: an anthology of poems for lovers of our animal friends, edited by Edwin Osgood Grover. New York, Crowell, 1929. xix, 288pp.

1808 HADFIELD, E C R
A book of animal verse, chosen by E C R Hadfield; illustrated by Erna Pinner. London, Oxford University Press, 1943. 64pp, illus. (Chameleon Books 21.)

1809 HILDITCH, Gwen
In praise of pets: an anthology for friends, compiled by Gwen Hilditch. London, Frederick Muller, 1957. 63pp.
Poetry and prose extracts; cats and dogs predominate.

1810 JONES, Rhodri
Men and beasts, edited by Rhodri Jones. London, Heinemann Educational, 1969. 72pp, illus. (Heinemann Themes series.)
Headings: Pets; Predators; Encounters; Victims.
Twentieth century poetry. Intended for schools.

1811 JACOBS, Leland B
Animal antics in Limerick Land, selected by Leland B Jacobs; drawings by Edward Malsbery. Champaign (Ill), Garrard, 1971. 63pp, illus.

1812 LEONARD, R M
Poems on animals, selected by R M Leonard. London, Oxford University Press, 1915. 128pp. (Oxford Garlands.)
Arranged by type of animal: Dog; Cat; Horse; Ox; Lamb; Fox; Hare; Lion; Tiger; Bear; Giraffe; Kangeroo; Bat; Toad; Lizard.
Poetry from the seventeenth to nineteenth century mostly by well-known poets.

1813 MacBETH, George
The Penguin book of animal verse, introduced and edited by George MacBeth. Harmondsworth (Middx), Penguin, 1965. 335pp.
Covers a very wide range of animals. Contains much twentieth century verse.

1814 MANNING-SANDERS, Ruth
Birds, beasts and fishes, compiled by Ruth Manning-Sanders; with illustrations by Rita Parsons. London, Oxford University Press, 1962. 247pp, illus.
Headings: An immense world of delight; Creatures great and small. Among green leaves and blossoms sweet; Morning and spring; Homestead, farm and garden; In field and meadow; In the woods; Evening and night; Winter;

Things which are little; To tell my loss; Fairy tales; Songs; Bright water and deep sea; Rhymes and riddles; Some more tales; In lonely places; To give him praise.
Intended for children; much familiar material.

1815 MANNHEIM, Grete
    Feather or fur: a collection of animal poems, compiled by Grete Mannheim. New York, Knopf, [1967]. illus. Intended for children.

1816 MASON, Kenneth A
    An anthology of animal poetry, compiled by Kenneth A Mason. Harmondsworth (Middx), Penguin, 1940. 112pp; (Pelican Books no 76.)

1817 PARKER, T H and TESKEY, F J
    Animals in captivity, edited by T H Parker and F J Teskey. London, Blackie, 1970. 58pp, illus. (Themes to Explore series.)
Headings: Taken prisoner; Behind bars; The sawdust ring; Around the house; Doomed to die.
Twentieth century prose and poetry. Intended for school use.

1818 REED, Gwendolyn
    Out of the ark: an anthology of animal verse, compiled by Gwendolyn Reed. London, Longman Young Books, 1970. xv, 228pp. Notes (pp 207-218).
    Originally published: New York, Atheneum, 1968.

1819 ROBINSON, Phil
    The poets and nature: reptiles, fishes and insects, by Phil Robinson. London, Chatto and Windus, 1893. x, 300pp.
Headings: The poets' reptiles: Crocodiles, turtles and lizards; Snakes in nature; Snakes in tradition; Snakes in poetry; The tuneful frog; The loathed paddock. The poets' fishes: Fish-monsters and myths; Fishes of the angle; Some poetic fish fancies; Some shell-fishes; The poets' dolphin. The poets' insects: Ants and butterflies; Night moths and day moths; Arachne and the poets; Flies: 'the hosts of Achor'; Grasshoppers, crickets and locusts; Lucifers and the poets; Deborah, 'the honey-bee'.
Consists of numerous extracts and pieces, with a running commentary.

1820 ROBINSON, Phil
    The poets' beasts, by Phil Robinson. London, Chatto and Windus, 1885. 356pp.
Headings: The king of the beasts; The heptarchy of the cats; Bears and wolves; Some beasts of reproach; Asses and apes; Some harmless beasts; British wild beasts; Beasts of chase; The poets' flock; 'The beard-blown goat'; The poets' herd; Some poets' horses; Some poets' dogs; Some poets' cats;
Consists of numerous extracts and pieces with a running commentary.

1821 SALT, Henry S
    Kith and kin: poems of animal life, selected by Henry S Salt. London, Bell, 1901. 95pp.

1821a SAUNDERS, Dennis
    Creatures small, poems selected by Dennis Saunders; photographs by
Terry Williams. London, Evans, 1974. 32pp, illus (Poems and Pictures
series.)

1822 SMILEY, Marjorie B and others
    Creatures in verse, compiled by Marjorie B Smiley, Florence B Fredman,
Domenica Paterns. New York, Macmillan, 1967. xix, 103pp.

1823 SPEARMAN, Diana
    The animal anthology, compiled by Diana Spearman; foreword by Peter
Scott. London, John Baker, 1966. 208pp.
Headings: The hunted; Friends, companions, servants; The animal for itself;
The common fate; Man's guilt; The continuing protest.
A wide-ranging anthology, covering prose and poetry of all periods.

1824 WILLIAMS, Eric
    Dragonsteeth, edited by Eric Williams. London, Arnold, 1972. 95pp,
illus (photographs).
'Poems explore man's physical setting—the seasons, weather, elements, sea,
landscape, etc, and the crises and emotions they arouse in him; and particularly man's relations with the other animals that surround him . . '
Twentieth century poetry.

See also: 228, 418, 663; Farming 796-801

Studies and criticism

1825 FISHER, K A
    The growth of humanitarian feeling towards animals as shown in English
poetry. MA thesis, University of Wales, 1929.

1826 HARRIS, Robert B
    The beast in English satire from Spenser to John Gay. PhD thesis, Harv-
ard University, 1932.

1827 JAGER, M
    The development of the idea of the animal as a symbol of harmony in
English literature. PhD thesis, University of Cambridge, 1932.

1828 LEVIE, Dagobert de
    The modern idea of prevention of cruelty to animals and its reflection
in English poetry. New York, S F Vann, 1947. 109pp. Bibliography (pp
102-108).
Originally presented as a thesis at the University of Basel.

1829 ROBIN, P Ansell
    Animal lore in English literature, by P Ansell Robin. London, John
Murray, 1932. 196pp, illus.
Chapters: The sources and uses of animal lore; The birth and death of ani-
mals; Animals as types of character; Some fabulous animals; Other

mammalia and a few insects; Marine creatures; Some reptiles; Birds of the air.
Illustrations from medieval sources.

1830 ROLT-WHEELER, Ethel
   Super-animals in English poetry (in Transactions of the Royal Society of Literature, second series, Vol 34, 1916, pp 47-86).

1831 SELLS, A Lytton
   Animal poetry in French and English literature and the Greek tradition, by A Lytton Sells. London, Thames and Hudson; Bloomington, Indiana University Press, 1958. xxxiv, 329pp, illus.
A chronological treatment of the subject. Illustrations are photographs of paintings and sculpture.

1832 STUART, Dorothy Margaret
   A book of birds and beasts, legendary, literary and historical, by Dorothy Margaret Stuart. London, Methuen, 1957. xii, 226pp, plates.
Chapters: Birds in the ancient world; Medieval birds; Birds of the English Renaissance; Birds under Stuart skies; Birds, Augustan to Victorian; Dogs in the ancient world; Medieval dogs; Dogs of the English Renaissance; Stuart dogs; Dogs, Augustan to Victorian; Horses in the ancient world; Horses, eleventh to sixteenth century; Tudor and Stuart horses; Horses Augustan to Victorian.

1833 WATSON, E A F
   The animal world in the poetry and drama of the sixteenth and seventeenth centuries, with special reference to Spenser, Shakespeare and Milton. BLitt thesis, University of Oxford, 1963.

1834 WESTACOTT, Charles A
   The poet and the animals, by Charles A Westacott. Letchworth (Herts), 24 Redhoods Way East, [1953]. 44pp.
References to animals in the poetry of Herrick, Thomson, Crabbe, Blake, Bloomfield, Cambell, Byron, Clare, and Keats.

Mammals

Cats

1835 ABERCONWAY, Christabel
   A dictionary of cat lovers, fifteenth century BC-twentieth century AD, with five legends concerning cats, and with notes on 'The cat in ancient Egypt', etc, compiled by Christabel Aberconway. London, Michael Joseph, 1949. 466pp, illus.
Alphabetical arrangement by author. Poetry and prose, with a number of French pieces in the original.

1836 BLEGVAK, Leonore
  Mittens for kittens and other rhymes about cats, chosen by Leonore Blegvak. London, Hamilton, 1974. [26pp], illus.
Originally published: New York, Atheneum, 1974.

1837 CARR, Samuel
  The poetry of cats, edited by Samuel Carr. London, Batsford, 1974. 96pp, illus, plates.
Mostly twentieth century poetry. Illustrations consist of prints, drawings and paintings.

1838 CRAWFORD, Nelson
  Cats in prose and verse, compiled by Nelson Crawford; drawings by Diana Thorre. New York, Coward-McCann, 1947. xxvii, 387pp, illus.

1839 FOSTER, Dorothy
  In praise of cats, compiled by Dorothy Foster, illustrated by Alan Daniel. London, Harrap, 1975. 129pp, illus.
Headings: The proud, mysterious cat; The hungry cat; The hunter; The curious cat; The kitten; Rhymes and ballads; The tomcat; The lover; The friend; Epitaph.
Mostly twentieth century poetry. Some foreign pieces in translation.

1840 FYFE, Hamilton
  Poems in praise of cats: a collection of poems about cats, compiled by Hamilton Fyfe. London, Bannisdale Press, 1949. 84pp. pp 9-19: Introduction.
Poetry mostly of the nineteenth and twentieth centuries.

1841a GOODEN, Mona
  The poet's cat: an anthology, compiled by Mona Gooden, with a frontispiece engraved by Stephen Gooden. London, Harrap, 1946. 115pp, front. pp 13-21: Introduction.
Poetry from the seventeenth to the twentieth century. Some foreign items in translation.

1841b HAMILTON, Lynn
  Sophisti-cats: poems for cat lovers, compiled and edited by Lynn Hamilton. The compiler, 1952. 368pp. pp 11-15: Introduction.
Mostly twentieth century American poetry.

1842 HILDITCH, Gwen
  In praise of cats: an anthology for friends, compiled by Gwen Hilditch. London, Frederic Muller, 1949. 62pp, illus.
Poetry and prose extracts.

1843 LEE, Elizabeth
  A quorum of cats: an anthology, selected by Elizabeth Lee, illustrated by Maurice Wilson. London, Elek, 1963. 172pp, illus.
Prose and poetry by twentieth century authors.
  Reissued 1976 with new drawings by Maurice Wilson.

1844 MacBETH, George and BOOTH, Martin
  The book of cats, edited by George MacBeth and Martin Booth. London,
Secker & Warburg, 1976. viii, 288pp, illus, col plates.
Headings: Cat's youth; Cat's meat; Cat's games; Cat's love; Cat's magic;
Cat's killings; Cat's age; Cat's death; Cat's resurrection.
Poetry and prose by mostly well-known writers of the twentieth century.
Includes new short stories specially commissioned from Patricia Highsmith,
Roy Fuller, and Giles Gordon.
Illustrations are photographs of paintings, engravings, drawings and sculp-
ture of all periods.

1845 MEIGHN, Moira
  Children of the moon: a booklet concerning cats, compiled by Moira
Meighn. London, Medici Society, 1929. 83pp.
Mostly prose extracts (pp 74-78: The signboard and the cat, from 'Cat gos-
sip' by H C Brooke).

1846 SCOTT, W S
  A clowder of cats: an anthology in prose and poetry for all cat lovers, by
W S Scott; with drawings by Edwin Smith. London, John Westhouse, 1946.
175pp, illus (some col).
Headings: Cats of old time; Cats in religion; Eighteenth century cats; Non-
sense cats.

1847 SHAW, Richard
  The cat book: an anthology of poetry and prose, compiled and edited by
Richard Shaw. London, Kaye and Ward, 1974. 48pp, illus (mostly col).
Prose and poetry. Intended for children.
  Originally published: New York, F Warne, 1973.

1848 TOMSON, Graham R
  Concerning cats: a book of poems by many authors, selected by Graham
R Tomson; and illustrated by Arthur Tomson. London, Fisher Unwin,
1892. 136pp, illus.

1849 WELLS, Carolyn and LUELLA, D Everett
  The cat in verse, compiled by Carolyn Well and D Everett Luella; with
illustrations by Meta Pluckebaum. Boston, Little and Brown, 1935. xii,
289pp, illus.

Studies and criticism

1850 (BIBLIOGRAPHY) DENHAM, Sidney
  Poet's cats (in 'Cats between covers: a bibliography of books about cats'.
London, H Denham, 1952, pp 16-20).
A brief review of some of the above anthologies and various cat poems.
Bibliography lists sixteen items, consisting of anthologies, individual poems
and collections by individual poets.

1851 (BIBLIOGRAPHY) NECKER, Claire
   Four centuries of cat books: a bibliography 1570-1970, compiled by
Claire Necker. Metuchen, Scarecrow Press, 1972. vii, 511pp.
Covers anthologies, individual poems and collections by individual authors.

Dogs

1852 BARNET, F M
   Our dog's birthday book, arranged by Mrs F M Barnet, with twelve pictures of champion dogs. London, George Allen, 1902. 143pp, illus.
Very short extracts of verse, all connected with dogs, for each day of the
year.

1853 BICKNELL, Ethel E
   Praise of the dog: an anthology, compiled by Ethel E Bicknell. London,
Grant Richards, 1902. 225pp.
Poetry and prose from the seventeenth to the twentieth century.

1854 BLEGVAK, Leonard
   Hark hark, the dogs do bark and other rhymes about dogs, chosen by
Leonard Blegvak. London, Hamilton, 1975. [26]pp, illus.

1855 BURTIS, Edwin
   All the best dog poems, an anthology of poetry about dogs, collected
by Edwin Burtis; illustrated by Nils Hogner. New York, Crowell, [1946].
231pp, illus.

1856 CARR, Samuel
   The poetry of dogs, edited by Samuel Carr. London, Batsford, 1974.
96pp, col plates, illus.
Mostly well-known poets from the eighteenth to twentieth century. Illustrations range from the fifteenth to nineteenth century.

1857 FROTHINGHAM, Robert
   Songs of dogs: an anthology, selected and arranged by Robert Frothingham. Boston, Houghton Mifflin, 1920. xvi, 167pp.

1858 HARNETT, C M
   In praise of dogs: an anthology in prose and verse, compiled by C M Har-
nett, illustrated with sixteen plates from chalk and pencil sketches by G
Vernon Stokes. London, Country Life Ltd, 1936. 112pp, plates.

1859 LEONARD, R Maynard
   The dog in British poetry, edited by R Maynard Leonard. London,
David Nutt, 1893. 350pp. Notes: pp 293-332.
Headings: Narrative poems; Sporting poems; Elegiac poems; Miscellaneous
poems.
Covers poetry from medieval period to the nineteenth century.

1860 MENZIES, Lucy
   The first friend: an anthology of the friendship of man and dog, compiled from the literature of all ages, 1400 BC-1921 AD, by Lucy Menzies.

London, Allen and Unwin, 1922. 199pp.
Prose and poetry.

1861 MILLER, Conrad Jenness
   Dogs of all nations in prose and rhyme, edited by Conrad Jenness Miller. New York, J S Ogilvie, 1903. vii, 243pp, illus.

1862 MONGREL, PUPPY, WHELP AND HOUND
   being a booklet in praise of dogs of all kinds. London, Boston, The Medici Society, [1929]; 79pp.
Poetry and prose from the seventeenth to nineteenth century.

1863 PARSON, J
   The friendly dog: an anthology, edited by J Parson. London, Kegan Paul, Trench, Trübner, 1912. 120pp.
Overlaps in the selection of nineteenth century poems with those in the collection by R M Leonard.

1864 RICHARDSON, Elizabeth
   Poet's dog, collected and arranged by E Richardson. New York, Putnam, 1895. x, 192pp.

1865 RUTTER, Owen
   Dog days, compiled and arranged by Owen Rutter; with decorations by Dilys Watkin. London, Clement Ingleby, 1925. 97pp, illus.

1866 STAMPA, G L
   In praise of dogs: an anthology for all dog lovers, compiled and illustrated by G L Stampa. London, Frederick Muller, 1948. 63pp, illus.
Poetry and prose extracts.

1867a WOODS, Ralph Louis
   A treasury of the dog, edited by Ralph Louis Woods; illustrated by Lumen Martin Winter. New York, Putnam, [1956]. 432pp, illus.
Dog legends, stories and poetry.

Donkeys

1867b WALKER, Stella A
   Enamoured of an ass, edited by Stella A Walker. London, Angus & Robertson, 1977. 224pp, plates, illus.
Headings: Donkeys defined; Donkeys diverse; Donkeys delectable; Donkeys delinquent; Donkey deals; Doctrines and dictums; Donkeys triumphant.
Prose and poetry of all periods on all aspects of the donkey.

Elephants

1868 SILLAR, F C and MEYLER, R M
   Elephants ancient and modern, compiled by F C Sillar and R M Meyler. London, Studio Vista, 1968. 255pp, illus.
Prose and poetry extracts; more prose than poetry.

Foxes

1869 SHAW, Richard
The fox book, compiled and edited by Richard Shaw. London, Kaye and Ward, 1972. 48pp, illus (mostly col.)
Poetry and prose. Intended for children.
Originally published: New York, F Warne, 1970.

Horses See: Riding 958-967

Pigs

1870 SILLAR, F C and MEYLER, R M
The symbolic pig: an anthology of pigs in literature and art, by Frederick Cameron Sillar and Ruth Mary Meyler; original drawings and decorations by Oliver Hott. Edinburgh, London, Oliver and Boyd, 1961. 193pp, plates, illus.
Headings: The charm of pigs; A pig's a pig for a' that; A glossary; The pig in art; Ecclesiastical pigs; Some fictional pigs; Revolutionary pigs; Pigs and learning; Legendary pigs; The nursery pig (pigs in nursery rhymes); Drawing pigs; Poor man pigs; Pigs and place names; Pigs in the oven; Pigs and devil; Pigs and water; The straying pig; The advantages of being a pig; Fly pigs; Pigs and music; Pig and whistle.
Poetry and prose; more prose than poetry.

Amphibians

Frogs

1871 SHAW, Richard
The frog book, compiled and edited by Richard Shaw. London, Kaye and Ward. 1973. 48pp, illus (mostly col.)
Poetry and prose. Intended for children.
Originally published: New York, F Warne, 1972.

Fish See: Fishing 938-946

Birds

1872 CARR, Samuel
The poetry of birds, edited by Samuel Carr. London, Batsford, 1976. 88pp, col plates, illus.
Mostly well-known English and American poets from the seventeenth to twentieth century. Illustrations range from the fifteenth to nineteenth century.

1873 CARRUTH, Hayden
The bird poem book; poems on the wild birds of N America, selected by Hayden Carruth, illustrated by Mel Hunter. New York, McCall, 1970. xii, 51pp, illus.

1874 CHANDLER, A R
  Larks, nightingales and poets: an essay and an anthology. Columbus, the compiler, 1938. viii, 190pp, illus. Music. Bibliography (pp 167-182).

1875 CHAPIN, Christina
  The bird-lover's book of verse, collected by Christina Chapin; and illustrated with linocuts by Raphael Nelson, foreword by Arthur Waugh. London, H F and G Witherby, 1937. x, 185pp, illus.
  Headings: The Birds; Birds and the poet; Birds and mankind; Birds and the universe.
  Mostly nineteenth and twentieth century poetry.

1876 HARPER, S A
  Twelve months with the birds and poets, [compiled] by S A Harper; illustrated by Ralph Fletcher Seymour. Chicago, R F Seymour, 1917. 295pp, plates, illus.

1877 HILDITCH, Gwen
  In praise of birds; an anthology for friends, compiled by Gwen Hilditch. London, Frederick Muller, 1954. 62pp, illus.
  Extracts of nineteenth and twentieth century prose and verse.

1878 KNOWLES, Susanne
  Chorus: an anthology of bird poems, compiled by Susanne Knowles. London, Heinemann; New York, Funk and Wagnalls, 1969. 253pp.
  Headings: The birds by name; General chorus; Myth, story and symbols.
  Covers a substantial amount of twentieth century poetry.

1879 MASSINGHAM, H J
  Poems about birds from the Middle Ages to the present day, chosen and edited with an introduction and notes by H J Massingham. London, Fisher Unwin, 1922. 415pp. Preface by J C Squire, pp 6-12; Introduction: pp 15-30.

1880 OSGOOD, Irene and WYNDHAM, Horace
  The winged anthology: a collection of representative poems relating to birds, butterflies and moths, from 1536 to 1914, selected and arranged by Irene Osgood and Horace Wyndham. London, John Richmond, 1914. 365pp.
  As with 1878, covers a very wide range of birds.

1881 P, M A and others
  The time of the singing of birds, [compiled by M A P, M S, and G M F]. London, Henry Frowde, 1910. 126pp.
  Headings: Spring, Summer, Autumn, Winter.
  Some overlap with 1891. Mostly nineteenth century verse.

1882 PATON, Frederick Noel
  Bards and birds, selected and arranged by Frederick Noel Paton; with illustrations by Mrs Hugh Blackburn and Hubert Paton. London, Reeves and Turner, 1894. xx, 514pp, plates.

Headings: General; Dawn; Spring-morning; Spring-nesting; Swallows-
summer-garden; Summer-woods; Woods-solitude-swallows-stream; Moorland-
skylark-sea; Eagles-afternoon-evening; Evening-night; Morning-autumn; Com-
panions-migration-winter.
Much unknown poetry, biased towards the nineteenth century.

1883 POOLE, Charles Henry
    A treasury of bird poems, selected and edited by Charles Henry Poole.
London, Simpkin, Marshall, Hamilton and Kent, [1911]. xxvii, 511pp.
Introduction, xix-xxvii: Birds, bards and naturalists.
Headings: Birds—nests and nestlings; Birds—musicians and their music;
Sonnets and songs of birds; Bird elegies and memorial lines; Places of birds;
The flight and feeding of birds; Legends and bird lessons; Tunes and seasons
of birds; The woodland and its people; Birds in captivity; Habits, plumage
and meeting; Biblical birds; Birds after their kind.
Poetry from the sixteenth to twentieth centuries.

1884 PORTER, Rose
    A charm of birds: poems, chosen and arranged by Rose Porter. New
York, Herrick, 1897. 206pp.

1885 PRIESTLEY, Mary
    A book of birds, [compiled] by Mary Priestley; with 82 wood engrav-
ings by C F Tunnicliffe. London, Gollancz, 1937. 384pp, illus.
Prose and verse mostly of the twentieth century. More prose than verse;
Extracts and pieces on over 150 birds.

1886 REED, Gwendolyn E
    Bird songs, compiled by Gwendolyn E Reed; drawings by Gabriele Mar-
gules. New York, Atheneum, 1969. 64pp, illus.

1887 ROBINSON, Phil
    The poets' birds, by Phil Robinson. London, Chatto and Windus, 1883.
x, 490pp.
Part I: introductory remarks on the poets' treatment in general of birds.
Part II: a synopsis of the poets' references to birds, arranged alphabetically
according to species.

1888 ROHDE, Eleanour Sinclair
    The bird lover's days: an anthology and diary, compiled by Eleanour
Sinclair Rohde. London, The Medici Society. 1930. 116pp, col front.
Prose and poetry extracts of the seventeenth, nineteenth and twentieth
centuries; mostly of the nineteenth century.

1889 SANDERSON, L F
    Birds of the poets, edited by L F Sanderson. Boston, Brown, 1899.
197pp.

1890 SCOLLARD, Clinton and RITTENHOUSE, Jessie B
    Bird-lover's anthology, compiled by Glinton Scollard and Jessie B Ritten-
house. New York, Houghton, 1930. xvi, 229pp.

1891 SICKERT, Robert
   The bird in song: a collection of poems, edited by Robert Sickert. London, E Grant Richards, 1906. vii, 179pp. (The Halcyon series no 1.)

1892 SNELL, Ada Laura Fonda
   Where birds sing, compiled by Ada Laura Fonda Snell; illustrated by Freda Reiter. New York, Bookman Associates, 1960. 56pp, illus.
37 poems about birds. Authors range from Boethius to Robert Frost.

1893 SWOPE, Eugene and others
   The Roosevelt bird sanctuary, compiled by Eugene Swope, Mabel Maris Swope and Alice D Weeks; foreword by Frank M Chapman. New York, Sears, 1932. x, 298pp, plate.

Cuckoos

1894 Cuckoo songs and rhymes (in Notes and Queries, 4th series, 1868, vol I p 480, vol II pp 22, 144, 555; 1869, vol III pp 20, 94, 204, 365; 1870, vol V p 596, vol VI p 58; 1872, vol X pp 349, 368, 420).

Owls

1895 SHAW, Richard
   The owl book, compiled and edited by Richard Shaw. London, Kaye and Ward, 1972. 48pp, illus (mostly col.)
Poetry and prose, intended for children.
   Originally published: New York, F Warne, 1970.

Studies and criticism

1896 HARRISON, Thomas P
   They tell of birds: Chaucer, Spenser, Milton, Drayton, by Thomas P Harrison. Austin, University of Texas Press, 1956. xviii, 159pp.
pp 141-159: index to birds named by these poets.

1897 SPENCER, K P G
   Birds in English poetry from earliest times to the present, with special reference to the period 1700-1956. MA thesis, University of Leeds, 1956.

See also 1676

Nightingales

1898 TELFER, J M
   The evolution of a medieval theme; (the nightingale and its significance in early French and English verse). (in Durham University Journal, 1952, pp 25-34.)

Robins

1899 LACK, David
   Robin redbreast, by David Lack. Oxford, Clarendon Press, 1950. vii. 224pp, illus.

Chapters: The winter friend; The death of the robin; The covering of dead bodies; Prisoners and criminals; The robin song; Redbreast; The robin in politics; The robin's home life; The exploitation of robins; Robins abroad; Robins in the nursery; A Happy Christmas.
A cultural history of the robin, with many poems and literary extracts as examples.

Insects

Orthopteroids (crickets, grasshoppers, etc.)

1900 McE Kevan, D Keith
    The land of the grasshoppers: being some verses on grigs, collected and perpetrated by D Keith McE Kevan. St Anne de Bellevue, Quebec, Lyman Entomological and Research Laboratory, 1974. ix, 326pp, illus.
(Memoir no 2; Special Publication no 8.)
Headings: Grigs in general; True grigs—saltators in general; Locusts and injurious acridid grasshoppers; Non-injurious acridid grasshoppers; Ground-hoppers and false mole-crickets; Long-horned grasshoppers; Katydids or bush-crickets (the Tettigonioidea); True crickets; Mole-crickets; Other 'crickets'; Stick insects and their kind; Mantids or sooth-sayers; Cockroaches; Termites; Earwigs and their kind; Stone-flies; Soil lice; Rock-crawlers; Web-spinners.
An international anthology, covering all periods, with introduction and translations. Some of the pieces are concerned with insects in general, with only passing references to Orthopteroids.

Ectoparasites (fleas, lice, vermin)

1901 BUSVINE, J R
    Insects, hygiene and history, by J R Busvine. London, Athlone Press, 1976. vii, 262pp, illus.
Chapters 4 (The prevalence of ectoparasites) and 5 (human reactions to ectoparasites) contain prose and verse extracts from all periods, from English, French, German and Latin literature.

THE BOTANICAL WORLD

General

1902 ADAMS, Estelle Davenport
    Flower and leaf: their teachings from the poets, selected and arranged by Estelle Davenport Adams. London, Suttaby, 1884. xvi, 256pp.
Part 1: Flowers in general. Part 2: Individual flowers (includes some trees). Poetry from the seventeenth to the nineteenth century.

1903 BONHAM-CARTER, Victor
    A posy of wildflowers, gathered in the countryside of English literature and furnished with appropriate sentiments by Victor Bonham-Carter;

illustrated with wood engravings by Hellmuth Weissenborn. London, Allan Wingate, 1946. 124pp, illus.
Extracts of poetry and prose for fifty-one flowers; brief notes on flowering periods and name variants for each flower. Compiler acknowledges great debt to 1925.

1904 BROCK, Kate Ursula
The fragrance of flowers: a nature-lover's anthology, [compiled] by Kate Ursula Brock. London, Hodder and Stoughton, [1911]. 247pp.
Headings: Flowers—their characteristics, their beauty, their fragrance, their hues, their seasons, their evanescence; The sensitive plant; Flower images: Flower fancies; Flowers—their message; Flower miscellanies.

1905 CROMMELIN, May
Poets in the garden, compiled by May Crommelin. London, Fisher Unwin, 1886, 256pp, front, illus.
Alphabetical arrangement by flower name, covering a wide range of plants with some commentary; poetry mostly of the nineteenth century. Introduction: pp 1-4. Decorated borders and capital letters.

1906 FLORAL POETRY
and the language of flowers, with coloured illustrations. London, Marcus Ward, 1877. 264pp, col illus.
Preface is signed J H S.

1907 FLOWERS IN LITERATURE
articles in Notes and Queries, Vol 178 1940: 20th January pp 46-47; 3rd February pp 88-89; 10th February p 103; 9th March pp 175-6; 1st June p 394.
Answers in reply to a request for references in poetry to various flowers: love-in-the-mist, chrysanthemum, arabis, stichwort, pinguicula, michaelmas daisy, cyclamen, pink, peony, dahlia, saxifrage.

1908 GILMAN, Clarabel
Songs of favorite flowers: choice selections from less familiar poems of notable authors, compiled by Clarabel Gilman. Boston, J H West, 1900. 40pp.

1909 HILDITCH, Neville
In praise of flowers: an anthology of enjoyment, compiled by Neville Hilditch. London, Frederick Muller, 1954. 63pp, plates.
Prose and poetry extracts, of the seventeenth, nineteenth and twentieth centuries.

1910 JOHNSTONE, Mary A
The poets and the flowers, by Mary A Johnstone. London, Glasgow, Blackie, 1927. 86pp.
Extracts from the major poets dealing with flowers, with brief commentary at beginning of each chapter.
Covers Tennyson, Keats, Shelley, Scott, Burns, Wordsworth, Milton and Chaucer. Conclusion: brief notes on types of flowers favoured.

1911 THE LANGUAGE AND POETRY OF FLOWERS
   with floral illustrations printed in colour and gold. London, Marcus
Ward, 1874. 193pp, col illus.

1912 NUTTAL, G Clarke
   Ye flower-lover's booke, [compiled] by G Clarke Nuttal, with four plates
photographed in colour direct from nature. London, Cassell, 1911. xvi,
238pp, col plates.
Headings: Flowers of every hue; Ye scent of them; Fancies aboute them;
Their influences on man; Ye lover and his flowers; Flowers and death;
Flowers in their season.
Mainly nineteenth century poetry; some prose. Covers forty-one different
flowers.

1913 THE POETRY OF FLOWERS
   being a collection of verse illustrating the nature, beauty, sentiments,
teachings and associations of the floral world. London, Ward, Lock and
Tyler, 1877. 123pp, illus.
Alphabetical arrangement by flower name; mostly nineteenth century
poetry.

1914 THE POETRY OF FLOWERS
   a collection of blossoms gathered from the garden of the English poets.
London, Ward, Lock and Tyler. 1877. 64pp.
A miniature book.

1915 RAWLINGS, Alfred
   A flower anthology, selected and illustrated by Alfred Rawlings. London,
Philip Lee Warner, 1910. 163pp, col illus.
Covers gardens, flowers in general and specific flowers. Mostly seventeenth
and nineteenth century poetry.

1916 RUTTER, Joan
   Here's flowers: an anthology of flower poems, compiled by Joan Rutter;
with an introduction by Walter De la Mare and wood engravings by John
O'Connor. London, Golden Cockerel Press, 1937. 197pp, illus. Limited
edition of 200 copies—in perpetua type on hand-made paper; also an un-
limited edition on machine made paper.
Headings: Flowers of spring; Spring nosegays; Flowers of summer; Summer
posies; Summer gardens; Flowers for remembrance.
Covers all periods; mostly well-known poets.

1917 SITWELL, Edith
   A book of flowers, compiled by Edith Sitwell. London, Macmillan,
1952. 314pp.
Headings: Plants and planets; The virtues; The flower; The soil; Of seeds;
Of garden heroes and gallants and of hortolan saints; Of ancient gardens;
Some garden necessities; Nature and names of those called usually English
flowers; Early spring in the orchard; The gardener; The fields near the
garden; Early spring; Some recipes; The primrose; Daisies; The birds; The

crocus; The anemone; Auriculas; Hyacinths; Violets; The daffodils and narcissus; The crowne imperial; Tulips; Lilies; The breath of flowers; The iris;
Lilac; The gifts; The rose; The strawberry; Gillyflowers; Pinks; Sweet johns
and sweet williams; Campions; The cherry; The fountain; Marigolds; The
mallow; The bee; The later pomp; Of fruits; Of other virtues; Rosemary;
Night in the garden.
Prose and poetry extracts from works by poets, gardeners, philosophers,
etc. An historical anthology featuring the medieval period and the sixteenth
and seventeenth centuries.

1918 WILLIAMS, Iolo A
Where the bee sucks: a book of flowers; poems chosen by Iolo A Williams;
the paintings by Katharine Cameron. London, The Medici Society, 1929.
87pp, col plates.
Headings· Garlands, posies and bouquets, Rose, Violets; Primroses; Daffodils;
Daisies; The small celandine; Hawthorn; Wallflowers; Various other flowers.
Poetry of the first half of the nineteenth century and earlier.

Daffodils

1919 CHALFONT, Edward
The daffodil: an anthology of the daffodil in poetry . . , edited by Edward
Chalfont. Woodstock (Vermont), Elm Tree Press, 1949. 117pp, illus.
Headings: The rank of the daffodil in poetry; The daffodil in English and
American poetry; Quotations of poems—fragments, allusions and trans-
lations concerning the daffodil, arranged alphabetically by author (pp 9-74);
Popular versus botanical names; Plant names of the daffodil; English deri-
vations and some of the synonyms; Daffodil and narcissus—synonyms; The
narcissus in mythology; The English nativity of the daffodil challenged.

Roses

1920 ADAMS, Estelle Davenport
Rose leaves: poems and passages about the rose, selected and arranged by
Estelle Davenport Adams. Glasgow, David Bryce. 1884. 124pp.
Extracts from the seventeenth to nineteenth century. A miniature book.

1921 TEMPERLEY, Helen
The rose upon her briar: an anthology compiled by Helen Temperley.
London, John Lane The Bodley Head, 1941. 229pp.
Headings: Garden roses; Queen of flowers; Brides; Conserved roses; 'Knoppes';
Cupid; Lovers; 'The warbling of musick'; Two Greek maidens; 'Halesome
herbes'; Beauty's short life; Wild roses; Philomel; Author's pother; Victorian
rose-buds; Thorns; 'Apparayle'; Persian roses; Good-night and good-morning;
Poetry from the sixteenth to nineteenth century.

Studies and criticism

1922 FLOWER LORE
The teachings of flowers: historical, legendary, poetical and symbolical.
Belfast, McCraw, Stevenson & Orr, [1879]. 233pp, illus.

Chapters: Sacred plants of the monks; Superstitions connected with various trees, plants and flowers; Heraldic badges—floral games of Toulouse; Plants frequented by bees; Sensibility of plants; Sleep of plants; The order in which flowers and trees come into leaf and bloom; Sacred trees and plants; Perfumes; Emblems of time; The language of flowers; Funeral flowers.
A study with numerous extracts.

1923 FOLKARD, Richard
Plantlore, legends and lyrics: embracing the myths, traditions, superstitions and folk-lore of the plant kingdom, by Richard Folkard. London, Sampson Low, 1884. 610pp, illus.
Chapters: The word-trees of the ancients; The trees of paradise and the trees of Adam; Sacred plants of the ancients; Floral ceremonies, garlands and wreaths; Plants of the Christian church; Plants of the fairies and Naiades; Sylvans, wood nymphs and tree spirits; Plants of the devil; Plants of the witches; Magical plants; Fabulous, wondrous and miraculous plants; Plants connected with birds and animals; The doctrine of plant signatures; Plants and the planets; Plant symbolism and language; Funeral plants.

1924 HULME, F Edward
Bards and blossom; or the poetry, history and associations of flowers, by F Edward Hulme. London, Marcus Ward, 1877. 232pp. Notes (pp 175-215).
Chapters: Introductory—plants valued for their useful service; Plants enjoyed for their beauty; Plants studied for their teaching.
A study with numerous extracts.

1925 RENDALL, Vernon
Wild flowers in literature, by Vernon Rendall. London, The Scolartis Press, 1934. 372pp.
A wide ranging study, with many quotations, of references to flowers in English prose and poetry.

1926 STEVENS, Neil Everitt
Botany of the New England poets (in Scientific Monthly Vol 12, February 1921, pp 137-49).

1927 WILSON, H M
Flowers in poetry (in Poetry Review Vol 32, May-June 1941, pp 153-62).
A brief consideration of types of flowers favoured by poets.

Trees

1928 CRESSWELL, Ruth Alston
Spirit of the trees: an anthology of poetry inspired by trees, compiled by Ruth Alston Cresswell; with a foreword by V Sackville-West. Abbotsbury (Devon), Society of the Men of the Trees, 1947. xlv, 434pp.
Covers all kinds of tree; ranges from the Bible to the twentieth century.

1929 HARE, Maud Curey
   The message of the trees: an anthology of leaves and branches, edited by
Maud Curey Hare; with a foreword by William Stanley Braithwaite. Boston,
Cornhill, [1918]. xiv, 190pp.

1930 MASE, Georgina
   The book of the tree, edited by Georgina Mase. London, Peter Davies,
1927. xliv, 239pp. Introduction: pp ix-xliv.
Poetry and prose. Some overlap with 1928.

1931 MELTON, Wightman Fletcher
   Poems of the trees, edited by Wightman Fletcher Melton. Atlanta, Banner
Press, 1932-4. 4 vols. Vol 3 has imprint: Oglethorpe University Press. Vol
4 has imprint: Curtiss Printing Co, Atlanta.

1932 POETRY OF THE WOODS
   passages from the poets descriptive of forest scenes. Philadelphia, P Hubbard, 1873. xv, 128pp, plates. (The Parlour Treasury of Gems of Poetry,
Vol 6, no 2.)

1933 PRICE, Nancy
   In praise of trees: an anthology for friends, chosen by Nancy Price. Lon-
don, Frederick Muller, 1953. 64pp, plates.
Poetry and prose. Considerable overlap with 1928 and 1930.

1934 SONGS OF THE WOODS
   a gift book from the poets; with 100 illustrations by Giacomelli. London,
Edinburgh, Nelson, [1886]; 128pp, illus.
Poetry depicting wood and forest scenes from the seventeenth to nineteenth
century.

Epping forest

1935 TONKIN, W G S
   A forest garland: Epping Forest in poetry and prose, edited by W G S Ton-
kin. Waltham Forest, Libraries and Arts Department and Walthamstow
Antiquarian Society, [1967]. 28pp, illus.
Contains poetry by Addison, Breton, Jonson, Clare, Betjeman, and Elen.
Based on the 'Forest garland' presented on 29th June, 1967 at the Forest
School, Snaresbrook, as part of the first Forest Festival.

Gardens

1936 BIKLÉ, Lucy Leffingwell Cable
   The voice of the garden, compiled by Lucy Leffingwell Cable Biklé; with
a preface by George W Cable. London, John Lane The Bodley Head, 1912.
265pp.
Headings: The delights of gardens; With herbs and flowers; The march of
the seasons; The singing of birds; The last and least of things; The lover;
The child in the garden; Of the days gone by; Some famous gardens.
Prose and poetry from the seventeenth to the nineteenth century.

1937 COX, E H M
   The gardener's chapbook, edited by E H M Cox. London, Chatto and Windus, 1931. ix, 258pp, illus.
pp 1-80: anthology of prose and poetry pieces, mostly from the nineteenth and twentieth centuries; pp 183-192: garden proverbs.

1938 HADFIELD, Miles and HADFIELD, John
   Gardens of delight, by Miles and John Hadfield. London, Cassell, 1964. 192pp, plates.
Headings: The fabulous and the ideal. Come, my spade; Fantasia of flowers; Fruits of the earth; The oriental vision; Landskip and design; The garden of love; The return to paradise.
Prose and poetry extracts of all periods, with a running commentary.

1939 HAY, Roy
   In praise of gardens: an anthology of enjoyment, compiled by Roy Hay. London, Frederick Muller, 1959. 47pp, illus.
Mostly prose pieces. Poetry by De la Mare, Thompson, Clare, Tennyson, Arkell, and Sackville-West.

1940 LAMPLUGH, Anne
   The garden book: an anthology for all who love gardens, collected by Anne Lamplugh. London, Herbert Jenkins, 1937. 245pp, illus.
Headings: Of gardens; Certain gardens; Birds, bees and other creatures; Flowers and perfume; Trees; Water and weather; Activity; Twilight, tranquillity and night.
Poetry and prose covering all periods.

1941 LYDALL, G O E
   Anthology of gardens and flowers, by G O E Lydall. London, Allman, 1939. 168pp.
Headings: Spring flowers; Summer flowers; Autumn; Winter; Old world gardens; The laying out of a garden; The garden bed; Lessons from the garden; The garland; Old herbals; Earthly paradise; Flowers in the wild.
Some overlap with 1940.

1942 NENDICK, Eva
   Silver bells and cockle shells: an anthology for garden lovers, arranged in 6 parts, by Eva Nendick; drawings by Andrew Dodds. London, Michael Joseph, 1971. 220pp, illus.
Chronological arrangement: sixteenth to twentieth century. Prose (extracts from novels) and poetry.

1943 OSGOOD, Irene and WYNDHAM, Horace
   The garden anthology: a collection of representative poems relating to gardens and their contents from 1535 to 1914, compiled by Irene Osgood and Horace Wyndham. London, John Richmond, 1914. 311pp.
Only a small proportion of the poems are devoted to gardens; most are on flowers.

1944 RICHARD, Gertrude Moore
   The melody of earth: an anthology of garden and nature poems from present-day poets, selected and arranged by Mrs Waldo Richard. Boston, New York, Houghton Mifflin, 1918. 301pp.
Headings: Within garden walls; The pageantry of gardens; Wings and song; The gardens of yesterday; Pastures and hillsides; Lovers and roses; Underneath the bough; The lost gardens of the heart; The garden overseas; The homely garden; Silver bells and cockle shells; The garden of life.
American poetry.

1945 ROHDE, Eleanour Sinclair
   The garden lover's days, compiled by Eleanour Sinclair Rohde. London, The Medici Society, 1929. [116] pp.
Mostly nineteenth century poetry and prose extracts about flowers and gardens.

1946 SPENCER, Sylvia
   Up from the earth: a collection of garden poems, 1300 BC-AD 1935, chosen and decorated by Sylvia Spencer. Boston, Houghton Mifflin, 1935. xxi, 305pp.

1947 SCOTT, Temple
   In praise of gardens, compiled by Temple Scott. New York, Baker & Taylor, 1910. 240pp.

1948 SHAYLOR, Sidney J
   In praise of gardens, compiled by Sidney J Shaylor. London, Truslove & Hanson, 1911. 152pp, illus.
Headings: In praise of gardens; Flowers; The wild garden; The seasons in a garden; The formation of gardens; Of poeple in a garden; The orchard; Sundial mottoes.
Poetry and prose mostly of the nineteenth century.

See also: 990, 997

Studies and criticisms

1949 COMITO, Terry A
   Renaissance gardens and Elizabethan romance. PhD thesis, Harvard University, 1968.

1950 IZOD, K J
   The garden in English poetry, 1590-1690. PhD thesis, University of Leeds, 1971.

1951 KLEINBERG, Seymour
   A study of the image of the garden in English literature in the sixteenth and seventeenth centuries. PhD thesis, Michigan University, 1963.

1952 SMITH, Thomas N
The garden image in medieval literature. PhD thesis, Connecticut University, 1968.

1953 STEWART, S
The enclosed garden: the tradition and image in seventeenth century poetry. Madison, University of Wisconsin Press, 1966. xiv, 226pp, illus.

1954 SYMES, M W R
The theme of the garden and its relation to man in the poetry of Spenser, Milton and Marvell with consideration of some other poetry of the time. MPhil thesis, University of London, 1968.

1955 THOMAS, William Beach
Gardens, by Sir William Beach Thomas. London, Burke, 1952. xviii, 302pp, plates. (Pleasures of Life series.)
Chapters: Edens; Gardeners; Nature's garden; Great gardens; Small gardens; Flowers; Pleasure gardens; Garden philosophy; Denizens; Ornaments; Garden romances; Academies; Calendar.
A general cultural history of the garden with many extracts of prose and poetry quoted.

MEDICINE

1956 (BIBLIOGRAPHY) DANA, Charles L
Poetry and the doctors: a catalogue of poetical works written by physicians with biographical notes and an essay on the poetry of certain ancient practitioners of medicine, illustrated with translations from the Latin and by reproductions of the title pages of the rarer works, by Charles L Dana. Woodstock (Vermont), The Elm Tree Press, 1916. xxiii, front, plates, 83pp.

1957 ERICHSEN, Hugo
Medical rhymes: a collection of rhymes of ye ancient times, and rhymes of the modern days; rhymes grave and rhymes mirthful; rhymes anatomical, therapeutical and surgical; all sorts of rhymes to interest, amuse, and edify all sorts of followers of Esculapius, selected and compiled from a variety of sources by Hugo Erichsen; with an introduction by Professor Willis P King. Atlanta, J H Chambers, 1884. xx, 220pp.

1958 HUTCHISON, Robert and WANCHOPE, G M
For and against doctors: an anthology, compiled by Robert Hutchison and G M Wanchope. London, Edward Arnold, 1935. 168pp.
Headings: Proverbs; The ancients; Medieval; Fifteenth to seventeenth century; The eighteenth century; Moderns.
Poetry and prose; some foreign pieces in translation.

1959 LILLARD, John F B
  The medical muse, grave and gay: a collection of rhymes by the doctor, for the doctor and against the doctor, collected and arranged by John F B Lillard. New York, I E Booth, 1895. 140pp.

1960 McDONOUGH, Mary Lou McCarthy
  Poet physicians: an anthology of medical poetry written by physicians, compiled by Mary Lou McCarthy McDonough. Springfield (Illinois), C C Thomas, 1945. xiii, 210pp. Biographical notes.
Chronological arrangement—sixteenth to twentieth century; mostly poetry of the nineteenth and twentieth centuries by Americans.

1961 THE MEDICAL MUSE
  a cheerful entertainment . . . directed by Fritz Spiegl. A recital of poetry, song and prose given at the Queen Elizabeth Hall, London, 8th June, 1974. The programme lists pieces performed, together with reproductions of the sheet covers.

1962 SERGEANT, Jean and SERGEANT, Howard
  Poems from hospital, compiled by Jean and Howard Sergeant. London, Allen and Unwin, 1968. 169pp.
Headings: The urgent bell; 'the pitiable and the private war'; 'Out of darkness rose the seed'; 'The glistening theatre swarms with eyes'; 'Rituals of grace'; 'Lamps burn all the night'; 'A weather in the head'; 'The cured man goes home'; Portraits and appreciations; 'The whole earth is our hospital'. Mostly twentieth century poetry.

1963 STRAUSS, Maurice B
  Familiar medical quotations, edited by Maurice B Strauss. London, J & A Churchill; New York, Little & Brown, 1968. xix, 968pp.
Short prose and poetry extracts.

1964 WARREN, Ina Russelle
  The doctor's window: poems by the doctor, for the doctor and about the doctor, edited by Ina Russelle Warren; with an introduction by William Pepper. Buffalo, New York, C W Moulton, 1898. viii, 288pp.

See also: 421, 1549

APPENDIX

POETRY INDEXES

BROWN, C F and ROBBINS, R H
Index of middle English verse. New York, Index Society, 1943. xx, 785pp.
Covers over 4,000 poems on religious and secular subjects written before 1500. Subject and title index.

Supplement:
ROBBINS, R H and CUTLER, J L
Supplement to the Index of Middle English verse. Lexington, University of Kentucky Press, 1965. xxix, 551pp.

BRUNCKEN, Herbert
Subject index to poetry: a guide for adult readers. Chicago, American Library Association, 1940. 201pp.
Indexes 215 anthologies by author, title, first line and subject.

CHICOREL, Marietta
Chicorel index to poetry in anthologies and collections in print. New York, Chicorel Library Publishing Group, 1974. 4 vols. 1798pp. (Chicorel Index series Vol 5.)
Indexes about 1,000 anthologies and some collections by individual poets, by author, title and first line. Entries for all works indexed showing total contents.

CRUM, M
First line index of English poetry, 1500-1800 in MSS of the Bodleian Library, Oxford. Oxford, Clarendon Press, 1969. 2 vols. 1257pp.

CUTHBERT, Eleonora Isabel
Index of Australian and New Zealand poetry. New York, Scarecrow Press, 1963. 453pp.
Indexes 22 anthologies of UK and Australasian origin by author, title and first line.

GRANGER'S INDEX TO POETRY
First edition: edited by Edith Granger. Chicago, A C McClurg, 1904. 970pp.

Second edition: edited by Edith Granger. Chicago, A C McClurg, 1918. xv, 1059pp.

Supplement: 1919-1928. Chicago, A C McClurg, 1929. ix, 519pp.

Third edition: edited by Helen Humphrey Bessey. Chicago, A C McClurg, 1940. xxiv, 1525pp.

Supplement: 1938-1944 [edited by Elizabeth J Sherwood and Gertrude Henderson]. New York, Columbia University Press, 1953. xvi, 415pp.

Fourth edition: edited by Raymond J Dixon. New York, Columbia University Press, 1953. xxxvii, 1823pp.

Supplement: edited by Raymond J Dixon. New York, Columbia University Press, 1957. xvi, 458pp.

Fifth edition: edited by William F Bernhardt. New York, Columbia University Press, 1962. xxxix, 2123pp.

Sixth edition: edited by William James Smith. New York, London, Columbia University Press, 1973. xxvii, 2223pp.

CHILDREN'S POETRY INDEXES

BREWTON, John Edmund and BREWTON, Sara Westbrook
Index to children's poetry. New York, Wilson, 1942. 965pp.
Indexes 130 anthologies by author, title, first line and subject.
Supplement: 1954. 405pp.
Indexes 66 anthologies.

MacPHERSON, Maud Russell
Children's poetry index. Boston, Faxon, 1938. 453pp.
Indexes fifty anthologies by author, title and subject.

MORRIS, Helen
Where's that poem: an index of poems for children. 2nd ed. Oxford, Blackwell, 1975. xiii, 287pp.
Indexes 309 anthologies by subject and author.

SELL, Violet
Subject index to poetry for children and young people. Chicago, American Library Association, 1957. 582pp.
Indexes 157 anthologies by subject only.

AUTHOR AND COMPILER INDEX